Thinking in Public

INTELLECTUAL HISTORY
OF THE MODERN AGE

Series Editors:
Angus Burgin, Peter E. Gordon,
Joel Isaac, Karuna Mantena,
Samuel Moyn, Jennifer Ratner-Rosenhagen,
Camille Robcis, Sophia Rosenfeld

THINKING
═ IN ═
PUBLIC

Strauss, Levinas, Arendt

Benjamin Aldes Wurgaft

PENN

UNIVERSITY OF PENNSYLVANIA PRESS

PHILADELPHIA

Published by
University of Pennsylvania Press
Philadelphia, Pennsylvania 19104-4112
www.upenn.edu/pennpress

Printed in the United States of America on acid-free paper
1 3 5 7 9 10 8 6 4 2

Library of Congress Cataloging-in-Publication Data
ISBN 978-0-8122-4784-8

For my parents

CONTENTS

═════

Contents

Introduction

A specter haunted Hannah Arendt from her youth in Weimar Germany to her maturity as a political theorist in the United States: the specter of the intellectual. In 1964, she described her haunted condition during a rare public appearance, a television interview with the journalist Günter Gaus.[1] Meditating on the National Socialist rise to power and the ensuing *Gleichschaltung*—the forced Nazification of all existing cultural, intellectual, and political institutions, whose officials had to either demonstrate loyalty to the new government or leave their posts—Arendt recalled having felt betrayed by friends and colleagues:

> The problem, the personal problem, was not what our enemies did but what our friends did . . . . I lived in an intellectual milieu, but I also knew other people. And among intellectuals *Gleichschaltung* was the rule, so to speak . . . . I never forgot that. I left Germany dominated by the idea . . . [that] I shall never again get involved in any kind of intellectual business. I want nothing to do with that lot.[2]

Arendt's indictment of the behavior of German "intellectuals" after 1933 should not shock us. Many witnesses to Nazification understood that the professions, including law, medicine, and the professoriate, had been wrapped up in the process and that education had not, in the terms used by the former Nazi jurist Carl Schmitt during his de-Nazification hearings, acted as an "inoculation" against the National Socialist "bacillus."

If Arendt's indictment of the intellectuals who participated in Nazification was unsurprising, she went further in the interview. She claimed that it was somehow natural for intellectuals to capitulate to the powers that be: "Also I didn't believe then that Jews and German Jewish intellectuals would have acted any differently had their own circumstances been different. That was not my opinion. I thought it had to do with this profession, with being an intellectual."[3] However we might define "an intellectual" (and one of the most remarkable things about the word is its protean resistance to final definition), Arendt was willing to venture a damning claim, namely that intellectuals are people who "make up ideas" about the world around them. They can find a theory to validate any state of affairs, including National Socialist rule.[4] She could easily have been thinking of her teacher, Martin Heidegger, who became a Nazi Party member at the height of his influence and claimed that the priorities of his own *Existenzphilosophie* harmonized with the practical aims of National Socialism. She was, after all, attributing to intellectuals a failure she often attributed to philosophers, namely the tendency to give up on public life, facilitating what Bertolt Brecht called "the permission of great political crimes." Arendt was not naïve regarding the power of culture workers. She did not expect literature, philosophy, or art to somehow bolster the Weimar Republic against its enemies. But neither did she expect educated and introspective producers of culture to participate in Nazification.

Arendt's claim was strange. For one thing, by linking intellectualism to capitulation she effectively mocked an old idea in Germany, namely that education, or *Bildung*, is not only the accumulation of knowledge or skill but also self-cultivation, the improvement of one's character. Presumably the most cultivated people should also be moral ones. And she ran against the comparatively more recent French and thereafter pan-European enthusiasm for "intellectuals," which imagined intellectuals as public guardians of truth and justice and opponents of political corruption. Arendt told Gaus that as a young woman she had felt the need to abandon the "intellectual circles" she had known as a student in order to see political events as they truly were. While Arendt never truly succeeded in leaving those ranks—at no point in her life did she cease to socialize with writers, journalists, political thinkers, and, yes, philosophers—she found worldly work in refugee organizations, wrote on politics as well as on philosophy, and for much of her career held no university post. She tried to become something more than the unworldly character conjured by the German (and Yiddish) *Luftmensch*, meaning someone who "lives on air." And she succeeded in becoming a public figure, sometimes intentionally and often not—an intellectual herself, perhaps, for all that she struggled against the term.

The year before her interview, Arendt had launched into the public realm what would become her most famous phrase, the "banality of evil," attacking not thinking but rather the failure to think. In her 1963 *Eichmann in Jerusalem*, she described and analyzed the Nazi bureaucrat Adolf Eichmann's ability to treat participation in genocide as a form of everyday office work. Whereas Eichmann had achieved a banal form of evil by failing to think through the consequences and the meaning of his actions, Arendt's colleagues had achieved the same result by indulging in theory without judgment. Years after her escape from Nazi Germany and following a long sojourn in Paris, Arendt found herself writing to her old mentor Karl Jaspers with reports of the new acquaintances she had made in New York. She remarked that in America she had met thinkers who, through their oppositional and nonconformist nature, helped her to admire the social type of "the intellectual" once more. For her, these politically engaged writers, critics, and activists, many of whom would later be known as the "New York Intellectuals," embodied precisely the resistance to corrupt politics that the name "*les intellectuels*" had conjured during the Dreyfus Affair. And yet the pleasures of socializing with New York's literati could not fully ease Arendt's mind regarding what she had observed in Germany. The specter stayed with her long after the parties ended, almost as if "the intellectuals" were cousins of Eichmann, their political banality no cure for the "the banality of evil."

This book is an attempt to puzzle through Arendt's thought on intellectuals, their publics, and the larger political and philosophical problems they brought to mind. It also follows the same trains of thought in her generational peers and fellow Heidegger students Leo Strauss and Emmanuel Levinas. Strauss, a dedicated Platonist, once insisted "the whole work of Plato may be described as a critique of the notion of 'the intellectual.'"[5] Levinas, by contrast, was critical of any attempt to apply ethics to politics, resisting the politically *engagé* versions of philosophy prevalent among his colleagues in postwar Paris. Their reflections on the intellectual question were outward expressions of a much more complex concern, for the question of the social task of philosophy weighed heavily on Arendt, Levinas, and Strauss throughout their careers. While their approaches to philosophy differed greatly, they each took for granted that in the twentieth century philosophers had to consider the possible political implications of their work. But they did not take it for granted that publicness was a boon either for politics or for philosophy, nor that philosophy was a boon for the public. While Strauss's animosity toward the public is well-known and Levinas never committed himself to a political cause in the manner that came into vogue in postwar France, Arendt's harsh words about intellectuals should surprise us. After all, she has been celebrated as one of the foremost "public intellectuals" of the twentieth century.[6]

Because so much has been written on the figure of "the intellectual" it is useful to address what this book is not. First, it is not a study of Arendt, Levinas, and Strauss as political intellectuals themselves, contextualizing their varied pronouncements on politics while searching for a common pattern between them and ultimately defining what sort of intellectual each was. Nor is this book a comprehensive examination of "the intellectual" as a social role, either descriptive or normative in its intention, though the history of that role forms a crucial part of my story. This book runs against the conventional grain of studies of intellectuals in public life, which tend to be strongly normative in character. That is, even when they couch themselves as empirical investigations of a single figure or a group of figures, often clustered around a single publication, school of thought, or movement, such studies are invested in promoting or damning the efforts of their subjects. They usually make politics the crucial horizon line for all intellectual work, judging the life of the mind purely in terms of the political provocations to which it responds, or because of its consequences for politics. Instead of following this well-worn course this book examines the way the figure of "the intellectual" and the idea of the "public" served as provocations for Arendt, Levinas, and Strauss. In a century whose political life seemed increasingly defined by mass publics, the questions of address, of recognition, of argument and agreement, were pressing ones. The figure of "the intellectual" brought to mind many of the ideals of liberal thought—not only the foundational divide between privacy and publicness, but also the ideal of reasoned discourse accessible to the public at large. But that figure also conjured apparent failures of the liberal order, including the Dreyfus Affair itself, the moment when the term established a footing in European discourse.

This book also offers the first comparative examination of Arendt, Levinas, and Strauss's thought and seeks to restore the shared cultural and intellectual matrices in which their thought was formed.[7] Not only were Arendt, Levinas, and Strauss all students of Heidegger, they shared the experiences of exile and refugee status during the Holocaust. All immigrated to liberal Western democracies, where they found shelter and conducted the bulk of their scholarly careers. All three maintained a strong interest in the political dimensions of the modern Jewish condition, though Strauss and (most especially) Levinas were scholars of the Jewish religious tradition as well. All three were deeply interested in the phenomenon of political persecution, whether that of the Jewish people or that of other peoples living under tyranny. Certainly their mature works flew off in different directions as they responded both to their own shifting interests and to the horrors of war and genocide. Arendt was preoccupied by political practice, Strauss by Platonic political philosophy, and Levinas was obsessed with the ethical reform of philosophy *tout court*. Nevertheless, even on these disparate trajectories they displayed a common preoccupation with the question of philosophy's place in public life, a question for which "the intellectual" sometimes served as shorthand.

Arendt, Levinas, and Strauss's meditations went further than the obvious problem of the "lure of Syracuse," the strange attraction political tyranny seemed to hold for certain prominent philosophers like Heidegger. That phrase recalls Plato's onetime journey to the Island of Syracuse, where he hoped to advise the tyrant Dionysius the Younger and perhaps, by doing so, produce a "perfect" regime.[8] Nor did their thinking on the issue stop with the insight that philosophy could degenerate into mere ideology when made to serve a parochial political cause, as they had all seen happen in both Germany and France. Instead, observing the encounters between philosophy and public life made Arendt, Levinas, and Strauss think about the nature of philosophical practice itself. It alerted them to what Michael Theunissen terms its inherent "social ontology," the way our lives with others condition our accounts of knowledge and of being itself.[9] Philosophy, for them, was a practice caught between certain "monological" elements, such as an emphasis on the power of an isolated mind to reason its way to the truth, and the alterity of encountering other persons, which offered the possibility of "dialogical" exchange. Philosophy's social ontology was tied to still more problems, in particular, the relationship between philosophers and audiences, and the relationship between private philosophical thoughts, their public expression, and their potential political effects. Simply put, in the decades following Heidegger's public support for Nazism, Arendt, Levinas, and Strauss came to ask if publicness always informed philosophical work.

In this study I will not force together such very disparate individual works as Arendt's *The Human Condition*, Strauss's *Natural Right and History*, or Levinas's *Otherwise Than Being*, as though reflection on philosophy's social role were the meta-task each work attempted. Levinas's praise for "exteriority," for example, has little to do with Arendt's account of public political life driven by "action." Rather than imposing such meta-considerations from above, I will instead employ a notion given specialized meaning by Ludwig Wittgenstein, "family resemblance," to describe the commonalities linking Arendt, Levinas, and Strauss. "Family resemblance" signifies here in two registers. Arendt, Levinas, and Strauss were all aware both of their own status as Jewish thinkers and of their relationship with the lineage Heidegger established though his *neue Denken* or "New Thinking." In his *Philosophical Investigations*, Wittgenstein suggested that we use "family resemblance" to describe likenesses between groups of things that are irreducible to a single trait, and are instead based on overlapping resemblances. When we survey the full set of activities we call "games," we observe that across the full set of games (ball games, card games, board games, etc.) a sufficient number of traits appear and reappear to justify the claim of membership in a family, but no two games are guaranteed to display the same linking trait. Just so, Arendt, Levinas, and Strauss each possessed a different understanding of the relationship between their identity as Jews and their intellectual labors. They derived very different lessons from Heidegger's teachings, as well as from those of Karl Jaspers, Franz Rosenzweig, and others associated with *Das neue Denken*.[10]

Notably, one of the reasons to keep Wittgenstein's "family resemblance" with us is that it offers an alternative logic to that of the canon itself, and one our protagonists might have endorsed, though they would likely have refused to recognize the parallels between their work and concerns.[11] "Family resemblance" might have appealed because though each declined to participate in Jewish essentialism (with the occasional lapse on Levinas's part), they recognized that, given common origins and common problems, common ideas appear again and again. Each was aware that it is in the nature of Judaism to resist both categorization and essentialism, including the essentialism of the term "nature" itself. None of them were eager to celebrate what Leora Batnitzky has termed the "German Jewish invention of the idea of Jewish religion," the process by which the set of laws, practices, and beliefs we term Judaism was made to fit within the modern European and Protestant understanding of "religion" as an individual's credo or belief.[12] Levinas noted that this process forced Judaism to become a private practice sequestered from the public world, causing a division alien to traditional Jewish life.[13] And yet in rejecting this assimilatory legacy of the German Jewish experience (or, in Levinas's case, the legacy of the nineteenth-century Jewish infatuation with French Republicanism) Arendt, Levinas, and Strauss never adopted the Zionist practice of "negating the Diaspora," and remained resolutely European Jews, even (in Arendt and Strauss's cases) when they became appreciative citizens of the United States of America.

Given their substantial commonalities of concern and their membership in the same philosophical generation, not to mention their iconic status in twentieth-century intellectual history, it seems surprising that no prior study has compared Arendt, Levinas, and Strauss. The explanation most likely lies in their divisive effects on readers, some of whom become passionate and devoted exegetes while others simply walk away. For his part, Levinas is most often read by scholars of continental philosophy, modern Jewish thought, and religious studies. He has often (mistakenly) been characterized as Judaism's authentic voice within French philosophy. When Levinas is not read as a religious thinker, there is a tendency to interpret his thought mainly as part of the story of French postwar philosophy. While in part correct—Levinas was an important influence on the younger Jacques Derrida, to name just one— this tendency may have distracted readers from the comparison of Levinas's thought with that of Heidegger's other students.

This book's comparative treatment of Arendt and Strauss may alarm readers who assume that the ideological gulf between them indicates the absence of any correlation between their works. To be sure, their differences were great: Arendt praised a public political process in which opinion-sharing was central, whereas Strauss emphasized the philosophical practice by which serious minds rise from opinion to truth, and he thought most members of the public were simply incapable of partaking in it. But the disinclination to compare the two thinkers likely arises from differences in the political attunement of their readers. Strauss's celebrants have tended to cluster at the conservative end of the political spectrum, whereas both liberals and leftists have claimed Arendt as their own. If one task of intellectual history is to clear away the ambiguities created by its own classifications (for example, by addressing the problems inherent in categories like "modern Jewish thought"), another is to dispel the illusion that political disagreements between thinkers are always perfectly mirrored in their theoretical works. Such thinking reflects our rush to see every philosophical reflection ramify at the level of politics or practical action; ironically, Arendt and Strauss both rejected this way of thinking about philosophy's ramifications, while Levinas denied his ethics could be "embodied" by a practical politics.

Political events have widened the already impressive gulf between Strauss's celebrants and critics. A flood of journalistic articles published in 2003 linked Strauss's name with a group of "neoconservative" government officials, politicians, and think-tank members, some of whom had studied either with

Strauss himself or with Strauss's immediate students. These "Straussians" seemed to justify U. S. president George W. Bush's wars in Iraq and Afghanistan using arguments derived from Strauss's writings. These articles described the rise of the Straussians (sometimes "Leocons") in Washington, and while Strauss's sudden and long-posthumous fame may have garnered him additional scholarly attention, it yielded distorted readings of his thought. In her otherwise insightful *Why Arendt Matters* (2006), Arendt's most important biographer Elisabeth Young-Bruehl contrasted Arendt's praise for opinion shared in public against the "Platonic prejudices" of Strauss and his students, while also employing Arendt's thought in a series of arguments against the official rhetoric used by the Bush administration in defending its wars. As it happens, the journalistic effort to link Strauss to the Bush administration (on which Young-Bruehl seemed to base her claim) was founded on exaggeration. Many of the major figures named by journalists, including Paul Wolfowitz, were more students of Strauss's Chicago colleague Albert Wohlstetter (architect of the Cold War strategy of nuclear deterrence) than of Strauss himself. Still, the animus against Strauss lingered in the years of this book's writing. While discussing the idea of comparing Arendt and Strauss, at a conference, I was once told (by a group of senior scholars who had known both Arendt and Strauss personally) that the comparison should be simple—Strauss had been "a bad man," Arendt a saint. Arendt and Strauss's political differences were very real, to be sure, but our attention to those differences has obscured the ways their works illuminate one another both by opposition of views and by commonalities of concern.

One of this work's more controversial claims is that Levinas and Arendt shared a view normally associated only with Strauss. Robert Pippin has observed that for Strauss the folly of modern philosophers is to believe that philosophy can play a public role, providing guidelines for the right conduct of our lives. Pippin aptly quips that, "If Straussianism were a religion, its central icon, rivaling the crucified Christ, would be Socrates drinking the hemlock."[14] I will demonstrate that Arendt and Levinas essentially agreed with Strauss at many points in their careers.[15] This assertion runs counter to many of our received images of Arendt (most especially) and of Levinas, who are often seen as having desired to play a role in public life. Certainly, they spoke out on issues of public concern or interest in a fashion Strauss never adopted. It is impossible to imagine Strauss writing on school desegregation in the American South, as Arendt did, or writing with enthusiasm about the orbital flight of Russian cosmonaut Yuri Gagarin, as did Levinas. But notably, for philosophers to speak in public they need not believe philosophy has a special public function. Heidegger attempted to "commit" his philosophy to a political cause without claiming that philosophy was improved by a form of exchange within a figurative "public sphere," or that philosophers had any special responsibility to the political world in which they lived. Similarly, Arendt and Levinas each sometimes tried to reach broad and nonacademic audiences; yet both associated philosophy, as historically practiced in European universities, with monologue rather than dialogue, and they criticized it for its enclosure within the selfsame, its separation from the social world.

This study avoids invoking the canonical category of "modern Jewish thought" to link its protagonists on the premise that this gesture would actually obscure rather than illuminate Arendt, Levinas, and Strauss's engagements with Jewish political experience, with Jewish texts (in the case of Levinas and Strauss), and with Jewish history. Peter Eli Gordon has suggested that "a certain romanticism of the outsider" may stand behind our tendency to associate Jewish philosophers with Jewish thought rather than with European philosophy proper, even if they identified their own context as primarily European.[16] However, a certain romanticism of the insider may be at work as well; both Jewish scholars and philo-Semitic non-Jewish ones have been eager to discover as Jewish a range of figures once primarily associated with existentialism, Marxism, psychoanalysis, and so forth. This tendency to categorize may be an unavoidable dimension of intellectual-historical writing, but it usually produces more noise than signal. Arendt, Levinas, and Strauss were all keenly aware of themselves as Jewish participants in conversations taking place in non-Jewish precincts, and their desire for their own work to signal in a universal rather than a particularistic register was obvious—even as they took Jewish historical cases as the particularistic basis for many of their claims. Importantly, to affirm Arendt, Levinas, and Strauss as thinkers in the traditions of European philosophy and political theory is not to deny their Jewish experiences, which influenced the philosophical and political-theoretical questions they chose to ask, and this can be seen most obviously in their shared interest in the themes of exile and persecution.

Arendt, Levinas, and Strauss (1906–1975, 1906–1995, and 1899–1973, respectively) grew up in the wake of the Dreyfus Affair, which shook both Europe and Jewish Europe, marked a high water mark for French nationalist sentiment, and performed a curious alchemy by which "intellectual," an adjective, became the noun, "an intellectual." Dreyfusards like Émile Zola—supporters of the innocence of the French Jewish artillery officer Alfred

Dreyfus, who had been falsely accused of providing military secrets to the Germans—insisted that they spoke on behalf of justice and truth, and that such outspoken speech was their right and duty *as intellectuals*, as scholars or artists, even as their opponents accused them of meddling in political affairs beyond their ken. When Arendt, Levinas, and Strauss encountered the term "the intellectual" years later, it carried the flavor of the Affair itself. It proposed a curious relationship between the contemplative life and action in society, in which the former not only legitimated but somehow mandated the latter—and which, with great consequences for later generations of scholars, made the merely contemplative life seem inert. And Arendt, Levinas, and Strauss knew that the Affair had also been an event in Jewish history. Zola and his friends had grounded their arguments in a claim to universal truth at a moment when the political universalism of Republican France, and very specifically its 1790–1791 extension of citizenship to Jews, was being challenged by anti-Semitic French nationalists. The universalistic version of "fraternité" celebrated in the Revolution turned out to be, at the time of the Dreyfus Affair, weaker than the chauvinistic blood-and-soil version. The role of the intellectual was created in non-Jewish society during an event itself marked as "Jewish." In the eyes of many observers, including founder of political Zionism Theodor Herzl, not just Dreyfus the man but the entire (and by now centuries-old) process of Jewish integration into modern European society stood on trial.

As noted earlier, this book is not an empirical study of the social institution of "the intellectual" as it emerged in European life. Rather, it is a sustained reflection on the *idea* of the intellectual and, secondarily, on its North American variant, the "public intellectual," and it builds from recent work on the myths and cultural baggage those ideas bring with them. Stefan Collini observes that while "the intellectual" is in the strictest sense a mere construct, it is a construct that can teach us lessons about its human makers, serving as an index to their political fears, hopes, and desires.[17] Likewise, we learn less by asking how Arendt, Levinas, or Strauss *acted* as politically engaged intellectuals (an inquiry that might rest on tendentious claims about what an "intellectual" or "public intellectual" *is*) than by asking how they came by their ideas about what an intellectual was, and why the question of the intellectual's social role was a significant one.[18] For example, Arendt's 1964 statement on intellectuals during the Gaus interview seems driven by a sense of disappointment or even betrayal. What was it about the "intellectuals," with whom she had once identified, that made them seem so untrustworthy, so politically blind?

The label "an intellectual," as circulated during the Dreyfus Affair, had no singular or stable set of definitional ideas behind it, philosophical or otherwise, but rather a set of rough intuitions. Intellectuals spoke and wrote not in the service of specific class, religious, or ideological interests but rather on behalf of society in general. Their responsibility was neither capricious nor volitional, but rather connected to a relationship with the values of truth and justice. Furthermore, their pursuit of a form of universal truth mapped, by an ineluctable logic, onto the pursuit of the interests of everyone, who were presumably served by the same truth. This same mapping bridged a gap between the interior space of reflection and the outer space of action: intellectuals sought truth and wanted the outside world to conform to "justice," understood as a political manifestation of the truth. Publicity was the means by which this conformity was to be achieved, and publicity was always already a necessary condition for the intellectual's existence in the first place. As Peter Winch has pointed out, the idea of "the intellectual's" responsibility "[was] not only an admission of accountability but a claim to power,"[19] but it was never entirely clear where either responsibility or right comes from. The condition of publicness thus seemed to generate both needs and rights in an arbitrary fashion.

Interestingly, the activity of intellectuals most often took the form of bearing "witness" to the truth (a phrasing especially beloved of Levinas) rather than engaging in forms of truth-producing dialogue. Julien Benda's *La trahison des clercs* (*The Betrayal of the Clerks*), written between 1924 and 1927, is paradigmatic of this trend in its reliance on what Ernest Gellner calls, "Platonic metaphysics and universalistic ethics."[20] A fierce defender of the autonomy of intellectual life, Benda insisted that *les clercs* were those who tried to articulate, albeit with the unreliable tool of human language, transcendental truths that existed independently of their efforts. On Benda's account it was this transcendental attitude that *les clercs* had abandoned, turning instead to party politics and nationalist struggles. But as Gellner points out, Benda's claim for the importance of a "transcendentally grounded" intellectual life was actually pragmatic in intent rather than a claim for the reality of a Platonic realm of ideas. For Benda, it was crucial that intellectuals act *as though* there were a transcendental realm of ideas, because if they did not, they contributed to the dire political and social crises that were on the rise in interwar Europe.[21] Thus there was a very nontranscendental heart to Benda's argument for the defense of the transcendental attitude.

Arendt, Levinas, and Strauss were hardly celebrants of Benda's position (Strauss at one point singled him out for criticism), but the motif of betrayal appeared in their respective visions of "engagement" through public writing or speech. Each understood philosophical and political practices to be basically incompatible. Usually discussion of "intellectuals" functioned, for each of them, as a means by which to explore the underlying and more pressing issue of the distinctions between philosophy, politics, and sociality more broadly. The question of whether it was in philosophy's nature to be a public practice loomed large. Arendt and Strauss in particular would reflect on this issue, while Levinas's work was marked by his ambivalence about whether philosophers should leave the private realm of their own reflections and address a popular audience. Levinas's two full-length philosophical works, *Totality and Infinity* and *Otherwise Than Being*, vibrate with the desire for philosophy to find its relevance in the political world, even as they conclude that every past philosophy has wrongly sought relevance by offering rules for the proper conduct of life. Whether his work was productively animated by the idea of a gulf between ethics and politics, or hampered by his inability to cross that gulf, remains a living issue in the study of his thought.

Intellectuals, Public and Private

Arendt, Levinas, and Strauss's responses to the "intellectual question" will only be fully comprehensible after a deeper examination of the history of "the intellectual." Much of the existing scholarship on intellectuals is unhelpfully normative in character, written not so much to examine the role as to endorse or in some rare cases condemn it. Some of these works propose strategies that might help intellectuals to engage in public life more successfully. Others, perhaps most famously Russell Jacoby's *The Last Intellectuals* and Richard Posner's *Public Intellectuals: A Study of Decline*, sound a death knell for the category or suggest that current generations are incapable of reaching the "heights" of engagement to which their predecessors soared.[22] But between the usually nonrigorous forms of the manifesto and the dirge fall a welcome set of studies whose goal is not to determine the intellectual's proper place in society, but rather to investigate the cultural logic that would invest such persons with moral authority.[23] This book follows from these latter studies in its emphasis on the discursive construction of the intellectual's public role.[24] To state this book's methodological claim in a formula, the stories we tell about intellectuals are most useful when we read them as barometers of our political hopes and fears.[25] Like the adjective "intelligent," both the adjective and the noun "intellectual" derive from the Latin *intelligere,* or "understanding." As Peter Allen points out, the term "an intellectual," as used to describe a person devoted to cultural pursuits, only began to appear in British English in the 1870s, the successor term to others such as "man of letters" or "moralist."[26] Prior to the 1870s, "intellectual" was in wide circulation as an adjective. In 1859, the poet and critic J. A. Symonds wrote to his sister of his plans to establish a club of seven "intellectually-pursuited men" at Oxford, meaning men whose primary interests were cultural in nature. It was only through a slow process that "an intellectual" came to mean a member of an educated elite with a particular role to play in society, and in fact this social role was essentially established beforehand, in the British case largely through the efforts of Victorian "public moralists." While interest in cultivating "intellectual" lifestyles was widespread as a trend in the Britain of the 1870s and 1880s, as evidenced by P. G. Hamerton's self-help book, *The Intellectual Life* (1873), and as satirized in Gilbert and Sullivan's operetta, *Patience* (1881), it was the Dreyfus Affair across the Channel that lent new political valences to the term.

Most accounts of the French history of the term go only as far back as Georges Clemenceau who, as editor of the newspaper *L'Aurore,* referred to the signatories of an 1898 *Manifeste* on behalf of Dreyfus as "*les intellectuels.*" However, some literary scholars have found earlier uses in which *intellectuel* was clearly intended to carry political meaning.[27] While Paul Bourget may have been the first to use *l'intellectuel* as a noun, in an 1882 essay on Flaubert, Henry Bérenger popularized the term and used it in explicitly political ways.[28] In his early essays and novels, published in the 1880s and 1890s, Bérenger presented intellectuals as persons crippled by education, unable to grapple with their own lives or with politics, but his thought took a different turn in 1895 when he published *L'Aristocratie intellectuelle,* in which he argued for politically engaged thinkers to play a role in society. After 1895, he used the term to describe educated men who played a specific sort of political role, providing a "transcendental" perspective on political and social problems without any of the constraints of party ideology. Bérenger's idealism can be seen clearly in his 1895 essay: "If a free solidarity is possible between all the members of the social organism, it is the intellectual aristocracy which alone may prepare and maintain it." Ironically the type of *engagement* occasioned by the Dreyfus Affair was precisely the opposite of what Bérenger, in whose works Clemenceau himself may have first encountered the term "*intellectuel*," had imagined.

Importantly, Clemenceau's use of the term in *l'Aurore* only caught the general public's eye when Ferdinand Brunetière, the anti-Dreyfusard writer, critic, and member of the Académie Française (the learned body that presides over the French language), attacked Clemenceau. Brunetière seems to have felt no need to dispute Clemenceau's use of *les intellectuels* to describe a specific social group. He *did,* however, dispute the idea that intellectual status brought political expertise or authority, thus his remark, "I do not see that a professor of Tibetan has the credentials for governing such matters."[29] However, Brunetière's complaint did nothing to diminish the increasingly political resonances of *intellectuel.* In the terms of Brunetière's colleague Maurice Barrès, Clemenceau had already succeeded in setting up "a trademark for the elite," making "intellectual" a term of public—and international—discourse that might answer the question of what social function highly educated people might fulfill.[30] Barrès linked "intellectuals" with other groups, including Protestants, Jews, and foreigners, under the general label *les déracinés,* "the uprooted." Zola was French-born, but he counted as uprooted on the grounds that his father was an Italian engineer, born in Venice.

While all types of knowledge-workers would try to apply their expertise to political life throughout the twentieth century, the popularization of "the intellectual" by both Dreyfusards and anti-Dreyfusards meant that this term would have lasting literary and philosophical connotations. It was not scientists, nor engineers nor doctors, but *cultural* experts who attempted to derive political clout and moral authority from their expertise. Much as Victorian public moralists had done, the Dreyfusards linked their status as cultural experts with their responsibility to stand against injustice in the public realm, as though the latter followed from the former. Thus did "publicness" come to inhere in the term *l'intellectuel* itself. One was not writing for posterity or for literary immortality, but as a "voice that proclaims itself a *conscience.*"[31] Speaking was acting. But a strange kind of acting, and one that would be rearticulated decades later by Levinas, as *témoignage,* "witnessing," or sometimes "prophetic witnessing." Brunetière's contestation of the term "an intellectual" would also find its echoes throughout the twentieth century. Not only in France but throughout Europe and the Americas as well, the same legitimation crisis regarding the scope of an intellectual's expertise and moral authority would reappear again and again.

The term "intellectual" and its associated traits were as controversial in Germany as in France. While *der Intellektuelle* did not come into widespread use until the mid-nineteenth century—and would not take on strong political resonances until well after the Dreyfus Affair—the idea that a cultural elite might have an important political role to play appeared much earlier, in the late eighteenth century. This idea manifested during the debate over the role of "guardians" (*Vormünder*) in the development and spread of Enlightenment culture, a debate in which Immanuel Kant was among the most influential voices. In his 1784 "An Answer to the Question: What Is Enlightenment?" Kant deliberately used "guardian" to describe a notion that had recently been employed in debates over the freedom of the press; the jurist Ernst Ferdinand Klein had insisted that the princes of the German-speaking lands grant their subjects "the freedom to think and to share their thoughts," and by doing so act as better guides for those Klein called the "immature children" of God.[32] While Kant seconded Klein's call for freedom of the press, his deployment of Klein's term "guardians" was not intended as a compliment. He accused the "guardians, who have graciously taken up the oversight of mankind," of forcing mankind to remain in a condition of immaturity (*unmündigkeit*) by effectively overparenting them.[33] However, he allowed that these enlightened "guardians of the masses" could do a great service if they allowed their subjects to think for themselves. A public (*das Publikum*) that had been granted freedom would gradually enlighten itself and thereby escape from immaturity. It was Kant's essay on Enlightenment that drew the counter-Enlightenment criticism of thinker Johann Georg Hamann.[34] Hamann's criticism of Kant nevertheless revealed a subtle shift in the debates over free speech. Whereas for Klein the guardians were explicitly political rulers, for Kant and Hamann the emergence of a recognizable *Publikum* meant that one could become a "guardian" through literary skill rather than political clout, and indeed, over the long term, the cultural guardians might make the greater difference through their educative work.

Kant's ambivalence about guardianship would find echoes at later moments in German history. While by the 1840s the term *Intelligenz* had come into common use, referring to an educated person who could represent his nation's cultural life, it was *der Intellektuelle* that Karl Marx gave a lasting place in debates between Socialists. In *The German Ideology* (1845), Marx used it to describe a mental rather than a material laborer, and he further described the intellectual as the class ideologist par excellence and thus as a potential enemy of emancipation and social change. However, in *The Communist*

Manifesto, Marx and Friedrich Engels gave the intellectual a more positive role as a "traitor" to the ruling classes who takes sides with the workers because of his insight into the grand trajectory of history. Not only was the intellectual a significant figure, whether for or against social change, he was also a figure whose role could shift and take on different dimensions—much as Kant had imagined. As we will see, Marx's use of *der Intellektuelle* would be significant for twentieth century reformulations of this role, less because of the specific uses to which he put it, and more because he had tied "intellectual" status to a knowledge of the course of world history. This Hegelian accent would turn up again and again among Marxists of all stripes, from Karl Mannheim to Antonio Gramsci.

Germany's dramatic industrialization between 1870 and 1933 transformed the academic world and forced the chiefs of that realm to investigate their own status as guardians.[35] Industrialization and attendant social change furthermore prompted the "mandarins" (in Fritz Ringer's terms, "a social and cultural elite which owes its status primarily to educational qualifications, rather than to hereditary rights or wealth"[36]) to reconceptualize their relationship to German society at large. This elite was not entirely literary or academic, and included bureaucrats, lawyers, and other professionals, but as Ringer points out there was a recognizable tendency for university professors to contribute to public debates on cultural issues with greater regularity than others did. In time they grew confident enough to challenge the German state's view of the university system as "purely technical," a factory for turning out administrators. Among the fundamental debates in German intellectual life during this period was that over utilitarianism, which the mandarins frequently attacked as a foreign and specifically Anglo-French tradition; Arendt and Strauss would offer their latter-day echoes of such criticisms, casting a critical eye on their colleagues in American departments of political science. These they suspected of aspiring to become "social engineers."[37] However, the crisis and eventual "decline" of these mandarin intellectuals was itself part and parcel of Germany's continuing modernization. It became harder and harder to argue for the relevance of an educated scholarly elite, or to sing the virtues of disinterested *Kultur* or *Wissenschaft*.[38] After 1890, the critical struggle in the German academy was that between the advocates of utility and those who hearkened back to the German Idealist and neohumanist traditions as articulated by Humboldt, Schleiermacher, and Fichte.[39]

While the term *Intellektuelle* was not central in all these debates, it came into common use after World War I when the political status of the intellectual was fiercely debated once again. The state-supported role of the mandarin had become impossible, the university system seemed increasingly politicized, and many writers found themselves subject to the whims of the literary and journalistic marketplace. In his 1918 essay on German national character, *Die Betrachtungen eines Unpolitischen* (*Reflections of an Unpolitical Man*), Thomas Mann used *Intellektuell* in a tellingly ambivalent manner. He spoke of his desire to create a work that would appeal to an *intellectual* public, while at the same time deriding "those intellectual swells and elegant ones who wear the most recent catchwords just as they wear their monocles."[40] And Mann wrapped "*die Intellektuellen*" together with the advocates of democracy, which in 1918 he held to be "foreign and poisonous to the German character."[41] He was not so different from Julian Benda in this regard; for Mann, it was "the *politicization* of the intellect" (my emphasis) that ran against the German spirit, and in his view, in Germany, "reverence for the intellect makes one skeptical of programs of action for its political 'realization.'"[42] It was also in this spirit that Max Weber argued for a *Wissenschaft* "without values," and extended his definition to cover the practitioners of both *Geistes-* and *Naturwissenschaften* (the humanities and natural sciences). Weber used the term *wissenschaftliche Arbeiter* (a scientific worker) to describe his ideal scientist, rather than *Intellektuelle*, a term that he generally used for thinkers who in his view ignored the pursuit of the truth via science and effectively returned to the "bad faith" of irrational religion. The example of Weber is extremely important because, as Peter Uwe Hohendahl has shown, Weber's brief against *der Intellektuelle* meant that all who would identify as such had to do so against his influential defense of value-neutrality. A number of thinkers, including Georg Lukács, did much to rehabilitate the term *Intellektuelle* and to dispute the hegemony of science Weber had proposed; however, their efforts did not entirely remove the negative connotations that the word had developed. The National Socialist tendency to heap invective upon *die Intellektuellen* may have been one of the reasons why, after 1945, the term could recover some of its earlier positive connotation.[43]

Learning to Love (and Hate) the Hidden King

Worrying about philosophy's place in the political world came naturally to Heidegger's students, but Heidegger's own early thought contained little sustained reflection on politics. Heidegger's early social ontology did not yield a political theory, but manifested instead in the idea of *Mitsein*, the notion that we can recognize each other as subjects on the grounds that we are already sharing a world with them; *Mitsein* and *Dasein* are equiprimordial.[44] *Mitsein* was constitutive of *Dasein*'s capacity for authenticity, or in other words, we know ourselves most truly when we acknowledge the condition of mutuality that subtends our isolation, and makes true isolation impossible. While it is intriguing that Heidegger emphasized the danger that reliance upon *Mitsein* might reduce us to a state of inauthenticity, rather than the positive or "communitarian" promise of *Mitsein*, Strauss may have expressed an even more striking consequence of the flaws in Heidegger's *Mitsein* when he suggested that Heidegger had been unable to speak of politics because he thought of nothing but Being.[45] Mutuality's importance seemed, for Heidegger, to lie in its nonmutual consequences for each individual. Levinas, for his part, found in the equiprimordial nature of Heidegger's *Mitsein* and *Dasein* the trace of an openness toward others, though it would be many years before he could derive an intersubjective ethics from Heidegger, whose thought could be called nonintersubjective insofar as it described not the meeting of isolated and agentive subjects but their primordial connectedness, already in place before they discovered themselves as independent entities.[46]

Even before the revelation of his Nazification, some of his students had begun to criticize as defective Heidegger's approach to *Mitsein*.[47] Both Arendt and Karl Löwith responded to Heidegger's insistence that we are never truly alone, the former beginning in her doctoral dissertation on St. Augustine. In his *Habilitationsschrift, Das Individuum in der Rolle des Mitmenschen: Ein Beitrag zur anthropologischen Grundlegung der ethischen Probleme (The Individual in the Role of Fellow Man: A Contribution to the Anthropological Foundation of Ethical Problems)*, Löwith judged that despite the immersive sociality implied by *Mitsein*, Heidegger nevertheless presented the self as solitary and always up against society.[48] Michael Theunissen's argument about Heideggerian social ontology follows closely from Löwith: as if he were a master of sleight-of-hand, Heidegger offered togetherness with one hand and took it away with the other. The "mutuality" of *Mitsein* in *Being and Time* was not an argument on behalf of our fundamental mutuality—such as might have yielded a "communitarianism"—but just a description of the primordial condition of togetherness that would serve Heidegger as a foil for the "empty" public social life that the individual self always confronts.[49] Much of Löwith's first important philosophical work was devoted to countering

Heidegger's conclusions about isolation and social alienation, arguing that such experiences were hardly inevitable.

Mitsein was not, importantly, an attempt to work through the existential meanings of communication, and on the worth of publicness as a category of communicative life the Heidegger of *Being and Time* was dismal. Seeing in publicness nothing more than the shallowness of mass culture, Heidegger concluded that those who allowed the public world to define their private worlds would never achieve a genuine relation to "the heart of the matter," *Dasein* itself. As he famously put it, "The light of the public obscures everything, and what has thus been covered up gets passed off as something familiar and accessible to everyone."[50] But from his beginnings as a little-known academic, Heidegger, whom Arendt called "the Hidden King," became a kind of public figure. In 1933, Heidegger gave his *Rektoratsrede* (Rector's Address) "The Self-Assertion of the University," having just taken charge of the University of Freiburg under the auspices of the new National Socialist government. In that speech he affirmed the priority of practice *over* theory. In addition to demanding that German students accept that academic freedom be replaced by the "true freedom" of "labor service" and "knowledge service" to the *Volksgemeinschaft* ("the community of the people") Heidegger called for the reassessment of theory itself as "the supreme realization of genuine practice." Most strikingly (and with a telling disregard for history), he denied that for the Greeks *theorein* (to speculate or examine) had ever had "unengaged" associations at all:

> It was not [the Greeks'] wish to bring practice into line with theory, but the other way around: to understand theory as the supreme realization of genuine practice. For the Greeks science is not a "cultural treasure" but the innermost determining center of their entire existence as a Volk and a state. Science is also not merely the means of making the unconscious conscious, but the force that keeps all existence in focus and embraces it.[51]

Theory was never autotelic. It had served the Greeks much as it now served Heidegger, as a means by which to crystallize and understand a course of political action already underway. Theory or "science" was, for the early Heidegger of the *Rektoratsrede*, directly linked to will, but this was not the free will of the neo-Kantians (whom Heidegger had held his *neue Denken* to supersede), but rather the will to know oneself in the terms given by one's existence. Self-examination, including the "making the unconscious conscious" that science enables, was thus subordinated to self-assertion. It was appropriate that Heidegger chose to cite Aeschylus's statement, "knowledge is far less powerful than necessity,"[52] and that he presented this statement as paradigmatic for all Greek philosophy. While Heidegger allowed that science or *theoria* would always imply questioning, he nevertheless accepted that questioning and throwing oneself into one's fate could go hand in hand. Interestingly, the "self-assertion" Heidegger described, which led inexorably to political practice, was not simply the assertion of the individual but rather possessed a "group" character.

Heidegger did not discuss the figure of the intellectual in the *Rektoratsrede*, but the rhetorical terms of his address tacitly rejected the intellectual's medium of choice, words shared in public. He effectively disregarded the public realm as a space for rational debate or collective judgment about the potential ends of action. In keeping with the antipathy toward "publicness" (*Öffentlichkeit*) he had displayed in the 1927 *Being and Time*, Heidegger suggested that knowledge workers simply place theory at the service of the National Socialist movement, using channels arranged by the movement. While it would be simple to read Arendt as championing the public in order to correct a flaw in Heidegger's thought, the path she actually traveled was determined less by Heidegger's criticisms of publicness (which she in fact inherited and displayed in her own criticisms of forms of fallen or degraded publicness) and more by his account of the subject's fundamental isolation. In her early works on St. Augustine and on the German Jewish *salonnière* Rahel Varnhegen, Arendt dealt with the themes of inwardness and the struggle for an authentic life with others, and Levinas and Strauss would take these themes up in their own work. In so doing, all three responded to the "pathos of isolation" that, as Gordon notes, infused the *Existenzphilosophie* of Heidegger's *Being and Time*, and could be detected even in such notions as *Mit-Dasein* itself.[53] Our protagonists' considerations of sociality, which sometimes drew on Heidegger's treatment of the experience of being with others but often went beyond it, can themselves be read as challenges to Heidegger's picture of the subject's fundamental isolation. And critically, Arendt, Levinas, and Strauss were all deeply concerned about Heidegger's apparent demotion of theory in favor of its more immediately demanding "other," practice. Practice gone wild could be just as oppressive as theory gone totalitarian. Even in Arendt's most ardent articulations of the priority of political action, she did not gainsay the need for independent reflection. Late in her career, in a series of lectures on the faculties of the mind, she would fully acknowledge the dignity of thoughts and words unconnected to deeds.

One great irony of the Heidegger case is that many of his Jewish students shared a reason for studying with him that we might call circumstantially (but of course not essentially) "Jewish": Heidegger was a critic not only of the Enlightenment but also of its implicit belief in the virtues of progress and modernization, an attitude many German Jews born around 1900 would grow to share.[54] Heidegger's doubts about the equivalence between modernization and progress were strikingly at odds with the views of some of his most prominent Jewish counterparts, including Ernst Cassirer, Hermann Cohen, and Edmund Husserl.[55] For Heidegger's Jewish students, his rejection of the Enlightenment may have harmonized with their own growing doubts—sometimes fueled by Zionist commitments—about the Enlightenment's downstream political consequences for Jews. Those doubts in turn led many to rebel against established lineages of German Jewish thought, such as Hermann Cohen's neo-Kantianism, which seemed to articulate in new terms an underlying harmony between Judaism's morality and the teachings of idealist philosophy. Strauss in particular found in Heidegger a critique of liberalism that buttressed his own growing conviction that the emancipation bargains of the Enlightenment had been a disaster for Jews in Europe, qua Jews. Long after his own disillusionment with Heidegger, Levinas voiced the same anxiety regarding the way emancipation shaded off into assimilation and the loss of Jewish distinctiveness, as did Arendt in her more forthrightly historical works on European Jewry.

While Arendt's relationship with Heidegger was made more complex by a romantic relationship that has become the object of much scandal, and Levinas spent much of his career trying to rehabilitate elements of Heidegger's thought after the revelation of Heidegger's Nazism, Strauss's relationship with Heidegger has received less attention.[56] In some ways this is appropriate, for Strauss did not study Heidegger's works as long or as intensely as Arendt or Levinas. Despite Strauss's obvious admiration for Heidegger, his failure to adopt the language of existentialism and phenomenology makes it difficult to refer to him as a "Heideggerian" thinker. However, Strauss's preoccupation with the conflict between ancient and modern thought was structurally similar to Heidegger's attempt to "return" to the pre-Socratics and forget the mistakes of modern philosophy. Furthermore, and as Eugene Sheppard and Daniel Doneson have shown, Strauss's method of reading texts "between the lines" was indebted to Heidegger's idea that ancient texts could be understood through a method Heidegger called *Destruktion*.[57] Strauss's gnomic statement on readership, "The problem inherent in the surface of things and only in the surface of things is the heart of things," can be understood as an adaptation of Heidegger's transformation of Husserlian phenomenology to the task of reading.[58] If Strauss was a very different *kind* of Heidegger pupil than either Arendt or Levinas, this may itself constitute an argument for his inclusion in the minor "canon" of Jewish students of Heidegger, for by observing his differences from them we might learn more about the figurative "garden of forking paths" that led from Heidegger's Freiburg workshop.

PART I

Leo Strauss and the Problem
of "The Intellectual"

Only because public speech demands a mixture
of seriousness and playfulness, can a true
Platonist present the serious teaching, the
philosophic teaching, in a historical and hence
playful, garb.

              —Leo Strauss, "Farabi's *Plato*"

CHAPTER 1

Moderns and Medievals

In 1950 Leo Strauss made his grand claim that "the whole work of Plato may be described as a critique of the notion of 'the intellectual.'"[1] Near the middle of his scholarly career Strauss found himself defending Plato from Max Weber's description of the Greek philosopher as "an intellectual," a potentially innocuous labeling but for the fact that Strauss abhorred such persons. Ever since his years as a young scholar in Weimar Germany, Strauss had been fascinated by the relationship between the philosopher and the polis. He had observed potential models for that relationship in many places: in the works of the medieval philosophers al-Farabi and Moses Maimonides, in the "bible science" of Baruch Spinoza, in the existentialism of Heidegger, and in Plato's Socratic dialogues. In each case he found morality tales urging the philosopher to measure his public words with care and keep his distance from politics. In 1950, Strauss's skepticism about publicly engaged philosophers became an attack on the premise that it was proper or natural for intellectuals to influence political life through speech in the public realm. The figure of "the intellectual" was a modern dodge by which one could pretend that the practices of reason not only did not conflict with political life, but could guide it. When Strauss used the term "intellectual" in his own writings, which he did sparingly, he meant someone who had fallen from wisdom because, like the public-spirited *philosophes* of the French Enlightenment, they thought philosophy was a tool for the improvement of man's estate on earth, especially effective when used in the public realm.

Strauss once observed that "all merely defensive positions are doomed," and indeed he not only defended the territory of philosophy against a modern, public-oriented instrumentalism, but also endeavored to understand the social obligations of philosophers.[2] He labored over that understanding from Paris to London, New York to Chicago, but he first caught sight of his goal while laboring over medieval Jewish texts in the politically fragile climate of Weimar-era Berlin. Strauss did not begin his career with the Greek and Latin classics. Rather, he wrote a doctoral dissertation on the counter-Enlightenment writer F. H. Jacobi's theory of knowledge and then moved backward in time, working first on Spinoza's bible science and then on the very same medieval figure—Maimonides—whom Spinoza attacked. It was while studying medieval philosophy that Strauss found his bridge back to Plato. In 1962 Strauss observed that, when he wrote his 1930 *Spinoza's Critique of Religion* (completed in 1928), he had been "a young Jew born and raised in Germany who found himself in the grip of the theologico-political predicament."[3] During the intervening thirty years Strauss concluded that since Plato, philosophers had often been anxious about the social and political contexts in which they operated.

After Strauss's death, the political theorist Allan Bloom denied that his teacher had ever "looked over his shoulder" while writing. The claim should startle us because Strauss was preoccupied by the linked questions of how philosophers anticipate their audiences, of how writing and reading influence society, and of how mentors shape their students.[4] Strauss's preoccupation with the issue of audience predated the revelation that Heidegger, Strauss's onetime teacher, had placed his philosophy in the service of National Socialism, but the revelation of Heidegger's Nazism strengthened Strauss's interest in the question of philosophy's social role.[5] This interest further intensified after Strauss came to the United States and worked alongside colleagues, at both the New School for Social Research and the University of Chicago, who devoted themselves to a "socially engaged" version of social scientific work.

But if Strauss read Plato's corpus as a critique of the intellectual, then what kind of creature was Strauss's "intellectual"? Chronologically incongruous with his own description of Plato critiquing intellectuals, for Strauss intellectuals descended from the authors of the eighteenth-century *Encyclopédie*, that Enlightenment compendium of knowledge about science, art, and culture whose express purpose had been to improve human life—to "change the way people think," in the words of one of its authors, Denis Diderot. Diderot and his colleagues contended that truth itself could flourish in a public realm more expansive than a privileged republic of letters, provided that the multitudes received the proper education. Strauss's intellectuals were vehicles for and symptoms of the Enlightenment's instrumentalization of knowledge. They crossed an invisible but crucial line between philosophy and politics, a line created by the natural difference between the philosophically minded and their less gifted counterparts, who were unable to understand philosophy as anything but the corrosion of binding social mores and traditions.

Strauss's critique of the intellectuals superficially resembles one written in France while Strauss was a young researcher in Berlin. This was Julian Benda's 1927 *La trahison des clercs*, in which the former Dreyfusard claimed that many of his contemporaries had abandoned their duty to the abstract truth by placing their intellects in the service of immediate political causes. If in *Natural Right and History* Strauss would agree that "since the seventeenth century, philosophy has become a weapon, and hence an instrument," he also complained that Benda "committed the fatal mistake . . . of ignoring the essential difference between intellectuals and philosophers. . . . For the politicization of philosophy consists precisely in this, that the difference between intellectuals and philosophers . . . becomes blurred and finally disappears."[6]

The category of the "intellectual" emerged from the transgression of the distinction between pursuing the truth and pursuing immediate political goals. Strauss would eventually find, and grapple with, a far more influential version of this transgression in his friend Alexandre Kojève's Hegelianism. Kojève's belief in the philosopher's role as an agent of social progress did not keep Strauss from paying him the compliment that he was "a philosopher and not an intellectual."[7] But if an intellectual is a thinker who believes that the requirements of society and the requirements of truth can be harmonized through social engineering or social progress, a philosopher recognizes irreconcilable differences between the real and the ideal and knows that the ideal city can only be founded in speech, never in stone and mortar.

Strauss's attack on intellectuals was the flip side of what might be called a theory of philosophical citizenship, and Strauss once called Socrates a "citizen-philosopher."[8] "Philosophical citizenship" is perhaps a surprising phrase with which to describe Strauss's understanding of how philosophers relate to society, given that Strauss seldom reflected on the concept of citizenship and had few kind words for the democratic public sphere. Whereas citizenship of the classical republican variety is grounded in the possibility of common deliberation, for Strauss the discussions held in our public squares consist only of "opinion," inferior to philosophical truth. On the question of the "end" or ultimate goal of the political community Strauss was Platonic, envisioning an end for man in virtue and excellence that only a few are capable of seeing. Strauss's "philosophical citizenship" was not a model of communal participation in any rich sense but rather a set of principles that kept the thinker and the polis from interfering with one another, while still allowing the latter to enjoy the benefits of the former's wisdom.

If philosophy was the contemplation of truths beyond politics, there were nevertheless political philosophers whose task was to understand what happened when the most "unpolitical" art or science entered the polis. In the 1945 essay "On Classical Political Philosophy," Strauss described such philosophers beginning with the material of everyday life—the common speech of the marketplace and "pre-philosophical" relations such as familial and religious ties—and then determining how the real might be shifted toward the ideal, not through social engineering but by rhetoric. [9] As Strauss put it, "Philosophy, being an attempt to rise from opinion to science, is necessarily related to the sphere of opinion as its essential starting point, and hence to the political sphere."[10] Because political philosophy has to account for a form of life that is pre-philosophical, it couches itself in the language of opinion and casual conversation; for Strauss this is how and why Plato's Socratic dialogues got their form.

If political philosophers helped to "create, by persuasion, agreement among the citizens,"[11] they did so by serving as the teachers of legislators, who would be equipped to foresee and preempt social conflict.[12] But Strauss's philosophers had an additional special task. Where the interests of philosophers and the interests of the political community seemed to diverge, philosophers had to make apologia, "to justify philosophy before the tribunal of the political community."[13] He first glimpsed that process of making apologia not, of course, in Plato's account of the trial and death of Socrates, but rather in the writings of medieval Muslim and Jewish philosophers who were mindful of the authority of religion and guarded against the charge that philosophy was heretical. They understood that philosophical skepticism could have corrosive effects on the social order at large, with disastrous effects both for philosophers and for their neighbors. Medievalism eventually led Strauss to "exoteric (or "esoteric") writing," according to which theory the great texts of philosophy have always presented one version of truth to the masses, another to an elite properly educated to understand them.[14] These texts perform good "philosophical citizenship" through their care for the relationship between society and philosophers, between the masses and the elites. But to understand Strauss's path, from the medieval to an esoteric approach to philosophical citizenship, we must first attend to the Weimar context of Strauss's education. During the tumultuous years of the Weimar Republic, the apparent weakness of liberalism and its politics of public deliberation led many young women and men to radical and seemingly anachronistic views; some turned away from modernity and toward the imagined temporality of the medieval.

Strauss's Existential Medievalism

Strauss's objection to that modern social type, "the intellectual," began with his youthful conviction that medieval Islamic and Jewish accounts of religion as law had a pressing contemporary relevance and could serve as correctives to modern philosophical mistakes. Medieval thinkers, thought Strauss, had been keenly aware of the difference between religious and philosophical truth-claims, and out of necessity (for they lived under the scrutiny of religious censors) they understood religion to operate in a political field in which philosophy was an interloper. In other words, they maintained the very line between philosophy and the public that moderns had begun to transgress.

Strauss developed this view slowly and out of diverse influences ranging from the neo-Kantianism of Hermann Cohen and the "New Thinking" of Heidegger and Rosenzweig, to the political theology of Carl Schmitt, with other stops in between. After finishing his doctoral dissertation on Jacobi, Strauss was awarded a research position under the direction of Julius Guttmann at the Berlin Akademie für die Wissenschaft des Judentums (Academy for the Scientific Study of Judaism). Guttmann, who would become Strauss's first intellectual sparring partner, seemed to Strauss an exponent of the German Jewish liberal tradition that had to be superseded both politically and philosophically. But Guttmann would also inadvertently introduce Strauss to the problem of philosophy's political context, for he charged Strauss with the study of Spinoza's bible science. By examining Spinoza's attempt to understand the bible by means of a "natural history of religion" and thereby deprive religious authorities of the basis for their political dominance, Strauss came to the question of the public political functions of philosophy and religion, respectively. He came to ask whether or not Spinoza's Enlightenment critique of religion had succeeded, banishing a legislative version of religion from the public realm.

Between 1926 and 1928, Strauss wrote *Die Religionskritik Spinozas als Grundlage seiner Bibelwissenschaft Untersuchung zu Spinozas Theologisch-politischen Traktat* (*Spinoza's Critique of Religion*), in which he explored

Spinoza's bible science as it had appeared in the 1670 *Tractatus Theologico-Politicus*.[15] As he put it, "The most general definition of the task of the Tractate reads: radical separation of the philosophy (reason) from theology (scripture)."[16] For Spinoza this separation meant that if we ascribe ethical, and thus political, authority to the Bible, it is because its manmade contents conform to the dictates of reason. As Strauss would later observe in a 1962 Preface written for the English translation of his book, "The purpose of [Spinoza's *Tractatus*] is to show the way toward a liberal society which is based on the recognition of the authority of the Bible."[17] Spinoza understood his bible science as a necessary step toward the advent of a society in which religion's authority would never exceed that of reason. As Strauss wrote, "The establishment of such a society required in [Spinoza's] opinion the abrogation of the Mosaic law in so far as it is a particularistic and political law, and especially [the abrogation] of the ceremonial laws."[18] Spinoza's state would be liberal and neither Christian nor Jewish in any theocratic sense even if it recognized the Bible's moral authority. It was while studying Spinoza's division of philosophy from theology that Strauss came to believe that he himself was the child of a German Jewish generation that had forgotten that division, a generation that had reshaped Judaism so that its dictates never conflicted with philosophical reason. Modern Jews no longer needed miracles.[19] Crucially, Strauss was not interested in becoming a *baal tshuvah* ("master of the return," that is, a returnee to Jewish observance) like his friend Rosenzweig, but rather in recovering the understanding of religion's social function that secular modernity had jettisoned.

Strauss's recovery effort put him at odds with Guttmann, who, despite his own doubts about Hermann Cohen's rendition of Judaism as a "religion of reason," nevertheless shared his teacher's view that Judaism was philosophically and politically compatible with secular liberalism. When Strauss dedicated his book to Rosenzweig, who had died in the winter of 1929, he was not only honoring a friend but also subtly identifying his study with the existentialism of Rosenzweig's "New Thinking," itself a rebellion against Cohen's neo-Kantianism. If the atheist Strauss could never fully embrace Rosenzweig's thought, he admired the emphasis Rosenzweig placed on the personal experience of divine commandment in his 1919 *Stern der Erlösung* (*The Star of Redemption*).[20] Rosenzweig had successfully evoked the force that Strauss would later ascribe to revealed legislation.[21] Strauss would ultimately crystallize his critique of Guttmann in a substantial 1935 review of Guttmann's 1933 opus, *Die Philosophie des Judentums* (*Philosophies of Judaism*), demonstrating a willingness to fight the internal battles of Weimar Jewish thought even after the National Socialists' rise to power. Guttmann never responded in print, but an unpublished reply to Strauss, found among Guttmann's papers after his death, indicates how seriously he took Strauss's challenge.

While a full account of Strauss's rebellion against Guttmann lies beyond this chapter's scope, a brief account is useful for understanding the political dynamics of Strauss's turn to the medieval, and for understanding the way this turn served as a crucible for his later esotericism. Strauss held that the two traditions with which Guttmann identified most closely—neo-Kantianism in philosophy and historicism in the mode of the early nineteenth-century Wissenschaft des Judentums school—had led his teacher to miss Judaism's political character. As Strauss put it, "scientific knowledge of Judaism is purchased at the price of belief in the authority of revelation." Guttmann devoted much of *Die Philosophie des Judentums* to medieval thinkers but nevertheless depicted modern thinkers, including Cohen, as having achieved a more developed and refined vision of Judaism's ethical content than their predecessors.

Guttmann's reading of medieval Jewish thought, and especially that of Maimonides, derived to a great degree from Cohen, who in 1908 had contributed the important "Characteristics of Maimonides' Ethics," and in whose (posthumously published) 1919 *Religion of Reason Out of the Sources of Judaism* Maimonides appeared prominently. In the former work, Cohen claimed, "There is no greater testimony to Maimonides as the most vital and most genuine representative of philosophy within Judaism than the fact that his ethics constitutes the core and effective center of his metaphysics."[22] In the latter, Cohen described Maimonides as maintaining that proximity to the Divine was "*knowledge* of God," a closeness of the mind. This account of Maimonides was itself part of Cohen's broader effort to present Judaism as a system of ethics entirely compatible with Kant's moral philosophy. Strauss understood quite well that this was an effort with an extra-philosophical dimension, namely demonstrating that there was only harmony between, as Strauss put it, "Judaism and culture" or "Torah and derekh eretz." To pursue such harmony in late nineteenth and early twentieth century Germany meant demonstrating that Judaism, and Jewish identity more broadly, were compatible with the modern liberal state, and that the vision of early champions of Jewish emancipation (such as Moses Mendelssohn) had been correct and was now being fulfilled. But this also meant ignoring Judaism's political content and its original vision of God as a lawgiver.

Strauss contended that Guttmann was carrying on Cohen's domestica-
tion efforts after the master's death by considering religion to be just one
aspect of "culture," available for study through "the philosophy of culture,"
which Strauss saw as an intellectual limb of liberalism. Guttmann was not
uncritical of his teacher, conceding in *Die Philosophie des Judentums* that
Cohen had transformed "god into an idea, involving the denial of his metaphysical claims and personal character."[23] But Guttmann clung to Cohen's
notion that the development of Jewish philosophy had always been an attempt
to reach beyond the Bible and Talmud and toward "a universal ideal of intellectual culture," fully realized only in the present.[24] It was in his progressive
modernism that Guttmann most recalled Cohen and offended Strauss: Guttmann was too focused on the superiority of modern Jewish thought to see
that its medieval antecedents might challenge it. He had replaced the fundamental choice between religion and reason, which the "ancients" had understood quite well, with Cohen's "harmonizing decision that the teachings of
revelation are identical with the teachings of reason."[25]

Strauss pointed out that even Guttmann had to grant what the medieval
held over the modern. As Guttmann wrote, "the medieval thinkers are more
strongly rooted as total personalities in the Jewish tradition and way of life,
and belief in the divine authority of the revelation is more self-evident in
them."[26] Importantly, Strauss suggested that in the meeting between Islamic,
Jewish, and Greek thought that took place in the medieval period, the social
practice of philosophy was profoundly altered as Jewish or Muslim Aristotelians had to either find a way to *harmonize* the conflicting claims of religion
and revealed law, or else make apologia to religious authorities on behalf of
philosophy and restrict the claims of philosophy so as not to infringe upon
religion's legislative territory. Thus Strauss arrived at a new understanding
of the "philosophy of religion" of the medievals: it was essentially a practice
of "exoteric" writing—Strauss here used the term for the first time in his
career—intended for a nonphilosophical audience, defending philosophy's accordance with the terms of the Law.[27] Furthermore, Strauss suggested that
a fundamental unbelief lay beneath the medieval philosophers' insistence
on the compatibility between reason and revelation. Their publicly broadcast
understanding of revelation was "pedagogical," intended for masses un-
equipped to do philosophy but in need of the political guidance the Law
would provide.

In later years Strauss would devote himself to attacking modern political
philosophers' fixation on "natural right," often targeting Thomas Hobbes's

account of self-preservation as the core natural human right. In his review of Guttmann, Strauss argued that medieval thinkers were guided not "by the derived idea of natural right, but by the *primary, ancient* idea of *law* as a unified, total regimen of human life; in other words . . . they are pupils of *Plato* and not pupils of Christians."[28] Modern Jewish thought had been so influenced by Christian thinkers (like Kant) that it could not countenance the essentially theocratic dimension of revealed Law; it preferred the liberal notion of "natural right" and the corresponding project of seeking to define and protect basic human freedoms. But Guttmann was not, in fact, as soft on Cohen (and his liberal understanding of Judaism) as Strauss claimed, allowing that much was lost in Cohen's transformation of Judaism's God into a regulatory ethical ideal. And despite his confessed modernism, in his own treatment of Maimonides Guttmann had attended to the same issues that fascinated Strauss, including the tension between esoteric and exoteric expression (the very terms Guttmann used) and the division between philosophical elites and unphilosophical masses. Strauss's attack on Guttmann was, in fact, excessive, the result of overdetermination by several sources of inspiration and influence. These collectively drove Strauss to recover a version of "law" more authoritative than the law of liberalism.

One such source was the sheer fact that some German Jews held out for a political interpretation of Jewish law. In the 1925 essay "Ecclesia Militans," Strauss contemplated the theological significance of neo-Orthodox Jewish groups while reflecting on the political challenge Frankfurt's separatist orthodox community posed for German Zionism.[29] Despite his atheism, Strauss was fascinated by the Orthodox emphasis on law as revealed legislation, and he was particularly interested in the variation offered by Isaac Breuer, a Frankfurt neo-Orthodox thinker who opposed Zionism on the grounds that it threatened to supplant Divine Law and replace it with secular law. For Breuer, the existence of Orthodox communities in the modern world meant that Jews had to ask whether "God and the Torah are primary over the Jewish nation or if the historical relation is primary," as he put it in the 1925 *Das Jüdische Nationalheim* (The Jewish National Home).[30] Even as Strauss found neo-Kantianism limiting for the study of Jewish thought, Breuer and his Orthodox colleagues turned on its head Kant's old dismissal of Judaism as a "collection of mere statutory laws upon which was established a political organization."[31] Where Kant derided Judaism for its legalism, they celebrated Judaism's revealed, living legislation against the modern account of law as mere convention. While Strauss ultimately criticized Breuer for his dismissal of political Zionism, he was impressed by the idea of returning to Judaism's original political authority rather than imitating the nation-state formations of the European powers, as Herzl and other Zionist leaders had done.

Strauss's critique of Guttmann was also informed by the political theology of Carl Schmitt.[32] Though Strauss would ultimately disagree with Schmitt over whether what Schmitt termed "the political" had its source in theology, the young Strauss endorsed Schmitt's anti-liberalism and shared his taste in premodern texts that appeared to validate a politics of obedience to a law not subject to democratic process.[33] In 1932, Strauss published a critical but basically friendly review of Schmitt's 1927 *Concept of the Political*, in which he examined Schmitt's critique of liberalism.[34] Whereas liberal thought tended to divide "the totality of human thought and action" into different spheres— into different "provinces of culture"[35]—Schmitt understood that "the political" was not really a separate sphere unto itself; politics and religion were the two forces that supplied men with existential promises and threats and thus transcended the merely "provincial" limits proposed in the culture model. In his review of Guttmann, Strauss called religion and politics the "original facts" that transcend culture, proposed that a "theologico-political treatise" could accomplish the critique of the philosophy of culture, and referred his reader back to his earlier "Notes" on Schmitt's text.[36]

Strauss was drawn to the way Schmitt's political theology reached from culture back toward nature. As Strauss wrote, "If it is true that the final self-awareness of liberalism is the philosophy of culture, we may say in summary that liberalism, sheltered by and engrossed in a world of culture, forgets the foundation of culture, the state of nature, that is, human nature in its dangerousness and endangeredness."[37] Schmitt's version of the political was directly analogous to the very "nature" that always lay beneath "culture," though culture denied it. While nature here meant primarily Hobbes's *status naturalis*, Strauss's implication was that the "human order of things" below culture was the meaningful subject of political-philosophical inquiry *as well* as of political theology. But if Strauss clung to the philosophical analysis of nature as an internal goal for philosophy, by 1932 he had certainly learned that the very gulf between philosophy and religion, and between the former's private nature and the latter's public function, could benefit philosophers— they need not become political theologians themselves to benefit from political theology's critique of liberalism, and from its teaching that a permanent climate of existential threat demanded the strong rule of law. The implications of Strauss's reading of Schmitt for his 1935 criticism of Guttmann were, simply put, that when Strauss accused Guttmann of operating within the provinces of the philosophy of culture, he meant that Guttmann could not see the true existential stakes of religion, which had been clearer for ancients than they were for moderns.

The degree to which Heidegger influenced Strauss, and the question of whether Strauss ever truly moved from the philosophical preoccupations of his youth to embrace Platonism, has bedeviled many interpreters, especially those who ascribe to Heidegger a brand of nihilism and suggest that Strauss shared it not only in his youth (when Strauss read Friedrich Nietzsche with enthusiasm), but also in his maturity, when he seemed to subscribe to a version of Platonism.[38] The influence was real, but it was partial. During his postdoctoral studies in medieval Jewish thought, existentialism helped Strauss to emphasize political philosophy as a way of understanding the *pragmata* we encounter in the world around us, but he did not follow Heidegger in affirming the priority of the question of Being or the priority of the pre-Socratics. Strauss was slowly moving toward the view that philosophy's social context was crucial, and existentialism's attention toward the life-world provided him with a vital key, even if he would come to take the question of politics rather than Being as first philosophy.

In fact, Heidegger's existentialism prepared Strauss to accept the reading of Plato conducted by the Islamic Aristotelians al-Farabi and Avicenna, who transformed Platonic politics "into a philosophic foundation of the revealed law," as Strauss himself put it.[39] The Islamic Aristotelians, in other words, read Plato's *Laws* as suggesting that the only law deserving of the name comes from a divinity, a teaching an atheist could easily interpret to mean that such a law must be proclaimed divine for the sake of governance alone. Daniel Tanguay has suggested that Strauss's thought took a "Farabian turn" when Strauss was exposed to al-Farabi's reading of Plato's *Laws*, ultimately influencing Strauss's "exoteric writing" thesis itself.[40] Strauss was most likely introduced to al-Farabi by the scholar of medieval Islam Paul Kraus, with whom he examined al-Farabi's paraphrase of Plato's *Laws* as well as al-Farabi's *al-Milla* and *al-Fadila*, in the late 1920s—long after he studied with Heidegger, and after he completed *Spinoza's Critique of Religion*, but before he penned his critique of Guttmann.[41]

Strauss published the essay "Eine vermiate schrift Farabis" in 1936 followed by "Some Remarks on the Political Science of Maimonides and Farabi," that same year.[42] But only in 1945, after publishing "Persecution and the Art of Writing," would Strauss publish "Farabi's *Plato*," in which he would

provide the fullest formulation of his views on the Aristotelian and his reading of Plato.[43] Here Strauss seemed merely to comment on al-Farabi's reading
of Plato's *Laws*, all the while subtly articulating his own claims about the
political nature of philosophizing through the proxy of al-Farabi. According
to Strauss's al-Farabi, the very question of the "political meaning of philosophy" presents a paradox because philosophy itself is unconcerned with political things, but, because man is a social animal, philosophy will always
be conducted in a political context. Thus it is not philosophical inquiry
into political questions but rather a surrounding political context that
produces the political meaning of philosophy: the philosopher finds himself in confrontation with his fellow citizens precisely *because* he attempts
to give a nonpolitical answer to the conventionally political question of
the good life. Al-Farabi well understood the tragic character of the trial
and death of Socrates.

And while al-Farabi seemed to draw a parallel between philosophy and
the "Art of Kingship," in what might seem to be a naïvely literal reading of
Plato's *Republic*, Strauss suggested another meaning for the parallel. Philosophy is akin to kingship in the sense that both arts seek to produce happiness, but kingship is doomed to failure and philosophy has some chance of
success. If real political regimes are always flawed, the "city" produced by the
philosopher only in speech can possess the quality of perfection. As Strauss
wrote, "We contend that [al-Farabi] uses the identification of philosophy
with the royal art as a pedagogic device for leading the reader toward the view
that theoretical philosophy by itself, and nothing else, produces true happiness in this life, i.e., the only happiness which is possible."[44]

But al-Farabi's claim is inevitably an undemocratic one, debarring the
many from the philosophic happiness only an educated elite can enjoy. Al-
Farabi is then obliged to provide the philosopher with a series of ruses for
turning aside his neighbors' suspicions: these are, first, the idea that philosophy only seeks *perfection* rather than happiness, and second, the idea that
religion might be necessary to secure such happiness; that philosophy on its
own is inadequate to the task. Given that we are by nature political and finite beings, it makes sense that we require human society on the one hand,
and divine aid on the other, to enjoy true happiness. It was in this context
that Strauss made one of his few direct observations about the nature of public speech: "Only because public speech demands a mixture of seriousness
and playfulness, can a true Platonist present the serious teaching, the philosophic teaching, in a historical and hence playful, garb."[45] This form of public

speech can praise an imperfect government or a religious authority toward the goal of defending the philosopher's freedom to dwell "in perfection" within an imperfect (and perhaps easily threatened) regime. Having cleared away misunderstandings in our interpretation of al-Farabi's equation of philosophy and kingship, we can see the philosopher as a "hidden king" of a sort, in fact the only true king.

All the rudimentary elements of Strauss's mature understanding of the philosophy-society relation seem present in "Farabi's *Plato.*" A letter Strauss sent to Guttmann on August 20, 1936, suggests that he was becoming convinced al-Farabi was the key to the medieval problem of the philosophy-religion relation; Strauss referred to plans for an "interpretation of Farabi's writing on Plato, for which I have already gathered the material. I believe, that the last research will not only be of interest relative to al-Farabi, but rather also for medieval Platonism: it is this medieval, and not the new Platonism, for which al-Farabi's conception of Plato was determined." This statement is of interest because of what it omits. It was not al-Farabi read alone but al-Farabi and Maimonides read under the influence of existentialism, that guided Strauss toward the distinction between religion's public function and the philosopher's need for privacy.

Strauss Responds to Heidegger

In "An Introduction to Heideggerian Existentialism," a lecture probably given in the mid-1950s, Strauss claimed that "everyone who had read his first great book and did not overlook the wood for the trees could see the kinship in temper and direction between Heidegger's thought and the Nazis."[46] This statement undoubtedly reflects Strauss's retrospective judgment, but it seems likely that from the late 1920s Strauss had understood Heidegger's thought as a reaction to contemporary crises both philosophical and political. Yet "temper and direction" falls short of Karl Löwith's suggestion that there was an "inner nihilism" or an inner "national socialism" hidden within Heidegger's emphasis on resolve.[47] Strauss's more moderate formulation of the link between Heidegger's thought and politics can be variously interpreted. Further from Heidegger than some of his generational colleagues, particularly Arendt, Löwith, Hans Jonas, and Herbert Marcuse, Strauss may have felt less fear of "theoretical contagion," to use Wolin's apposite phrase.[48] Strauss the political Zionist had been a very different reader of Heidegger than

most of the teacher's "children." He was more stridently antiliberal, receptive to models of political conflict that were abhorrent to many German Jews,
and furthermore he was receptive to Schmitt. Strauss wrote to Löwith in
praise of "the Roman idea" of fascism six days before Heidegger delivered his
infamous *Rektoratsrede*, the Rector's Address in which he stated his intention to place his philosophy in the service of National Socialism. Strauss's
restrained reference to "temper and direction" may have been intended to
divert attention from his debts to Heidegger precisely *because* of his anxiety,
not about "intellectual contagion," but about simply having Heidegger's mark
on his work recognized.

In fact, the question of whether Strauss was in fact a "closet Heideggerian" has become a flash point for conflict between Strauss's critical and sympathetic interpreters. Some have claimed that the two shared nihilistic views,
or, more modestly, have proposed that Strauss saw Heidegger as a nihilist,
found that nihilism resonant, and then hid his own Heidegger-influenced
nihilism behind a filigreed screen of Platonism.[49] This has caused some
defenders of Strauss's legacy to attend closely to his infrequent comments
on Heidegger, producing animated and combative readings of Strauss's
thought—often couched as readings of what Strauss *really* thought and thus
raising the suspicion that Strauss was playing shell games. Interpreters who
have seen Strauss as truly anti-Heideggerian—among them Allan Bloom and
Eugene Miller—have identified Heidegger as the source of the historicism
that Strauss opposed throughout his career, and have read Strauss's antihistoricism as opposition to value-relativism and the nihilism that often seems
to follow from it.[50] Any fixation on the question of Strauss's putative "Heideggerianism" is also fixation on the possibility of the theoretical contami-
nation of his work by "national socialist" and "nihilist" philosophy, and
rests on the questionable judgment that Heidegger's philosophy is itself con-
taminated by his politics. Even more problematically, the fixation on Heideggerian elements in Strauss's thinking misses the complexity of Heidegger's
influence on Strauss, the fact that it was a matter of "elements" rather than
wholesale ideological transfer. Strauss made it very clear that he had been impressed by, and felt a need to respond to, not only the question of Being that
Heidegger had presented in *Being and Time*, but also Heidegger's style in addressing his publics, both academic and extra-academic.

Because Heidegger was not his primary teacher, Strauss most likely
understood him within the full matrix of his other Weimar influences, as he
indicated in the 1962 Preface to *Spinoza's Critique of Religion*. Here, Strauss

made plain the close connection he saw between "the new thinking" of Heidegger's thought and Nietzsche's "philosophy of the future."

> The philosophy of the future is distinguished from traditional philosophy, which pretended to be purely theoretical, by the fact that it is consciously the outcome of a will: the fundamental awareness is not purely theoretical but theoretical and practical, inseparable from an act of the will or a decision. The fundamental awareness characteristic of the new thinking is a secularized version of the Biblical faith as interpreted by Christian theology. What is true of Nietzsche is no less true of the author of *Sein und Zeit*.[51]

Carl Schmitt's presence in these lines is clear, if curiously unstated, for Strauss's emphasis on "will" in both Nietzsche and Heidegger suggests that he understood their thought in precisely the same light as he had understood Schmitt's political theology many years before. Their philosophies were decisionist, centered on acts of will, and rested on the secularization of religious motifs just as Schmitt had once claimed that "all modern concepts of the state are secularized theological concepts."[52] While Strauss did not say so in 1962, it had been this dimension of Heidegger's thought that had compelled him as a young man awake to the possibility that intellectual life is a matter of both theory and practice, whatever the pretenses of "traditional" philosophy might have been. It seems likely, too, that it was Heidegger's understanding that philosophizing was an act not merely of intellect but of will that had so impressed the young Strauss.

Despite the considerable differences that emerged between their bodies of work as Strauss matured, the young Strauss and Heidegger had been united in their interest in the prephilosophical and prepolitical "life-world" where we express our wills. Strauss was drawn to Heidegger's thought by the master's belief in the "crisis of the West," his conviction that modern rationalism was essentially self-destructive, and his desire to reengage with the texts of the Greek philosophical tradition through a new practice of reading he termed *Destruktion*. While Heidegger's emphasis on the prephilosophical was vaguely congruous with Nietzsche's insistence, in *Beyond Good and Evil*, that one "play *the* dangerous game" by living " 'unphilosophically' and 'unwisely,' above all *imprudently*, and bear[ing] the burden and duty of a hundred attempts and temptations of life" and with Schmitt's emphasis on the existentially demanding engagement with risk entailed by "the political," Heidegger's work touched Strauss in ways beyond the categories supplied by Nietzsche or, eventually, by Schmitt (Strauss's commentary on Schmitt was, of course, published and presumably written years after Strauss's time studying with Heidegger).[53] It was Heidegger who Strauss said was the "name" behind the "nameless" movement of existentialism.[54] Even Strauss's return to Greek thought began along the path Heidegger had walked, although it then forked onto a different route—for while Strauss would follow Heidegger in staging a return to the classics in order to think beyond the crisis of modernity, Strauss reached the urban environment of classical political philosophy whereas Heidegger had struck out for the wilds of the pre-Socratic question of Being. In fact it was Heidegger's very preoccupation with Being that Strauss would later assess as a root cause of his teacher's abandonment of ethics and politics and his disdain for the Greek classics' treatments of both, or as he would eventually reflect in a letter to Alexandre Kojève, "we both apparently turned away from Being to Tyranny because we have seen that those who lacked the courage to face the issue of Tyranny, who therefore . . . . were forced to evade the issue of Being as well, precisely because they did nothing but talk of Being."[55]

Strauss implied that the "issue of Being" was somehow tied to politics, but that talk of Being could obscure access to that issue. Heidegger's emphasis on Being and its conditioning by temporality was bound up, for Strauss, with the problem of Heidegger's historicism. Heidegger had refused the distinction between nature and convention that would become crucial for Strauss, and by accepting that values are determined by will along the horizon line of historical time Heidegger had lost his powers of political discernment.[56]

Before engaging in a closer reading of Strauss's scattered discussions of Heidegger, it is useful to review the intellectual tools Strauss took from Heidegger, the patterns of thought into which Heidegger led him, and the styles of thinking Heidegger displayed and that Strauss rejected. To the first category belong the lens of existential phenomenology itself (though as we will see Strauss refocused it on the pragmata of politics and allowed the question of Being to fuzz into incoherence in the background) and the technique of *Destruktion*. In the second we might place the felt need to return to tradition while reading it with new and radical eyes, and the sense that in its crisis modern rationalism cried out for conversation with religious sources—the Bible in particular. To the third belong Heidegger's onetime desire for philosophy to "lead" politics and his historicist rejection of the nature/convention distinction. Strauss would see both as mistakes into which the question of Being had led Heidegger.

Heidegger described *Destruktion* as a method necessary for properly engaging with Greek thought, shaking off mistaken readings of texts that had accrued over generations of scholarly practice.[57] Strauss would later describe Heidegger's method as follows: "By uprooting and not simply rejecting the tradition of philosophy, [Heidegger] made it possible for the first time after many centuries . . . to see the roots of the tradition and thus perhaps to know, what so many merely believe, that those roots are the only natural and healthy roots."[58] But of course the engagement with tradition had a pressing philosophical meaning for Heidegger, who at the time Strauss studied with him imagined *Destruktion* as a reading practice that did more than merely uncover the meanings of texts below their accumulated traditional readings—it actually "rendere[d] uncertain one's own existence [*Dasein*]." As Sheppard points out, becoming uncertain about one's own existence was, for Heidegger, an experience that paralleled becoming uncertain about one's relationship with philosophical tradition. Forgetting the question of Being and forgetting the philosophical origins of one's own practice went hand in hand—so recovering the question (and thus the uncertainty) of Being meant recovering a question about the origins of the philosophical method one practiced. While Heidegger himself did not want to return to the teachings of Plato and Aristotle, whose metaphysical framework had, in his view, obscured the question of Being, Strauss found in Heidegger's reading practice a way to read post-Socratic thought afresh. As Strauss made it very clear in his "An Introduction to Heideggerian Existentialism," his Plato was no morally decisive antidote to the relativism he found in Heidegger, but rather a figure of doubt and questioning, unsure about the extent of his own knowledge and ignorance.

Strauss approached Heidegger's express desire for philosophy to lead politics (Heidegger had once stated his wish to "lead the Fuhrer" [*den Führer führen*]) far more obliquely than his friend Löwith, who meditated on it directly in his 1946 "The Political Implications of Heidegger's Existentialism." Löwith claimed that Heidegger "took on political responsibilities and involvements in a manner consistent with the fundamental thesis of *Being and Time*."[59] For Löwith, Heidegger's emphasis on "resolution"—one version of the expression of will—was disastrous because it was not joined to a method of judging the worth of different goals, the objects of resolve. In contrast, Strauss seemed as struck by Heidegger's influence on his audience as by his thought. Whereas Max Weber had done much to aid scholars' understanding of charisma in social and political life, Heidegger actually possessed that quality in abundance, and in Strauss's eyes Heidegger made Weber, "the incarnation of the spirit of science and scholarship" seem "an orphan child."[60] Strauss said he "had never seen before such seriousness, profundity, and concentration in the interpretation of philosophic texts." And yet Heidegger's charisma ultimately inhibited intellectual inquiry. In Strauss's retelling of Heidegger's 1929 disputation with Ernst Cassirer in Davos, Switzerland (which may well have been a secondhand retelling; there is no evidence that Strauss was at Davos himself), Heidegger's charisma inspired a "paralysis of the critical faculties" in all who heard him. Strauss deepened the claim by expressing his suspicion that for the students of existentialism, "philosophizing seems to have been transformed into listening with reverence to the incipient *mythoi* of Heidegger."[61] The religious overtones of that description are notable; so is the close relationship between "listening" and waiting for Being to come into itself in historical time. As Wolin points out, when Heidegger pushed his philosophical investigations into historical terms, as in an infamous 1949 lecture in which he compared industrial agriculture facilities to concentration camps, his philosophy of Being only produced "judgmental incapacities," both in himself and in his audience.[62] While Strauss studied with Heidegger for only a short time, and never lingered long enough in Freiburg to become a part of the "charismatic community" (to use Max Weber's term) of students gathered around to hear the master think, he certainly would have recognized that community's existence.

Whatever "unrest" and "dissatisfaction" ran through his audience, Strauss's Heidegger could calm listeners through his sheer "clarity and certainty." Strauss chose two lines from Virgil's *Aeneid* to describe this effect: "Tum, pietate gravem ac meritis si forte virum quem / Conspexere, silent arrectisque auribus adstant"[63] ("If then some grave and pious man appear, they hush their noise, and lend a listening ear"[64]). Here Virgil compares Neptune's ability to calm the waves to the power of a masterful orator, and in quoting him Strauss both underscored the authoritarian dimension of Heidegger's influence and effectively colluded with Heidegger in his "mythic" aspirations by inscribing him into the *Aeneid* itself.[65] In the epic, Neptune calms the waves that batter the hero Aeneas's ships, having ascertained that his sister, the goddess Juno, had summoned them on the basis of an old grudge she held against Aeneas's mother Venus, who had been chosen as the most beautiful of the goddesses by the mortal Paris. Thus Neptune's intervention not only saves Aeneas and the refugees he leads away from the ruins of Troy, it also plays an indirect role in the foundation of the Roman state, which is the political denouement of the entire epic. Strauss certainly knew Heidegger had been unsuccessful in his efforts to influence the National Socialist movement through his philosophy, but, given the range of quotations from the classics available to Strauss, his choice of the *Aeneid*'s myth of the state must have been self-consciously made. Levinas, notably, looked back on Heidegger with similar concern. In a late interview he opined, "there is in Heidegger the dream of a nobility of the blood and the sword," a statement that recalls the "crusading" spirit Strauss had once observed in Weimar medievalism, though he did not name Heidegger explicitly.[66]

Delivered after the important midcareer works *On Tyranny* and *Natural Right and History*, "An Introduction to Heideggerian Existentialism" has an autobiographical quality Strauss's more formal written works lack, as Strauss relates to his audience what it had felt like to be personally caught up in Heidegger's revolution in thought. And yet the lecture began by dragging Heidegger (very much alive at the time of Strauss's lecture) *out* of his time and into the Greek temporal horizon where Strauss, by this time, felt most at home: "Existentialism has reminded people that thinking is incomplete and defective if the thinking being, the thinking individual, forgets himself as what he is. It is the old Socratic warning."[67] Strauss was forthright on one point: Heidegger had faced the critical challenge present to German philosophers in the 1920s, namely that of ethics, which had been such a strong presence in the teachings of Hermann Cohen and which Strauss felt Cohen's student Cassirer had simply dropped. At the Davos disputation Heidegger had implied that Kant's conclusions, regarding the finitude of reason itself, should actually lead to a critique of Western metaphysics (and thus the ethics that depends on metaphysics) at its very foundation.[68] From the perspective of the question of Being, ethics had no ground and thus Heidegger ruled it impossible and faced the "abyss" left open by his judgment. Strauss then led his audience to conclude that, if one accepted that Heidegger had been right, there could not really *be* philosophical positions of any kind, at least not the kind of positions that might support a faltering "rational liberalism" (his term).[69] Strauss's term "abyss" alluded to the relationship between "abyss" (*Abgrund*) and "ground" (*Grund*) in Heidegger. Michael Inwood points out that for Heidegger *Grund* conjured the Greek *arche*, which means a first principle, beginning, or rule, in the sense of either a way of doing something or a way of ordering and controlling something.[70] The term *Abgrund,* then, means not the simple lack of these things, but connotes depth and a downward trajectory as well; Heidegger's *Abgrund* is not so much an abyss for *Dasein,* which "is in existing, the ground of its ability-to-be" or in other words can root itself in itself, but clearly denies first principles to any philosophy incapable of grounding itself in itself. Strauss's actual remark, "I am afraid that we shall have to make a very great effort in order to find a solid basis for rational liberalism," was thus carefully and ironically phrased. For a Heideggerian, solid bases are not so much found as they are encountered as the already-present terms of one's existence (Heidegger's term to describe this was *Geworfenheit* or thrown-ness) and then chosen in an act of self-grounding.

Strauss acknowledged that the problem of an "abysmal" liberalism was only a problem if Heidegger's philosophy was in a strong sense correct—but the great difficulty was that no philosopher besides Heidegger was capable of reading *Being and Time* and properly judging its merits. Strauss denied his own ability to judge on the grounds that he was a mere "scholar" next to Heidegger, a gesture with the fortunate side effect of allowing Strauss to continue to entertain the potential truth-content of existentialism; Strauss even acknowledged that he was passing over the opportunity to dismiss Heidegger's thought on the grounds of his Nazism, which he described as being "akin" to Heidegger's philosophy at its core.

The remainder of Strauss's lecture simply dropped the problem of Heidegger's Nazism and the anxiety that it might be a philosophically communicable infection. In the next paragraph, Strauss proceeded from the premise that it was "insufficient" to simply protect liberal democracy from outside threats (and Strauss intimated that Nazism and fascism were such threats) because liberal democracy faced graver dangers from within, dangers Nietzsche had already described in his critique of modernity. According to that critique, heightened professional specialization, expanded knowledge of the world through newspapers and other media, and our acquisition of greater comfort pulls us away from true self-knowledge. The problem summarized by the familiar adage that we "know more and more about less and less" is that science cannot tell us what to do with the power science gives us, a problem that worried Arendt in *The Human Condition,* published in 1958 and thus written just a few years after Strauss probably gave his lecture. And the most extreme form of this thought, for Strauss (or for Arendt) is that scientists and engineers do not simply lack political acumen, but display political stupidity when they imagine that fixing a polity's problems is like fixing a cantilever bridge.

In a lecture that would become famous as the essay, "The Question Concerning Technology," Heidegger had emphasized the way the phenomenal dimensions of science and technology distracted moderns from their essences unless they could return to a more primary understanding of *techne* in its original sense as "revealing." Strauss's critique was less oriented toward science and technology themselves and more toward their abandonment of true rationalism, which Western liberals had left behind wholesale when they adopted the "Epicurean" mindset of Francis Bacon and Thomas Hobbes, embracing instead the thought that science and engineering are here to perfect the human estate on earth. In the process, those liberals reached the same problem as the existentialists: they shirked the (quintessentially Socratic) responsibility to question the values of their society.[71] By framing the problem of modernity in this fashion, Strauss strove to go beyond the simple categories of conservative *Kulturkritik* he had received during his youth, from sources ranging from Nietzsche to Paul de Lagarde. He arrived, as we know, not at the prephilosophical and prescientific version of Greek thought Heidegger formulated, but rather at a version of classical rationality that required none of the "grounding" affirmations of the life-world found in Heidegger or even in Nietzsche.

Strauss claimed to find a gap in Heidegger's thought, a gap the size of the idea of the whole. If Heideggerian existentialism's insight into the limits of our knowledge can be expressed in the statement, "we cannot know the whole," does this insight not rest on at least an intuition of the existence of a whole, and thus an Archimedean point from whence we might glimpse that whole? This perspectival problem found its parallel in existentialism's inability to gauge its own situation in history. Both existentialism and historicism, Strauss implied, claim that there can be no atemporal truth but do so in a specific location in time, and thus must forget or cover up their own essential situatedness. This led thinkers like Heidegger to miss the way their own thought belonged to "the decline of Europe" (Strauss's term) or, in other words, that Heidegger's thought was less a *solution* to the crises of European modernization than a symptom thereof. Strauss's Heidegger is actually very similar to Nietzsche in the "untimely" quality of his thought—its need for an ahistorical and extra-worldly point of measurement—but Heidegger is unaware of this, because unlike Nietzsche he is convinced that his philosophy is timely.

But Heidegger's "timely" engagement with the problems of the present had the merit of opening up possibilities foreclosed upon by modernity's version of *techne*. If *techne* resulted from an "unmastered" or "unlimited" version of the Greek philosophical desire to understand "the whole," thereby mastering Being on the plane of theory, Heidegger's thought gestured toward an abandonment of that stance of mastery. The "deepest roots" of Western thought in Heidegger, Strauss said, tangled underground with the roots of an Eastern counterpart. Those "deep roots" were biblical—the Bible (Strauss likely meant the Hebrew Bible) is the trace of the East within the West, offering a (to once again use Strauss's terminology) "counter-poison" to Western thought, the attitude of *Gelassenheit* or "releasement." The notion of "deep roots" suggests, of course, that what for Heidegger was an *Abgrund* or abyss was also—as one literal meaning of "Ab-grund" (down-ground) suggests—a path down into historical time. At the close of his lecture Strauss suggested that Heidegger's thought, and thus existentialism as a movement, would always combine Plato and the Bible—that is, both would hover between the desire for knowledge of the whole, and an inclination to place limits on the search for knowledge and operate in a life-world both prerational and prescientific. Heidegger's *Esse*, Strauss said somewhat gnomically, "is a synthesis of Platonic ideas and the Biblical God: it is as impersonal as the Platonic ideas and as elusive as the Biblical God."[72]

Strauss would later extend these reflections in the 1962 Preface to *Spinoza's Critique of Religion*—that autobiographical text in which he returned to the crucible of his earlier existential medievalism and poked the embers beneath it—and in the process shed light on his gnomic "synthesis" statement. Strauss claimed that Heidegger rejected one account of the human subject, namely, "the Greek understanding of man as a rational animal" and replaced it with "the Biblical understanding of man as created in the image of God." Heidegger was thus very close, in Strauss's view, not only to the exoteric versions of Maimonides and al-Farabi, with their emphases on the human subject's vulnerability and debt to an extrahuman force that nevertheless infuses the human, but also to that other "new thinker," Franz Rosenzweig.

Heidegger had been a compelling speaker in part because in speech and manner he presented himself as an outsider to the academy, expressing himself in everyday language rather than in the parlance of academic philosophy. But he was not a master of public speech. Toward the end of his career Strauss expressed his views on public speech in conversation with his lifelong friend Jacob Klein. "Philosophy," he said, is the attempt to replace opinion by knowledge; but opinion is the element of the city, hence philosophy is subversive, hence the philosopher must write in such a way that he will improve rather than subvert the city. In other words, the virtue of the philosopher's thought is a certain kind of "mania" while the virtue of the philosopher's public speech is "sophrosyne."[73]

Interestingly, Strauss's remark about "opinion" being the "element of the city" came remarkably close to Heidegger's use of *Gerede* or "idle talk" in *Being and Time*. There, *Gerede* indicated a means of communication used by those dwelling in "inauthenticity" and often discussing experiences they had not had themselves. But whatever Strauss thought of the truth-content of existentialism—and it is not clear that his mind was fully made up about Heidegger's claims—he saw Heidegger as guilty of engaging in publicly "manic" behavior when "sophrosyne" had been required. Heidegger was an expert manipulator of academic audiences, but even in his fear of the intellectually "leveling-down" effects of the light of the public, Heidegger made the mistake of speaking, in public, truths that were better expressed in private. Indeed, the key to Strauss's attitude toward Heidegger may lie within Strauss's continued references to the religious or mythic dimension of Heideggerian philosophy. Although Strauss never said so explicitly, he made about Heidegger a claim he had only previously made for a handful of medieval thinkers, namely that Heidegger brought together the lessons of Eastern and Western thought. But Heidegger fell short of Maimonides and al-Farabi because he failed to grasp the fundamentally political nature of the field of human experience onto which his thought opened. A richer understanding of that field might have led to precisely the "sophrosyne" Maimonides had displayed, which involved limiting philosophy in such a way that it did not infringe on the sphere of revealed religion, both for the sake of political stability and for the security of both rationalist and religious frames of mind. For Strauss, the real import of Heidegger's *Geworfenheit*, or "throwness," for philosophers, was that they always found themselves mired in the political even in their efforts to dig beneath it. As he said, in what Seth Bernardete calls Strauss's "Golden Sentence," "the problem inherent in the surface of things, and only in the surface of things, is the heart of things."[74] Strauss cultivated his interest in surfaces in full awareness of Heidegger's interest in depths, the *Abgrund*, and roots.

CHAPTER 2

The Exoteric Writing Thesis

If Strauss composed any of his works in a spirit of irony, surely it was the 1941 "Persecution and the Art of Writing." Published in *Social Research*, a journal whose authors often depicted social scientists as agents of progressive social change, the essay implied that the journal's editors had misunderstood the public audience intellectuals might hope to reach. Whereas many *Social Research* authors focused on the influence intellectuals might have on political life as commentators, activists, or consultants, "Persecution and the Art of Writing" imagined the public as an uncomprehending and potentially hostile crowd rather than a receptive audience for the teachings of sociologists, economists, political scientists, and others.

Strauss's "exoteric writing" thesis, put forward in the essay and more commonly referred to as the "esoteric writing thesis," would become one of his most famous (for some, infamous) contributions to the history of philosophy. The thesis was simple enough: throughout the ages scholars, philosophers, and critics have written "between the lines" in order to avoid censorship and penalties as harsh as death. In the most succinct summary of his argument, Strauss presented exoteric writing as a form of ethical action. As he wrote, "Exoteric literature presupposes that there are basic truths which would not be pronounced in public by any decent man, because they would do harm to many people who, having been hurt, would naturally be inclined to hurt in turn him who pronounces the unpleasant truths."[1]

Employed at the New School for Social Research where *Social Research* was based, Strauss served as an associate editor at the journal under the sociologist Hans Speier, whom he had known in Berlin. Both were members of what was termed the "University in Exile," a collection of émigré scholars, many of them refugees from Nazi Germany, many of whom had known one another in Europe. Old relationships often carried over to the New School.

Speier had himself served under the economist Emil Lederer, one of *Social Research*'s senior contributors and a dean at the New School, when Lederer was editor of the *Archiv für Sozialwissenschaft und Sozialpolitik* at the Berlin Hochschule für Politik. In his own *Social Research* essay, "Freedom and Science," Lederer stressed the intellectual's obligations to the world beyond himself, and he was joined by many of the journal's authors who insisted on a scholar's responsibility to speak regardless of the personal consequences.[2] Strauss's emphasis on the consequences of speech was therefore a subtle response to his colleagues at his new academic home. Late in "Persecution and the Art of Writing," Strauss praised Plato's "noble lie," which he had not yet mentioned in any of his extant writings, saying "these imitations of the resourceful Odysseus were perhaps merely more sincere than we when they called 'lying nobly' what we now call 'considering one's social responsibilities.'"[3]

Some background about the New School for Social Research, Strauss's progress through its ranks, and the journal *Social Research* is necessary for a full appreciation of the ironies and scholarly contributions of "Persecution and the Art of Writing." Strauss arrived in New York in 1937 and in 1938 Alvin Johnson, president of the New School, offered him a position. Between 1938 and 1948 Strauss's life transformed. He made the slow transition from poorly paid lecturer to tenured full professor, his wife and stepson joined him from Europe, and he took American citizenship.[4] But Strauss's chance arrival at the New School as a lecturer—in one of the happenstance occurrences that shape academic careers, he had been recommended to Johnson by Harold Laski of the London School of Economics, who had met Strauss during his stint as a Rockefeller Foundation fellow pursuing research on Hobbes—placed him under a new kind of pressure, for he was bound to resist the New School's ethos.[5]

The New School had been born out of a 1917 struggle for free speech at Columbia University. Professors Charles A. Beard and James Harvey Robinson resigned to protest the firing of two of their colleagues, political historians James Cattell and Henry Dana, in retribution for their opposition to America's entry into World War I.[6] Beard and Robinson's departure led to a debate over questions of academic freedom and precipitated the discussions leading to the New School's formation. The institution's founders (who included Beard and Robinson, as well as philosopher John Dewey and sociologist Thorstein Veblen) had been preoccupied, appropriately enough, by the question of the intellectual's social role, the very question that had shadowed

Strauss from Germany.[7] Their chosen name, the New School, implied an alternative to all that was stagnant and conservative in American higher education, and they planted the first version of their institution in the West Village, at the other end of Manhattan from Columbia's Morningside Heights campus.

Not only did these founders believe that scientific knowledge had a socially as well as a technically progressive character, some of them, including Veblen, believed the United States had inherited a mantle of sorts following the devastation of so many European universities in the Great War. In his 1918 essay "War and Higher Learning," Veblen described the United States as a guardian of scholarship, and depicted American scholars as having a special responsibility to aide their European counterparts.[8] It was precisely such an attitude of stewardship that Strauss encountered and rejected a generation later. This posture only became more widespread after 1933 when the New School enjoyed a "second founding" of sorts through a real act of stewardship, the establishment of the "University in Exile," renamed the Graduate Faculty in 1935. While this second founding was in the main an attempt to assist refugee scholars fleeing Europe, many of them Jews or socialists, it also fulfilled Alvin Johnson's longstanding dream of building the New School into a powerhouse of social scientific research. In addition to establishing the University in Exile, Johnson created *Social Research* in 1934 to provide his new faculty with an organ in which to publish their research and views, and to bind them together morally; as he put it in a letter, "Social Research was an instrument in maintaining the collective spirit of the continental scholars comprising our faculty."[9] *Social Research* was also intended as a platform from which refugees from the liberal Weimar Republic (like Speier and Lederer) might pursue the Republic's ideals on new soil, and thus, as Eugene Sheppard notes, Strauss would feel a need to respond not only to the progressivist American liberalism of Johnson and his colleagues, but to specters from his own past.[10] In "Persecution and the Art of Writing" and other essays of this period, Strauss emphasized education precisely because he felt that the liberal educators of Weimar had mishandled the upbringing of the youth, allowing them to fall under the sway of political extremists.[11] Anxieties about civilization's collapse fueled Strauss's fear for future generations, even as his colleagues expressed far shorter-term anxieties about the outcome of the war and the possible consequences of fascism in contemporary Europe. Strauss was, in other words, learning to think in the long term.

Certainly Johnson had Germany's hostile new regime on his mind when he penned a foreword for the inaugural issue of *Social Research*, celebrating the new feeling of openness and freedom enjoyed by the school's émigré scholars. He called *Social Research* the mouthpiece of a new cosmopolitan intellectual movement that would oppose the nationalism rising in Europe.[12] That opposition came in the form of numerous essays on the intertwined themes of free speech and the social responsibility of intellectuals by luminaries ranging from Lederer to novelist Thomas Mann and theologian Paul Tillich.[13] Strauss never singled out these worthies for criticism in his contributions to the journal, but the subversive character of his offerings would have been clear to anyone who knew him.

Strauss's first essay for *Social Research*, the 1939 "The Spirit of Sparta or a Taste of Xenophon," recommends itself as a kind of precursor not only to *On Tyranny*, Strauss's major study of Xenophon's *Hiero*, but also to "Persecution and the Art of Writing." Here Strauss explored the Athenian historian, mercenary, and Socrates-pupil Xenophon's criticism of the politics of the city-state of Sparta, which offended him by (as Strauss put it) "subject[ing] everything to the requirements of public virtue," meaning the visible performance of virtuous behavior.[14] According to the rules laid down by the ruler Lycurgus, Spartans were educated more by compulsion than by education in letters and speech, all to the end of maintaining public decorum and order in the city. In Xenophon's view, as in Strauss's, this was disastrous because "Lycurgus compelled all the Spartans to practice all virtues publicly: that is, he did not (and he could not) compel them to practice virtue in private." The development of the habit of "brachylogy," or brief speech, was just one of the ways they maintained private vices. Strauss added a footnote connecting Xenophon's observations about Sparta, the *Constitution of the Lacedemonians* (II, 2) with its reference to "private pedagogues," to Plato's *Laws* (666e), which contains a similar admonition to teach the young to cultivate private as well as public forms of virtue. After his reading of Plato's *Laws* through the lens of al-Farabi, Strauss had come to view that text as encouraging a modification of Socrates's harsh moralism, which would have allowed Socrates to function in the Athenian city-state, by simply showing one face to the public and the other to private philosophical audiences, while carefully employing pedagogical methods that might improve the young from the inside out.[15]

Strauss also described another text of Xenophon's, the *Memorabilia*, in which Xenophon presented his most important (and apologetic) account of

Socrates—but a public and not a private Socrates, the philosopher as he behaved and not how he thought or believed. Strauss discovered in the *Memorabilia* a perplexing tension between what Socrates did and what he thought, or as Strauss wrote,

> In the main [the *Memorabilia*] openly states his public views, i.e., the opinions which he uttered in public and in private conversation with people who were merely members of the public. Their not quite serious nature is indicated between the lines, i.e., by occasional remarks which are in flagrant contradiction to his public views and which, therefore, are apt to be deleted by modern editors . . . in order to discover Xenophon's and Socrates' private views one must do some private thinking, and especially one must in each case deduct from Socrates's statements that deliberate distortion of the truth which was caused by his compliance with, and adaptation to, the specific imbecility of the interlocutor with whom he happened to talk.[16]

In short, Strauss discovered a mode of writing that presented philosophy's findings in terms compatible with the public's notions of the true and the good. Faced with the brachylogical Spartans, Xenophon (who, as an exile from Athens, was politically vulnerable) adapted himself to their mode of expression, an achievement "which is surpassed only by Plato's *Laws*."[17] While this essay was not a direct assault on the principles of liberalism, it tacitly implied that there was something tyrannical about the very expectation that philosophers pass a test for "public-spiritedness," and traded on an opposition between philosophy and the public life of politics already familiar from Strauss's prior works. As Strauss put it, "political life, if taken seriously, meant belief in the gods of the city, and philosophy is the denial of the gods of the city."[18] But Strauss's essay also introduced a new emphasis on writing as the materialization of philosophic teaching and on the political consequences of publicizing the truth in written form—something the students of Socrates had to discover for themselves, for their teacher had written nothing down.[19]

Strauss drew his essay to a close by noting that while the wisdom of exoteric literature appeared "in all epochs" "in which wisdom was not separated from moderation," modernity was dominated by philosophical systems with immoderate hopes and world-transforming aims.[20] Jean-Jacques Rousseau's philosophy was paradigmatic of this earnest modern trend, and thus "the restitution of a sound approach" to philosophy "is bound up with the elimination of Rousseau's influence."[21] In *The Political Philosophy of Hobbes: Its Basis and Its Genesis*, published just three years before his Xenophon essay, Strauss had compared Rousseau (unfavorably) to the Greeks, saying that he had broken from the Greek view of Man as a "rational animal" (*zoon logikon*). Rousseau replaced the Greek view not with the ancient biblical view Heidegger would choose (Man as created being in the image of the Divine), but rather with a new view of Man as a being with no fixed nature but instead a fluid one that could be subordinated to Rousseau's famous "general will."[22]

That same year Strauss explored similar concerns in "The Literary Character of *The Guide of the Perplexed*," which approached the exoteric writing thesis from the precincts of Talmudic and Platonic thought. Strauss understood quite well that his essay was a work of heresy. As he said in a 1938 letter to Jacob Klein, written when he was just beginning "The Literary Character," he was claiming that "Maimonides was absolutely not a Jew in his belief." On his reading, in the famous *Moreh Nevukim* (Guide of the Perplexed), Maimonides held there to be an "incompatibility in principle of philosophy and Judaism."[23] Fortunately Strauss's essay did not make its claim in a bald-faced manner but rather proceeded to cast Maimonides as a guide who explained how best to maintain heretical positions in a circumspect manner.[24]

Maimonides had served as Strauss's paradigmatic exoteric writer ever since Strauss learned to read the "Great Eagle" through the lens of al-Farabi. It had been Maimonides' strategy, Strauss held, to render apologia for philosophy in the face of Jewish orthodoxy by claiming that philosophy was a central concern and presence in Jewish texts. But he himself had been a philosopher at his core and stood in two traditions of concealment, one whose source was Plato and the other the Talmud. That is, as a reader of al-Farabi, Maimonides received al-Farabi's rendition of Plato's *Laws* and their injunctions for philosophers to observe the distinction between public and private modes of speech and behavior. And, as Strauss noted, the sages of the Talmud had always disapproved of any disclosure of the Bible's secrets, especially when it meant writing them down: "explaining secrets in a book is tantamount to transmitting those secrets to thousands of men. Consequently, the Talmudic prohibition mentioned implies the prohibition against writing a book devoted to their explanation."[25] By couching the *Moreh Nevukim* as a dialogue between himself and his student Joseph, Maimonides achieved the appearance of an appropriate oral transmission of knowledge even as he engaged in an act of conscious transgression.

Importantly for Strauss, Maimonides' act of transgression was made necessary by a set of political circumstances akin to those that had inspired
Xenophon's art of exoteric writing. Xenophon was himself an exile from Athens; Maimonides and his student Joseph were Jews in the Diaspora (or exile;
galut) and Joseph was about to go on a journey that would likely separate him
from his teacher forever. Maimonides thus had to render his teachings in a
transportable form, and a form that might survive the passing of fragile human relationships. Strauss published his essays on exoteric writing as a member of the University in Exile, and the references to the modern period he
scattered through "The Literary Character" made it plain that he understood
the parallel between his own position and that of Maimonides. Strauss drew
close the implicit comparison by noting that both he and Maimonides had
written against dominant public opinion—belief in revealed religion in Maimonides' time, "historic consciousness" in Strauss's. Strauss even claimed—
controversially for a refugee scholar sheltered by a liberal regime—that he was
writing in a time that required the exoteric technique: "Freedom of thought
being menaced in our time more than for several centuries, we have not only
the right but even the duty to explain the teaching of Maimonides, in order
to contribute to a better understanding of what freedom of thought means."[26]

Strauss did not say just *why* freedom of thought was in jeopardy, but he
completed this consideration in "Persecution and the Art of Writing," which
began with a reorientation of his earlier treatments of the problems of public
speech and free thinking. Whereas Strauss had previously examined cases
in which philosophers might experience the actual curtailment of their liberties to teach or publish, in "Persecution and the Art of Writing" he asked if
the "freedom of thought" afforded by the democratic public sphere might
in fact be false freedom. As Strauss put it, "What is called freedom of thought
in a large number of cases amounts to—and even for all practical purposes
consists of—the ability to choose between two or more different views presented by the small minority of people who are public speakers or writers."[27]
This is what had become of freedom in many countries that had enjoyed relative legal freedom of public debate since the mid-nineteenth century and
Strauss implied that there was something about the *public* conditions of
speech and thought that inherently limited said speech. Turning to the definition of the term "persecution," Strauss claimed that between the harshness
of the Spanish Inquisition and the gentleness of mere social ostracism there
existed types of persecution of great interest for the intellectual historian, and
that those types were present in putatively liberal regimes.[28]

For Strauss the dissemination of knowledge through publishing provided channels through which the truth could travel and spread, but not in the manner for which Enlightenment philosophes like Diderot and d'Alembert might have hoped. The art of exoteric writing, of presenting the "truth about all crucial things" "exclusively between the lines,"[29] had enabled generations of philosophers to reach out through public channels to individuals Strauss called "reasonable friends,"[30] usually young men just waking to their own philosophical potential. Strauss was not describing a code that implied the existence of a secret conspiracy throughout philosophy's history, but rather, a longstanding practice of making oneself alert to contradictions in texts, of watching for inconsistencies that seem somehow deliberate and indicate a writer is presenting multiple levels of truth. Strauss noted that whereas scholars before him understood internal contradictions to indicate that a writer had altered his position on a subject, he understood contradiction as an explicit signal to likeminded readers, alerting them to search for hidden meanings. Crucially, for Strauss the receptive reader of an exoteric text is likely to be in political accord with the author—Strauss thus discovered, in the exoteric writing phenomenon, a kind of proof for his claim that philosophers display greater loyalty to one another than to their nonphilosophical fellows. Optimistically, he believed that the lovers of the truth would cooperate rather than compete among themselves.[31]

Strauss observed that the thinkers of the Enlightenment, in contrast with premodern thinkers who did not believe popular education could bridge the gap between the educated few and the vulgar many, "looked forward to a time when, as a result of the progress of popular education, practically complete freedom of speech would be possible, or—to exaggerate for purposes of clarification—to a time when no one would suffer any harm from hearing any truth."[32] Either education would disseminate truth so broadly that the ideology-dissolving effects of skeptical philosophy no longer seemed corrosive, or popular education and technocracy would work together so that, through development, the various components of society would come to operate in general conformity with the requirements of truth. Modern thinkers living in expectation of such developments rejected the "noble lie," while their premodern counterparts endorsed the "noble lie," the "pious fraud," or, to use an elegant euphemism of Strauss's coinage, the "economy of the truth."[33]

Strauss's "economy of the truth" is a premodern solution necessary until the ultimate success of the modern project of popular education, but Strauss expressed no optimism about such developments coming to pass. As long as one maintains the Platonic view that philosophical contemplation is a private activity in tension with the modalities of popular discussion (although individuals can be led, through dialogue, toward philosophy), exoteric writing offers the writer a distinct educational advantage, the power to lead students from a world of outward appearances to one of inner truths. In fact, "Persecution and the Art of Writing" was the first essay in which Strauss actively attended to pedagogy as one of the philosopher's central concerns. Pointedly, he concluded the essay by saying, "Education, [the philosophers] felt, is the only answer to the always pressing question, to the political question par excellence, of how to reconcile order which is not oppression with freedom which is not license."[34] In a journal that published little on literature or aesthetics, Strauss counseled reading texts for their "inner beauty," but that beauty's import lay in its power to mold the ethical instincts of society's future leaders and to draw potential philosophers out of the public sphere whose mode of discourse was so close to Heidegger's *Gerede*.

Strauss did not flee Germany as a refugee from the Nazis, but rather left in the spring of 1932 to pursue his research abroad, first in Paris, then in England. However, by the time he reached the New School in 1938, he was as much an exile as his colleagues who had fled after Hitler's rise to power in 1933, and he shared their sense of embattlement and crisis. As Sheppard points out, Strauss had by this time had the chastening experience of being a refugee, having been joined by true refugees (both Jewish and not) in even more dire circumstances than his own during his stay in Paris, and then arriving in England to continue his research on Hobbes with meager financial resources.[35] Strauss was an "intellectual in crisis," to employ the title Alvin Johnson chose for one of his own essays in *Social Research*; yet if his experiences of privation would leave him deeply appreciative of the support individuals like Johnson could provide, they did not convince him to share Johnson's instrumentalist understanding of the role of intellectuals in society—and Johnson had at this point even edited an *Encyclopedia of the Social Sciences*, which faintly echoed the Enlightenment encyclopedists themselves.[36] Not only did Strauss never abandon his critique of liberalism (it was, after all, from his first station of exile in Paris that he wrote to Löwith of his unwillingness to "crawl to the cross" of liberalism so long as a glimmer of "the Roman idea" somewhere twinkled), he had learned lessons in his first five years away from Germany that convinced him that serious scholars needed concealment rather than the action-oriented stance Johnson promoted. The year before Strauss's arrival, Johnson had claimed that while "the soldiers and statesmen who dictated the Treaty of Versailles commanded all the force of the world" but "could not create a peace," "the intellectuals and poets" might have succeeded in doing so "given time, adequacy of numbers, sufficient trained abilities."[37] For such a remark to appear after Johnson had also insisted "if we are indeed living in times of emergency we can not pause to weigh values, even eternal values," must have seemed both offensive and like high comedy to Strauss, who had corresponded with that great exploiter of states of emergency Schmitt, and who knew most intellectuals were hardly capable of taking advantage of such states. Johnson also described his graduate faculty as part of a "rational intellectual strategy," by which he could only mean an intervention in public affairs and plausibly on the international stage.

Strauss could have observed similar praise for action in Lederer's 1937 "The Search for Truth," in which Lederer harmonized with Johnson's insistence that intellectuals make decisions, or as Lederer said while reflecting on the causes of the current political crisis, "trust in mere analysis caused the intellectual to forget that every question he asks involves a decision." To be sure, Lederer intended that intellectuals act to defend their freedom. But in Lederer's view the responsibility to act in order to secure freedom subtended all activities done in freedom. "To be free is a burden," Lederer wrote, but this thought had a consequence he did not see. It meant that the value of freedom itself was never questioned, subtly but definitively limiting the territory intellectuals could investigate. Speier, writing in the same issue of *Social Research*, offered a more nuanced account of the way the intellectual's role was determined by a set of special activities. Speier acknowledged that the life of the mind was characterized by sometimes-incompatible needs (solitude in order to think, but also interlocutors and audiences), and he allowed that the unique nature of each historical case meant that no grand unified theory of the intellectual's role was plausible. But universalism crept into his account nevertheless, as Speier claimed that "the community of intellectuals is ultimately based on reason," meaning that intellectuals in exile could always hope to find their fellows even in a strange land. Speier noted that the trauma of exile marked a kind of suspension of values and thus forced intellectuals to account for their relationship with tradition anew, but he also observed that this very alienation essentially produced "an external detachment from local or historical values and a comprehension of the universality of the spirit." Strauss could easily have identified with Speier's account of the inner commonality shared by men who had chosen the life of the mind, for it resembled his own claim about the transhistorical "community" of philosophers, but Speier still made the error of which Strauss would accuse many. Namely, he found transcendent rationality in men who Strauss would have derided as mere social engineers, essentially mechanics of the mind.

Many similar essays appeared in the pages of *Social Research* in the years before Strauss arrived at the New School, and many more would appear after his arrival; the Yale political scientist Harold Laswell made the virtue of cross-pollination out of the necessity of the European intellectuals' exile, Max Lerner, editor of *The Nation*, emphasized intellectuals' need for an audience above all else, and the philosopher Max Wertheimer tied freedom of inquiry to the value of truth in science. It was of course appropriate for the journal of the University in Exile to focus so much attention on the intellectual's present predicament and potential useful function in society, but also understandable that given the embattled and threatened circumstances under which the Exiles worked, early *Social Research* essays on the role of the intellectual contributed more to esprit des corps than to a historical or sociological understanding of the intellectual as a figure. The authors of these essays tended to agree on a few major points: first, that one could speak meaningfully of "the intellectual" as a type; second, that one did not need to say too much about the definitions of that type, or in other words, little ink was wasted arguing over who belonged to the category of "intellectuals" and who was outside it. Third, they agreed that the intellectuals had both the responsibility and the right to take action in a time of political crisis, or in other words that they constituted a special elite by virtue of education and training whose sphere of action (i.e., the range of phenomena about which they could opine or comment) was not limited by their scholarly specialization. Many scholars—like the members of the Frankfurt Institute for Social Research who went to work on Paul Lazarsfeld's Princeton Radio Research Project—had to labor in fields or in jobs that were new to them, expanding their range whether they enjoyed their new tasks or not.[38]

The fourth, and perhaps most overarching, common point that linked the *Social Research* authors was a bias toward what the sociologist Zygmunt Bauman calls a "legislative" rather than an "interpretive" understanding of the role of the intellectual, or as Bauman puts it: "The typically modern strategy of intellectual work is one best characterized by the metaphor of the 'legislator' role. It consists of making authoritative statements which arbitrate in controversies of opinions and which select those opinions which, having been selected, become correct and binding."[39] In contrast, "interpretive"

intellectuals focus their attention on textual and other sources of knowledge, sometimes translating works from one cultural tradition into the literal or figurative idiom of another. And some of the *Social Research* authors
seemed anxious to be acknowledged for their legislative skill, in contrast to
Percy Bysshe Shelley's famous description of poets as the "unacknowledged
legislators of the world."[40] Shelley's claim for poets was based on his notion
that language itself reveals the deep order of the universe, and that our social institutions are ordered through the beneficial mediation of language
itself. The *Social Research* authors tended to root the intellectual's legislative
role not in specific competencies (politics, history, economics, etc.), but rather
in abstract reason, and they were thus distant inheritors of Shelley's sensibility. And yet where Shelley's "unacknowledged" left the poet out of the public
sphere of politics altogether, Johnson and his colleagues were also more
proximate inheritors of the tradition Zola and company had initiated a little
over three decades before, the tradition of the intellectual whose very role
was constituted by the existence of an audience and by the hope that, given a
democratic public sphere, public testimony to the truth could be broadly appreciated and acted upon. Not all the General Faculty's membership looked
beyond the offices and classrooms of the New School and attempted to reach
a journalistic audience, to engage with the American government itself, or to
participate in other forms of activism, but many did, especially the economists; for example, Karl Brandt served on the American Council of Economic Advisers on the strength of his expertise in agriculture.[41]

It naturally does a historical injustice to lump together the diverse group
of American and European expatriate thinkers in the General Faculty under a
single label. However, most of the authors published in *Social Research* shared
an ideological commitment not only to what Nils Gilman calls the "macrohis-
torical quantum known as modernity," but also to the modernization process
that brought it about—and which, for many social scientists, entailed a theory
of history.[42] Max Weber, who did so much to uncover both the benefits of the
"rationalizations" inherent in modernization and the deep costs of that process (the "disenchantment of the world" and the production of "specialists
without spirit" and "sensualists without heart" were just two of the pessimistic assessments of modernity Weber made famous), was among the most cited
authorities in *Social Research*'s early articles. The *Social Research* authors
hewed to varied models of modernization: some favored a human-driven
model of progress that dated back to the Enlightenment, whose sense of the
agency of the individual person was expressed by Kant's motto *sapere aude*

(have the courage to use your own reason) and whose boundless optimism was expressed by the marquis de Condorcet's "nature has set no limit to the realization of our hopes." Others favored a version of Hegelian historicism according to which history itself was the progressive unfolding of reason through its instantiation in a series of human institutions, such as the modern bureaucratic state in which Hegel himself labored. But most of the authors were also indebted to Karl Marx's transformation of Hegel, which made human actors into the crucial (and sometimes revolutionary) agents of historical processes far larger than any individual.[43] Broadly speaking, many of the General Faculty's members were committed to the role of the intellectual in contributing to social progress, regardless of how active or legislative they imagined that role would be—and conversely, social progress was the metanarrative that formed a backdrop for their scholarly projects.

Certainly Strauss arrived at the New School long before the modernization concept's zenith of influence. His colleagues were living and working in parlous times and were insufficiently optimistic to imagine that modernization promised (say, by wiping away political problems using scientific solutions) the "end of ideology," as Raymond Aron would put it in his 1955 *The Opium of the Intellectuals*.[44] But Strauss's anxieties, rooted in his opposition to the idea of humanity setting itself up as master of its own fate, essentially anticipated the later conversation American modernization theorists would create around Aron's phrase. As Gilman points out, "the end of ideology" became a full-blown hypothesis in American social scientific circles in part through the efforts of Karl Mannheim's student Talcott Parsons.[45] One young celebrant, Seymour Martin Lipset, longed for a shift "from ideology to sociology," which would require political scientists to leave the classic works of political theory on the dusty shelves for which they were destined and devote themselves to quantitative research instead. Certainly, the "end of ideology" meant the rising stock of Weber's model of value-free social science, which had attracted Strauss's ire many years earlier. As we will see, Strauss would later interpret his "Persecution and the Art of Writing" as an attempt at an anti-Weberian "sociology of philosophy," opposing the inherently progressive version of the rationalization thesis at work in Weber's "sociology of knowledge." Whereas the champions of the "end of ideology" would long for social scientific research and government problem-solving to replace political argument, Strauss worried that modernization itself entailed an end run around the fundamental question of values over which philosophers had always labored. Modernization's essential promise, in Strauss's view, was not

so much Weberian rationalization, technological progress, or the enshrine-
ment of science as the first principle of society, but rather the autonomy of
Man and his permanent freedom from heteronomy, whether he gave his
"other" the name of God, political strife, or nature.

Strauss's first use of the term "public discussion" in "Persecution and the
Art of Writing" simply describes a negative freedom enjoyed in some countries, the freedom to express one's views regardless of their content. Strauss
says that this freedom has recently been suppressed not by "compulsion," but
rather by the elimination of freedom of thought, which has been replaced by
"the ability to choose between two or more different views presented by the
small minority of people who are public speakers or writers." Strauss's footnote, following "writers," is to Milton's 1644 *Areopagitica*, whose central
thesis is "Reason is but choosing."[46] Milton's tract, a defense of freedom of
speech and expression, was directed at the English Parliament and demanded
the repeal of a Licensing Order, issued June 16, 1643. That order had created
a series of government-appointed censors with control over any material released by a press.[47] But Strauss's ironic footnote indicated that Milton had
been a member of precisely the type of minority of writers whose dominance
limited true freedom of thought. Public discussion may have been "enhanced"
by the presence of figures like Milton, but the quality of publicness—meaning
the availability of an utterance or document or image to a group beyond an
intimate group of conversation partners—does not, in and of itself, serve freedom of thought.

Just before "Persecution and the Art of Writing" appeared, Strauss gave
a lecture to the New School for Social Research's General Seminar in which
he revealed the civilizational vision that was developing, in ways both subtle
and gross, through his essays on literary expression and freedom of thought.
In "German Nihilism," delivered on February 26, 1941, Strauss attacked precisely the principle of the open society for which Milton had labored. It was
a strange effort, and strangely timed—Strauss presented his lecture to an all-
faculty seminar (attendance was a contractual duty for New School faculty)
known both for its liberal progressive views and for its combativeness, even
as Britain still stood very much alone against Germany. The lecture combined
a potted intellectual history of German nihilism with a comparison of "England" (i.e., Great Britain) and Germany. Both states had developed, Strauss
told his audience, out of conflict between a "modern ideal" and its classical
counterpart, a conflict that naturally arose through the modernization process. [48] Whereas England had, Strauss said, managed to preserve civilization

through a "working amalgamation" of the classical ideal with its modern counterpart (he offered little explanation of this, unfortunately), the Germans had been unable to achieve such a feat, and in rejecting modernity they had come to reject the principles of civilization themselves. England, and not Germany, Strauss said, in a statement as unqualified as it was in hindsight disturbing, deserved an empire.

Strauss was careful to distinguish between Hitler's regime and a broader tendency in German thought that he called "nihilist." Criticizing the former he applauded the latter, validating the critique of modernity within German nihilism by placing it in a common lineage that linked Glaucon's criticism of the city of pigs in Plato's *Republic*[49] to Rousseau's critique of the superficial qualities of civilization in *The Social Contract* and both of these to Nietzsche's persistent critique of modernity. The German nihilists were correct to attack the principle of the "open society," Strauss said, on the grounds that said principle could not be reconciled with a truly moral life—for (as Strauss explained) the open society was a goal for those who sought only pleasure and power without responsibility, whereas the loyal members of *closed* societies pursued virtue.[50] Strauss would articulate this idea more fully in *Natural Right and History*, but its genesis lay in his confrontation with the New School and the University in Exile and their joint promotion of openness and publicity without attendance to the consequences of each. In 1941, the same civilizational vision that produced the exoteric writing thesis allowed Strauss to explain to his colleagues that one could be on the right side of the war while remaining on the wrong side of a larger clash of civilizations, in which the war was just one moment.

Very similarly, in "Persecution and the Art of Writing" Strauss suggested that an interest in public speech and the freedom to pursue it was quintessentially modern, as was the belief in popular education that always seemed to follow belief in the public: "What attitude people adopt toward freedom of public discussion, depends decisively on what they think about popular education and its limits."[51] It was in mid-seventeenth-century Europe that both sprang up—the time and place of Milton's *Areopagitica*. As Strauss said, "premodern philosophers were more timid in this respect than modern philosophers."[52] At that point, Strauss said, authors like Milton began to publish not only to express their thoughts but to fight for their right to do so, to abolish "persecution as such." Such authors hoped for a time when popular education would make totally free speech possible, for such speech would no longer have potentially injurious consequences. Their faith in the public was, in other words, couched in a faith in the universal human capacity for understanding. If the very definition of "intellectual" as used affirmatively by his colleagues at *Social Research*, conveyed a sense of a person with a potential (and potentially appreciative) audience, Strauss implied that the hoped-for public was potentially capricious, unresponsive, and likely to strike back at an author judged to be offensive. In his *Areopagitica*, Milton insisted, "A good book is the precious lifeblood of a master spirit, embalmed and treasured up on purpose to a life beyond life." Strauss's point was that such gestures required not only trust in a future posterity whose value and intentions could not be known, but trust in the purposes of readers much closer at hand.

If "Persecution and the Art of Writing" began as an ironic rejoinder to the trends displayed in the pages of *Social Research*, Strauss would later understand the essay as his first step toward a new type of critical practice, as he made clear in the Introduction he wrote for a 1952 essay collection that borrowed its title from the 1941 essay and which gathered together many of his works of the 1940s. Here Strauss meditated on the field of the sociology of knowledge, whose most important representatives were (for Strauss) Mannheim and, of course, its founder Max Weber. In a little-known 1927 essay, "Konspektivismus," Strauss had criticized Mannheim's formulation of the "sociology of ideas" for its inattention to the distinction between philosophical ideas and other types of conceptual formations. In the early 1950s, Strauss contemplated a "future sociology of philosophy" and offered up his own essays as a modest first step toward establishing that practice. In his view Mannheim and Weber's discipline had been a scientific byproduct of the progressive Enlightenment: the "sociology of knowledge emerged in a society which took for granted the essential harmony between thought and society or between intellectual progress and social progress."[53] In other words, while Weber's sociological approach enabled scholars to understand how thought's development mirrored and perhaps aided the technological improvement of man's estate on earth—as the Encyclopedists had once imagined—it was incapable of illuminating the other possible relationships between thought and social life. As Strauss made plain, the sociology of knowledge can only help to make sense of philosophy if philosophy has first been made to resemble other forms of intellectual endeavor. More pointedly, such a sociology counts on philosophy having been made subject to the same protocols of purpose associated with the applied natural sciences. For such sociologists, the philosopher appeared "eventually or from the beginning, as a member of a motley crowd which they called the intellectuals or the Sages."[54] For Strauss this instrumentalization was symptomatic of the post-Enlightenment forgetting of the distinction between philosophy and other forms of thought, a distinction based on the *zetetic* or skeptical character of philosophy and the solitary and nonpolitical nature of philosophical life—or to put the point in almost deceptively simple terms, philosophers share more with one another than they share with their nonphilosophical fellows. The "sociology of philosophy" underscores the fundamental antagonism between the philosophical life and other forms of existence. Said antagonism, in keeping with Strauss's antihistoricism, was not linked to any particular period.

The final lines of the Introduction to *Persecution and the Art of Writing* yoked together the critique of Weber's sociology of knowledge and the medieval reading of Plato. Strauss liberally mined "Farabi's *Plato*" for the Introduction and included much of this material unchanged. However, he also underscored the importance he had, by 1952, come to attach to the medieval recovery of Plato in general and to Farabi's reading in particular:

> Farabi ascribed to Plato the view that in the Greek city the philosopher was in grave danger. In making this statement, he merely repeated what Plato himself had said. . . . But the success of Plato must not blind us to the existence of a danger which, however much its forms may vary, is coeval with philosophy. The understanding of this danger and of the various forms which it has taken, and which it may take, is the foremost task, and indeed the sole task, of the sociology of philosophy.[55]

The "sociology of philosophy" was a mode of risk assessment. If Strauss described the dangers faced by philosophers as "coeval" with philosophy and thus eternal, and criticized Mannheim and Weber for the modernist character of their assumptions about the function of ideas in society, his "sociology of philosophy" was nevertheless itself a modern project by dint of its very antimodernism—it was defined through the very conflict in which it was locked. Notably, when Strauss considered such a future sociology, he had already moved from the New School to the University of Chicago, the institution where he would influence generations of students, and with which his name is now most closely associated. Even as he arrived, at the end of the 1940s, he prepared works that developed the critique of the Enlightenment, and of its social and political projects most especially, that had remained latent in "Persecution and the Art of Writing."

CHAPTER 3

Natural Right and Tyranny

Shortly after moving from the New School to the University of Chicago, Strauss gave a series of lectures, sponsored by the Charles Walgreen Foundation and later published as *Natural Right and History*. It was in these lectures that he criticized Weber's claim that Plato had been "an intellectual." Open to the public, the lectures were hardly popular in the strictest sense, and Strauss told his audience that philosophy was a practice of, as he said, "ascend[ing] from public dogma to essentially private knowledge." He went on: "The public dogma is originally an inadequate attempt to answer the question of the all-comprehensive truth or of the eternal order."[1] But public dogma is necessary. As Strauss noted, immediately before commenting on the ascent from the public to the private, "Men cannot live, that is, they cannot live together, if opinions are not stabilized by social fiat. Opinion thus becomes authoritative opinion or public dogma or *Weltanschauung*."[2] Thus at the very beginning of his lectures Strauss announced the tension between our need for public speech and speech's incapacity to express the truth. *Natural Right and History* told the story not only of the ascent of the liberal principle of natural right through the teachings of Hobbes and his predecessors, but of the emergence of the principle by which "intellectuals" functioned, namely, that of the public. Thus the lectures applied the lessons of Strauss's *Social Research* essays to the history of modern political thought.

Even as Strauss championed "classical" natural right against a modern usurper in *Natural Right and History*, he was engaged on a different front of the *quarelle des Anciens et des Modernes*, in which the figure of the "intellectual" likewise stood significant symbolic duty. In 1948 Strauss had written to his close friend Alexander Kojève, arguably the twentieth century's most influential exponent of the philosophy of G. W. F. Hegel. Strauss mentioned that he was awaiting the publication of his study of Xenophon's dialogue,

Hiero, or Tyrannicus, a dialogue on the subject of political power, happiness, and tyranny.[3] He requested that Kojève review it, flattering his friend by telling him he was one of the few thinkers alive capable of understanding the project. Referring to Kojève's 1947 *Introduction à la lecture de Hegel*, he wrote "No one has made the case for modern thought in our time as brilliantly as you."[4] While the two friends, who had known each other since Strauss's Berlin days, would discuss the content of *Hiero*, their debate would ultimately address the distinction between ancient and modern ways of being a philosopher. In the course of this, Strauss depicted the temptation to political action as a kind of gateway drug leading to life as a "mere" intellectual. It was not political tyranny itself that dominated the Strauss-Kojève debate, but rather the question of the relationship between philosophy and tyranny, and, most specifically, the distorting effects of the will to rule.

On its face, *Hiero* is a dialogue between the eponymous Tyrant, who complains of the pains and limitations that come with his role, and Simonides, a wandering poet who tries to show Hiero a path toward a more benign despotism, promising that when Hiero wins the love of his people he will find tyranny less constraining. Simonides begins by reminding Hiero, whose status as Tyrant makes him a "public" man, of the pleasures available to men in private life.[5] While Simonides insists that these are nothing when compared to the pleasures of the all-powerful Tyrant, Hiero argues that the Tyrant is constrained in his ability to enjoy his riches, or the personal attention his position might bring. After all, even feasts pale when they become mundane affairs and sexual pleasures are diminished when they are readily available but do not come with love, "For love takes pleasure in longing not for what is at hand, but for what is hoped for."[6] Nor does Simonides's praise for the Tyrant's power please Hiero.[7] The latter rejoins that power only brings worry and fear—moreover, the political struggles in which the Tyrant must engage make of his whole life a war.[8] And a Tyrant cannot safely abdicate from power, because his former subjects would doubtless seek revenge against him for past injustices.[9] A break in Hiero's complaints allows Simonides to observe that Hiero's greatest desire is to be loved—and what if one could serve as a benign Tyrant, securing the love of one's subjects by giving gifts, improving the city, and becoming the benefactor of as many friends within the city as possible? In consequence of doing these things, Simonides says in closing the dialogue, "You will acquire the most noble and most blessed possession to be met with among human beings, for while being happy, you will not be envied for being happy."[10]

While *Hiero* might seem a simple tale of political reform achieved through philosophical dialogue, its core emphasis on the erotic life (understood in the broadest sense) piqued both Strauss's and Kojève's philosophical interest. Xenophon raised the question of how erotic drives can be satisfied in politics, a central question for Kojève, who understood eros as the engine driving Hegel's social morality, whose basis is our pursuit of "recognition."[11] For Kojève Xenophon's *Hiero* prompted meditation on whether universal recognition could be possible for a mass public given sufficient education; the problem of eros might be resolved by a sufficiently advanced and benign state. For Strauss on the other hand, eros was the human longing to be whole, and the characters of Hiero and Simonides each represented a different form of longing, reflected in Simonides' frequent comments about eating and in Hiero's preference for talking about sex. Strauss's Simonides was effectively a philosopher seeking a state of contemplative grace for which other human subjects are unnecessary (represented by eating), whereas Strauss's Hiero longed for intersubjective happiness (represented by sex).[12] But while Strauss and Kojève agreed that the issue of eros was critical for understanding what motivated philosophical and political lives, respectively, Strauss took Simonides' and Hiero's different desires to indicate that philosophy and politics are mutually exclusive, whereas Kojève hoped the progress of history might bring them together.[13]

Seeming to anticipate Kojève's position, Strauss argued that Xenophon was not using Simonides to model an "intellectual's" program for governmental reform, but rather offering a meditation on the comparative pleasures of two modes of living: "ultimately, the dialogue serves the purpose of contrasting *the* two ways of life: the political life and the life devoted to wisdom."[14] Strauss explored various gaps in Simonides' description of the good life, especially his failure to present a strong argument for the political life as the happiest life, and claimed that Simonides by this means—and despite his efforts to convince Hiero of tyranny's potential virtues—preserved the possibility of the nonpolitical or private life being the happier.[15] Thus, Simonides subtly suggested that Hiero ought to return to private life if it proved possible, for the private life is the life of wisdom.

The issues of tyranny and of the "two ways of life" might seem worlds apart, but for Strauss they were linked by the problem of free speech. In the opening passages of *On Tyranny*, Strauss acknowledged that the special character of modern tyrannical regimes demanded that social scientists understand the roles played by technology and ideology. However, a prefatory passage Strauss quoted from Thomas Babington Macauley's *History of England from the Accession of James the Second* suggested an additional meaning, namely, that free access to technologies of publicity and opinion-sharing was paradoxically as injurious to a particular kind of freedom as jackboots, bullhorns, and propaganda films. Macauley, a Whig politician and historian who served his government under Victoria, noted that

> During a hundred and sixty years the liberty of our press has been constantly becoming more and more entire; and during those hundred and sixty years the restraint imposed on writers by the general feeling of readers has been constantly becoming more and more strict . . . . At this day foreigners, who dare not print a word reflecting on the government under which they live, are at a loss to understand how it happens that the freest press in Europe is the most prudish.[16]

Strauss's citation of Macauley implied not only that social scientists misunderstood tyranny when they ignored the roots of tyrannical impulses growing in the human soul, it also implied that to understand tyranny one had to first understand the basic predicament of the freedom of speech. Modern social scientists who could only see tyranny in the most obvious of places missed its true character; one read *Hiero* not to recognize a tyranny (the ostensible purpose of the dialogue is to teach Hiero how to be a *better* tyrant), but to understand the senses in which tyranny was a constant threat, and to understand how philosophers could respond to it productively. As Macauley knew, no one could philosophize safely if, like the pupils of Socrates, they would be understood as making "practical" proposals every time they raised theoretical questions, such as whether or not democracy is the best order.[17]

In his response to Strauss, first published as "L'action politique des philosophes" in the journal *Critique,* Kojève showed how well he understood Strauss's use of Macauley. Strauss was not championing the total withdrawal of philosophers, but rather their subtle and indirect manipulation of statesmen. Early in his response to Strauss, Kojève observed that Simonides did not exactly offer Hiero any practical advice, and by that omission he seemed "to have behaved not so much like a wise man as like a typical 'intellectual' who criticizes the real world in which he lives from the standpoint of an 'ideal' constructed in the universe of discourse," or in other words, Simonides seemed to offer a utopia that Hiero could readily view as mere theory and thus no threat. As Strauss put it, Simonides liked to appear only to be a "poet." By contrast, for his part Hiero behaves like a "good liberal" statesman by letting Simonides the dreamer go on his way in peace, though such a bold and well-spoken person might have seemed a threat to the insecure Tyrant's rule.[18]

Most fundamentally, however, Kojève questioned Strauss's assumption that the reformed and ideal tyranny described by Simonides was just a utopia. "Nowadays," he observed, many of Simonides's recommendations for reform were practiced by governments that might be judged tyrannical, and he referred to the establishment of "Stakhanovite" prizes for on-the-job performance in Stalin's Soviet Union, and to Antonio de Oliveira Salazar, who some credited with important economic reforms during his time as prime minister of Portugal.[19] Without suggesting that those particular regimes were themselves ideal, Kojève allowed that tyrants were not incapable of reform and that tightly managed states were capable of their own kind of perfection. He furthermore argued, following Hegel and as Strauss had invited him to argue, that tyrants, like all statesmen, were motivated by a desire for recognition.[20] Thus Hiero desires to be obeyed *willingly* by subjects who recognize the worth of his rule. And most importantly, a "successor" to Simonides could act as more than a mere "intellectual" for a properly motivated tyrant, offering concrete advice about how to produce conditions for maximal recognition across society—a first step toward something approaching Hegel's universal state.

Strauss's argument against philosophers playing a role in political reform rested "on a misunderstanding, on a total misconception of what philosophy is and of what the philosopher is."[21] In Kojève's view, Strauss's picture of a philosopher who can do no more than indirectly guide rulers, derived from an "Epicurean" conception of the philosophical life as a contemplative retreat from the public world.[22] An account of the philosopher as isolated, Kojève said, rested on the claim that the truth was itself ahistorical. He mentioned two versions of the ahistorical truth quite dear to Strauss, namely Plato's "intellectual intuition" by which one perceives the Forms, and divine revelation itself.[23] Such a "theistic" Truth, Kojève implied, was overthrown by the Hegelian equations "Being=Becoming" and "Being=Truth=Man=History," and any philosopher on the Hegelian model must needs act, must become a participant in the process of historical unfolding. Given the ultimate alignment between the philosopher's priorities and those of the statesman, there was no reason for the former not to advise the latter. And even if Strauss were to reject the historicist component of Kojève's Hegelianism, he would have to

concede the centrality of interpersonal encounters in philosophy: philosophical "friends" were necessary for all philosophers if they were to know
that their truths were not like the truths of madmen, who are convinced
they see a hidden truth that others miss. Philosophers need recognition too,
even if they may receive it from a select few people, and like tyrants they
want to be recognized for their actions.

How were philosophers to do their part? Clearly, they might come into
contact with the public through many channels. Even their basic functions
as pedagogues brought them into contact with the state because of the state's
interest in educating the young. There could be conflict at that point of contact,
or philosophers might "participate, in one way or another, in government
as a whole, so that the State might be organized and governed in a way that
makes his philosophical pedagogy both possible and effective."[24] An interest
in pedagogy, Kojève implied, could quickly lead to an interest in governance
more broadly. And yet this led to great difficulties, for philosophers' time
was not infinite, and they could not become statesmen themselves without
effectively giving up philosophy, ultimately ceasing to give truly philosophical advice. Kojève memorably stated that this, the conflict of the philosopher
and the Tyrant, left one with "the conflict of the intellectual faced with
action," "the only authentic *tragedy* that takes place in the Christian or
bourgeois world: the tragedy of Hamlet and of Faust."[25]

Kojève's solution to the problem was an express challenge to Strauss. He
allowed that philosophers themselves were unlikely to act effectively, but, using the career of Alexander the Great as an example, he argued that there
had been many successful attempts to actualize the logos of Greek philosophy in a universal civilization—and Kojève offered the further example of
the Roman Church as a more durable expression of philosophy's universal
principle having its political effect throughout history. In the modern period,
the goal of creating a homogeneous state—a state of relative equals—had led
to a new kind of social actor, namely the intellectual, who acts as a translator
between the philosopher and the statesman, making ideas less utopian but
making them practicable. Kojève rendered the proper relation between philosophers, intellectuals, and statesmen or tyrants in a formula: "In general
terms, it is history that attends to 'judging' . . . the deeds of statesmen or tyrants, which they perform (consciously or not) as a function of the ideas of
philosophers, adapted for practical purposes by intellectuals."[26] Symbolically
speaking, the "intellectual" served as the link between philosophy and practice on the level of history—the same intellectual Strauss was busy skewering

in *Natural Right and History*, a work devoted to combating the assumptions of historicism. Not only did philosophy affect politics; it was the only thing that ever really did.

Strauss called his response the "Restatement on Xenophon's *Hiero*," an honest title, for he was not shifting his position but merely rearticulating it.[27] He opposed Kojève's claim that universal recognition under a universal state could become possible, and more basically he denied recognition's central role in philosophy: "concern with recognition," he stated, "necessarily detracts from the singleness of purpose which is characteristic of the philosopher."[28] While Strauss agreed that philosophers had always been engaged with the political community both through pedagogy (entering the market place in search of students) and casual conversation (the very gadfly behavior for which Socrates was famous), he insisted that this was simply due to the philosopher's duty to undermine comfortable prejudices wherever they might be found.[29] And though Strauss acknowledged that the conflicts caused by a philosopher's entry into the marketplace constituted a form of political action, he denied that philosophers had any role as aids in decision-making, or that intellectuals were truly translators of philosophical insights.[30] As he put it, "[Kojève] does not belong to the many who today are unabashed atheists and more than Byzantine flatterers of tyrants for the same reason for which they would have been addicted to the grossest superstitions, both religious and legal, had they lived in an earlier age. In a word, Kojève is a philosopher and not an intellectual."[31]

Surveying Kojève's Hegelian theory of historical development, Strauss disdained to attack its inherent idealism—not really so different from his own Platonic "theism" (as Kojève called it)—and instead rejected the notion that "recognition" was an ultimate *telos* or end for humanity. It was not the experience of worth in the eyes of a respectable other person, but rather "wisdom" of a transcendental sort that was man's "end," although one would come to understand the former by drawing closer to the latter.[32] But if a suitably educated public in a universal state might enjoy recognition, not everyone could hope to achieve wisdom (the "ends" of most people would consist, more modestly, in different versions of satisfying happiness). Given that the end of history, as Kojève understand it, would involve something like the final satisfaction of man's erotic drives (broadly understood), human nature itself seemed to Strauss to supply the surest arguments against his friend. The end of history was a social vision of the fulfillment of the irremediable lacks at the core of the human soul.

In his "Restatement," Strauss claimed that Kojève well understood the impossibility of the total satisfaction of any human society. The end of history required the dissolution of the most fundamental difference between types of humans, namely, the division between those with the capacity for wisdom and those without it. Indeed, the idea of a final State acting with coercive force on its citizens was necessary precisely because of the impossibility of an end-of-history scenario yielding universal satisfaction. Strauss refrained from mentioning Nietzsche's "last man" in the "Restatement," for such a figure was not so much the antithesis of the philosopher as the antithesis of the "great man of action."[33] Having abandoned great deeds, he sought only comfort, unlike either true actors or philosophers. But Strauss never gave up his suspicion that Kojève's Hegelian-Marxian final State would produce "last men." In a letter of 1957 he reminded his friend: "The root of the question is I suppose the same as it always was, that you are convinced of the truth of Hegel (Marx) and I am not. You have never given me an answer to my question: was Nietzsche not right in describing the Hegelian-Marxian end as 'the last man'?"[34]

Regardless how much or little he pushed against Kojève's Hegelianism, glaring in Strauss's "Restatement" was a lack of reference to intellectuals, save for his early comment that Kojève was not one. Intellectuals, in Kojève's account, were interpreters who moved both political life and philosophy forward though they contributed directly to the substance of neither. They worked not with the public, but with "statesmen or tyrants," and thus did not break the veil Strauss insisted on maintaining between philosophers and the public—but Strauss must certainly have cast a skeptical eye on Kojève's intellectuals for their embrace of practical matters and history, and he may have been alarmed by the way they seemed to belong to neither the philosophers nor the statesmen, but worked between those two groups. Strauss understood politics and philosophy to be separate spheres, but did not acknowledge the validity of a third sphere between them—intellectuals had nowhere to stand.

But Strauss closed his "Restatement" with an oblique reference to the Heidegger case. Reflecting on his own career and on that of Kojève, he wrote:

> For we both apparently turned away from Being to Tyranny because we have seen that those who lacked the courage to face the issue of Tyranny, who therefore *et humiliter serviebant et superbe dominabantur,* were forced to evade the issue of Being as well, precisely because they did nothing but talk of Being.[35]

Strauss and Kojève had only mentioned Heidegger occasionally in their prior correspondence; Strauss provided Kojève with a reference to Heidegger's *Rektoratsrede* mere months after the speech was given, and Strauss at one point referred to the "cowardly vagueness of Heideggerian existentialism."[36] Here in his "Restatement," Strauss implied that Heidegger's choices of the early 1930s had been disastrous both philosophically and politically. The reference to Heidegger was striking. The philosopher was not only the one *modern* influence Strauss and Kojève shared, he also offered one of the most compelling accounts of history since Hegel, albeit one with no room for Hegelian idealism, for it yanked the pre-Socratic question of Being out of the heavens and placed it firmly on the horizon-line of history. But the attempt to realize his philosophical vision through action in history blinded Heidegger to the impossibility of such a realization. While Strauss's phrase "forced to evade the issue of Being as well" was vague, it captured the frustrated character of Heidegger's attempt to—in terms Heidegger had used in his *Rektoratsrede*— place knowledge in the service of necessity.[37] Kojève was naturally not Heidegger, but the danger of another Heidegger case was ever present if one forgot that not "the earth" (Strauss's chosen term was among Heidegger's favorites), but rather "the whole," which resonated with "the cosmos," was the proper home of the philosopher.[38] Here the Heideggerian emphasis on the earth as a horizon for philosophical meaning dissatisfied Strauss, much as the neo-Kantian and phenomenological emphasis on the human subject had dissatisfied him: he summoned an ancient cosmological model in which Man was not the maker of order, as both tyrants and intellectuals hoped to be, nor a world-making entity, as Heidegger had claimed, but just a part of a larger order.

If the problem of tyranny was linked to the role of "the intellectual" in *On Tyranny*, so were they linked in *Natural Right and History*. In his "Restatement," Strauss claimed "present-day tyranny, in contradistinction to classical tyranny, is based on the unlimited progress in the 'conquest of nature' which is made possible by modern science, as well as on the popularization or diffusion of philosophic or scientific knowledge."[39] Both tendencies, Strauss said, were known to the authors of the classics, but reviled by them as unnatural, "as destructive of humanity."[40] Kojève supported technological progress without limit, whereas Strauss condemned it. In *Natural Right and History* Strauss would similarly argue that the political crises of modernity (including but not limited to tyranny) were due to an immoderate faith in science and a linked belief in the efficacy of modes of political discourse that allow for the easy and transparent transmission of scientific knowledge. It was this type of thinking that produced the faith in popular education Strauss had criticized in "Persecution and the Art of Writing." Intellectuals, in *Natural Right and History*, were both the beneficiaries and the agents of the spread of popular education, and they embodied the technocratic mindset Strauss decried.

While *Natural Right and History* nowhere mentions factories, rockets, atomic bombs, or any other type of technology that caught the attention of mid-twentieth-century authors, it nevertheless belongs in a broad set of mid-twentieth-century works on the perils of technocracy, a set that would cut across political divides and unite Strauss with figures with whom he shared little, including Theodor Adorno and Max Horkheimer, who produced their *Dialektik der Aufklärung* (*Dialectic of Enlightenment*) only a few years before Strauss penned his text. The first page of that work had identified Francis Bacon as the Enlightenment's "father of experimental philosophy" who called for the mastery of nature.[41] Strauss hardly mentioned Bacon in *Natural Right and History*, but he did include him as one of the chief influences of Rousseau, whom he considered, with Nietzsche, one of the chief causes of the crises of modernity.[42] Strauss's Rousseau was no enemy of science, but he attacked (in his First Discourse) all those who sought to popularize philosophy and expose it to vulgar opinion. Strauss found in that Discourse an attempt "to warn away from science, not all men, but only the common men."[43] Strauss was no more a critic of science and technology in their own right than Rousseau (a son of Geneva, city of clockmakers) but, and analogously to the Heidegger of "The Question Concerning Technology," Strauss asserted that the dominance of science and its mechanistic worldview had come with costs, including the loss of the problem of natural right itself. Where Heidegger argued that technologists and their followers forgot the relationship with Being that the original Greek *techne* might afford, reducing the world to raw material for production and consumption, Strauss argued that an uncovering and restoration of the idea of nature and its limits could serve as a bulwark against the crises of modernity themselves.[44]

Whereas science, for Strauss, "is instrumental and nothing but instrumental: it is born to be the handmaid of any powers or any interests that be," the idea of nature can remind us of forces exterior to our will that act on us with the force of constraint.[45] While someone attending Strauss's lectures without prior familiarity with his works could easily have missed the meaning of his continued references to nature, the concept of natural right functioned precisely as the concept of the law of revealed religion had functioned for him, in the late 1920s and early 1930s, as a reminder of human limitations and the fact that philosophy always had and always would have to tangle with a set of necessities generated by our biological condition. Liberalism, Strauss suggested, had always dealt clumsily with both god and nature. That nature in the guise of "natural right" came to serve an argumentative function for Strauss that revealed religion previously had served, is vouchsafed by the references to Epicureanism he scattered throughout *Natural Right and History*. He referred to Epicureanism as "the most developed form of classical hedonism,"[46] and pointed to Epicurus and Lucretius as deep influences on the modern thinkers he addressed—including Hobbes, founder of modern "political hedonism." In *Spinoza's Critique of Religion*, Epicureanism had appeared both as the classic form of the critique of religion, and in a modified modern form embodied by thinkers like Spinoza. Rather than simply ridding humans of their fear of the gods, these modern Epicureans would transform society in order to perfect, insofar as it was possible, the human condition on earth—but the standards for "perfection" were in Strauss's view based on comfort and security, earning the title "political hedonism." Their views of nature were substantially different from the essentially Aristotelian view Strauss found in classical natural right theory. Aristotle's nature was teleological, a nature in which every organism has purpose and destiny written into it. For Hobbes, nature was merely matter in motion, in keeping with Epicurus' vision of atoms colliding without plan, purpose, or plot. Such a nature was, of course, available to a Bacon or a Hobbes as a resource for the satisfaction of human purposes.

The critical link between Strauss's early investigation of Epicureanism as the critique of religion, and his later examination of that doctrine as the abandonment of a teleological vision of nature and its replacement with a vision of nature as resource or raw material, is that he understood both as "heretical" positions, rebellions against sources of extra-human authority.[47] The moral tone of his charges against Hobbes and Rousseau in *Natural Right and History* was due to the fact that the problem of Epicureanism underwent a kind of secularization, but was still animated by the associations Epicureanism, as the critique of religion, had conjured for Strauss as a young man. At the time of *Spinoza's Critique of Religion* Strauss had, after all, been well aware of the pun between Epicurus and *Apikores*, or heretic (Hebrew), and it had informed his suggestion that "Epicureanism can lead only to a mercenary

morality whereas traditional Jewish morality is not mercenary."[48] And Strauss
had examined Hobbes's engagement with the Epicurean tradition in its full
complexity both in his 1936 *The Political Philosophy of Hobbes: Its Basis and
its Genesis*, in which he presented Hobbes as tempering his own critique of
religion for the sake of social harmony, as well as in an unpublished text over
which he labored in the early 1930s, *Hobbes's Critique of Religion*. However,
in *Natural Right and History* Strauss presented a simplified understanding
of Hobbes's Epicureanism. The Hobbes of this text abandoned any conception of natural right that relied on a harmony between the human political
order and a larger cosmic order, and embraced instead the consideration of
our "baser" needs—the defense of bodily health, property, and peace of mind.
This Epicurean emphasis on personal rights rather than the aspiration toward
virtuous duty seemed to the Strauss of *Natural Right and History* to be the
basis of modern liberalism itself.

A full understanding of *Natural Right and History* is most easily obtained
by starting with the scholarly project of the lectures and the book they became. While Strauss wrote *Natural Right and History* when he was beginning to abandon some of the devices of historical writing, it also constituted
an intervention in the existing historiography of the idea of natural right.
Where most historians of the idea associated modern natural law with a secularization of Stoic-Christian natural law, Strauss traced its origins back to
the very birth of political philosophy. *Natural Right and History* was an effort to rethink the modern history of natural right, with special attention paid
to a transformation Strauss associated with the work of Hobbes, and with
Locke and Rousseau as well. He took the premodern or classical idea of
natural right to be "identical with the actualization of a human possibility
which, at least according to its own interpretation, is trans-historical, trans-
social, trans-moral and trans-religious."[49] In such a context, natural right
could be understood to carry the force of law or "ethical correctness." In
contrast, the modern concept of natural right as it appeared in the work of
Hobbes, Rousseau, and others—that is, the reflection on the state of nature
prior to the establishment of civil order—was simply a response to the emergent consensus that law possesses only conventional validity.

Modern natural right rose on the tide of science, and the dominance of
science likewise transformed the tasks that the theorists of natural right found
available to them—and made it possible for them to understand themselves
as "intellectuals" in the public sense of that term. As Strauss put it, "Originally, philosophy had been the humanizing quest for the eternal order, and

hence it had been a pure source of humane inspiration and aspiration. Since the seventeenth century, philosophy has become a weapon, and hence an instrument."[50] For Strauss it was this very instrumentalization of philosophy in the service of politics that had provoked Julien Benda to denounce the "treason of the intellectuals." But Benda's critical mistake had been to disregard the fundamental distinction between intellectuals and philosophers. The problem was not the abandonment of the abstract truth by intellectuals, but the emergence of that category in its own right. And while Strauss would have understood that "the intellectual," as a rhetorical term, emerged at the end of the nineteenth century, he suggested that the conditions for the emergence of "the intellectual" as an instrumentalist social type had developed two hundred years earlier, during the century of Hobbes.

Strauss's description of a seventeenth-century transition toward instrumental conceptions of philosophy directly recalled the essays of his New School period in which he presented faith in public education as one of modernity's errors. The rise of public opinion, Strauss implied, led scholars to orient themselves more and more toward anticipated audiences. In *Natural Right and History* Strauss sharpened his criticism of the linked ascendancies of the public and of the intellectual by suggesting intellectuals were really little more than sophists. He suggested that whereas in Plato's day there had been a class of "gentlemen," moneyed citizens who were virtuous and partook of some of the philosophers' wisdom but who, unlike the philosophers, were "public-spirited" and concerned with government, in the modern period there are only sophists and rhetoricians. These intelligent men only used knowledge for particular political ends. It was Weber's inattention to the distinction between philosophers and mere experts that led him, Strauss said, to the unforgivable crime of calling Plato "an intellectual." Like Benda, Weber came to his mistake by virtue of a general occlusion of the distinction between properly philosophical wisdom and instrumental knowledge that was characteristic of modernity. Simply put, Strauss thought that the intellectual is a creature who accepts the historicist assumption that philosophy is restrained by an immanent political horizon. The intellectual thus becomes the figure who *performs* the historicist thesis that thought is limited to the immanent present that shapes it, and in which it can produce its effects, and the intellectual thus becomes the immediate agent of the negative political consequences of historicist relativism.

The public-spirited gentlemen were, according to the teachings of classical natural right, a necessary institution because of the impossibility of philosophers actually ruling; thus, rule by the gentlemen was left as the "practically" rather than "absolutely" best regime. Direct philosophical rule was impossible because of the need for the consent of citizens in general, or, in other words, the problem of public recognition. However, as Strauss had observed in his earlier essays on exoteric writing, in the seventeenth century the concept of consent and public recognition was transformed into a faith in the public as an important medium both for the transmission and the re-direction of power through the development of public opinion. As he put it,

> Plato had said that evils will not cease from the cities if the philosophers do not become kings or if philosophy and political power do not coincide. He had expected such salvation for mortal nature as can reasonably be expected, from a coincidence over which philosophy has no control but for which one can only wish or pray. Hobbes, on the other hand, was certain that philosophy itself can bring about the coincidence of philosophy and political power by becoming popularized philosophy and thus public opinion.[51]

In other words, like Milton in his *Areopagitica*, Hobbes maintained faith in popular enlightenment. Hobbes accused the classics—including Plato—of utopianism, of calling for a greater coincidence of philosophy and political power than was possible, of conjuring ideal city-states that could exist in speech only. But Hobbes was far more utopian, for he hoped that what was summoned in language might become brick and mortar.

Strauss composed the lectures that became *Natural Right and History* long before the widespread development of a literature on what Jürgen Habermas would call "the public sphere," a figurative space located between the private sphere of family life and the sphere of public authority itself. Strauss was not concerned with the social function of public opinion per se, but rather with the functions a group of social theorists and philosophers imputed to an amorphous and impermanent body of readers and listeners. Nor did Strauss attend overmuch to the sources on the development of printing and free speech he had cited in his essays on exoteric writing, or to other aspects of the infrastructure that underlay a flourishing public sphere.

But while *Natural Right and History* was, on one level, a study of natural right and its fortunes in an era of historicism, it was also a study of the influence of publicness on the enduring philosophical idea of natural right itself. Strauss examined how the anticipation of an audience or the internalization of an *idea* of audience affected philosophers, beginning in the seventeenth century, when new ideas about governance (and the central role of public opinion within governance) combined with the rising power of science to make the popular reception of philosophy a critical trope. For classical philosophers, the natural right teaching was impossible to teach publicly, and philosophizing meant moving away from the "medium" of public conversation—opinion—and toward truth. For moderns, science likewise promised a movement away from opinion (or, perhaps, folk-belief) and toward truth. But that truth can be publicized, or at least so runs the dogma of moderns as regards the public. In both periods, the public is actually necessary, providing a starting point from which one ascends to the truth; however, in the latter case, the public is both the point of departure and the ultimate destination.

Given Strauss's express belief that natural right's transformation in the seventeenth century was still relevant at the time he gave his lectures, it is curious that those lectures did not move forward in time past Edmund Burke, that famous foe of the French Revolution, an event Hegel understood as receiving its "first impulse" from philosophy. Burke attempted to recover classical natural right, siding with antiquity rather than with "the Parisian philosophers." Whereas modern natural right as articulated by Hobbes and Rousseau suggested that civil society was not natural, Burke argued that it was by forming social organizations that we fulfill our natures; the artifice of social life and culture is innately human, not to be disrupted by mythical or imaginary accounts of "rights of men" vouchsafed by an account of pre-civilizational modes of life. As Strauss put it, Burke "denies that natural right by itself can tell much about the legitimacy of a given constitution: that constitution is legitimate in a given society which is most suitable to the provision for human wants and to the promotion of virtue in that society; its suitability cannot be determined by natural right but only by experience," or, in other words, the experience of living in a particular society.[52] Experience and not the political equivalent of an Archimedean point is the best support for political judgment, and the universal lessons divulged by science ("the work of men who think about human affairs as geometricians think about figures and planes"[53]) only work as a universal solvent on the fragile but necessary social bonds local to a particular political community. Indeed, Burke's emphasis on politics as an enterprise of human practitioners rather than a matter of impersonal forces visible only to "speculatists of our speculating age" earned him the sympathy of Strauss, attuned as he was to the political field as a realm of pragmata on the most human of scales. Theory is insufficient as a guide for practice, which is better supported by tradition. Burke thought, in keeping with the principles of classical natural right thinking, that the best political constitution is that which comes into being over a long period of time, having the kind of unity displayed by natural organisms rather than the unity possessed by architectural designs. As Strauss explains at the conclusion of *Natural Right and History*, Burke's thought left more room for "individuality" than did the formulations of the modern natural right theorists.

Strauss suggested that Burke attempted his recovery of natural right "at the last minute, as it were,"[54] implying that after Burke such a recovery became impossible. The recovery of natural right was still feasible, Strauss implied, during Burke's eighteenth century despite the rise of science, which Strauss identified with Hobbes's previous century. What would render natural right irretrievable was the French Revolution itself, which Burke famously criticized. This was in part because the revolutionaries proposed principles of governance that were new and contrary to tradition, and in part because the Revolution itself marked a new way of making government accountable to its public: giving public opinion a role in government and thereby changing the very meaning of publicness itself. The classical natural right teaching Burke attempted to recover contained an attack on the idea of the public, and Strauss's decision to end his talk with Burke reflected his own dissatisfaction with the culture of publicness and transparency that marked the modern world. Never stating that *Natural Right and History* was a defense of classical natural right principles, Strauss nevertheless made it clear that the dominance of the public had led to a forgetting of those principles, and led to the dominance of historicism as well.

The quest to restore the question of natural right in a historicist age may have seemed purely theoretical. Criticizing intellectuals in *Natural Right and History* and *On Tyranny*, Strauss said less about his own vision of the social role of philosophers. However, six years after *Natural Right and History* appeared in print, Strauss articulated a model for practice in a commencement address, "What Is Liberal Education?," which he delivered to the tenth graduating class in the Basic Program of Liberal Education for Adults at the University of Chicago. In this address, among his most intemperate, Strauss criticized mass culture and its influence on democracy, defended an elite version of liberal education that he realized was available only to the few, and rooted both gestures in natural right teachings that underlay his conception of liberal education. And he concluded with an attack on intellectuals as participants in a "vanity fair," referring to the location first introduced in Bunyan's *Pilgrim's Progress*, a town called Vanity along the pilgrim's route where an endless festival carried on, representing humanity's attachment to worldly things. It was from Bunyan's novel that William Makepeace Thackeray drew the title for his satire of early nineteenth-century English society. Just as they had in *Natural Right and History*, in Strauss's address on liberal education, intellectuals stood for the instrumentalist impulse that made philosophy serve worldly ends, an impulse that Strauss traced to modern philosophy itself and that he implied was bound up with a mass culture in which one could only express oneself through a "loudspeaker." The masses have a Hollywood conception of happiness, as Strauss put it, which we can understand as a debased version of the Epicurean pursuit of happiness sketched in *Natural Right and History*. They were only willing to listen to those thinkers whose messages conformed to their tastes.

Liberal education was the "counterpoison" to mass culture and its "corroding effects," and a path back to a version of culture *not* in keeping with "mass democracy," which Strauss called "a culture which can be appropriated by the meanest capacities without any intellectual and moral effort and at a very low monetary price" but with true democracy.[55] Strauss insisted on a classical definition of "democracy" as a society that is rational because all its adults have developed their virtue and wisdom—qualities once possessed by aristocrats alone.[56] Liberal education was a means by which to produce virtue and wisdom. Strauss's phrase for this was "human greatness," recalling his emphasis in *Natural Right and History* on the distinction between the anthropocentrism of modern thinkers who would remake the world to suit humanity's needs, and the classical natural right teaching that would establish patterns of just living in conformity with the human condition as disclosed by nature. Liberal education was, in fact, a path back to nature in the guise of the natural human faculties of reason. Strauss emphasized the etymological origins of "culture" within agriculture, "improving the soil in accordance with its nature," and directly compared students to soil—but their ultimate teachers (the "farmers") were not necessarily the men in the classroom with them, but the authors of the "great" books of wisdom that motivated their teachers.

The logic of Strauss's brief address was simple. One had to reject mass culture and mass democracy and its expectations for philosophers and intellectuals to supply concrete answers or guidance for living, in order to truly

cultivate one's mind in accordance with nature. But there was an instrumental reason to reject instrumentality: it was by this means that true democratic
tendencies could be cultivated even within mass society. Strauss further
articulated this idea in his essay "Liberal Education and Responsibility," in
which Strauss identified himself fully with the task of the pedagogue ("education at its best or highest"[57]) and distanced himself from the concept of
"responsibility," which he rejected as a late arriving neologism that had dis-
placed the concept of "virtue." Once again, liberal education served as a
means by which to move from modern ways to classical ones, as Strauss explained that the beneficiaries of liberal education had originally been those
gentlemen who displayed proper "civic responsibility" for the cities in which
they lived.[58] From the perspective of liberal education, the role of the philosopher in the city was simply to provide for the education of the gentlemen,
whose rule might reflect a portion of philosophy's excellence. Liberal education becomes the means for the introduction of a kind of responsibility
superior to that neologistic one Strauss disdained, for liberal education can
bring a sense of responsibility that grows out of a concern for virtue. Strauss
bluntly proposed what he had left implicit in "What Is Liberal Education?,"
namely, that the "present predicament" of modern society was due to the decay of the liberal education of its leadership.

Strauss furthermore pointed out that an original meaning of "liberal" was
simply "free," a condition that only made sense in a social system that sustained the institution of slavery ("a free man, as distinguished from a slave"[59]).
The original "liberals" were actually gentlemen, for it took a degree of wealth to
be free from work and thus enjoy time for personal development. The gentlemen had once been the students of philosophers who also participated in
political life, and were themselves more political than philosophical, but they
still respected that questions of governance had to be answered in the light
of the wisdom disclosed by philosophy. In the absence of liberal education
that might produce such gentlemen, and due to patterns of education in keeping with the instrumentalism of modern philosophy, governance had itself
transformed. Whereas classical philosophy had understood the "ends" of
philosophers to be radically different from the "ends" of nonphilosophers,
modern philosophy understands the ends of all people to be more or less the
same. As Strauss put it, "The end of philosophy is no longer what one may
call disinterested contemplation of the eternal, but the relief of man's estate."[60]
Philosophy is now a tool for the improvement of human life—it is placed in
the service of a human power for making life "longer, healthier and more

abundant."[61] When understood loosely, Strauss tells his reader, the term "philosophy" becomes identical with "intellectual interests." Liberal education was formerly the type of mediation through which philosophy affected the city; modern thinkers have reformulated education to serve needs Strauss would have seen as essentially illiberal, or, in other words, the needs that preoccupied mere "intellectuals," the lesser descendents of Hobbes who preferred *physis* to *nomos*.

JewGreek Is GreekJew: Extremes Meet

Strauss's remarks on liberal education are distinctive because he rarely wrote anything so revealing of himself. He always tried to leave himself out of his work. While he emphasized the act of interpretation (i.e., esoteric reading) he never dwelled upon the necessarily individual character of a given critic or scholar's interpretation of a text. Certainly, this was the mode in which Strauss was trained to conduct himself as a student of classics and philosophy, but he had been an avid reader of Nietzsche as a young man. He was thus familiar with an author who had challenged the conventions of philology by inserting himself as a character into his own books. In fact, there were moments in Strauss's works when he crept back into his own texts—as in his comparison between the conditions under which Maimonides wrote and the working conditions that limited his own authorial freedom—but only rarely did he indulge himself in this fashion. Nor did Strauss like to reflect, at least in writing, on the way his biography had shaped his thought. The 1962 Preface to *Spinoza's Critique of Religion* and his late dialogue with Jacob Klein, "A Giving of Accounts," are two notable exceptions, but Strauss noted in a letter to Kojève that his Preface came "as close to an autobiography as is possible within the bounds of propriety," or, in other words, autobiography was somehow desirable but also somehow inappropriate.[62] The Preface does explain much about the young Strauss's influences and motivations, but it is hardly autobiography, and in any case it concludes when Strauss says his youth concluded, that is, when he realized a return to premodern philosophy really *was* possible.

It requires no reconstruction of Strauss's psychology to note the strange discord between his fixation on the position of the writer in society and his tactic of diverting attention away from his own position as an author. That discord itself invites the question of what Strauss was avoiding—and takes the interpreter into the oft-traveled but treacherous ground of asking "what Leo Strauss really thought" behind a pose Strauss himself termed "the immunity of the commentator."[63] No interlinear reading of Strauss's own works is necessary, however, to observe that throughout his career he was indebted to two cities, Athens and Jerusalem, and that he understood each city to contribute a radically different element to his thinking. The same year Strauss earned his doctorate in philosophy under Cassirer, James Joyce completed his masterwork *Ulysses*, a work rarely, if ever, invoked in readings of Strauss, but one helpful in understanding the relationship between Strauss's cities. At one moment the cap worn by one of Joyce's characters, Lynch, suddenly comes to life and mocks the protagonist Stephen Daedalus's pretensions toward knowledge: "Ba! It is because it is. Woman's reason. Jewgreek is Greekjew. Extremes meet." For Derrida, Joyce's line is Hegelian in its suggestion not only of a meeting between Jews and Hellenes but in the production, out of the clash of thesis and antithesis, of a new synthesis. It may even account for "the historical *coupling* [Derrida's emphasis] of Judaism and Hellenism."[64] Strauss was no celebrant of Hegel's model of historical progress by opposition and synthesis. After completing his doctoral dissertation, he spent years in the parallel study of Jewish sources and the central texts of European political philosophy, never bringing them together. As the last three chapters have endeavored to show, it was by observing Maimonides's refusal to synthesize Judaism and philosophy together that Strauss discovered an ideal "coordination" of philosophy and politics, where religion serves to regulate political life. Strauss, an avowed atheist, came to focus his work on the teachings of Plato and the classical natural right tradition rather than on Judaism. And yet he never abandoned his interest in Jewish figures, writing on Maimonides throughout his career and continuing to suggest that Athens and Jerusalem represented the poles of his thought. Strauss, in other words, never ceased to identify as a Jewish thinker himself, though he never claimed that works like *Natural Right and History* were "Jewish." In a public address of 1962 entitled "Why We Remain Jews," Strauss returned to the questions of his youthful Zionism, acknowledging the very real possibility of assimilation in the modern world and the threatened Jewish condition, but nevertheless insisting on "accepting" one's past, the practice of which he called the virtue of "fidelity."[65]

Strauss displayed "fidelity" to his own Jewish lineage by exploring precisely the political predicaments that had faced Jews in the Diaspora; persecution, exile, and the disorders to which liberal regimes are especially vulnerable, were all central concerns for him. In fact, one need not take recourse to ethnic determinism to see that Strauss's mature works remain entangled in precisely the political themes he first encountered during his Weimar years. Nowhere is this more evident than in the Preface to *Spinoza's Critique of Religion*, and the past three chapters have demonstrated that Strauss arrived at his particular brand of Platonism after beginning, as he related in his Preface, as "a young Jew born and raised in Germany who found himself in the grip of the theologico-political predicament." That Preface was written in 1962, the same year Strauss presented "Why We Remain Jews," and Eugene Sheppard points out that in the latter address Strauss was "less inhibited to be forthright," precisely because he was addressing a more intimate audience—and, because his talk was held at the University of Chicago's Hillel House and hosted by the B'nai B'rith Hillel Foundation, an audience that might be presumed to be largely Jewish. In "Why We Remain Jews," Strauss explored the notion of the Jews' status as a "chosen" people, but suggested that its true meaning lay in the forsaken nature of the human condition. The Jews had simply come to symbolize a universal problem, or as Strauss said, "The Jewish people and their fate are the living witness for the absence of redemption. This, one could say, is the very meaning of the chosen people."[66] As Sheppard points out, one meaning of this claim is that utopia is impossible, just as *u-topos*, or "no-where" would imply. At the same time Strauss performed this universalization of the Jewish condition—this expression of his "ontological pessimism"[67]—his contemporary and fellow Heidegger student Emmanuel Levinas was at work on the manuscript of his 1963 *Difficile liberté (Difficult Freedom)*, a gathering of his "confessional writings," attempts to find universal applications for the particular experiences of the Jewish people. Strauss learned many of his lessons about the public from Jewish sources. It was, after all, his youthful experiments in reading Maimonides and Spinoza that led him to his al-Farabi-influenced Platonism. Levinas, born in Lithuania, similarly derived much of his understanding of politics from Jewish history and from contemporary Jewish life in his adoptive France. Like Strauss, he remained fixated on the Jewish experience of exile throughout his career—but as the next three chapters of this book will show, Levinas did not share Strauss's pessimism about the potential consequences of philosophical speech in public. Deeply ambivalent about the phenomenon of the publicly *engagé* intellectual, and convinced, in Clausewitzian fashion, that politics itself was violence by other means, Levinas nevertheless pit philosophy against violence and tyranny, as if in a personal struggle against the ontological roots of injustice.

PART II

The Dog at the End of the Verse: Emmanuel Levinas Between Ethics and Engagement

I'm all for the Greek tradition! It is not at the beginning of things, but everything must be able to be "translated" into Greek. The Septuagint translation of the Scriptures symbolizes this necessity.

—Emmanuel Levinas, *Is It Righteous to Be?*

CHAPTER 4

Growth of a Moralist

Exodus 22:30 reads, "You shall be men consecrated to me; therefore you shall not eat any flesh that is torn by beasts in the field; you shall cast it to the dogs." Emmanuel Levinas, reading these lines playfully in his short essay "The Name of a Dog, or Natural Rights," found that the struggles of beasts in the state of nature reminded him of war and its horrors. It was enough, he said, to make one emulate Adam, the first man, and adopt vegetarianism.[1] But Levinas's real interest was not exactly the Biblical commandment itself and its implied divisions between human society and animals, but the identity of the dogs themselves. He asked, "So who is this dog at the end of the verse? Someone who disrupts society's games (or Society itself) and is consequently given a cold reception?"[2] Levinas was meditating on what it means to bear witness to the crimes of society, to structural forms of violence that mirrored wolves running down their prey, and illustrated just how much "inhumanity" existed within civilization. And Levinas had a very specific canine witness in mind, a dog named Bobby, who had visited him and his fellow French soldiers at a German POW camp in Fallingpostel, where he had been interned for four years during World War II after being captured. Where the Germans treated them as inhuman, Bobby the dog recognized them as men, "barking in delight." Levinas called him "the last Kantian in Nazi Germany, without the brain needed to universalize maxims and drives," and a "descendent of the dogs of Egypt" who did not snarl at the Israelites and thus served as witnesses to the injustice of their enslavement. Levinas could easily have gone on to mention the next verses of Exodus 23:1–3, which read, "You must not carry false rumors; you shall not join hands with the guilty to act as a malicious witness: You shall neither side with the mighty to do wrong—you shall not give perverse testimony in a dispute so as to pervert it in favor of the mighty—nor shall you show deference to the poor man in his dispute." That he did not stray into the next verse and its evocation of a formal justice system, that he stayed with the dog at the end of the verse who stands on the side of ethics rather than considerations of what is fair, says a great deal about how Levinas understood the activity of *témoignage*, or "witnessing," and serves as a symbol of one curious feature of his thought, namely his inability to explain how his ethics translated into a politics.

Levinas would eventually describe "witnessing," or "prophetic witnessing," as the task of the intellectual. It is tempting to say that the "dog at the end of the verse" was for him an outsiderly critic whose barking might alert us to structural forms of violence including racism, sexism, and economic injustice. But Levinas's views on these subjects were far more complicated than this pat description makes it seem, and his views were bound up with French national debates about just what an intellectual should be. While there is no evidence that he intended this, Levinas's reference to dogs cannot help but recall the communist Paul Nizan's 1932 "Les chiens de garde" ("Watchdogs"), a screed against idealist academic thinkers who ignored the sufferings of the poor, and on behalf of Marxists, whose critical work uncovered them. Levinas himself was no Marxist, though he would come to understand poverty as a form of violence that demands ethical response, and his attitude toward the most outspoken Marxist intellectual in postwar Paris, Nizan's friend Jean-Paul Sartre, was complex. Levinas criticized Sartre for instrumentalizing philosophy and literature in the service of politics, and while both used the term "witnessing," for Levinas it carried the sense of a public address whose power lay not in rhetoric or even in reason. "Witnessing" aspired to call attention to suffering and summon up an innate human ethical response. While Levinas wrote on issues of contemporary interest throughout his career, from the Cold War and the dawn of the Atomic age to the foundation of the state of Israel, his lifelong friend Maurice Blanchot was right to observe a fundamentally "untimely" quality in his thought, a rejection of "engagement," which served Sartre as a kind of God-term.[3] For example, while Levinas would ultimately construe his own mature philosophical works as responses to totalitarianism, he would avoid any engagement with concrete instantiations thereof. The great difficulty of moving from Levinas's ethics to a formal theory of politics or of social practice has frustrated many of his readers, and led some to judge his philosophical project a failure. Conceding that there is a caesura between philosophy and politics in Levinas's work, I will argue in this chapter, and in the two after it, that it is precisely by examining this difficulty that we can make historical sense of Levinas's projects.

He was hardly the only thinker in postwar France to maintain an ambivalent relationship with political engagement. Like his contemporaries Raymond Aron and Albert Camus, Levinas should be understood as a moralist rather than an ideologist, a thinker for whom abstract values were more compelling than concrete political projects allied with parties and—crucially, for Levinas's opposition to both Heideggerian and Hegelian historicity— elaborate imagined plotlines on which history was thought to move.[4] The puzzle with which Levinas left his readers (how could one move from an ethics founded in interpersonal encounter to a set of social and political practices capable of making ethical even impersonal systems like "the state" and "society"?) reflected his own struggle to preserve the French intellectual tradition of "the intellectual," as it had been performed by Zola (that "deracinated" son of a Venetian) and his confederates at the time of the Dreyfus Affair, against the revision of that role performed by Sartre and other "engaged" intellectuals in the years after World War II. Levinas declined to take what Vincent Descombes has called the "decisive test," for French intellectuals at midcentury, by affiliating his philosophy with a political position, and yet he meditated on political matters and often identified his own thought with, variously, monotheism, liberalism, and the French Republican project. From the perspective of many student radicals during the "May Events" of 1968, Levinas might have seemed a quietistic figure of the academic establishment. And yet this characterization would have missed Levinas's own prior engagement with the problem of "engagement," twenty years earlier, as well as his desire for a model of witnessing that would maintain a version of ethical experience within a flawed political world.

In an essay titled "Les vertus de patience," published in 1963 but plausibly written years earlier, Levinas had inveighed against intellectuals committing themselves to a course of action that involved violence, and most especially when they took their course of action to be mandated by a theory of history. As he put it, "Intellectuals are ashamed of their own condition, feeling powerless and decrepit. For almost fifty years now, they have been ashamed of contemplation."[5] Action, on the other hand, promised to cut the Gordian knots of problems that were themselves properly cognitive. Levinas tied all this to a prejudice on behalf of youth and its enthusiasms, and accused the unnamed intellectuals of "flattering adolescents."[6] True revolution, Levinas intimated, was tied to patience and to a willingness to suffer. However heartfelt, these sentiments only make full sense after a consideration of the broad sweep of Levinas's project, attendant to the contexts of its development. Levinas's stand against Sartrean engagement and his attempt to revive Zola's older model of the figure of the intellectual was just one part of his larger attempt to revise philosophy in the wake of the political disasters of the early twentieth century. Philosophy had been weaponized by the supporters of totalitarianism and, in the wake of tragedy, swords had to be beaten not into plowshares (too instrumental for Levinas) but into words.

Scholarly studies of Levinas often emphasize the difficulty of translating his ethics into politics understood in the "archic," or foundational sense of laws and procedures for civil order and rule.[7] He presented ethics as stemming from the obligation one feels to another person whose vulnerability is expressed through the appearance of a figurative "face." This ethics becomes politics only because of the presence of what Levinas called "the third," which in his terminology often referred to a social and inevitably political realm beyond the dyad of the first two individuals involved in a face-to-face encounter. Commentators eager to avoid certain objectionable dimensions of Levinas's ethics—such as his emphasis on "fraternity" as the basis of justice, his vision of a "fraternity" of men united as sons of a singular God of monotheism, and the androcentrism "fraternity" implies, to name only a few—have turned eagerly to Derrida's observation that Levinas was *deliberately* silent about how one could put his philosophy into practice as politics.[8] Derrida argued that for Levinas the impossibility of traveling from ethics to politics is "welcome" insofar as it leaves politics defined in terms of unconditional hospitality.[9] Following Derrida, Simon Critchley suggests that Levinas's thought produces not a politics, but rather an anarchist, nonfoundational "metapolitics," making us aware of the need for constant "invention" in political decision-making rather than a reliance on the structures established by classical political theory.

However, such interpretations of Levinas's failure to deduce politics from philosophy not only read that failure quite generously (after all, why should silence about political practice read as "hospitality" rather than as "neglect"?), they also neglect to situate Levinas's possible "metapolitics" in its historical and political context. As both Critchley and Howard Caygill point out, the Lithuanian Jewish Levinas was a French thinker insofar as he was devoted to the Republican spirit he associated with his adoptive country. If, as Caygill argues in his *Levinas and the Political*, Levinas's philosophy reflects the categories of "liberté, egalité, fraternité," nevertheless the most crucial Republican moment was not the foundational date of 1789 but rather the Dreyfus Affair a little more than a hundred years after that.[10] Even if the Affair revealed the fragility of liberal Republicanism it was also the moment when ethics publicly trumped politics. But Levinas would also have to respond to the obvious failures of liberalism during the Affair, failures registered in cries of "à la mort les juifs." He would theorize a version of fraternity universal enough to resist the blood-and-soil nationalism of the anti-Dreyfusards, who claimed that both Jews and intellectuals had no real place in France. Levinas's attempts to produce an ethics out of the subjective experience of human vulnerability itself, while rooted in his rereadings of Husserl and Heidegger, was also an attempt to trace a fraternity of truly human, rather than local, origins.

Levinas's continued and almost compulsive returns to the themes of the Dreyfus Affair confirm Michel Winock's claim that the Dreyfus Affair was repeatedly "reactivated" as an inaugural event throughout the twentieth century.[11] In his 1967 "Beyond Dialogue," Levinas paid the Affair the ultimate "compliment" by implying—incredibly, and we might say with Blanchot, in an "untimely" fashion—that it had been a crisis for European Jewry of the same magnitude as "Hitlerism" itself.[12] It was while taking a philosophy course taught by Maurice Pradines at the Université de Strasbourg that the young Levinas had first imagined the Affair as the public triumph of ethics over corrupt politics. Because of his Lithuanian background, Levinas had been perfectly attuned to find Pradines' lesson affecting. As he later put it, "everywhere in Eastern Europe, Jews knew about Dreyfus. Old Jewish men with beards who had never seen a letter of the Latin alphabet in their life, spoke of Zola as if he were a saint. And then, suddenly, there was a professor before me in the flesh, who had chosen this as his example. What an extraordinary world!"[13] It was in Pradines' courses that Levinas first encountered the question of the relationship between philosophy and politics, which he would develop in later works such as *Totalité et infini* (*Totality and Infinity*), *Autrement qu'être* (*Otherwise Than Being*), and others. And he was offered a promising model for that relationship in the person of Zola, who had written to President Félix Faure not in his own name, but rather in that of "humanity": "I have but one passion, that of the Enlightenment, in the name of the humanity that has suffered so much and that has a right to happiness."[14] His own relationship with the legacy of the Enlightenment would be complex, but Levinas found sufficient inspiration in French political and intellectual history to remain in France—which was among other things a nation in which all lycée students had to read at least some philosophy[15]—after he had completed his studies.

Despite the massive literature on Levinas that has accumulated since the 1980s, relatively little has been said about his views on the social responsibilities of philosophers and intellectuals. Our relative inattention to Levinas's political views may be due to the delayed reception of Levinas's work both in France and elsewhere, which has drawn attention away from the historical context in which Levinas's thought developed. While Levinas was among the writers responsible for introducing the thought of Husserl and Heidegger to French readers during the 1930s,[16] it was a full fifty years later that he found an audience eager to enshrine him as the figurehead of a transformed French philosophy. Julian Bourg describes the shift that took place between the student and worker rebellions of 1968 and the 1980s, as a shift "from revolution to ethics." In the ethical moment of the late 1970s and early 1980s, so-called New Philosophers like Alain Finkielkraut, André Glucksmann, and Bernard Henri-Levy rebelled against the generation for which Sartre had served as figurehead and deemphasized the links between philosophy and politics, embracing instead questions like the nature of "the good life," which may have been an essentially political question for the Greeks but could be depoliticized with surprising ease a decade after the May events.[17] When Levinas was read alongside such authors, his own lasting preoccupations with politics was deemphasized, although because of his clear identification with Judaism, Levinas's ethics always recalled the Holocaust and its symbolic victim, the "figural Jew," in Sarah Hammerschlag's deft formulation.[18] Furthermore Levinas was received as though his thought had not matured in the age of Sartre, Camus, and Aron, as if it was not just "untimely" but actually ahistorical. Ethan Kleinberg has rightly noted the emergence of a "myth" of Levinas as an authentic voice of Rabbinic Judaism in continental philosophy. This emergence, I suggest, is partly the result of the considerable time-lapse between the period of Levinas's intellectual maturation and greatest productivity, and the reception of his work by both European and American readers.

Levinas's philosophy of ethics has been interpreted in many ways, but most prominently as an attempt to replace what Derrida terms the "logocentrism" of European philosophy, which Levinas saw as ethically blind, with an ethics grounded not in universal rules but rather in the singularity and vulnerability of the other. There was still a universalism here, echoing that of Zola: Levinas's ethics of the other can be readily understood as a universalism secured by particular cases, an attempt to do away with the aspects of logo-centric thought that enact forms of representational violence while maintaining the transcendent view of the infinite toward which Western philosophy has aspired, and which Edmund Husserl had maintained within his original phenomenology. In this shuttling between universals and particulars, Levinas's thought responds to one of the central dramas of modern French intellectual life, the struggle for a form of political identity dominated neither by universalist nor humanistic notions of community.[19] During his youth, Levinas saw many European political parties attempt to put politics—and forms of political community such as blood and soil—before reason. This was the defining feature of the antiliberalism he rebelled against. And yet his own thought can be understood as the effort to place a form of community, albeit one founded on mere humanity rather than ties of blood, soil, or language, *before reason itself.* The radical character of this revision of Dreyfusard principles reminds us that Levinas did not slavishly emulate Zola and company, or, more to the point, emulate his received impression of them.

No formal theorist of the public or of public speech, Levinas nevertheless testified to the importance of a universal language in one late interview. This would be Greek, the historical linguistic vessel of logocentrism itself: "I'm all for the Greek tradition! It is not at the beginning of things, but everything must be able to be 'translated' into Greek. The Septuagint translation of the Scriptures symbolizes this necessity."[20] This statement is complex, not least because it takes as the symbol for translation the story of when the Five Books of Moses (often called the Pentateuch by Christians) were (as the story goes) rendered into Greek for the first time. As Levinas explained, King Ptolemy II of Egypt had ordered that seventy Jewish scholars be sent to an island near Alexandria and locked in seventy separate chambers to translate the story of the Five Books of Moses. All versions of the Septuagint legend, which has been retold by different tellers to different religious purposes, agree that all seventy scholars translated the text more or less identically. In Levinas's version, the scholars do not simply translate identically, they also agree on the "corrections" made necessary by the slight deviations between their renditions of the Five Books of Moses.

Levinas was certainly aware that Christian readings of the Septuagint story glossed parallel translation as a miracle, and that some Christian readers reveled in such details as the transformation of the Hebrew *almah*, or "young woman," in Isaiah as the Greek *parthenos*, or virgin, meaning that not a "young woman" but rather a "virgin" would give birth. But he must have also understood that Ptolemy II licensed the translation not for the use of future Christians—not yet extant in the third century B.C.E.—but rather for Alexandrian Jewish readers fluent in Koine Greek and less proficient in Hebrew. It was, in other words, a tool crafted for the Diaspora, and as such a powerful symbol for Levinas, a supporter of the state of Israel who never engaged in the "negation of the Diaspora" and furthermore insisted on exilic experience as a potential gateway to ethics. He understood that for the Jewish tradition to flourish in the Diaspora, the work of the translator was an absolute necessity. But translation into "Greek" meant more than the translation of Jewish thought into a universal language so that Diasporic Jews could access their heritage and perhaps share it with non-Jewish counterparts. It meant that for Levinas a universal language was tied to Hellenic philosophy, a means of expression tied to a style of thought. Greek, as he said, is "the universality of a pure knowing." He went on: "What I call Greek is the manner or mode of our university language as the heir of Greece. At the University—and even at the Catholic and at the Hebrew University—one speaks Greek, even when, and if, one does not know the difference between alpha and beta."[21] This was not a thought innocent of politics. Levinas saw Greek philosophy and the Bible as the meritorious achievements of human civilization and regarded all else as "dancing."[22] Many of his comments on "Asians" (usually Chinese) seem simply racist. But in the context of Levinas's own work, the logic of translation meant that the private religious world he experienced as an Orthodox Jew had to meet the public world for which he wrote as a philosopher. The very division Levinas struck between "Hebrew" and "Greek" was a division between public communication and private experience: "translation" meant rendering the language of one tradition into that of another, but this was "Greek" in masquerade as "no tradition," as pure rationality without cultural baggage.

Throughout his career, Levinas struggled to explain how his ethics met the world of politics; he struggled to explain how the particular tradition of Judaism could be translated into universal terms without irreparable loss of meaning. Levinas's attempts to speak in the universal "Greek" of the intellectuals were complicated by his desire to speak on Jewish topics, and, sometimes, to speak on behalf of Judaism or of the Jewish people. They were further complicated by his shuttling back and forth between philosophical and "confessional" writings, and by the resulting confusion over whether he was speaking "as a philosopher" or "as a Jew" at any given moment. These translational troubles found their philosophical parallel in Levinas's incapacity to move from ethics into politics, and sometimes they were the engines of that incapacity.

This chapter and the two that follow it propose that we approach the puzzle of Levinas's translational difficulties by viewing his projects as attempts to write, think, and act "in imitation of Zola," following an important shift in the political character of French intellectual life: the "Café de Flore crowd," associated with Sartre and the journal *Temps Modernes*, insisting on a politics of ideological commitment rather than an essentially apolitical defense of truth itself. But Levinas knew that for a Jew to act *in imitatio Zola* meant revisiting the great theme of both the Dreyfus Affair and the post-1789 debates over Jewish emancipation in France, the Jew described as *déraciné*, a rootless wanderer without connection to French soil. The Lithuanian-born Jew who had adopted his beloved France would attempt to recast the condition of rootlessness as an ideal preparation for ethics. And he did so in response to his teacher Heidegger, who had argued for the value of rootedness and whose Nazification had struck Levinas as a deep betrayal. Of all the injustices and sufferings to which Levinas tried to bear witness, the complicity of philosophy in tyranny was particularly painful to him. It was worth acting like a dog, figuratively speaking, to call such offenses to public attention.

From Kovno to Phenomenology

It was never so important to imitate Zola as when it became impossible to imitate Heidegger, never so important to find a model of the intellectual's social responsibility as after Heidegger joined the Nazi party in 1933. Levinas came to doubt the nature of the very philosophy he had endorsed as Heidegger's student at Freiburg and, more productively, he also began to write on political themes. After 1933, Levinas groped for a transcendent version of meaning and ethics he could pit *against* Heidegger's emphasis on immanence and historicity, which seemed to lead to a specific form of political life, or as Löwith put it in his 1939 "The Political Implications of Heidegger's Existentialism," "*Being and Time* . . . represents—and in a far from inessential manner—a theory of historical existence."[23] However, until Heidegger's work seemed Nazified, it was deeply appealing to Levinas, as it was to so many of his generational colleagues, including Hannah Arendt and Leo Strauss. Appropriately enough for a philosopher who would build an ethics out of vulnerability and the experiences of suffering and charity in the face of suffering, the young Levinas had been drawn to a philosophy that seemed, at least at first, to make room for feelings.

In 1923, seventeen-year-old Levinas traveled from his family's home in Kovno, Lithuania, to Strasbourg to pursue his education. The Université de Strasbourg had emerged in 1919 after Alsace-Lorraine had been reclaimed from the Germans, replacing the Kaiser-Wilhelms-Universität, a legacy of German occupation established in 1870. While Levinas's first priorities were linguistic—improving his French and German in what was, essentially, a bilingual city—Strasbourg's proximity to Germany made it easy for Levinas to catch wind of current trends in German philosophical communities, and when Levinas became interested in phenomenology he would travel to Freiburg to study with Husserl. In the years immediately following the reclamation of Alsace-Lorraine, the French government focused attention and resources on the Université de Strasbourg, strengthening it to announce France's renewed control of the region. Toward this end, the university recruited many of the most promising and innovative scholars of the day, including Martial Gueroult and Maurice Pradines in philosophy, Maurice Halbwachs in sociology, as well as Marc Bloch and Lucien Febvre, later known as founders of the *Annales* school of historical research. Levinas's preparation in philosophy was at this point limited to time spent in the Russian-language bookshop his family ran, reading the novels of Fyodor Dostoevsky and Leo Tolstoy. The first task set to him at Strasbourg was to learn Latin, and he spent a year immersed in that language while also improving his French and German. In 1924 he began his studies in philosophy, taking courses with Pradines, Henri Carteron and Charles Blondel, as well as with Halbwachs in sociology. However, he seems to have been less motivated to master a standing traditional curriculum than to pursue the newest developments in philosophy—and he absorbed a series of theological influences as well, including important Protestant ones.

Before he ever came across existential phenomenology, Levinas was drawn to the work of Henri Bergson, whom he read with Pradines and whose emphasis on sensation and the spiritual appealed to his literary sensibility. Bergson's emphasis on feeling was in part a side effect of the larger project he had initiated in his 1889 *Time and Free Will*, in which he tried to counter what he saw as a scientific tendency to imagine the world as a series of temporal moments divided from one another. Against this tendency Bergson offered the idea of "lived duration."[24] As Bergson wrote in his classic 1907 work, *Creative*

Evolution, "real time, regarded as flux, or, in other words, the very mobility of being, escapes the hold of scientific knowledge."[25] Initially fascinated by Bergson's understanding of lived duration, Levinas would in later years turn to Heidegger's understanding of temporality as a force conditioning Being, implying in the essay, "Martin Heidegger and Ontology," that Heidegger's emphasis on Being seemed (and in a fashion Heidegger failed to acknowledge) to pick up where Bergson had left off. But Levinas would show, not only in the 1947 *De l'existence à l'existant* (*Existence to Existents* in its English translation), but also in the 1961 *Totality and Infinity*, that Bergson's understanding of duration remained influential for him. Said understanding helped him to articulate a vision of temporality that emphasized the present moment and the infinite possibilities contained in the future.[26]

Bergson's emphasis on experience—not only the experience of the individual moment but of emotion, including laughter, about which Bergson wrote a book—gratified Levinas's desire for a philosophy of affect. He would soon find an even deeper influence in the new discourse of Husserlian phenomenology, which would in time bring him to Heidegger. It was Jean Hering, a former student of Husserl's and an instructor in the Protestant theological faculty at Strasbourg, and Gabrielle Peiffer, a fellow student, who introduced Levinas to Husserl's work, at that point not yet translated into French; Peiffer and Levinas undertook to translate the *Cartesian Meditations* together. Hering was a critical antecedent to the mature Levinas's theorization of the infinite, a theologian who as Samuel Moyn puts it, "interpreted phenomenology as the science of the transcendent infinite (divine rather than human),"[27] and Hering became a channel through which early German phenomenology entered France as a mode of reflection already inflected by an interest in the divine Other. As his *Phenomenology and Religious Philosophy* shows, Hering's phenomenology was in part a response to the development of Protestant theology in Germany, which had drifted, due to works by Karl Barth and others heavily influenced by Friedrich Schleiermacher's emphasis on religious consciousness, toward a psychology of religious experience that abandoned or ignored the transcendent character of the divine, instead attending solely to the world of religious experience located within the human subject.[28] Hering held that the theological turn to experience had been problematic insofar as it left no room for the reality of a divinity outside the subject. Inspired by Husserl's adaptation of work done by Husserl's teacher Franz Brentano, Hering hoped that phenomenological methods could find evidence—a phenomenological proof—of the existence of God "within the intuitions through which religion reaches its object."[29] That is, phenomenology offered a tool by which theology could be saved from the abyss of subjectivism into which the nineteenth century had cast it. Husserl's phenomenology provided Hering with a means by which to conjure the objectivity of the divine beyond the human subject and thus escape the problems of consciousness-oriented theology.

Similarly, Husserl seemed to offer a way out of the dominant methodological dilemma facing Strasbourg's philosophers. If Bergsonism was under attack by the French exponents of neo-Kantianism, Husserl's phenomenology provided a means to explore experience without Bergsonism's susceptibility to the charge of subjectivism, perhaps the most frequent broadside from the neo-Kantians. By traveling to Freiburg as a visiting student in 1928, Levinas would pursue studies at the world's foremost center of phenomenological research. Significantly, at this point in his training, Levinas's trajectory was not, despite his exposure to Pradines' interpretation of the Dreyfus Affair, marked by an interest in the relationship between philosophers and politics. Levinas's interest in Husserl and Heidegger was initially driven by purely philosophical concerns. In later years, Levinas would damn Heidegger's philosophy for its inattention to ethics—where others, like Strauss, accused Heidegger of being blind to politics—and he would point toward Heidegger's fundamental solipsism, his thought's inability to make room for the dignity of the other person. It was as though Levinas had been caught totally offguard by Heidegger's Nazism, attending to the political predicament of philosophy only after 1933.

Solipsism with Husserl and Heidegger

The mature Strauss would criticize Heidegger for having allowed talk of Being to distract him from politics and, similarly, Levinas would argue that Heidegger was blinded to ethics by a form of philosophical solipsism and was furthermore blind to the political ontology that characterized his own thought. In Levinas's case, a prior engagement with Husserl provides the crucial background for his originally enthusiastic and then deeply hostile engagement with Heidegger. Whereas Bergson's principle of intuition seemed vulnerable to the charge of relativism (for how could one subject validate the intuition of another?) and Léon Brunschvicg's neo-Kantian idealism seemed

incapable of addressing the elements of a concrete life in the world, phenomenology offered something very different.[30] However, during his studies
with Husserl, Levinas's initial enthusiasm gave way to the view that an inherent weakness—a tendency toward solipsism—undermined Husserl's approach. It would be on these grounds that Levinas turned from Husserl to
Heidegger, and in some senses *La théorie de l'intuition dans la phénoménologie de Husserl* (*The Theory of Intuition in Husserl's Phenomenology*; 1930),
Levinas's first book and the product of his year in Freiburg, illustrated these
shifts in his attitudes toward Husserl and Heidegger. Levinas's early enthusiasm for Heidegger was so evident that Hering, in a critical review of Levinas's book, noted that Levinas seemed to view Husserl through a Heideggerian
lens.[31] Hering was correct insofar as Levinas approached Husserl as though
he offered "a new ontology of consciousness."[32]

Levinas understood that for Husserl intentionality was the key concept
that helped to explain the connection between consciousness and reality, re-
solving the puzzle of how noumena and phenomena relate to one another.
Husserl proposed that a theory of consciousness must include a theoretical
account of the meaning of the objects contained within consciousness. Within
Husserl's system the term "reality" would be understood to contain two types
of being, first the being of consciousness itself, second the being of the objects perceived by the conscious mind. However, these modes of being are
united in the representational act itself. On the grounds that Husserl's phenomenology focused on understanding this coming-together of these modes
within the act of representation (*Vorstellung*), Levinas characterized Husserl's
thought (employing, as Adriaan Peperzak points out, Heideggerian terms)
as *vorstellende*, that is, "objectifying" or "representationalist." The representational process lay at the basis of all philosophical work within Husserl's system: even ethical and moral deliberations were complex constructs built out
of a series of representations.

Levinas also followed from Heidegger in observing that Husserl's appreciation of being was itself rooted in historical circumstance and thus in a very
particular instantiation of Being. Husserl's understanding of being was therefore inevitably limited by the horizons of his own representational para-
digm; under Heidegger's influence (and ironically, given his own later
anti-historicism), Levinas felt there was too much theory and not enough accounting for history in Husserl.[33] Husserl's preference for theory was in turn
linked to a belief in the autonomy of the subject. As Peperzak shows, it would
be in the 1940 essay, "The Work of Edmund Husserl," that Levinas radicalized

his earlier critique of Husserl by claiming that Husserl's desire for theoretical knowledge was tied to a desire for the sovereignty of the subject, and Levinas would effectively recapitulate these critiques in the 1961 *Totality and Infinity*.[34]

But Levinas's charge that Husserl was invested in a problematic version of autonomy would transfer easily to Heidegger. In Levinas's *Totality and Infinity* and *Otherwise Than Being*, Heidegger's characterization of Being would fall prey to the same criticism as Husserl's representation: despite Heidegger's efforts to overcome idealism he was effectively complicit with its intention to dominate others in order to secure the autonomy and freedom of the self. Some of these assessments of Husserl and Heidegger would, however, take years to fully develop. In 1930, Levinas still saw Heidegger's reading of Husserl not so much as marking the inadequate or inherently problematic nature of Husserlian phenomenology as preparing the program for its future development. If Husserl had, as Levinas put it, offered "for the first time a possibility of passing from and through the theory of knowledge to the theory of Being,"[35] it was Heidegger who could show how to take the theory of Being seriously and explore its deepest meanings. Again, it was Heidegger who helped Levinas to reach what may well have been his goal as a philosophy student with strong literary instincts: to engage with the philosophical valences of sensation, representation, and affect. However, once reeling in a state of betrayal, Levinas would turn away from Heidegger and back toward the version of spontaneous freedom he had identified in Bergson and, in *The Theory of Intuition in Husserl's Phenomenology*, already contrasted against Heidegger's emphasis on "destiny."[36]

Heidegger as Pagan: Levinas's First Political Turn

In his admiring 1932 "Martin Heidegger and Ontology," Levinas presented the findings of *Being and Time* for a French audience not yet familiar with Heidegger.[37] However, the 1934 "Some Remarks on the Philosophy of Hitlerism," published in the left-wing Catholic journal *Esprit*, marked Levinas's turn against ontology and a politically motivated return to a model of transcendence at odds with Heidegger's existential phenomenology. This work was also Levinas's first effort to apply philosophy to contemporary political problems, in this case by understanding Nazism not only through an analysis of its political and social dimensions, but in terms of its putative philosophical foundations—aptly summarized in the suggestion that Heidegger offered "the philosophy of Hitlerism."[38]

The author of "Some Remarks on the Philosophy of Hitlerism" seemed convinced that his discipline could somehow serve as a weapon against the Nazis. Levinas began by observing that Hitler's movement concealed a philosophy directly opposed not only to the liberal governments of the West, but also to the Christian church, "in spite of the careful attentions or Concordats that the Christian churches took advantage of when Hitler's regime came to power."[39] Levinas thus addressed himself to *Esprit*'s Christian readers to remind them that whatever political promises Nazi Germany made, it was committed to a series of ultimately anti-Christian philosophical positions. Levinas then charted a course into the territory of existential religion, presenting Jewish thought both as the original monotheism and as an alternative to Heidegger's fixation on "Being-Towards-Death": "Judaism brings with itself this magnificent message . . . . The human being discovers in the present elements to modify and to eradicate the past. Time loses its irreversibility. Enervated, it cowers at the human being's feet like an injured animal. And the human being frees it."[40]

In the 1932 essay "Martin Heidegger and Ontology," Levinas had found a similar emphasis on the present in Bergsonian temporality. There he had seen Heidegger's understanding of temporality as an extension of Bergson's notion of duration, but in 1934 he reversed the course of his earlier reflections. The Levinas of the "Hitlerism" essay insisted that the present is the temporal location of human agency, something utterly absent from "Hitlerism" with its emphasis on the inevitably or "fatedness" of the future. Levinas, as Caygill suggests, was here thinking not of the freedom of the liberal subject, but of Bergson's concept of freedom as a spontaneous display of creativity, transposed onto a religious conception of man's choices before God, a scene of choice stripped of any conceptions of the chooser's past or the futures that branch out from the moment of decision.[41] In Levinas's view, a community of human beings who lived by fulfilling their potential in the present would be superior to one based on a shared future interpreted as a "common fate" or a shared past understood in terms of heritage or blood. But this essay— appropriately, given its place in a Catholic journal—performed a universalization of Judaism's teaching of freedom, extending it to the readers Levinas imagined might pick up a copy of *Esprit*.

If Levinas's discussion of agency was influenced more by Bergsonism than liberalism, he did insist that liberalism offered a secularized version of the

transcendent freedom offered by monotheism. As he wrote, "If the liberalism of these last few centuries evades the dramatic aspects of such a liberation, it does retain one of its essential elements in the form of the sovereign
freedom of reason."[42] The free decision maker of liberalism does not feel herself weighed down by a past history or a future destiny: her choices can be
based on purely rational determinations. In contrast, the philosophers of Hitlerism do not just oppose liberty, they affirm that essential obstacle to freedom, the human body: "[The body] breaks the free flight of the spirit and
drags it back down to earthly conditions, and yet, like an obstacle, it is to be
overcome. This is the feeling of the eternal strangeness of the body in relation to us that has nurtured Christianity as much as modern liberalism."[43]

Hitlerist materialism relocated spirit so that it "no longer lies in freedom,
but in a kind of bondage."[44] The emphasis on blood and heredity and the
emphasis on history and temporality are tied together within "Hitlerism," for
as Levinas pointed out the body serves as an "enigmatic vehicle" for the past.
And bodies that are busy being vehicles for the past, have no room for literally
liberal minds. As Levinas would write of "Hitlerism" elsewhere, it was the
hardest test Judaism had endured precisely because it attempted to convert
Jewish election or chosen-ness into a racial and thus physical condition.[45]

Levinas's first essay for a nonacademic public must be understood in the
context of the journal in which it was published, and in light of the unique
orientation of Emmanuel Mounier, founder of *Esprit* and of his own philosophy, "Personalism." A response to the climate of crisis triggered by the
stock market crash of 1929 and by justifiable interwar doubts about Europe's
political future, Personalism attempted to combine Marxism's emphasis on
determinant material conditions with Kierkegaard's emphasis on the radical freedom of the will.[46] For Mounier, the "personality" was shaped by historical forces but still capable of free moral choice. Furthermore, and very
significantly for Levinas's decision to publish in its pages, *Esprit* was created
as a mouthpiece for Personalism beyond the academy. The goal of engagement in issues of public interest, and of the bond between Personalist thinkers and the working classes, was always close to Mounier's heart, earning one
admirer's comment that "[Mounier] thinks and judges in solidarity."[47]
Mounier called his journal a "laboratory of new solutions" to contemporary
problems from the start of its publication, and as David Schalk has noted,
that "laboratory" did much to popularize the term "engagement" long before
Sartre founded *Les Temps Modernes* and linked himself to the term. In a manifesto published in the journal's very first issue, Mounier called Christians

to political action, and a year later he tellingly described "the spirit" (*l'esprit*) as itself consisting of "an engagement": "one engages himself with all his soul and all his days before him. Our labor of revolutionary criticism is a position taken against injustice before being an effort to construct justice."[48]

"Some Reflections" would be the first of many "occasional" essays Levinas would pen for *Esprit* throughout his long career. It also marked the beginning of Levinas's habit of simultaneously implying that philosophy had political consequences and failing to give an account, either dialectical or directly causal, of how this worked. In the case of "Some Reflections," this resulted in a bizarrely abstract account of "Hitlerism's" development, as if Nazification developed directly out of tendencies in the history of thought. A year after "Some Reflections," Levinas wove this same pattern into "De l'évasion" or "On Escape,"[49] a longer essay best understood as a work of anti-Heideggerian Heideggerianism in which Levinas rejected the philosophy of *Dasein* while accepting the premise that thinking through the question of Being constitutes first philosophy.

Here Levinas assessed philosophy's traditional preoccupation with transcendence as a response to the essential fact of identity, understood as a "riveting" we can never undo—and while "On Escape" was not an explicitly political performance as "Some Reflections" had been, Levinas glossed transcendence as that deeply political concept, freedom. As he wrote, "The revolt of traditional philosophy against the idea of Being originates in the discord between human freedom and the brutal fact of Being that assaults this freedom."[50] In fact, "On Escape" attempted to rehabilitate Heidegger's question of Being by producing a new type of existentialism concerned with *both* Being and transcendence, with both the feeling of rootedness in one's own identity and the felt need to escape one's skin. Levinas's essay subtly suggested that a style of political thought followed from philosophy's basic encounter with the "riveted" character of being. This was the most important sense in which Levinas's 1935 essay anticipated Sartre's 1938 *La Nausée* (*Nausea*) and, indeed, anticipated Sartre's view of existentialism as a philosophy with its own distinctive approach to politics.

"On Escape" opened as the much later *Totality and Infinity* would open, by making a political problem out of the solipsism of the Western philosophical tradition, which emphasized an "ideal of peace" in which peace was a function of the individual subject's security and autonomy.[51] "No one is more proud than Rousseau or Byron, no one is more self-sufficient," Levinas wrote, linking the political philosopher to the romantic poet by way of their visions of the autonomous self, withdrawing from a society that threatens to inflict upon each the un-freedom of inauthenticity.[52] But such self-sufficiency was a pose, compensation for the subject's knowledge of his own finitude: "The insufficiency of the human condition has never been understood otherwise than as a limitation of being, without our ever having envisaged the meaning of 'finite being.' The transcendence of these limits, communion with the infinite being, remained philosophy's sole preoccupation."[53]

Levinas nowhere mentioned Rosenzweig, whose *Star of Redemption* began by discussing philosophy's characteristic and historical deceit—the attempts of philosophers to escape from their very mortality into realms of thought—but Rosenzweig's presence was clear.[54] Having already criticized eighteenth-century champions of individualism, Levinas extended his criticism to the bourgeois capitalist subject, whom he saw as an anxious, clock-watching figure preoccupied with maintaining control over time by predicting the future and preparing for it.[55] Levinas had attacked Marxism for the materialist basis of its thought in "Some Reflections"; here he attacked capitalism for the apparent philosophical basis of its preoccupation with "security," which led only to "imperialism."

Philosophers, Levinas implied, had understood transcendence as a correction of the imbalances and lacks we experience within our beings, replacing insufficiency with sufficiency. Or at least they had until the advent of a new "abandonment of . . . concern with transcendence," existentialism, against which a new generation—that of Levinas—was, in turn, rebelling. In other words, existentialism's disquiet with transcendence had led to a backlash manifest in the rising generation of writers and philosophers (Levinas was about twenty-nine when he wrote his essay) who preoccupied themselves with the motif of escape. To escape one's own identity now meant breaking with Western philosophy's traditional figuration of transcendence as the production of sufficiency. Levinas coined a new term for this escaping, "excendence" (derived from the Latin for "to climb out"), which implied for him not the possibility of ultimately finding "a peace become real at the depths of the I," but rather the hope to produce not contentment with self but rather a radical breaking of the identity principle, of the sheer possibility of riveting. Levinas never mentioned Heidegger, but it was clear that "excendence," or escape, offered him a way to pose Heidegger's question of Being in new terms. At the conclusion of "On Escape," Levinas returned to the political claim of the 1934 "Some Reflections," that the acceptance of Being was opposed to the values of Western civilization and was in fact barbarism.

Similarly, the question of Being had to be experienced as disquiet with Being, rather than as the acceptance of being Levinas seemed to find in Heidegger. "Excendence" was a way to have being without barbarism.

Having begun his essay with the distinctly political equation of philosophy's fixation on transcendence with personal freedom, Levinas returned to the same equation at the essay's end. Here he reconsidered the stalemate between idealism and existentialism he had observed at Strasbourg and probed its political content. As he put it, "The value of European civilization consists incontestably in the aspirations of idealism, if not in its path: in its primary inspiration idealism seeks to surpass being. Every civilization that accepts being—with the tragic despair it contains and the crimes it justifies—merits the name 'barbarian'."[56] Such language reflected not only Levinas's antagonism toward Heidegger in the mid-1930s, but also his growing tendency to see philosophy and politics running together. If excendence was meritorious (and European) insofar as it tried to get beyond the riveted character of Being, it nevertheless implicitly accepted the Heideggerian prioritization of the *Seinsfrage* (the question of Being), for its efforts always led to the same revelation of the rivet. Levinas hoped excendence could provide a purchase on the question of Being, more critical, and thus less likely to become a politically numbing affirmation of one's place in history, than Heidegger's existential phenomenology.

But the full meaning of Levinas's perception of a political conflict between idealism and existentialism is greatly clarified by his response not only to Heidegger's brief Nazi career, but also to Heidegger's 1929 debate with the neo-Kantian Cassirer at Davos, Switzerland, which Levinas attended while studying with Husserl. Decades after witnessing Davos he declared, "for a young student, the impression was of being present at the creation and the end of the world."[57] Levinas took Heidegger's side in the debate, choosing the *neue Denken* rising up from the spot where Cassirer's edifice of neo-Kantianism had fallen. He would later speak of having witnessed the end of "a particular type of humanism," or, in other words, he had seen the cracks in Cassirer's neo-Kantian humanism, which owed equal debts to Kant's *Critique of Pure Reason* and to Goethe's poetry, and which emphasized an "expressive" as well as a "knowing" version of the human subject.

A full accounting of the Davos disputation is naturally beyond the scope of this chapter, but several aspects of Levinas's perception thereof are helpful in explaining "On Escape" and the "generational" task Levinas sought to complete by writing it. First, while Cassirer and Heidegger both understood

themselves as philosophers operating within history, Cassirer championed neo-Kantian idealism while Heidegger approached things from the
existential-phenomenological position he had taken in *Being and Time*, published two years before the debate; it was easy for Levinas to map them onto
"idealism" and "existentialism," respectively. Second, and as both "Some Reflections" and "On Escape" demonstrate, Levinas became a partisan—and
with great swiftness, since the 1934 and 1935 essays followed closely on the
heels of the revelation of Heidegger's Nazification—of a political interpretation not only of Heidegger's philosophy, but also of his debate with the Jewish
Cassirer at Davos. This interpretation performed, to paraphrase Peter Eli
Gordon, an "inscription" of what had been a largely technical debate over
Kant's metaphysics and epistemology, directly onto the fields of culture and
politics. In 1929, Levinas (clearly deriving impish pleasure from the weekend
at Davos) had orchestrated a performance in which students acted out the
parts of Heidegger and Cassirer, which, as Gordon notes, was symbolic of
Levinas's desire to see the debate ramify in a worldly, material fashion.
Tellingly, the line Levinas (as Cassirer) repeated again and again was "I am
a pacifist," a statement intended to caricature Cassirer as a milquetoast when
compared to Heidegger. But this statement bore an added meaning, for the
ideal of "peace" was precisely the goal of Western philosophy that Levinas
would skewer at the beginning of "On Escape," complaining that it was
couched upon a failure to understand the basic predicament of being, or as he
wrote, "The revolt of traditional philosophy against the idea of Being originates
in the discord between human freedom and the brutal fact of Being that assaults this freedom," a statement which subtly accepted the Heideggerian
proposition that the "fact of Being" was *prior* to the other tasks of traditional
philosophy: we can only rebel against that which precedes us. Peace was vulnerable, Levinas implied, to the claims of existentialism, which of course did not
invalidate the goal of peace so much as demand a more secure foundation for
it than Cassirer had provided. Decades after the Davos dispute, on a rare trip
to the United States, Levinas would search for Cassirer's widow, Toni, in order
to apologize for his youthful choice—by 1935, he had already begun to see his
mistake as choosing "barbarism" over "Western civilization."

In that same year, Levinas also published "L'actualité de Maimonide" ("The
Currency of Maimonides"), written for a 1935 celebration of the medieval
philosopher in *Paix et Droit*, the journal of the Alliance Israélite Universelle
(AIU), the Jewish aid and educational organization for which Levinas had
begun to work as a young teacher and which would employ him for most of his

professional life.[58] On the 800th anniversary of Maimonides' birth, Levinas argued for his contemporary relevance as a counter-force against an "arrogant barbarism" at the heart of Europe, National Socialism barely masked. He repeated his claim that National Socialism was a "pagan" ideology that confused the distinctions between the sacred and the profane and threatened what Levinas called "Judeo-Christian Civilization." In keeping with the tenor of "Some Reflections," but also displaying the tendency toward political inscription apparent in "On Escape," Levinas emphasized (but did not explain) philosophy's applicability: "The value of a real philosophy is not found in an impersonal eternity . . . . The truly philosophical aspect of a philosophy is found in its currency [*actualité*]. The most pure homage one may pay to it, is to apply it to the preoccupations of the hour."[59] Like "On Escape," "The Currency of Maimonides" engaged with its philosophical subject while grafting it onto a set of worldly political positions.

Having implied that Maimonides's thought might serve as a weapon against Nazism, Levinas then took a detour into the technical matter of Maimonides's reconciliation of revealed legislation with the philosophy of Aristotle, generally considered one of the medieval sage's most important contributions to Jewish thought. Maimonides had explained how one might believe in the Biblical account of the creation of the world, while also agreeing with the Aristotelian account of the world's eternity: in his *Moreh Nevukim (The Guide of the Perplexed)* Maimonides insisted that God had made the world so that it would appear to be understandable through the methods of logic and science, appearing to obey apparently eternal laws that in fact had only appeared when both the material and temporal dimensions—Maimonidean "spacetime"—were created ex nihilo and de novo. Despite the lack of any obvious *actualité* or contemporary relevance of this resolution of philosophy and religion's conflict over creation, Levinas turned it and turned it again until it related directly to the conflict between paganism and monotheism. He claimed that, like the Aristotelian doctrine, the pagan doctrine is characterized by a "radical inability to leave the world." It was in surpassing "the thought which thinks the world" that Judaism enjoyed a "definitive victory over paganism," and it is Maimonides who brought us this "great consolation."[60] Heidegger may have been at pains to go back before Aristotle to the pre-Socratics (a fact Levinas seems to have found it convenient to ignore here), but Levinas compared the "pagan" thought of National Socialism to Aristotelianism and ascribed to them both an inability to take seriously the idea of a "beyond." Levinas seemed to suggest that just as Maimonides had managed to harmonize Aristotelianism and the Bible, he himself might find a point of harmony between existentialism and transcendence—just as "On Escape" had promised.[61] Beyond its invocation of Judaism, represented by Maimonides, against a barely concealed Heideggerianism, "The Currency of Maimonides" inaugurated a different trend: Levinas's pattern of associating his own new philosophical path with Judaism while allowing that association to pass undefined and un-theorized. This pattern would prove generative for so many of his later efforts, including the Talmudic Readings of the 1960s, which often offered commentary on contemporary political developments along with their close studies of rabbinic texts. Levinas's traumatic experiences of the intervening war, however, would lend this pattern an entirely different meaning, and it is to this transition that the next chapter attends.

CHAPTER 5

Resisting Engagement

The Holocaust would loom large in Levinas's later work, informing everything from his account of human vulnerability to his gradually deepening
identification of political ontology with totalitarianism and, simply put, evil.
However, a crucial turn in his thought took place between the first stirrings
of war and the time he became aware of the mass murder of European Jewry.
Levinas himself reflected on this turn in his aforementioned essay, "The Name
of a Dog, or Human Rights," in which he described his experiences at POW
camp #1492 at Fallingpostel, Germany. Levinas, captured by the Germans,
was imprisoned at Fallingpostel along with other Jewish soldiers fighting in
the French army. The POWs did hard labor in the forest, but—like their
non-Jewish counterparts—they were allowed care packages and letters from
relatives in France. "Books appeared," Levinas later said in an interview,
and he found time to read Hegel, Proust, Diderot, and Rousseau among others, the very writers he could easily have associated with that other great
"last Kantian in Germany," Cassirer. Levinas continued to deepen his animus against the tradition that he, following Heidegger, termed "Western
philosophy," and it was in this spirit that he wrote the fragment *Il y a*, which
would become the core of his transitional work *De l'existence à l'existant*. *Il y
a* took up the theme of being itself as an experience of enchainment or being
trapped, implying that "being" harbors an evil or malicious force. The
themes of "On Escape" had found the ideal situation onto which they could
rivet themselves.

Importantly, being a POW likely saved Levinas from the concentration
camps; camp #1492 was not far from Bergen-Belsen. In 1939 Levinas had been
mobilized and made an interpreter within the French 10th Army. By June
1940 the 10th had been captured by the Germans, and while the Jews were

separated into their own subcamp, they were spared shipment to the concentration camps due to a prior agreement on the treatment of prisoners of war, itself based on German fear of reprisals against their own POWs.[1] They were furthermore spared the indignity of wearing the Star-of-David badge imposed by the Nazis. Most of Levinas's relatives were not so fortunate. He lost his extended family in Lithuania, and his wife and daughter were able to hide successfully in occupied France only through the efforts of Blanchot.

Much like *On Escape*, *Existence and Existents* reads as a meditation in existential phenomenology in which sensuous elements such as the night, light, food, clothing, and so forth, all become material to think with. Moods such as indolence, fatigue, and desire predominate, and each becomes a stance an individual subject can take relative to existence. However, it was writing at Fallingpostel that further radicalized Levinas's already impassioned response to Heidegger as a "pagan." Here Levinas seemed to transform Being itself into a kind of evil. In Levinas's "il y a," a near-translation of Heidegger's "es gibt," there is a sheer horror at the unchosen-ness of existence with none of the positive and generous sense of a "giving truth" Heidegger would confer to "es gibt" in the 1947 *Letter on Humanism*. Levinas thus rendered ontology a more problematic category than it was in *On Escape*, where existence threw the subject back on the sheer fact of hypostasis by reminding it of its physical limitations.

Levinas's internment was thus the site of much creative work, albeit work conducted in the absence of the very face-to-face encounter whose advocate he would become in later years. Following his studies at Freiburg, Levinas had relocated to Paris and taken French citizenship, and he also had the opportunity to travel back to Kovno, where he met his future wife, Raissa. Back in France, he performed mandatory military service and began to work as a teacher and administrator at the École Normale Israélite Orientale (ENIO), the main educational institution of the Alliance israèlite universelle. He would later become the school's director in 1946.[2] Levinas left no conclusive statement as to the reasons why he did not immediately attempt to climb the familiar rungs of the French professoriate, which would have involved taking the *agrégation* (examinations to certify teachers in philosophy, as well as in other fields) and in time preparing the second doctoral thesis, the *thèse d'état*, which was required for teaching in the French university system.[3] He did, however, continue to attend seminars at the Sorbonne and the École Pratique des Hautes Études, such as those led by Alexandre Koyré and his successor Alexandre Kojève, and he maintained personal and professional relationships with colleagues in philosophy.

In a late interview, Levinas offered an ideological explanation for his long years of work at the AIU, stating he endorsed its pursuit of emancipation for Jews living in countries where they did not enjoy the right to citizenship.[4] In the AIU, Levinas had found an institution working to promote Jewish interests as interpreted within a distinctly French Republican political framework.[5] Founded in 1860, the organization had been established, Levinas said, "according to the French ideas of the rights of man," with the explicit goal of extending those rights to Jews living in the Levantine world, particularly in countries where France had had a colonial presence but where Jews could not become citizens. Because much of the organization's work consisted of providing education through a network of international schools—the first had been established in Tetuan, Morocco, in 1862—ENIO was a critical part of the AIU's mission, the site for training the teachers who would teach at those schools.[6]

Shut down during the Occupation, but reconstructed after Liberation under the direction of AIU president René Cassin, the AIU's political orientation shifted in the postwar years. Like Levinas, Cassin was convinced that a renaissance of Jewish life in France could only come about through teaching, and he felt that the AIU's efforts to train Jewish teachers from the French colonies represented a step in the right direction. Notably, during the postwar period ENIO began a slow transformation that would continue through the decades. Partly due to France's weakening influence on its former colonies, ENIO became less and less a training ground for future teachers who might return to the colonies and enrich Jewish education there. It slowly became a private Jewish secondary school, and increasingly served a pool of students born in France itself. Levinas would thus oversee a highly transitional period at ENIO, although his post still provided him with a unique perspective on developments in the Jewish world both in France and beyond. Levinas continued his work there until 1961, when—even as *Totality and Infinity* was published—he received an appointment as professor of philosophy at Poitiers. He would receive two more professorial appointments, first to Paris-Nanterre in 1967 and then to the Sorbonne itself in 1973, a scant three years before his retirement from teaching. However, it was while a Jewish school administrator that Levinas invented the philosophy of ethics he would later refine as a professional academic. Levinas's very removal from the precincts of French academic philosophy and public life helped him to approach the themes of politics and ethics away from the guiding stars of "engagement" and "responsibility" and under the anachronistic sign of Zola.

As his essay on the "philosophy of Hitlerism" shows, after turning away from Heidegger Levinas had sought a politically meaningful version of transcendence, and this long before he had developed his mature account of an ethics of intersubjectivity. More to the point, Levinas's progress toward an account of the other had been directly paralleled by his attribution of a political meaning to the *il y a* and a search for a counterforce that might oppose it, which he associated with monotheistic and liberal accounts of the freedom of the subject. During the postwar years this taste for freedom would lead Levinas to defend a set of essentially idealist positions against Jean-Paul Sartre's variation on existentialism, and in the process to oppose Sartre's account of the role of the intellectual-as-writer. A writer had to be bold to oppose the darling of the Parisian literati in the postwar years, and the editorial board of Sartre's journal and mouthpiece *Temps Modernes* would scold Levinas for his troubles. However, Levinas opposed Sartre not just on the social role of the writer, but also on what turned out to be an intertwined issue for both thinkers: the nature of being Jewish. When Levinas criticized Sartre's attempt to transform writing into a political tool, he was essentially claiming that the teachings of Sartre's *Being and Nothingness* did not apply to the work of intellectuals; similarly, and for the same reasons, Levinas resisted the application of *Being and Nothingness* to Jewish identity.

It was a polite kind of conflict. On Tuesday, June 3, 1947, Sartre stepped up to the podium in the AIU's lecture hall, Levinas having invited him to give a lecture on his 1946 *Réflexions sur la question juive* (in English, *Anti-Semite and Jew*). This work had marked a turning point both in French public discourse on anti-Semitism and in Sartre's career.[7] Claude Lanzmann, later the director of the 1985 film *Shoah* and a student at the time Sartre's book appeared, claimed that it had boosted French-Jewish pride just as Zola's famous "J'accuse" had once done. Certainly it was one of the first postwar acknowledgments of the acts perpetrated against Jews by French anti-Semites, and before Sartre took the stage the AIU's president Cassin praised him for his efforts to bring anti-Semitism into the light of day, expressing the sentiments of many within a French Jewish community still recovering from the experience of Vichy and aware that anti-Semitic elements continued to thrive in French politics and letters. The right-wing journals *Écrits de Paris* and *Aspects de la France* had resumed publication in 1947 and, even as Sartre labored over *Réflexions sur la question juive*, Maurice Bardèche—brother-in-law of collaborationist writer Robert Brasillach—was writing his Holocaust-denying *Nuremberg ou la terre promise* (*Nuremberg, or, the Promised Land*), which would appear in 1948. Short of active anti-Semitism, in 1946, a poll conducted by the Institut Français d'Opinion Publique determined that only about two-thirds of the French adult population considered French Jews to be "as French" as their non-Jewish compatriots.

Sartre's lecture was aimed at a broad, primarily Jewish public, and posters advertising his talk hung outside synagogues and in Jewish businesses throughout Paris.[8] However, once at the podium Sartre seemed almost sheepish about what he had written. Conceding his inability to represent the interests or experiences of France's Jewish community, he said, "it is only with great hesitation that one speaks of a condition one hasn't shared and in which one hasn't lived, in particular during the five years of the recent past."[9] Moving into the main body of his talk, however, Sartre effectively recapitulated the central arguments of *Anti-Semite and Jew*. In *Being and Nothingness*, Sartre had offered a picture of human subjectivity defined by the tension between a radically free consciousness and the social constraints it comes up against, constraints that originate when the individual subject encounters other persons. That encounter is mediated by the other's gaze, the experience of which illuminates the fact that consciousness is embodied in the world and *can be taken* as an object by another—thus the radically free consciousness has its erstwhile solipsism cruelly stripped away. Writing three years before *Réflexions*, Sartre had already used the example of the anti-Semite's persecuting gaze to illustrate his meaning: Jewishness could be understood as a quality projected onto the Jew, with no real content of its own, illustrating the general point that identity is itself a projection that not only objectifies, but also limits the radical freedom of the individual consciousness. For Sartre, the case of the Jew and the anti-Semite had always been a useful illustration of the human condition most broadly, if one that attracted Sartre because of its obvious contemporary significance. In both *Being and Nothingness* and *Réflexions*, the task of the individual subject is to accept the situation in which they find themselves—including, for example, the role of "Jew" as imposed by anti-Semites—and act within it, by opposing anti-Semitism in the Jewish case.

While *Réflexions* was anecdotal rather than systematic, at the core of Sartre's analysis were two prominent versions of anti-Semitism.[10] Sartre was strident in his condemnation of the "Manichaean" anti-Semite who divides the world into good and evil and blames the latter on "the Jews."[11] However, he also attacked the liberal democrat as a "weak protector of the Jews"[12] and submitted that democracy and anti-Semitism both imagined the Jewish Question being resolved by the actual or effective eradication of the Jews as a people. The anti-Semite would have them physically removed or killed whereas the democrat would see the Jews disappear as a markedly different social and cultural group. The democrat is thus guilty of a mild or weak version of anti-Semitism insofar as he cannot tolerate Jews as a separate type, but only as potential representatives of humanity enjoying "the universal rights of man and of citizen." Sartre's reference to the famous Declaration of the French Revolution inevitably recalled the terms on which France's revolutionary government had extended civic emancipation to France's Jewish communities, and the fact that emancipation had come with the expectation that the Jews, once emancipated, would cease to be "a people apart" and eventually lose all distinguishing marks of Jewish identity and religion.[13]

Levinas announced his disappointment with Sartre's understanding of Jewishness in a review of the lecture titled "Existentialism and Anti-Semitism." However, he praised Sartre for deploying existentialist ideas in the service of the Jewish people, making it clear that he saw this *not*—as some of Sartre's critics contended—as a self-serving appropriation of the idea of "the Jew" meant to provide existentialism with some purchase on political life: "This is not simply an event for the Café de Flore crowd," Levinas wrote. But Levinas was more critical in another essay of 1947, "Être Juif" (Being Jewish),[14] which demanded the positive account of "Jewish being" Sartre could not have provided. "Jewish existence," said Levinas, cannot be fit into the set of distinctions by which Sartre . . . attempts to grasp it."[15] No Jewish essentialist per se, Levinas nevertheless objected to the idea that one could observe the conditions of a Jew's existence and from them understand the predicament of the Jew in the modern world; to do so one needed to understand Jewish existence from within. Indeed, the version of freedom manifest in Sartre's notion of "assuming one's situation" was ultimately inapplicable to Jewish identity because it missed that signal element of traditional Judaism, obedience to the divine law. Levinas wrote, "even if it is true that the Jewish fact exists bare, indeterminate in its essence, and called to choose an essence for itself according to the Sartrean framework, this fact is, in its very facticity, inconceivable without election."[16] In fact, the core of Jewishness was for Levinas a relation between the ego and a primary other, or God understood as the primal parent who constructed that ego. Against Sartre's understanding

of freedom as radical and "negative"—as an absence of constraints—
Levinas offered a very different freedom based on preexisting relationships
between self and other.

Sartre would explore the literary implications of *Being and Nothingness*
in the 1947 essay "What Is Writing?," published in his journal *Les Temps Modernes*. That essay, like the launch of *Les Temps Modernes* itself, was a founding gesture of Sartre's postwar thought, part of his effort to make philosophy
an inherently political enterprise and to put himself on public view.[17] While
Sartrean existentialism kept the human subject from becoming a mere "reflex" of its material conditions by celebrating the subject's ability to act freely
in the world, Sartre's view of the function of prose in the world was effectively mechanical, and he rendered it a potential tool in the hands of activists. While poets, Sartre said, are men "who refuse to *utilize* language,"[18] he
said that he could "define the prose-writer as a man who *makes use* of words."[19]
However, for Sartre the simple act of writing also served to reveal one's attitudes toward the world, and thus "What Is Writing?" located the "value" of
a work of prose not in its aesthetic qualities but rather in its function as "action by disclosure."[20]

Sartre had political motivations for wishing to cast writing as action. With
an eye toward Marxist colleagues who were calling art "apolitical," Sartre
attempted to "rehabilitate literature before the bar of the advancing revolution," as Anna Boschetti puts it.[21] Yet preserving art in the form of committed writing also helped Sartre to keep his distance from one element of
Marxist thought he feared. The human subject whose freedom was so central
to existentialism, both as goal and puzzle, could be suppressed by crude
versions of the Marxist economic dialectic. In Sartre's view, the project of
committed writing could help to preserve a radically free human subject, and
make that subject's freedom compatible with the praxis-driven propositions of Marxism.[22]

It is surprising that the editors of *Les Temps Modernes* chose to publish
Levinas's criticism of Sartre at all. In "Reality and Its Shadow," Levinas presented the aesthetic experience as an encounter with the nature of Being, preserved from politics both by art's autonomy from the world of concepts in
which we live, and by many artistic mediums' ability to capture moments out
of time. In this he preserved and further adapted a motif he had first established in *Existence and Existents*, where in an almost Brechtian mode he
had described works of art as estranging or alienating otherwise familiar
representational subjects. As though anxious that his focus on Being might

be read as a backward slide toward Heideggerianism, Levinas suggested that alienation might call attention to the status of everyday objects as instantiations of Being and in so doing call us to ethics. "Reality and Its Shadow" thus tried to move the aesthetic toward the ethical while removing the tool-like qualities Sartre had grafted on.

As Jill Robbins argues, this essay—along with two other essays on literature, "The Transcendence of Words" and "The Other in Proust," also written in the late 1940s—began a denigration of visual representation Levinas would continue in the later *Totality and Infinity*. In these essays Levinas worried that visual and language-based art are totalizing forms of representation that deny difference, and are thus counter-ethical. But while Levinas *was* concerned about the totalizing effects of representational art, he also defended a version of the transcendence or sublimity of aesthetic experience against utilitarian views of art, in the process defending an idea dear to French intellectuals, namely that cultural artifacts are self-sufficient, detached from their environments, effectively autotelic. And after Levinas's own early experiments in making philosophy speak back to politics, these three essays mark an important turn toward a consideration of the public character of writing and speech acts.

The best evidence that Levinas wrote "Reality and Its Shadow" as a response to Sartre is the insulting *caveat lector* with which the editors of *Temps Modernes* introduced the essay:

> One has presented the writer as a bad partisan and, so to speak, a man without character . . . . In this regard the ideas of Sartre on the engagement of literature have not been examined carefully enough. Levinas has not taken note of the difficulties of literary communication, tending at each instant to return the writer to his solitude.

Levinas's misdeed lay in explicitly rejecting that key Sartrean term, "engagement." As he wrote, "art, essentially *disengaged*, constitutes, in a world of initiative and responsibility, a dimension of evasion."[23] He suggested that the so-called "problem of committed literature" began with the idea that art objects are more or less equivalent to speech acts.[24] Contrary to the committed writers whose roles were founded on such assumptions, Levinas proposed that artistic practices are essentially transcendent and that it is the role of the *critic* rather than the artist to explain how artworks bear on contemporary social life. Where Sartre had denounced art critics as "graveyard keepers" who preside over nothing of relevance to the world of the living, Levinas spoke of the necessity of both the critical enterprise and of the social role of the art critic. It was the critic who dwelled in the world of "interest" and who could thus convey, to the larger community, the ethical lessons contained within art.[25] Thus, "criticism exists as a public's mode of comportment. Not content with being absorbed in aesthetic enjoyment, the public feels an irresistible need to speak."[26] Without denigrating the public function of art—although he notably neglected to present a fully developed theory of such—Levinas shifted responsibility for that function away from the artists themselves. While no artist could ignore their audience, it was authorial intent rather than reception that justified the work of art and made it beautiful.

Levinas insisted he was not supporting "art for art's sake," but rather exploring the *disengagement* art required as a condition of its production, and which art could provide for its audience. Returning to the great theme of the earlier "On Escape," Levinas suggested that art represented human freedom from the world, and he wrote that the "element of art" that runs through "all human work" "bears witness to an accord with some destiny extrinsic to the course of things, which situates it outside the world."[27] In contrast, Sartre had written, in the "Présentation" that introduced the first issue of *Temps Modernes*, "we write for our contemporaries," rather than for literary posterity or "immortality."

Thus for Levinas, opposing "What Is Writing" meant opposing its utilitarian denigration of form, or the letter, and its preference for the meaning behind the letter. He wrote:

> The most elementary procedure of art consists in substituting for the object its image. Its image, and not its concept. A concept is the object *grasped*, the intelligible object. Already by action we maintain a living relationship with a real object; we grasp it, we conceive it. The image neutralizes this real relationship, this primary conceiving through action. The well-known disinterestedness of artistic vision, which the current aesthetic analysis stops with, signifies above all a blindness to concepts.[28]

But what was the nature of the "images" Levinas preferred over concepts? And what is the value of the image, which Sartre was too focused on the communicability of content to understand? Levinas argued that to perceive the image of an object, which he called its "allegory," was to enter into a meditation on the economy of being: "An allegory is not a simple auxiliary to thought . . . . It is an ambiguous commerce with reality in which reality does not refer to itself but to its reflection, its shadow. An allegory thus represents what in the object itself doubles it up. An image, we can say, is an allegory of being."[29] However, these "shadows" of reality, or, in other words, art objects, are not necessarily philosophically instructive or morally enlightening in and of themselves. Levinas wrote of the nightmarish quality of the "stopped time" visible in paintings and statues, whose subjects remain frozen in a form of bad eternity, and he could find no beauty in the representation of an incomplete picture of life. The *Mona Lisa*'s hint of a smile, he said, will (horribly) never broaden into fullness. In fact, it is on the basis of this problem of frozen *time* in art (Levinas referred exclusively to arts other than the "timed arts" of music, dance, film, and theater) that he could claim "the proscription of images is truly the supreme command of monotheism."[30] Jewish monotheism, in particular, turns us away from artistic evasions of responsibility and toward obedience to the law. Levinas never fully explained this argument, if indeed it was an argument—he never explained why frozen pictures of life turned his mind toward the proscription of images—although it certainly anticipated the critique of representation he would offer in *Totality and Infinity*.

But in historical terms, Levinas's criticisms of Sartre on art and Jewishness were most important because they stood as warnings to limit the scope of the existentialist project itself. In both "Reality and Its Shadow" and "Being Jewish," Levinas effectively implied that Sartre's privileging of politics obscured the ethical dimension of existence. Furthermore, he suggested that Sartre was wrong to gather together every aspect of life, including art and religious identity, as material for a broader and markedly voluntarist philosophical project in which all parts of human life were to be viewed as grounds for action. Levinas feared that Sartrean "engagement" would limit philosophy's horizons far too much, reducing its truth-claims to the status of ideological statements and denying philosophy's primary gesture of transcendence. While he never directly invoked Zola in his criticisms of Sartre, it was toward the Dreyfusard model that Levinas turned—and as Levinas made clear in *Totality and Infinity*, this was not because he shared Benda's naïve view of 1927, namely, that philosophy had once been apolitical, subsequently "fell," and now needed its guardians to return it to its former high pedestal. Rather, because certain patterns of philosophical thinking—the ones most conventional in the Western tradition—were linked to tyranny, a philosophy of ethics founded in fraternity was needed. Only a philosopher of ethics understood thusly could perform philosophy's ideal social function, which was not so different from the role Levinas attributed to the art critic in "Reality and Its Shadow." Thus did Levinas attempt to echo Zola and company, or echo his received impression of them—a pattern that would continue in the extended philosophical works that followed.

CHAPTER 6

Witnessing

Despite his early resistance to engagement, Levinas evidently wrote to the don of the intellectuals in 1964, just after Sartre had declined the Nobel Prize in Literature, to entice him to action. Levinas asked Sartre to embark on a diplomatic journey to visit Egypt's president Gamal Abdel Nasser and ask him to consider peace with Israel. Not a backslide from his opposition to *"engagement,"* Levinas's attempt to recruit Sartre was predicated on the belief that Sartre, by declining a high public honor, had in fact elevated himself above the rewards of Caesar and become an ideal witness for peace. Sartre's was a potential voice for ethics rather than politics, in terms Levinas had laid down in his first full-length philosophical study, the 1961 Thèse d'État, *Totalité et infini*. It had never been Sartre's orientation toward the public that troubled Levinas, but rather his orientation toward partisan action. In contrast, the ethical stance Levinas developed in his first major book could be called passivity—albeit a passivity that seeks to undermine all violence. Even language, which Sartre had made into a tool, for Levinas expressed a vulnerability that called for the ethical solicitude of other persons. In *Totality and Infinity* Levinas would maintain the same basic view he had relied on in earlier work, that political positions such as liberalism and fascism corresponded to philosophical stances: "The visage of being that shows itself in war is fixed in the concept of totality, which dominates Western philosophy."[1] Setting out from that starting point, the work eventually reached the conclusion that another form of thought (a thinking "otherwise") was possible, one purified not only of politics but of the aggression against others that lay at the root of all political thinking—and that lay at the root of all the representational strategies philosophy had employed to figure the truth as fixed ontological presence.

Through *Totality and Infinity* there winds a meditation on ethics in which Levinas mobilizes the concept of infinity, derived from Descartes's and Plato's discussions of the infinite, against the understanding of truth as an autonomous and self-sufficient whole that Levinas attributed to "Western philosophy" (as usual, understood in very broad strokes). To express *Totality and Infinity*'s central thought in a formula seems inappropriate, for Levinas was critical of representational strategies that do violence to the singularity of a philosophical problem, a natural phenomenon, or even a person. Such summary is nevertheless a useful exercise when engaging with such a complex work and the reader may have to be somewhat unfaithful to the spirit of Levinas's thought in order to understand the letter of his writing. The version of ethics that Levinas articulates in *Totality and Infinity* is based on overcoming the allergy to alterity, to the other person, which is caused by philosophy's emphasis on totality. Infinity is understood as the root of ethics, or as Levinas would later say, "to have the idea of infinity is already to have welcomed the Other."

In *Totality and Infinity* Levinas pushed forward ideas he had been developing since the 1930s and 1940s, moving him from the ranks of philosophical commentators on Husserl and Heidegger and marking his arrival as a constructive thinker in his own right. Following the publication of *Existence and Existents* and *Time and the Other* (both of which had appeared in 1947), Levinas had devoted much thought to the relationship between selfhood and the capacity for ethics.[2] Whereas in Levinas's earlier works a preexisting and independent self engaged in ethical relations with other persons, in *Totality and Infinity* he re-imagined the encounter with the other, the experience from which ethics follows, as taking place *prior* to the formation of the self, producing an "impingement" of the self by a primal ethical event. By doing so, Levinas preserved the emphasis on subjectivity that had marked his earlier works, but suggested that the solipsistic subject itself rested on an illusion of autonomous selfhood.

If *Totality and Infinity* marked a transition away from the relation between selfhood and ethics presented in *Time and the Other*, it was continuous and consistent with that text's program of ethical investigation.[3] *Time and the Other* had marked an important developmental stage in Levinas's thought, crystallizing the central insight of *On Escape* and *Existence and Existents*. For Levinas, experiences of our "riveted" nature, which call to consciousness our fundamental relationship with Being, are actually stages toward the realization of ethics. But *Time and the Other* also incorporated a response to Sartre's materialist existentialism and to his theory of commitment, and a more direct one than Levinas had offered in either "Reality and Its Shadow" or "Being Jewish."[4]

The trajectory marked by *Time and the Other*, as Richard Cohen notes, leads from existence considered as an abstract entity (Heidegger's *Dasein* as Levinas understood it) to the alterity possible between separated, living, and suffering beings, or "existents." The ultimate goal of the individual subject becomes not "completion," which is the objective of a solipsist, but rather to break out of circles of solipsistic self-sameness. Levinas reached his understanding of this movement through an investigation of our relationship with time, by now a familiar preoccupation for him, but now he went beyond the reflections he had offered in *Existence and Existents*. Time he considered in two dimensions: the individual subject's relation with temporality, on the one hand, and on the other the acknowledgment that another person exists according to his or her own time, not congruent with the subject's own. This talk of time, of course, gestured back toward Levinas's essays of the 1930s, especially "Some Reflections on the Philosophy of Hitlerism," in which he had compared Heidegger's "pagan" understanding of time with that furnished by Judaism. In *Time and the Other* the intention of that earlier essay remained visible, for against Heidegger's account of our existences in time as being-toward-death, Levinas tried to identify something liberating in temporality.

Recalling "Reflections on the Philosophy of Hitlerism," Levinas argued that our relation to temporality is not (contra Heidegger) a matter of struggling through our relation with our own finitude. Rather, this relation allows us to understand our relation to the infinite. While he presented *Time and the Other* as a philosophical and not a theological text, Levinas walked the line between these categories when he phrased his project as a question: "Is time the very limitation of finite being or is it the relationship of finite being to God?"[5] Levinas's setting of this thesis in a more secular key, in a Preface he wrote for *Time and the Other*, is helpful:

> The main thesis caught sight of in *Time and the Other* . . . consists in thinking time not as a *degradation* of eternity, but as the relationship to *that* which—of itself unassimilable, absolutely other—would not allow itself to be assimilated by experience; or to *that* which—of itself infinite—would not allow itself to be comprehended.[6]

While such an "infinite" can be located in the idea of the divine, Levinas also found it in the secular "other," the other person. Time became "the very relationship of the subject with the Other."[7] Levinas did not, of course, deny that solitude is a fundamental condition of our existence.[8] In fact, once an existent comes to understand the sheer fact that it exists, one of its first lessons is its solitude within that existence.[9]

Levinas's "solitude" seems directly indebted to Sartre's mid-1940s discussions of the relation between aloneness and freedom. Our freedom, as Sartre claimed in his 1945 public lecture "Existentialism is a Humanism," is the part of us that transcends our "situation," and allows us to respond to that situation creatively; and yet this transcendence is incomplete because our very solitude within ourselves renders us radically responsible for all our actions and their consequences. As Levinas put it, the temporality in which we exist is "incapable of loosening the tie of hypostasis."[10] What *can* perform this loosening—diminishing even our absolute, incontrovertible solitude—is the relationship between the present and the future accomplished by the relationship between the self and another person. Just as the future is the absolute *other* of the present, it also does more than merely continue the tasks of the present. "Time is," Levinas wrote, "essentially a new birth."[11] Solitude is broken by the encounter with another person whose temporality is absolutely other than our own, in ways that we cannot even assimilate to our own terms of understanding—as Levinas put it, "intersubjective space is not symmetrical."[12] When it comes to the other we are never simply concerned with another existent who exists in the same manner that we do. We are concerned with an "event of alterity."[13]

In *Time and the Other*, Levinas doubted that Sartre's subject could be solitary and world-transforming at the same time, and he offered the encounter with the other as one solution to this basic problem: "Can one not thus resolve a contradiction that all contemporary philosophy plays out? The hope for a better society and the despair of solitude, both of which are founded on experiences that claim to be self-evident, seem to be in an insurmountable antagonism."[14] In other words, Levinas claimed that existentialism's aspirations to stand as *the* premier philosophy of engagement were at odds with its picture of the human agent as fundamentally alone in the world. Even Sartre's robust publication record spoke against the claim of fundamental solitude. In writing a book on anxiety, Levinas noted, one always has an audience in mind.[15] Levinas furthermore disputed Sartre's notion that the workers' struggles provided a privileged perspective that might generate either intellectual or political freedom: "I do not believe that the oppression that crushes the working classes gives it uniquely a pure experience of oppression in order to awaken in it, beyond economic liberation, the nostalgia for a metaphysical liberation."[16] Instead, economic and spiritual struggles should be accounted as being on a par with one another.

Levinas did not attack Sartre by name here, but his intention is unmistakable. Perhaps it is the very indirectness of Levinas's discussion of Sartre that best communicates his continued ambivalence regarding Sartrean existentialism; it was only after pages of hand-wringing regarding the conflicts between existentialism and social justice that Levinas could give Sartre his due compliment as a thinker who carried philosophy beyond egoism, even if his thought remained compromised by its political engagements. Beyond the details of Levinas's commentary on Sartre, *Time and the Other* shows that it was only after careful consideration of Sartre's vision of solitude, freedom, and social life that Levinas began his own mature encounter with the idea of the other. The encounter with postwar existentialism, the very movement for which Levinas's early writings on Hussserl and Heidegger had provided fuel, now presented a distinctly political foil against which Levinas constructed his ethics.

The Argument of *Totality and Infinity*

In the first pages of his magnum opus, Levinas announced the link between war—including the war by other means that goes by the name "politics" in times of peace—and the philosophy of totality that dominated Western thought. The warlike character of European philosophy stemmed from its central solipsism (the very problem that had gripped Levinas during his student days) and he opened *Totality and Infinity* by describing the philosophical subject for whom totality was the unquestioned mode of philosophical inquiry. It was only by understanding the problem of solipsism, Levinas suggested, that one could understand how the self could be moved toward ethics by the plight of another, its reverie of ego interrupted. As he put it, egoism, enjoyment, sensibility, and the whole dimension of interiority are in fact necessary for the idea of infinity, "the relation with the other that opens forth from separated and finite being."[17]

In order to argue that our status as existents can interrupt the representational process by which solipsism is maintained, Levinas needed something

akin to Heidegger's view that life experience has a "pre-philosophical" significance that can in turn affect philosophy. For Levinas, this type of *erlebnis* (experience) held a very different significance from what Heidegger had
found in it. The experience of corporeal life did not itself lead to a stress on
decisively choosing a particular path of action, as it did for Heidegger and
Sartre. Rather, it challenged the "representationalist" bias on which philosophy has operated from the Greeks through Hegel. Drawing on a theme he
had explored many years earlier in "On Escape," and which had showed
very clearly in *il y a* and in his postwar writings, Levinas observed that the
embodied subject's physical experiences exposed it to its own existential
condition.

Levinas described the experience of the body in terms of "enjoyment."
We taste the world around us, consuming it both figuratively and literally.
While this "alimentary" process potentially leads to solipsistic consequences
as we cease to see the world around us as anything but material for consumption, it was nevertheless necessary for subject-formation to take place
at all. As Levinas insisted, "Subjectivity originates in the independence and
sovereignty of enjoyment."[18] The process of first differentiating one's self from
something outside oneself, and then *absorbing* that thing into one's self, is a
phase in the establishment of the self. Interiority is not an inward-dwelling
"mood" of the subject, but rather an essential characteristic of personhood.

The break from interiority into exteriority was to be accomplished through
a departure from the solipsist's logic of representation, for the transcendent
other must be encountered through a modality that does not reduce difference to sameness. Levinas described this departure as follows:

> If the transcendent cuts across sensibility, if it is openness preemi-
> nently, if its vision is the vision of the very openness of being, it cuts
> across the vision of forms and can be stated neither in terms of con-
> templation nor in terms of practice. It is the face; its revelation is
> speech. The relation with the Other alone introduces a dimension of
> transcendence, and leads us to a relation totally different from expe-
> rience in the sensible sense of the term, relative and egoist.[19]

Where Levinas used the metaphors of vision and alimentary consumption
to characterize totality, it was "language" or "speech" that accomplished the
revelation of infinity.[20] Speech inaugurates true intersubjective relations,
moving us beyond vision's tendency to reduce its objects to the terms of their

intelligibility. As Levinas had put it in "Reality and Its Shadow," expressing the anti-ocular bias that would manifest throughout his later work, "The proscription of images is the truly the supreme command of monotheism."[21] Even more importantly, Levinas suggested that it is the very *structure* of language that "announces the ethical inviolability of the Other."[22]

Despite the fact that Levinas alternately described the Other as a stranger or neighbor throughout his later works, in *Totality and Infinity* the Other did not originate in an "elsewhere" and then penetrate the bounds of my interiority or ego in the manner of a foreign object breaching a cell membrane. Instead the other somehow "overflows" subjectivity from within. In describing this process Levinas drew directly from the argument of Descartes's Third Meditation, in which the "infinite" idea of God somehow exists within my finite mind, somehow persisting in a vessel too limited to contain it: "The idea of infinity, the infinitely more contained in the less, is concretely produced in the form of a relation with the face."[23] Furthermore, Levinas implied that it is our innate desire for some substantiation of our idea of the infinite that produces the "epiphany" of the face of the Other.[24] He argued, in other words, that there was a "fit" between our inherent receptivity to otherness and the encounter with an actual "other" person, but *Totality and Infinity* was given over not to an account of philosophy somehow interrupted by social life, but rather to an account of the forces within the individual that then produce ethical effects within social life.

Our idea of the infinite might be internal, but it is in our relations with others that we are reminded of our preexisting receptiveness to alterity, because of the very "resistance" they provide. On Levinas's account we see other people as "resistant" when we acknowledge that we cannot simply absorb them into ourselves or make them into tools for use. "The face resists possession, resists my powers," as Levinas put it.[25] But resistance to my powers can still provoke the desire to kill, for complex reasons. The Other has resisted my attempts to dominate it, but murder is not the "domination" achieved by the victor of Hegel's master-slave struggle, but rather the total annihilation of the loser. For a philosopher, the desire to "negate" something has special meaning. It means acknowledging that this thing cannot be comprehended, must in fact be removed from the realm of potential comprehension.[26] However, Levinas argued, the ethical command issued by the proximity of the other makes such a murder impossible. The very infinitude of the other person that we see in a face is, effectively, "the first word: you shall not commit murder."[27] The other's resistance is not concrete, but rather a power of a different order, a power that subtends our ability to kill.[28] While the commandment not to kill thus loomed large as the foremost articulation of ethics in *Totality and Infinity*, this does not mean that the text only characterized ethics "negatively," via a prohibition. Levinas also articulated a corresponding "positive" duty: the duty to make sacrifices so that the other person not only survives but flourishes.

After explaining the philosophical prohibition against murder leveled by the face, Levinas returned to his earlier pronouncement that the very structure of language announces the other's ethical inviolability. Language is not an expression of representational mastery, but instead a revelation of the speaker's needs and vulnerabilities. This is why it functions as a reminder of the ethical encounter: it is one version of what Levinas described as "sociability," which gently but insistently returns us not only to our desire for alterity but also to the infinity of that alterity. Words are not, as a nominalist would have it, the instruments of convention, nor are they instruments of mastery. Instead, and as Maurice Merleau-Ponty observed, they "incarnate" thought, and give to the thought thereby incarnated the vulnerability that corporeality gives to mind and soul. The metaphor Levinas used for this type of speech was "witnessing," recalling his earlier experiences with *Esprit* and the interests he shared with Mounier.[29] Levinas wrote, "The event proper to expression consists in bearing witness to oneself, and guaranteeing this witness. This attestation of oneself is possible only as a face, that is, as speech."[30] Thus, witnessing became a way of accounting for—or narrating—one's perspective on the world while simultaneously accounting for one's intimate vulnerabilities as part of that perspective. The term "witnessing" also conjures the image of an observer at a remove from some scene of activity, and Levinas made it clear that the renunciation of action is a necessary part of language becoming expression.[31] In a turn that directly recalls his earlier rejection of Sartre's "committed writing" argument, language must cease to be utilitarian before it can take on the salutary functions Levinas finds within it; language, in *Totality and Infinity*, is a medium of "witnessing"—of witnessing one's own vulnerability and calling others to witness it—rather than a tool.

The Third

Perhaps *Totality and Infinity*'s weakest point is its account of how the ethical relation between self and other extends to a social world of selves and others *beyond* the initial self-other dyad. The need for such an account followed from Levinas's conviction that sociability was a constituent part of prephilosophical experience. Having accorded the other a degree of infinite difference, Levinas then came to a problem, which quickly grew into more problems: can two others be equally infinite, relative to me? And if there are three of us, does the triangular relation established between us diminish my others' otherness by rendering it relative? How could I be so totally, so "asymmetrically" responsible for so many beings at once? The problems arising from this "triadic" dimension of *Totality and Infinity* are critical for our understanding of how politics features in this text. This is because the "triadic" *is*, for Levinas, the dimension of the political; we enter into it through the introduction of what Levinas calls a "third term." As mentioned earlier, Levinas normally viewed ethics, which emerges in the dyadic relation, as absent from the political realm, which is characterized by the emergence of the triadic. Without an account of the way ethics might be carried over from the former to the latter, Levinas could not bring ethics to politics.

Levinas attempted to address this problem in a subsection of *Totality and Infinity* titled "The Other and the Others." Here he claimed that a public world provides the setting in which the encounter with the Other takes place: "Everything that takes place here 'between us' concerns everyone, the face that looks at it places itself in the full light of the public order, even if I draw back from it to seek with the interlocutor the complicity of a private relation and a clandestinity."[32] The medium of language itself reveals that the social world preexists the dyad. My language is not exclusive to me, betraying the existence of the broader world in which I exist. But language also serves to carry the force of the laws that regulate our shared social world: "The third party looks at me in the eyes of the other—language is justice."[33] Thus, in perceiving the face of the other we also find ourselves confronting the social order writ large and we feel the impact of the laws that affect us. But from whence does the power of the law, carried by language, come? According to Levinas, society's law only has power to the extent that it can recall the transcendent encounter with a personal Other—the law regulating the triadic relation originates within the dyad. Levinas warned against the tendency to imagine society in abstract terms—as a "genus," he wrote—and he suggested that the ethical encounter enables us to see our fellow community members in their full individuality rather than subsuming them under a whole. The word that summarized this feeling for Levinas was "fraternity," though even strangers could be brothers. Needing a common "father" to secure this

fraternity, Levinas turned to the idea of monotheism, which, at least symbolically, underwrites the idea of the fraternity of Man.

Even a generous reader willing to endorse Levinas's notion that the feeling of the dyadic encounter might infuse the triadic, must note the brief and
incomplete nature of *Totality and Infinity's* discussion of ethics on the level
of the social. Intriguingly, the vagueness of Levinas's account of the Third in
Totality and Infinity may be due to his having abandoned a different line of
thinking in the years prior to *Totality and Infinity's* publication. This different course would have been an explicitly humanist political theory articulated against a politics of totality whose effects were felt not only in the
Holocaust, but also in the Cold War—not a "constructive" or "archic" theory, then, but an argument against concrete instances of the style of thought
Levinas attacked in *Totality and Infinity*. Levinas's very short essay "On the
Spirit of Geneva," published in *Esprit* and occasioned by the 1955 meeting of
the "Big Four" nuclear superpowers at Geneva, was perhaps his most explicit
engagement with the Cold War. As Levinas pointed out, for anyone anxious
about the possibility of nuclear war, the Geneva summit provided a cause
for optimism. Meeting with Soviet premier Nikolai Bulganin, British prime
minister Anthony Eden, and French prime minister Edgar Faure, American
president Dwight D. Eisenhower proposed his "Open Skies" plan, which
called for mutual U.S.-Soviet weapons inspection and an exchange of military blueprints. This would have produced an unprecedented degree of
transparency for the two powers. "On the Spirit of Geneva" displayed the
same style of thinking the relationship between politics and philosophy Levinas had shown in his essays of the 1930s. Here he was struck by the new style
of conflict the Cold War represented and understood that mode to rest on a
particular form of political ontology.[34] When paired with the 1960 "Principles and Faces," another short *Esprit* essay, "On the Spirit of Geneva" illus-
trates the fact that Levinas understood his philosophy as an antidote to a
dangerous mode of political thought. It also shows that he came to juxtapose
his ethics against not "politics" in general, despite the vagueness of *Totality
and Infinity's* language, but against specific types of political thought.

In "On the Spirit of Geneva," Levinas targeted for criticism those political decisions conceived on the "inhuman scale" of technology and he called
for a restoration of a human scale in political deliberations, particularly between contending powers of the Cold War. In criticizing the impact of technology on modern political life, Levinas was not so different from many of his
contemporaries, including Arendt and Hans Jonas, as well as the philosopher

and theologian Jacques Ellul, who insisted in his 1964 *The Technological Society* that the embrace of "technique," understood broadly, led to the subjugation of nature and the impoverishment of humanity. And he drew close to Heidegger, for his former teacher had turned his gaze to such issues in the 1954 "The Question Concerning Technology."[35] "On the Spirit of Geneva" belonged to a period marked by the end of the Holocaust, the beginning of the Cold War, and the development of nuclear deterrence, which led to modes of war characterized by weapons and strategies that did not wear, to use Levinas's term, "faces." Even a philosopher like Levinas, who never displayed nostalgia for the soldier's life, could claim "the old meaning of combat between men is lost."

"The third" appeared early in the essay, albeit with a different meaning. Levinas described "warriors" and "diplomats" having difficulty dealing with a "third party" in the room who is *not* "the third man." "It is not a man," he wrote, "it is faceless powers."[36] Here the third was not the additional "other" who forces us to ask a question of distributive justice. The third was the Bomb, the specter of nuclear annihilation haunting all Cold War talks undergone in the interests of détente. However, in Levinas's view it was this very replacement of a *human* "third" with an inhuman one that signaled the need for a renewed humanism that "begins with the wars where the forces of Nature are forgotten."[37] And puzzlingly, Levinas insisted on the very thing that he would later seem to condemn—"politics"—or as he said: "Giving politics precedence over physics is an invitation to work for a better world, to believe that the world is transformable and human."[38] Here there is something "nonpolitical" about the Cold War, or at least about the atomic physics that underlies it: "Reason resides not in the wisdom of politics but in truths without historical condition that forecast cosmic dangers. Politics is replaced by cosmo-politics, which is physics."[39]

That Levinas entertained a lost version of the political as a responsible alternative to this "cosmo-politics" may seem hard to square with his antipathy toward all models of politics in *Totality and Infinity*. However, in "Principles and Faces," also published in *Esprit*, Levinas would summon the "Spirit of Geneva" once more.[40] In the latter essay Levinas understood there to be a clear connection between the version of politics on display in the Cold War, and Western metaphysics. Essentially a commentary on a speech given by Nikita Khrushchev on the occasion of his departure for a diplomatic mission to the United States, "Principles and Faces" suggested that Khrush-

chev's defense of the Soviet Union was itself an extension of a style of thinking of which Hegel is the most famous exponent, in which the state became
the incarnation of reason within whose institutions the humanity of all citizens can be fully "accomplished." Against this vision of the State as a manifestation of universal reason, Levinas asked if another model of universality
might be found, one that also reached beyond the "concretization" of the
universal found in Marx and Hegel. The great irony toward which Levinas
gestured, in closing his essay, was that despite Khrushchev's politics, the
Russian's diplomatic voyage demonstrated "the importance, beyond universal structures, of the person-to-person, man-to-man relationship; it proves
that man must see behind the anonymous principle the face of the other
man."[41] For the optimistic Levinas, diplomacy thus trumped the "totality"
principle that ran the official structures of the Soviet Union, and the "human" scale triumphed over the scale of state power.

That these essays appeared a few short years before *Totality and Infinity*
helps us read that work's condemnation of the political in a different light.
By the time *Totality and Infinity* appeared, Levinas no longer employed the
term "politics" to describe the interpersonal, ethical order he would celebrate,
suggesting he had abandoned the new humanist politics that "On the Spirit
of Geneva" and "Principles and Faces" had invoked. If we read *Totality and
Infinity* as a call for an ethics of vulnerability *rather* than an ethics substan-
tiated through political institutions, we must bear in mind that it could easily have become an articulation of a politics based on the face-to-face. *Totality
and Infinity*, taken on its own terms, is not a work that easily admits interpretation in light of historical events, but Levinas's earlier engagement
with politics makes the unworldliness of *Totality and Infinity* seem like a
choice, deliberately made, but with awkward consequences for philosophical practice.

Judaism, Publicity, Fraternity

Regardless of the way contemporary events played on Levinas's mind, *Totality and Infinity* was an academic text and the scene of address that haunted
it was not the intellectual's act of writing for a popular journal, a radio broadcast, or a public speech. Levinas had, in fact, given a number of talks on
Jewish themes as a guest on the radio program "Ecoute Israel" during the

1950s—several of which were published as short essays in his 1963 volume, *Difficile liberté: Essais sur le judaisme* ("Difficult Freedom") and he had continued to write essays, primarily on Jewish themes but (as we have seen) also on international politics, throughout the 1950s. He continued to do so after *Totality and Infinity* appeared, and while one reading of *Totality and Infinity* produces a condemnation of any form of politics that falls short of the requirements of ethics, Levinas clearly did not see his own critique of representation as a "guide" to behavior in public. The text's anarchic approach to politics is not, after all, intended to short-circuit speech, for speech is the very medium in which vulnerability and need can register. The "truth" to which Levinas hoped to give witness in his work was the truth of human vulnerability.

Levinas spoke most frequently on Jewish issues. While in his *Talmudic Readings* Levinas was careful to present himself as an *amateur* rather than a true expert, he was willing to speak as an authority on matters of Jewish tradition, either in defense of the Jewish people or of Judaism, or simply when issues of interest to a Jewish readership were raised in the French media. In fact, following Levinas's engagement with Sartre, his frequency of public writing only increased, perhaps confirming it was not the fact of Sartre's public engagement but the character of that engagement that gave Levinas pause. However, and as many commentators have noted, Levinas's Jewish writings contain an unstable combination of undisguised partisanship and the proposition that the Jewish people stood outside the field of contestation he called politics. His remarks on the state of Israel were animated by ambivalence about the simple fact of the state's existence qua state. His occasional writings on Jewish identity can most satisfactorily be understood not as advocacy efforts per se, but as experiments in "applying" his apparently un-applicable ethics. Levinas examined Jewish life and Jewish struggles in order to locate real-world cases in which ethical life, or at least the promise of ethics, flourished, and he regarded the Jewish condition as being defined by particularity even as he emphasized the universal import of that condition. Ironically, the statements Levinas was wont to make, in his guise as an intellectual writing for nonacademic audiences, seemed to give lie to his insistence that *Totality and Infinity* had not been a Jewish book.

Levinas called Rosenzweig's *Star of Redemption* a crucial influence on *Totality and Infinity*, "too often present in this book to be cited."[42] Like Rosenzweig, Levinas suggested that a version of redemption (here figured as ethics) could be experienced in the midst of the political world, although always athwart politics. Rosenzweig had written, "Because the Jewish people is beyond the contradiction that constitutes the vital drive in the life of the nations—the contradiction between national characteristics and world history, home and faith, earth and heaven—it knows nothing of war."[43] Levinas similarly allowed that ethical encounters could take place even "within the political order," and he argued that despite the immorality of much of political life, one could still behave ethically in a world dominated by politics. He implied that minor spheres of ethical life come into being through interpersonal ethical encounters between members of larger political communities, and in his occasional writings on Jewish subjects Levinas seemed to call for Jews to bring those spheres into being. Adamant that *Totality and Infinity* had been a secular text, Levinas frequently treated the Jewish people as the very embodiment of the encounter with the other.

This Rosenzweig-influenced vision shone through clearly in Levinas's essay "Honor Without a Flag," written in the context of the "Treblinka Affair," which raged following the publication of Jean-François Steiner's *Treblinka: The Revolt of an Extermination Camp.*[44] Comparable in fervor if not in international scope to the controversy around Arendt's *Eichmann in Jerusalem* a few years earlier, the "Treblinka Affair" inspired French Jews to debate the implications of the Holocaust for contemporary Jewish life, and to contemplate the painful question of Jewish resistance or passivity in the face of murder. Steiner, a young journalist with literary aspirations, published an account of the 1943 uprising at Treblinka, the concentration camp where some 750,000 persons both Jewish and otherwise were murdered during the Holocaust. The book attracted a reproach very similar to the one leveled against Arendt's book, for Steiner was taken to describe Jewish victims as agents in their own suffering and deaths.[45]

In fact, by focusing on the prisoner uprising at Treblinka, Steiner revealed himself to be on a search for Jewish heroes to replace the Jewish victims he found in other Holocaust narratives. However, Steiner defined Jewish heroism rather narrowly. It meant not only the willingness to fight but also the desire to fight for life. Comparing the Treblinka revolt to the famous Warsaw Ghetto uprising, which had also taken place in 1943, Steiner noted that while the Warsaw rebels knew their efforts were in vain (they were in effect choosing their own way of dying rather than allowing themselves to be killed as the Nazis saw fit), the Treblinka revolt, which freed 600 people, was driven by the hope of success. Steiner hoped to demonstrate that there was a "Jewish" dimension to this revolt for life: Jewish heroism was characterized by its respect for life's continuity, which disqualified suicide missions from being considered "Jewish" in the sense Steiner intended.

Steiner's book was immediately praised and condemned in the press by Jewish and non-Jewish critics. He was catapulted both to the stardom for which he had hoped and to a notoriety he might not have anticipated. The resulting debate also contributed to many discursive shifts in the way the Holocaust was understood by French Jews and by the broader French public. Perhaps most importantly, *Treblinka* helped to divide the Holocaust from the war, emphasizing the special fates reserved for Jews at the hands of the Nazis and distinguishing them from other victims of Nazi violence. Steiner's book also forced the French-Jewish community to deal with a critical voice from within, one coming from a younger generation that had not lived through the Holocaust and knew it primarily through communal memory, history books, and public trials. When Levinas responded to Steiner with an essay titled "Honneur sans Drapeau" (Honor Without a Flag), published in the AIU journal *Les Nouveaux Cahiers*, he opposed Steiner's heroic vision of Jewish rebels and offered an alternate view of the Holocaust's implications for Jewish identity.[46] However, Levinas accepted some of the discursive shifts and terms of debate that Steiner had introduced, as well as the need to understand the Holocaust's implications for Jewish identity, which was of course not Steiner's alone.

The title "Honor Without a Flag" expressed Levinas's core belief that Jews could pursue honor without participating in any martial endeavors or carrying the implied battle standards. As he put it, he saw honor "In not concluding, in a universe at war, that warlike virtues are the only sure ones; in not taking pleasure, during the tragic situation, in the virile virtues of death and desperate murder; in living dangerously only in order to remove dangers and to return to the shade of one's own vine and fig tree."[47] While Levinas nowhere mentioned Steiner by name, he forthrightly repudiated Steiner's vision of a Jew who would struggle through military means to ensure life and offered a different vision instead, one that saw the Jews as preserving their ethics above all else—including self-preservation or the preservation of any specific social institutions. Thus the violent struggle to preserve life was as un-Jewish for Levinas as it had been Jewish for Steiner. Levinas emphasized the passivity and the "witnessing" function of the Jews, rather than their ability to become active participants in historical events like the members of other nations.[48]

Levinas gladly took up the generational gauntlet thrown down by Steiner, reflecting (in a pedagogical spirit) on the lessons that should be taught to the first post-Holocaust generation raised in France. He asked, "And what of our children, who were born after the Liberation, and who already belong to that group? Will they be able to understand that feeling of chaos and emptiness?"[49] Levinas proposed an educational program consisting of three lessons drawn "from the experience of the concentration camps."[50] The first was that assimilation, which brought modern European Jews greater material wealth and greater comforts, offered no lasting security—that the dream of *fraternité*, in France, had been a mere castle in the sky, easily blown apart by the winds of nationalism. While Levinas did not expand on this point, he clearly implied that the Holocaust demonstrated the persistent danger that the non-Jewish world might turn on the Jews. The second was that the highest duty—which Levinas interestingly did not define as a "Jewish" duty—was to maintain a life of ethical rather than warlike behavior. The third lesson was consistent with Levinas's vision of a Jewish life defined by its "apolitical" character: he enjoined the new generation to be strong in isolation, to retreat into themselves rather than to place their faith in the political world. Although scarcely a philosophical exercise, "Honor Without a Flag" nevertheless reflected the fundamental distinction between ethics and politics established in *Totality and Infinity*. The Jews became passive witnesses to historical events, but their very passivity gave them the power to preserve ethics in a space beyond temporal flux. Despite the horrors brought upon the Jewish people, Levinas suggested that resistance would have meant participation in precisely the same categories of thought and action that were inimical to ethical life; by resisting, the Jews would have given up a salutary part of Judaism.

The most curious aspect of "Honor Without a Flag" was its call for an apolitical interpretation of Jewish life almost twenty years after the establishment of the state of Israel. It is thus worthwhile to ask just what Zionist views Levinas had articulated at the time he published "Honor Without a Flag," and of what larger project the essay must be considered a part. Among Levinas's first pronouncements on the subject was the 1951 essay "The State of Israel and the Religion of Israel," which rejected the idea (articulated by some ultra-Orthodox Jews) that establishing and supporting the state was a form of idolatry.[51] However, Levinas's argument was not founded on the idea that Israel somehow "normalized" the Jewish people, making them akin to every other nation in the world, but rather on the proposition that the ethical idea of Judaism could be found even in the everyday political dealings of Israelis. The state of Israel, he said, "finally offers the opportunity to carry out the social law of Judaism."[52] Absent any argument about *how* Judaism's social law might be carried out, such a statement seems merely (and, it must be said, thoughtlessly) partisan. Levinas seemed to suggest that Israel's relationship with the Jewish tradition itself supplied it with a source of ethics to counter the inevitable violence any political activity produces.

More dramatically, and at greater risk, in the 1968 "Space Is Not One Dimensional," Levinas transferred the claims of "Honor Without a Flag" to an Israel that had just triumphed in the Six-Day War of 1967.[53] The essay seems to have been inspired not by the war alone but by French president Charles de Gaulle's remark, immediately following the conflict, that the Jews were an "elite people, self-assured and domineering," who might transform their Passover expression of hope, "next year in Jerusalem," into "a burning ambition of conquest."[54] More important than self-assurance were potentially split loyalties; de Gaulle was concerned about French Jews who had supported Israel in a war toward which France had been officially neutral. De Gaulle referred to the massive amounts of "money, influence and propaganda" that Israel received from Jewish circles worldwide, and suggested that the Israeli government had been harboring expansionist hopes since 1956. In full awareness of the severity of de Gaulle's charges, Levinas spoke of the multiple "dimensions" of loyalty, insisting that Jewish and French identities were compatible: "An avowal of active sympathy for the State of Israel does not stem from any duplicity or clandestine allegiance, and does not constitute treason," he wrote.[55] From there, Levinas launched into his own views on the religious meaning of Israel's existence. Founded after what he called the "Passion of the Shoah," Israel embodies a biblical dream, and *not* a political dream, but rather one embodied by the deprivations faced by the Jewish settlers who had worked to build the new state:

> It is not because the Holy Land takes the form of a State that it brings the reign of the Messiah any closer, but because the men who inhabit it try to resist the temptations of politics; because this State, proclaimed in the aftermath of Auschwitz, embraces the teaching of the prophets; because it produces abnegation and self-sacrifice.[56]

Levinas acknowledged that the state played the important role of "resuscitating the Holy land," but the significance of Israel was in his eyes ethical rather than political. Thus, Jewish sympathy for Israel could be construed as an expression of religion. It was no threat to Frenchness to engage in the "spiritual adventure" of being Jewish.

Against de Gaulle's charge that Jewish loyalty was divided, Levinas invoked what he saw as a special relationship between France and the Jews dating back to 1789, to the coming-together of "political and moral life" in a universalistic ideology that welcomed Jewish citizens—the ideology of *fraternité*. To be loyal to the French state was, Levinas said, "a metaphysical act," a commitment to a country that displayed its trinitarian emblem "on the front of its public buildings."[57] Levinas implied that being attached to the existence of the state of Israel marked no transformation of or interruption in the French nationality of "les Israèlites," but rather was an attachment consistent with the very universalism enshrined within the French republic.[58] While de Gaulle's implication had been that Israel's founding had produced an occasion for split loyalties for French Jews, Levinas named the Dreyfus Affair as the fracture point in the Republican dream of 1789. The ultimate triumph of justice in the Affair could not hide the fact that during it, the very "fragility of reason" and "the possibility of its failure" had been revealed.

Levinas's idealization of Israel, or the abstract project of Israel, must be taken in the context of the much broader renaissance in Jewish culture in France ongoing in the late 1960s and early 1970s. While this renaissance received a boost from the fervor of 1967, it began before the Six-Day War and involved a new enthusiasm for Jewish textual study and even orthodox or semi-orthodox religious practice. Just as important, and as Judith Friedlander points out, after 1967 many younger Jews—including those involved in the famous student uprisings of 1968—hoped to challenge the very distinction between public and private that had governed French-Jewish life for so long, insisting that they had a right to expressions of Jewish identity "in the street" as opposed to solely in private.[59] They understood this challenge to be directed against the values of 1789, or more properly, against the staged emancipation of separate communities of Ashkenazi and Sephardic Jews by the French Revolutionary government shortly after the Revolution had ended. Said emancipation had itself been predicated on the expectation that Jewish difference would gradually disappear in the years and decades to come.[60] In his influential 1980 memoir *Le juif imaginaire*, Alain Finkielkraut similarly described the way many younger Jews insisted on being Jewish as publicly as possible.[61] While Levinas himself seems to have only recognized this moment as a "renaissance" in Jewish life in France, he had been keenly interested in the way a social logic of public and private affected Jews ever since his 1959 essay, "How Is Judaism Possible?" Writing in the wake of the events of 1967, Levinas commented on the present and future of Jewish life in France in his "La renaissance culturelle juive en Europe continentale."[62] Levinas saw his essay as a small catalogue of efforts to "search for lost Judaism," as he put it with a Proustian flourish. Taking as his starting point the modern Judaism of the late nineteenth century, which was emancipated but cut off from its traditional roots, Levinas cast the Dreyfus Affair as the first important turning point for French Jews. The Affair did not simply catalyze Zionist activity, but also stirred up nostalgia, especially in Eastern Europe, for Jewish traditions past. Levinas suggested that this nostalgia had made Martin Buber and Rosenzweig possible in Germany and Edmond Fleg and André Spire possible in France.

Far more tragically, it was the Holocaust that truly triggered the desire for *techouva* (a return to Judaism) among surviving French Jews, a response to the existential feeling of solitude that overtook the survivors. Levinas pointed, as signs of this return, to the foundation of new Jewish schools and the establishment of the *Colloque des intellectuels juifs de langue française* in 1957, a series of yearly meetings which would bring together a wide range of French Jewish thinkers concerned not only with the restoration of Jewish life after the Holocaust, but with the applicability of Jewish thought to contemporary problems. Their efforts, like all such purposeful returns to tradition, involved not just mere recovery, but reinterpretation. One hallmark of post-Holocaust Jewish scholarship in France was that a new cadre of teachers re-imagined Judaism as "the Bible read through the Talmud," effectively restoring rabbinic literature to the position of eminence it had enjoyed before the advent of modern liberal Judaism. Accompanying this philo-rabbinic attitude was a fresh appetite for the observance of *mitzvoth* and for the full embrace of Orthodox practice, particularly among younger Jews.

Despite the new emphasis on traditional scholarship and observance, and a new attitude of "publicness," Levinas still sought grounds for calling the *techouva* movement "universalistic" in its orientation. First, he said, it sought a Judaism purified of all mystical or magical elements, and second, it was characterized by an adherence to Western intellectual values. While rationalism carries the risk of atheism, it also serves as a powerful tool to augment religious thought. Most importantly, Levinas saw the truths of rabbinic Judaism as applicable even for non-Jews. That tradition, in fact, was most important to him as a gateway to a universal set of values that could only be accessed via particularity. Ironically, in Levinas's view it was precisely by acting as a Jew in the street that one could act as a "universal man."

It is useful to read Levinas's reflections on France's Jewish "renaissance" against one of the crucial interlocutors of his later career, the aforementioned Finkielkraut. Although Finkielkraut (born in 1949) was, like Levinas, keenly interested in the revival of Jewish identity following the Holocaust, he was part of a younger generation of Jews that had known neither the Holocaust nor pre-Holocaust Jewish society. Often compared to Franz Kafka's famous "Letter to His Father" due to its accusation that those Jews surviving the Holocaust declined to pass on the remaining fragments of Jewish culture, Finkielkraut's book described the psychological motivations for crafting an "imaginary" Jewish identity—motivations Finkielkraut himself found deeply dubious.[63] The "imaginary " Jews of postwar Western Europe were those who, whatever their Jewish heritage, invented Jewish identities out of elements borrowed from their parents' generation, usually in an effort to tie themselves to a dramatic narrative of victimization or martyrdom. The "Jew," understood as victim, became a role available even—under certain extraordinary circumstances—to non-Jews, as in the chant heard during the student revolts of 1968: "We are all German Jews,"[64] meant to connect the chanters to the German-born Daniel Cohn-Bendit, prohibited from reentering France by de Gaulle's government. It was, as Sarah Hammerschlag notes, a high moment of *fraternité* for the protesters, and one that echoed the Dreyfusard defense of a Jew accused of being un-French. This time, however, *fraternité* was presented as the state of being bound together in difference—Jewishness—rather than by the universalism of the Enlightenment. Despite his antipathy toward such figurations of the Jew as a role effectively available to all, Finkielkraut nevertheless maintained his hostility to any jargon of "authenticity" and harbored no hope of understanding Judaism or Jewishness at the level of "essences;" Sartre's *Quelques réflexions sur la question juive* may have influenced him deeply as a youth, but as he matured he saw the need to escape its restrictive logic of the authentic and the inauthentic.[65] Against the political logics of liberal humanism and the Left, both of which suppressed ethnic difference as politically irrelevant, Finkielkraut sought a public form of Jewish identity simultaneously true to pre-Holocaust Jewish life and consistent with the logic of 1960s protests, which made everything "private" into "the political." Jewish visibility—including public displays such as the wearing of yarmulkes and other garb—thus became politically significant for Finkielkraut, for whom ritual observance was a way out of the version of the imaginary he feared.

But for Levinas, Jewish public visibility found its ultimate meaning not in the promotion of Jewish ends, but as a challenge to the very logic of publicness and privacy that had dominated modern Jewish life. As Levinas made clear in many of his occasional essays, it was the transformation of Judaism into a "confessional" category in modern Europe that had facilitated the dominance of that logic. It was in the impassioned call for Jewish renewal, in "How Is Judaism Possible?," published in *L'Arche* in 1959, that Levinas explored this production of Judaism as "confession," asserting its centrality for the modern Jewish condition itself. As Levinas put it, "The difference between nation and religion, universal and particular, public and private, political life and inner life, places within its just limits the Jewish destiny and stems the potential overflowing of the Jewish soul."[66]

Beyond following from the classic association between religion and private life and politics with public life, this statement alluded to the poet Judah Leib Gordon's famous or infamous injunction that one should "be a Jew at home but a man in the street," the very same injunction that the young Jews of the French "renaissance" would try to reverse in the later 1960s. Levinas observed that the production of Judaism as confession had "admirably regulate[d] our duty to the nation."[67] However, it ran the risk of making Judaism into a "museum" religion and betraying "its profound essence."[68]

Another, subtler, challenge lay in the fact that Christianity itself only *seemed* to have been relegated to the status of "confession." It still permeated the public sphere or, as Levinas said: "The rhythm of legal time is scanned by Catholic feast days, cathedrals determine towns and sites."[69] Thus, the division between public and private, and the institutional scheme of the confession, was misleading, and Levinas called for a revival of Judaism beyond the bounds presented by the category of the confession. Rather than challenging the sanctity of French citizenship defined as loyalty to the state with no regard to creed or religion, Levinas asked how Jewish institutions could work against the negative effect that the "confessional" interpretation of Judaism had on Jewish spirituality and religious practice. Toward this end, Levinas called for a new type of school that could stand at the forefront of a new movement in Jewish learning, not unlike the center for adult Jewish education in Berlin that Rosenzweig had established. Such schools might emphasize biblical and rabbinical texts studied in Hebrew, but the students would be laypeople rather than future rabbis, and the bearers of a new cultural politics that might breach the very public-private distinction running through the notion of "confession."[70] As was his wont, Levinas the Jewish educator saw education as a form of action; Jewish education, in this case, was intended to counterbalance the potentially pernicious effects of the public-private distinction itself. This was a moment when Levinas declined to invoke the motif of translation, which guided so much of his thinking about the relationship between Jewish particularism and the universalism he called "Greek."

Otherwise Than Being

The frontispiece of Levinas's second major philosophical work, *Otherwise than Being*, invites the reader to translate between the two halves of a Dedication split in two languages. The frontispiece includes one paragraph dedicated to the memory of those killed in the Holocaust (in French) and another dedicated to Levinas's immediate relatives who had been killed (in Hebrew). Only fully accessible to a bilingual reader, the Dedication leaves Hebrew readers with a deeper insight into the personal nature of the statement and leaves those who read only French with, perhaps, a "trace" (to use a term Levinas favored) of the author's relationship with the Jewish tradition. For any reader, the split Dedication works to undo Levinas's insistence on the division between his philosophical and Jewish works. The Dedication's other clear semantic effect is to root the book in the Holocaust, promising the reader that the work's presentation of a philosophy of ethics constitutes a response to the great crisis of the Shoah—much as *Totality and Infinity* had promised a response to totalitarian politics in its Preface.

The concluding pages of *Otherwise Than Being* seem to offer the response to political disaster promised by the Dedication, by asking that "intellectuals" (a group not mentioned in the intervening pages of the text) make themselves "hostages" to the welfare of those around them. The suggestion is surprising given the actual content of *Otherwise Than Being*, which is far from a sociological treatise on the responsibilities of intellectuals. However, this manifesto in miniature is in keeping with the volume's tendency to revise the wholesale rejection of the political found in *Totality and Infinity* and replace it with "an ethical qualification of ontology."[71] That is, read in the context of the book's overall argument, a call for intellectuals to make themselves hostages becomes legible as a form of political activity that has nothing to do with the bad form of ontological thinking Levinas connected with totalitarianism in *Totality and Infinity* and earlier works.

Performing vulnerability by making oneself a hostage was not, of course, part of a constructive or "archic" politics, nor was the term "hostage" to be taken literally. Rather, Levinas called for intellectuals to acknowledge the suffering of others and to express it through speech or writing—giving voice to experiences of suffering endured in passivity, in a manner that questioned the very distinction between "passivity" and "activity," as in the gnomic epigram from Jean Wahl with which Levinas opened the book's first chapter: "There is something to be said, Novalis wrote, in favor of passivity. It is significant that one of Novalis' contemporaries, Maine de Brain, who wished to be the philosopher of activity, will remain essentially the philosopher of two passivities, the lower and the higher. But is the lower lower than the higher?"[72] Whereas in *Totality and Infinity* language was a medium in which one's own vulnerability was revealed, in *Otherwise Than Being* language could be a means by which to express the suffering of a third party. *Totality and Infinity* had operated by moving through the history of philosophy and questioning the ethical implications of its representational and ontological claims; as Jacques Derrida put it, Levinas "summon[ed] us to a dislocation of the Greek logos, to a dislocation of our identity, and perhaps of identity in general," and Levinas called that dislocation the route toward ethics.[73] In contrast, *Otherwise Than Being* gestured at a theory—albeit not a clear or simple theory—of justice, in so doing addressing precisely the problem of distributive justice with which *Totality and Infinity* had left its readers, the impossibility of extending infinite care beyond the personal to the social, or from the dyadic to the "triadic."

Much of the text between the "political" bookends of *Otherwise Than Being* consisted of a meditation on language and its relationship with representation, ontology, and mastery, rather than any formal engagement with the political. But the distinction between two types of language—"saying" and "the said"—which Levinas introduced, related directly to the distinction between personal encounter and representation he had relied on for many years, with "saying" corresponding to a pre-ontological use of language, addressed to a neighbor in a manner that exposes our vulnerability and can have promissory effect, and "the said" corresponding to a symbolic register that made ontological claims about what it symbolized, rendering them intelligible according to a set of rules.[74] The saying, Levinas claimed, "holds nothing back," but "the birthplace of ontology is the said. Ontology is stated in the amphibology of being and entities."[75] Without aiming to reject "the said" and its order of intelligibility and ontologization ("Western philosophy has never doubted the gnoseological, and consequently ontological, structure of signification," he wrote[76]), Levinas argued that language was capable of expressing both ontology and the "outside of being," as if by "betrayal," communicating the fact that being was in part an "event" rather than a brute fact—thus his distinction between the "saying" and "the said" bears a resemblance to J. L. Austin's understanding of speech acts that can have the "illocutionary" effect of delivering semantic content with some intended outcome, as well as the "perlocutionary" effect of acting on the addressed person with persuasion, intimidation, charm, or other personal effect.[77]

It was in the realm of saying, which is the realm of personal encounter, that Levinas situated the experience of realizing one's responsibility for another person. Recalling the central argument of *Time and the Other*, he wrote, "The freedom of another could never begin in my freedom, that is, abide in the same present, be contemporary, be representable to me. The responsibility for the other can not have begun in my commitment, in my decision."[78] Thus Levinas presented responsibilities for other persons as unchosen and inalienable, in a turn that renders the very concept of political freedom questionable, and which he glossed as "substitution," or in other words being willing to take the place of another in suffering, and to embrace their vulnerability as our own. If signification could inscribe the ontological, it was also the means by which one became vulnerable to others, as well as sensitive to their needs—aware "that a subject is of flesh and blood," as Levinas put it, and as he graphically added, "capable of giving the bread out of his mouth, or giving his skin."[79]

While Levinas never explicitly defined "justice" as a concept in and of itself, describing what it meant to treat an other justly or to institute justice at the level of society, he associated justice with signification itself—with the understanding of the needs of the other that comes with the proximate relationship mobilizing by the "saying"—and thus made the interpersonal encounter the font of justice. Even the judge, he wrote, is a person who deals with the law "in the midst of proximity," even as "society, the State and its institutions, exchanges and work are comprehensible out of proximity."[80] The art of justice is to treat every person as if her vulnerability worked upon us with the same power as the person ("the closest") actually proximate to us.

But if the responsibility for the other that is carried out as "justice" is born out of proximity itself, the process of signification in language also produces the presence of a third party, a term that produces order and can serve to regulate a social group beyond the basic dyad of the self-other encounter.[81] The third and justice are not simple extrapolations from the dyadic to the triadic as they appeared in *Totality and Infinity*; they are inherent in all relations of proximity between humans. Levinas went so far as to say that consciousness itself is a form of justice on the most purely formal of levels.

Otherwise Than Being's concluding plea for intellectuals to act through passivity was perhaps its most curious feature, and it demands interpretation. Levinas referred to the "utopian" impulse of "intellectuals" of his time, who "feel themselves to be hostages for destitute masses unconscious of their own wretchedness."[82] And Levinas complained that those very intellectuals had grown wary of the universalistic humanism that made such a gesture of radical substitution possible. While Levinas never mentioned Sartre's name, it seems likely that he was referring to the turn that Sartre had taken, away from a humanism compatible with Levinas's concept of fraternity and toward a philosophy of pure struggle necessitated by the waves of decolonization that split France from its former colonies between 1946 and 1962. In an Introduction written for Frantz Fanon's 1961 study of the psychic violence of colonialism, *The Wretched of the Earth*, Sartre accepted the need for violence in anticolonial struggles such as the Algerian War. For Sartre, Fanon "shows clearly that this irrepressible violence is neither sound and fury, nor the resurrection of savage instincts, nor even the effect of resentment: it is man re-creating himself."[83] In the 1972 *Plaidoyer pour les intellectuels* (*A Plea for the Intellectuals*) (originally a series of lectures given in 1966, in Kyoto), Sartre had argued against precisely the universalistic version of the intellectual first manifest during the Dreyfus Affair. Sartre suggested that not universals, but rather attention to the details of particular historical conflicts would allow intellectuals to contribute to the struggle against racism and colonialism.[84] This was, of course, a recapitulation of the doctrine of "situatedness" developed in *Being and Nothingness*.

While Levinas certainly would have had time to read Sartre's *Plaidoyer* before publishing *Otherwise Than Being*, he made no explicit reference to that work, in which Sartre had offered a potted history of the figure of "the intellectual." This history began with the medieval cleric who acted as a bearer of general (and ideological) knowledge for his society, and proceeded to the emergence of true knowledge specialists, which was an effect of the rise of the bourgeoisie and their ideology of mercantile capitalism.[85] It had been the *philosophes* of the eighteenth century, Sartre said, who made the mistake of thinking that they were the champions of universal interests rather than of the narrower class interests of the bourgeois. The important question, Sartre suggested, was what it meant for the "grandsons of the *philosophes*" to become "intellectuals" at the time of the Dreyfus Affair, and his Marxist answer was that within late modernity it became possible for knowledge-workers to recognize the inherent contradiction between their universalist beliefs and their own rise to prominence in society. Understanding that their rise was due to privilege and that an individual's potential was figured by the opportunities their place in society afforded them, intellectuals of middle-class origins found themselves in sudden conflict with themselves. Memorably, Sartre wrote that those unable to live with those contradictions and offer their services to the ruling classes (thereby becoming, in his terminology, "false intellectuals") could only become "monsters," that is to say, true intellectuals who were "monstrous" in their inquires into their own way of living and the ways of living of those around them. Sartre did not deny the universalism inherent in the intellectual's existence or function, noting that among the intellectual's tasks was to understand her or his own ends as being "shared by all those in struggle." Yet he also insisted that the intellectual always began in a particular "situation" in society, a "situation" characterized by contradictions one could never transcend through reason and remediable only by engagement in political struggle.

In contrast to Sartre's plea, Levinas made no reference to class struggle. He identified intellectuals as elites but gave no indication that he understood them to experience internal conflict over that status. His intellectuals were possessed of a universalism that began with the singularity of an encounter with another, but was in no wise the projection of the class interests of one particular group. While Levinas forewent any detailed description of the "intellectuals," beyond noting that they were found in "agglomerations" or "dispersions" across the face of the earth, he did call them "chosen," in the sense of embodying the attitude of responsibility his book had described. His intellectual also embodied a kind of utopianism, albeit one that referenced a utopia to be brought about not by "action" but rather by a form of passivity, a method of registering in speech or writing the vulnerabilities of the dispossessed, a method at which "intellectuals" excelled. Levinas's vision was, of course, very much the opposite of Sartre's call for a "radical-ization" of intellectuals, and naturally would have left no room for the vio-lent overthrow of French colonial rule—Sartre, for his part, could never have endorsed a philosophy that would render activity one of "two passivities."

Despite the gulf between Levinas's understanding of the role of the in-tellectual and Sartre's—just as wide in 1974 as it had been in the late 1940s—the parallel Levinas struck between the chosen "intellectuals" and the Jews recalled Sartre's ongoing identification of those categories with one another, and likewise recalled both philosophers' understanding of the condition of both Jews and intellectuals as a "crystallization" of the human condition more generally. The link between the universalist intellectual and the particular Jew was, of course, in keeping with Levinas's vision of the relationship be-tween particular and universal instantiations of ethics: the trauma of the Jew-ish people, announced in the Dedication to *Otherwise Than Being*, became by the end of the book not only a story of unmitigated vulnerability but also of capacity, namely the capacity to stand witness to the suffering of others and to perform a type of fraternity that could have repaired the damage dealt to that concept by the eruptions of nationalism, racism, and totalitarianism from the Dreyfus Affair to the end of the Holocaust itself. Levinas's use of the term "utopian" in this context was far from incidental, registering an awareness of the "no-where" (*u-topos*) in utopia, of the nature of justice and ethics as processes impossible to "fix" in place and of the nature of intellec-tuals as themselves rootless and diasporic—of being "no-where" in particular, but capable of a perspective only rootlessness can provide. The intellectual, like the Jew, was connected to the very quality of rootlessness that had come under attack during the Dreyfus Affair, a quality Levinas connected to an appreciation of the fragility of human life and the infinite ethical demand issuing from that fragility, which requires us to accept a responsibility sub-tending and limiting our freedom. Levinas did not speculate directly on the public character of the work of the intellectual, but clearly, if the hostage be-havior of Levinas's intellectuals was to have an effect, this witnessing would itself require witnesses, or in other words, a public.

While Levinas said little about the mechanism by which "witnessing" might have an effect on unnamed publics, there was a deeper problem with his encomium to the intellectuals. For Levinas, such persons (including, pre-sumably, himself) were elites who arrogated to themselves the responsibility to speak on behalf of others. They had the capacity to substitute themselves as hostages for suffering peoples, but such a gesture had to be founded on their judgment of what constituted suffering, and their assessment of the best interests of these "peoples." Indeed, the Levinas of 1974 anticipated a controversial claim he would make in a 1991 interview: "I often say, although it is a dangerous thing to say publicly, that humanity consists of the Bible and the Greeks. All the rest can be translated: all the rest—all the exotic—is dance."[86] Indeed, it seemed that Levinas's intellectuals, who presumably were readers of the Bible and of the Greeks, were capable of placing themselves as hostages for the suffering of "peoples" of which they were not themselves members witnessing to their suffering, precisely because they preserved their freedom of judgment, a freedom grounded in Western traditions. Ironically, in order to make intellectuals into ethical agents capable of witnessing in public, Levinas had to endow them with a universal capacity in tension with his own ethics of encounter with a proximate and particular other. There was, in this special sense, a "trahison des clercs" in Levinas's plea to the intellectuals. The very "translation into Greek" Levinas associated with philosophy and with intellectuals seemed to run against his career-long attempt to reform philosophy from the standpoint of an ethics of alterity.

Levinas would not dwell on the figure of the intellectual again, nor explain the mechanism by which he imagined "witnessing" to have a concrete effect on political life. However, this expression of faith in the power of witnessing, inserted somewhat surprisingly at the end of a volume dedicated to the ethical remedy of philosophical ontology, must be understood as an effort to reactivate the cultural logic of the Dreyfus Affair itself. Levinas imputed to the intellectual a certain custodian status, a capacity to speak to the political powers that be from a position beyond them, and an ability to communicate with a public audience that he did not define, but which presumably could receive the intellectual's performance of vulnerability and respond accordingly, echoing Dreyfus's ultimate exoneration—but Levinas did not linger to describe precisely how this last effect might be brought about. This leaves the reader with a "translational" difficulty that echoes the translational challenge posed by the Dedication that opens *Otherwise Than Being*. It is unclear how the intellectual's capacity to register the pain of others, and to respond to that feeling by making her or himself a symbolically passive and suffering "hostage" (notably more a matter of the capacity for empathy than a matter of the capacity for thought), "translates" into politically effective action. Levinas made the intellectual into the agent of his ethics, at the close of his book, but the very ambiguity of that figure echoed the gulf between ethics and politics in Levinas's thought, which the concept of "justice" in *Otherwise Than Being* had intended to bridge.

The last three chapters of this book have endeavored, through a re-construction of Levinas's encounters with Heidegger and Sartre, to make historical sense of his difficulties sorting through the public tasks of philos-ophy. The apparent betrayal of philosophy in politics cast a very long shadow over Levinas's career, accounting not only for his equation of ontology with totalitarianism, but also for his refusal to derive any "archic" politics from philosophy. Levinas evidently felt no need, at the end of *Otherwise Than Being*, to explain how "witnessing" the vulnerability of others would have an effect on the broader public world. The next chapter will explore the work and career of Levinas's contemporary, Hannah Arendt. An equally if differ-ently devoted student of Heidegger, Arendt shared many other influences with Levinas, including a fascination with the Dreyfus Affair, and she was similarly preoccupied with tyranny. Unlike Levinas, Arendt abjured the view that philosophy could somehow remedy political injustice if it were itself first reformed. Surprisingly, Arendt's famous praise for a participatory demo-cratic politics, conducted in public, was accompanied by a deep ambivalence regarding the proper role of philosophers, intellectuals or, in a term that she once used more approvingly, "*hommes des lettres.*"

PART III

Against Speechless Wonder:
Hannah Arendt on Philosophers
and Intellectuals

All thinking, strictly speaking, is done in solitude
and is a dialogue between me and myself;
but this dialogue of the two-in-one does not
lose contact with the world of my fellow-men
because they are represented in the self with
whom I lead the dialogue of thought.
  —Hannah Arendt, *The Origins of Totalitarianism*

CHAPTER 7

Arendt's Weimar Origins

Hannah Arendt never devoted a major work to the place of philosophers in politics. Her thoughts on the subject lie scattered throughout her writings and one of her most significant and puzzling reflections is buried in a footnote toward the end of her 1963 book, *On Revolution*. Here Arendt bemoaned the ancient parting of ways between "men of thought" and "men of action," a parting that (on her account) dated from the trial and execution of Socrates.[1] She judged that this parting had been a tragedy for both politics and philosophy, and observed that its effects were still being felt in the mid-twentieth century. It is the task of the next three chapters to explore the meaning of this gnomic statement, and many others like it. The "speechless wonder" (*thaumazein*) philosophers experienced in a state of contemplation was, for Arendt, the opposite of the glories of political life that ring out in speech. Arendt's criticisms of "intellectuals," which also lie scattered throughout her writings, were tied to her attempts to understand the implications, for the modern world, of the ancient split between philosophy and politics and of efforts to reunite them. While she harbored hopes for such a reunion, she was quick to criticize anyone arrogant enough to "apply" philosophy (or for that matter the natural sciences or social sciences) directly to matters she understood as "political."

Of course, Arendt's own career might have convinced the casual observer that the parting of ways between thinkers and actors had never taken place. By the time *On Revolution* hit the shelves, Arendt was known not only as a scholar but also as a journalist, cultural critic, and political commentator.[2] The breadth and depth of her writings on history, politics, and literature seemed to qualify her as a perfect representative of the "intellectual" type. Furthermore, as a formerly stateless German Jewish refugee, Arendt gratified expectations for intellectuals to be outsiders, examining states and societies from a perspective that could only be called productively alienated. Attempts were made to place her in various ideological categories that her works seemed to invite: Zionist (and anti-Zionist) Cold War liberal, intellectual of the German Left. One praiseful American reviewer even said, "what she thinks about and says would, if it were attended to in the proper quarters, help alter the course of the century."[3] Yet Arendt fit no category, and she seems to have had no desire to play such a world-historical role. As she put it in 1954, writing in order to "educate others and elevate public opinion" turned words into weapons, causing them to "lose their quality of speech" and become mere instruments of indoctrination.[4]

Asked in a 1964 interview if she wished to "achieve extensive influence" through her works, Arendt acknowledged that it was not a simple question. She had written many essays on thinkers and writers who became influential either by accident or design, including her mentors in *Existenzphilosophie*, Heidegger and Jaspers, and if the former's attempt to influence the Nazi Party struck her as catastrophic, she heaped praise on the latter for his public interventions. But she insisted, "when I am working, I am not interested in how my work might affect people."[5] Arendt went on to offer her opinion of the desire for influence. In a word, it was "masculine": "Men always want to be terribly influential, but I see that as somewhat external. Do I imagine myself being influential? No. I want to understand. And if others understand—in the same sense that I have understood—that gives me a sense of satisfaction, like feeling at home."[6]

To the right listener, Arendt's answer might have recalled the bodily etymology of "public," deriving from the Latin *poplicus*, or "people." *Poplicus*, as Michael Warner points out, was transformed into *publicus* through association with *puberes*, referring to adult men.[7] But this was something of a red herring, implying a depth of engagement with gender questions Arendt did not, in fact, maintain. Asked how she felt about being a woman in philosophy, she replied that she herself was old-fashioned on issues of gender and of "proper" work for women, even saying "it just doesn't look good when women give orders." Arendt attributed her aversion to influence not to her desire to play a "feminine" role, but rather to her writing practice, whose goal was to promote understanding in sympathetic readers rather than to reach a mass audience and persuade them; argumentation for peers, then, rather than rhetoric intended to reach and persuade a broad public, or to "legislate" on the basis of absolute truth.

Arendt's avowed desire to remain a critic and commentator rather than a pundit, coupled with her dislike of ideological positions—especially positions that, like Marxism, came with their own future-oriented philosophies of history—recalls her basically tragic view of the modern world. While she disdained pessimistic and doom-filled perspectives on humanity's future, it often seemed she was more animated by the fight against naïve progressivism and its teleological readings of the past. As she once put it, the best we can hope for is "to see precisely what [the past] was, and to endure this knowledge."[8] She was, after all, a refugee from one of the worst regimes the modern world ever produced, understood herself as a member of the last generation of German Jews, and wrote on a series of tragedies, from the rise of totalitarianism to the Holocaust, because she felt a responsibility to confront them. It is possible to read her works, from her first historical project *Rahel Varnhagen* through *The Origins of Totalitarianism* to *Eichmann in Jerusalem*, as studies of the ill effects of modernization on every level of human social experience, from politics down to personal identity. What is remarkable is that Arendt sustained a tragic view without becoming attached to a theory of historical decline. As she put it in *The Origins of Totalitarianism*, she wrote against a background of "reckless optimism and reckless despair," and she said that "Progress and Doom" were nothing more than "two sides of the same medal."[9] The modern was neither demon nor hero for Arendt, and she simply insisted that historical events be viewed as the works of men, rather than as the material working-through of a pattern, whether construed as transcendental or emergent. Like so many thinkers of her generation, coming of age amid the aftershocks of World War I, Arendt could see no "sense" in history.

Even a brief rehearsal of Arendt's accomplishments makes it hard to accept her avowed disinterest in influence. As though to make this point, at the conversation's close, her interviewer, the journalist and later politician Günter Gaus, brought up a remark Arendt had once made in praise of her mentor and friend Karl Jaspers: "Humanity is never acquired in solitude, and never by giving one's work to the public. It can be achieved only by one who has thrown his life and his person into the 'venture into the public realm.'"[10] It was not clear what Arendt had meant by implying that humanity is an "acquired" state, but intertwining humanity and publicness was a telling gesture. To a knowing member of her audience this might have recalled her 1958 *The Human Condition,* in which she wrote of the value of appearing in public and making the kinds of political speeches that might win fame. She called this behavior "action." Action, for her, was autotelic. It found its purpose within itself, and while it might have an effect in the realm of politics it was never justified by that effect.[11] One could perform it only after becoming free of the body's animal needs, which were fulfilled by "labor:" laboring man was the *animal laborans*, not quite human. Only freedom from worry regarding the needs of the body (e.g., economic security) allowed one to enter public life and by doing so, acquire humanity.

Arendt's praise for her teacher and friend raised questions about what she herself sought to do in the public realm, questions that remained unasked in the interview. The action of entering public life was crucial for the attainment of full humanity, but what mattered was paradoxically not the works one "gave" to the public, but one's presence. Why place oneself in public view, save in pursuit of influence? Why act as a witness or judge of world events? Why did the subject of one's writings matter at all? And what of the "understanding" between writer and reader Arendt named as her goal earlier in the interview? Or was the autotelic "action" just a kind of regulatory ideal, "regulatory" because Arendt knew it could never be realized? In her 1962 essay "The Crisis in Culture," Arendt articulated a view of "humanity" that somewhat clarified her *laudatio* to Jaspers. Here she praised humanists, in the sense of nonspecialists who nevertheless practice a diverse array of arts and sciences. In her view they

> exer[t] a faculty of judgment and taste which is beyond the coercion which each specialty imposes upon us. This Roman *humanitas* applied to men who were free in every respect, for whom the question of freedom, of not being coerced, was the decisive one—even in philosophy, even in science, even in the arts.[12]

In other words, humanists were truly free because they were never hemmed in by the *déformation professionelle* that develops during years of training in a discipline. They were thus akin to the political actors who pursued politics for its own sake, free even from considerations of the outcome of their acts. "Giving one's *work* to the public," was less the point. More important was the development of a sense of judgment detached from the content of individual works. Arendt's praise for the generalist was, of course, in keeping with the impressive range of her own writings, but she could also have been referring to Jaspers's scholarly and popular productions on subjects from psychopathology to higher education to the Atomic Age.

Ironically, Arendt would not have been speaking on the nature of publicness in a formal interview had she not desired public engagement at least
some of the time.[13] Jaspers himself had encouraged her to manage her public
reputation carefully, so that she might serve as a "sovereign figure for the Jewish
question."[14] In the same interview in which she disavowed a desire for influence, she meditated on the obligation to speak truths in public, recalling the
rhetoric of the Dreyfusards and their sense that the public, when properly
addressed, might function as a kind of tribunal, and then act on the truth
once it was known. But even as a proponent of the public conduct of political life, and as a contributor to journals and magazines including the *New
Yorker*, *Partisan Review*, and *Dissent*, Arendt could remain skeptical about
many of the elements that made up what we might call the twentieth-century
folk theory of "the intellectual."[15] In keeping with her opposition to ideology,
she was suspicious of those who wrote on politics in the name of one philosophical school or another, she distrusted the deployment of technical expertise when essentially political questions were at hand, and she dismissed the
idea that the educated knew a greater share of the truth about politics than
their fellows. As her career moved on, the Greek she praised was Socrates,
and she often remarked on his egalitarian, maieutic method, which had
sought to bring nascent truth out of the *doxa* of his fellow Athenians, regardless of their social status.

But the significance of the apparent contradictions between Arendt's
statements on publicness, action, and thought does not lie in the contradictions themselves.[16] After all, though Arendt is often celebrated as a theorist
of publicness, she did not offer a grand and unifying theoretical account of
public life, nor of the role of philosophers and intellectuals in politics. Simply put, there was nothing for contradiction to undermine. The contradictions are important because they indicate Arendt's ambivalence about the
importance and meaning of appearing in public as a writer or thinker. Her
statements in the Gaus interview remind us that participation in public intellectual life can coexist with curiosity and doubt about such participation.
Arendt was not only impossible to categorize, she was capable of taking
remarkably heterodox stances. Similarly, she was heterodox and unsystematic
in her understanding of what it meant to be "an intellectual." For example,
while Arendt knew full well that the term "an intellectual" had, since the
Dreyfus Affair, been associated with outsider (she often said "pariah") status,
and with a critical approach to established political institutions, she often

used the term to describe individuals who placed themselves in the service of the status quo.

Arendt also understood that to speak or write in public meant risking misunderstanding, misrecognition, and worse. She learned this lesson the old-fashioned way, by getting into trouble. Arendt made her 1963 statement on the "parting of ways" the same year she published *Eichmann in Jerusalem: A Report on the Banality of Evil*, her account of the Jerusalem trial of National Socialist bureaucrat Adolf Eichmann. This book, which began as an article commissioned by William Shawn for the *New Yorker* (and which grew into five articles before becoming a book), would toss Arendt into the greatest controversy of her career.[17] Critics would assess her claims about Eichmann himself, the conduct of his trial, and the Holocaust, and they would make numerous inquiries into her own character. The controversy surrounding *Eichmann in Jerusalem* has been assessed time and time again,[18] but it was Gershom Scholem who supplied the most succinct assessment of Arendt's "error," in a now-famous letter. The historian of Jewish mysticism wrote to Arendt and accused her of lacking *"ahavat Israel,"* love of the Jewish people (the cruder form of this charge was that Arendt was, in the classic phrase, a "self-hating Jew").[19] This was notably a sign of Scholem's disappointment in his erstwhile friend; he had once described Arendt as "a wonderful woman and an extraordinary Zionist," thinking of the Arendt who had worked for the rescue and repatriation organization Youth Aliyah in Paris in the 1930s.[20] Arendt responded that she could not love a collectivity.[21] She only loved her friends: "the only kind of love I know of and believe in is the love of persons."[22] But while Arendt tried to reject the love of groups and the practice of arguing on the basis of group identity, she could not help but appear to reject the love of Jews.[23]

Arendt's praise for face-to-face connection would not convince those critics who felt she lacked the proper spirit of Jewish solidarity. She had hardly been sympathetic to the Israeli court, accusing it of violating the demands of justice by putting not only Eichmann himself, but the entire history of European anti-Semitism, on trial.[24] To her mind, the trial should not have emphasized Jew-hatred at all, but rather the universally important crimes against humanity in which Eichmann participated, and the potentially universal nature of Eichmann's thoughtlessness, a bad precedent for future generations. New Eichmanns, new *hostis humani generis* ("enemies of humanity") could rise up around the globe. Perhaps even worse in the minds of her critics, Arendt discussed the role of the *Judenräte*, the councils of Jewish elders faced with the horrible task of selecting victims for deportation from the ghettos, and this led many to think (erroneously) that she was blaming Jews for participating in their own destruction.[25] Her critics portrayed her as attacking the still-young Israeli state and its developing culture as much as she criticized Eichmann himself for the "banal" quality of his evil actions.[26] Arendt's real goal, which was to understand Eichmann's failure to think, was often lost in the storm. By the time of her 1964 interview with Gaus, she had already received ample critical attention over Eichmann; Judge Michael Musmanno, who had been an American prosecutor at Nuremberg, produced a savage review only two weeks after *Eichmann in Jerusalem* appeared.[27] Arendt had more than enough reminders of the complexity of public life, of the way not only one's writings but also one's persona inevitably fell under scrutiny.

Arendt had defined Eichmann himself as a kind of intellectual, albeit not a public one, and she focused on his puzzling inability to think. He was not just a bureaucrat whose "only language was officialese" (as he put it), but a product of good German schools capable of quoting Kant and a man who held his job because of his logistical expertise.[28] His participation in great political crimes thus flew in the face of the old idea that *Bildung* provided moral improvement and refined the faculty of judgment. Most prominently in 1958 *The Human Condition* (but also in other works), Arendt complained about the intrusions of "experts" into political life. These "intellectuals," as she wrote, were technocrats eager to treat political problems as though they could be remedied using technical solutions. Interestingly, in his letter to Arendt, Scholem used the term "intellectual" as follows: "In you, dear Hannah, as in so many intellectuals who came here from the German Left, I find little trace of [*ahavat Israel*]." In her response, Arendt distanced herself from the category: "I am not," she wrote, "'one of the intellectuals who comes from the German Left.' You could not have known this, since we did not know each other when we were young . . . . If I can be said to 'have come from anywhere,' it is from the tradition of German philosophy."

Arendt criticized Eichmann's "banality" and thereby implied that there was a form of independent reflection of which he had been incapable, and which could have kept him from participating in genocide. But Arendt's own desire for a standpoint independent of any group—political *humanitas*—proved an irritant to her critics. Some of her Jewish critics attributed it to a German Jewish tendency toward individualism and insensitivity to the concerns of other Jews, especially those from Eastern Europe.[29] Such accusations of "yekke" prejudice seem harsh, and it might be more appropriate to attribute to Arendt a modernist disinclination to base her speech upon tradition or group identity. She never attempted to speak "as a Jew" any more than "as a woman," refusing the representational logic this would have invoked.[30] One of the mysteries surrounding her book on Eichmann is why Arendt wrote it as provocatively as she did, given that she was not without foresight. Her 1959 essay on school desegregation in the American South, "Reflections on Little Rock," had caused significant uproar.[31] Nor did Arendt acknowledge relishing the good or bad publicity she received for any work, calling it "a nuisance."[32] She was, however, not an expert on the *practice* of predicting and meeting the expectations of her public, but rather a theorist of the meanings of public life. *Eichmann in Jerusalem* and the resulting scandal reinforce the impression that Arendt was overly optimistic about the potential for publics to function in the ideal terms she had traced in *The Human Condition*— ironically, she fell prey to the same weakness she once noted in Socrates, namely that he held his interlocutors in too high an esteem to try to persuade them through rhetoric, and took their opinions seriously as vessels in which truth was latent.

Much of this chapter and the two after it will deal with works from Arendt's mature period, in this case meaning the writings she produced following her 1941 arrival in the United States. These include the aforementioned *The Human Condition* and *The Life of the Mind*, as well as essays and addresses on pressing issues of the day. But influences from Arendt's Weimar youth shadowed her later observations on intellectuals and philosophers in politics, and I will attend to those as well. As is well known, these included her relationships with the philosophers Heidegger and Jaspers and their respective accounts of what Michael Theunissen terms "social ontology," as well as her sometime affiliation with Zionism, and her politicization in the course of flight from Nazi Germany. As this chapter will show, Arendt was also driven, in her examinations of publicness, by her early projects in Jewish history, including the study of assimilation in nineteenth-century Prussian salon society, *Rahel Varnhagen,* and the chapters on anti-Semitism in the mammoth 1951 study *The Origins of Totalitarianism*. She crafted her most positive portrayal of publicness, in *The Human Condition*, only *after* she had examined a series of Jewish failures to properly understand the public dimensions of modern European political life, and then spent years puzzling through philosophy's historical disinterest in the muddiness of daily political life. In *The Human Condition* Arendt criticized intellectuals and philosophers for their fumbling designs on politics, and demonstrated that she had no faith in the progressivist liberal picture of the public sphere as rational. While Arendt never moved away from these criticisms of politically engaged thinkers, in the years after the Gaus interview she began to reflect on the very thing whose influence *The Human Condition* had attempted to counter—the *vita contemplativa*, the life of philosophy. In her final lectures, Arendt explored a kind of publicness she had first considered during the scholarly exercises that led up to *The Human Condition*, a publicness that lay within the basic representational structure of thought itself. In returning to the thinkers she had first read in her youth, Arendt found a way to reclaim the very philosophical tradition she had abjured years earlier, while re-creating herself as a political theorist.

Love and Saint Augustine

As was the case with Emmanuel Levinas and Leo Strauss, the works of Arendt's maturity displayed important filiations with her youthful studies. The rough and ready truth of Arendt's claim that she had abandoned philosophy for politics and history belies the way her 1929 doctoral dissertation, *Die Liebsbegriff bei Augustin* (rendered as *Love and Saint Augustine* in its English translation), can help us to understand her development. In particular, it demonstrates that from the very start she understood philosophy to be marked by a private and inward orientation, a turning-away from other persons. The dissertation offers a window onto Arendt's early account of social ontology, but it also illuminates her original leave-taking from Heidegger's version of *Existenzphilosophie* and her search for the limits of Heideggerian social ontology, which actually began before her interests became primarily "political." Years later she would, in a letter to Jaspers, complain of philosophy's failure to deal more than tangentially with the "fact of plurality."[33] It was here that she had first approached the problem, albeit obliquely, through the surrogate of writing on a father of the Christian Church.

Arendt wrote *Love and Saint Augustine* in 1928, five years before her shift away from philosophy and toward politics. In his comments on *Love and Saint Augustine*, Jaspers, writing as her dissertation advisor, suggested that Arendt had been drawn by something beyond philosophy: "The impulse behind this work is ultimately something not explicitly stated: through philosophical

work with ideas the author wants to justify her freedom from Christian possibilities, which also attract her."[34] But there is a crucial difference between an
interest in theology writ large, which Arendt certainly had, and an interest
in "Christian possibilities,"[35] which she did not. Samuel Moyn has explored
Arendt's dissertation as the site of her consideration and subsequent abandonment of a transcendental approach to ethics. This would derive ethics from the
recognition that one and one's neighbor are both God's co-creations.[36] Arendt's central concern about such an approach had to do with its fundamental
denial of worldly alterity—mirroring Heidegger's prior critique of Husserl's
failure to adequately account for the world in his own transcendental phenomenology. In Augustine's view, mutual recognition between two persons
who see one another as co-creations of God, involves a shift from loving the
features of this world (including the characteristics of the other person) to
loving God: from *cupiditas* to *caritas*, in his terms. In Arendt's view, the negative result is that in loving one's neighbor as a co-creation we must efface
her distinguishing and "worldly" features, shifting focus from what Augustine termed the "city of man" to the "city of God." While the young Arendt
did not invoke the language of publicness and privacy, she seemed troubled
by the way Augustinian *caritas* involved abandoning the same phenomenal
realm she would in later years view as critical to the establishment of a
healthy public life. This worry would find its echo in *The Human Condition*,
where Arendt claimed that Augustine exemplified the Christian tendency to
find a replacement for the world itself in the bond between the faithful.[37]

While she first encountered Augustine's thought in a Marburg seminar
led by Heidegger's friend and colleague, the Protestant theologian Rudolf
Bultmann,[38] the theological dimensions of Augustine's thought seemed to interest Arendt only insofar as they reflected an underlying Platonism. Like
Heidegger, she tended to secularize Christian themes. Notably, this reach for
abstract philosophical content was in keeping with Bultmann's own "demythologizing" approach to religious narratives, including the story of the life
of Jesus. Arendt observed that even Augustine's interest in love was somehow a vestige of his own non-Christian past. "Insofar as Augustine defines
love as a kind of desire, he hardly speaks as a Christian," but rather as an observer "of the deplorable state of the human [desiring] condition."[39] In emphasizing Augustine's preoccupation with eternity, the object of our most
noble cravings, Arendt drew him back to his great influence Plotinus, who
had described eternity, in his *Enneads,* as a kind of "eternal present" with

neither past nor future, temporalities that require us to "lose" one moment in order to gain another.[40]

Arendt came closer to drawing political lessons from Augustine in a fascinating but brief 1930 essay for *Frankfurter Zeitung*, "Augustin und Protestantismus," in which she managed the curious feat of producing a de-Christianized rendering of Augustine by discussing the legacy of his thought *for Christians*. This gymnastic was accomplished by arguing for a "Protestant" interpretation of Augustine's teachings. Arendt stated that undue attention to his activities as a founder of the Church could blind readers to the "empire" of internal religious experience he had founded in his *Confessions*. It was this empire that linked Greek philosophical discourse on the soul to Luther's eventual celebration of an internal relation to God. With grossly unhistorical flourish, Arendt positioned Augustine at the parting of ways between two versions of Christianity: Catholicism, with its explicitly worldly political presence (she called it the heir to the Roman Empire), and an unworldly and internal Protestantism. But her implication was that Augustine belonged to philosophical inwardness rather than to a lineage of religious thinkers concerned with worldly matters. This recalled the central question she asked about *Existenzphilosophie* in her dissertation, through the proxy of Augustine. Was it capable of embracing action in the world, or would its reflections remain stuck in the solitude (or failed sociality) Heidegger had offered in *Being and Time*, ultimately no great improvement over the solipsism of Husserl's system?

How Arendt engaged with Heidegger's *Existenzphilosophie* by writing about Augustine will become clear after a brief consideration of her argument. Arendt's work consists of three sections. The first focused on the nature of love as a craving (*cupiditas*), the second on God as the object of love (*caritas*), and the third on the love of the neighbor.[41] About *cupiditas* Arendt wrote, "the trouble with human happiness is that it is constantly beset by fear. It is not the lack of possessing but the safety of possession that is at stake."[42] *Caritas*, the love of God, can set us free from such fear of loss. We learn to love not the things of this world, but only God, and to love our neighbors solely in their capacity as co-creations. But as if to frustrate any temptation to read that tripartite structure as bespeaking a dialectical progression in which the conflict between *cupiditas* and *caritas* is resolved in neighborliness, Arendt's final section imagined the Augustinian Christian community bound together not by love for one another as worldly creatures, but by a mutual decision to choose the afterlife over the present world. Her implication was that this was no model for true community.

Though Augustine was no existentialist (he was, for example, Platonic in his understanding of being as something unconditioned by time[43]), his thought on love resonated with key themes in Heidegger's and Jaspers's respective variations on *Existenzphilosophie*. Augustine's decision to convert, made during a crisis over mortality, recalled Jaspers's notion of the "limit situation" in which dread and anxiety serve as catalysts toward transformation and the surpassing of past limitations, articulated by Jaspers in the 1919 *Psychology of Worldviews*. Augustine's preoccupation with death also conjured the Heidegger of *Being and Time* with his understanding of *being-towards-death*. In *Love and Saint Augustine*, otherness (with which both Heidegger and Jaspers had been preoccupied) takes several main forms, one of which is the eternal, another of which is the future, with a third being death. Further, the work concludes with the alterity of the neighbor.[44] Curiously, perhaps, there are only two direct discussions of Heidegger, a parenthetical reference to his emphasis on being-towards-death, and a significant footnote.[45]

In that footnote Arendt addresses Heidegger's own understanding of Augustine's concept of "the world," as articulated in his essay "Vom Wesen des Grundes."[46] Heidegger had acknowledged the two meanings Augustine granted the word *mundus*. On the one hand it meant "ens creatum" (created thing), and on the other, the world as known by those who love it. According to Arendt, though, Heidegger focused only on the world as humans relate to it. In ignoring the all-important tension between those two modalities of "world," Heidegger missed Augustine's significance for thinking through the problem inherent in his own social ontology. While Arendt did not present Augustinian *caritas* as a successful model for intersubjective ethics (which could have made the young Arendt a kind of Levinasian *avant la lettre*), she saw that the recognition of createdness was essential to Augustinian ethics, flaws and all. Indeed, Arendt's dissertation dealt with a perceived "failure of otherness" in Heidegger's *Existenzphilosophie* through the surrogate of uncovering that failure in Augustine. The Augustinian neighbor never appears as he truly is, save as a sign of either grace or sin; similarly, Heideggerian *Mitsein* ignored particularity and the authentic community that might emerge in a congregation of particulars. Arendt further noted that Augustinian inwardness was disabling when it came to performing deeds in the world. She quoted Augustine's realization that he was not one "who can act well within [himself] so that actual deeds will result from this."[47] Not only real neighborliness, which accepts alterity, but also action, was blocked for Augustine.

Die Liebsbegriff bei Augustin is also significant because in the 1960s Arendt took up the work again, revising it for English-language publication at a pivotal moment in her own career when she was reconsidering her relationship with philosophy. Certainly, events in Arendt's life, especially the controversy surrounding the 1963 *Eichmann in Jerusalem,* conspired to keep her preoccupied, and the revised study of Augustine never appeared. But this attempted revision placed the lessons of her dissertation squarely in view as she worked through a late-career rapprochement with philosophy, whose inwardness she had tried to leave much as she had abandoned "the intellectuals" she had known in her youth. In her dissertation Arendt dealt with concepts that would remain alive in her thought for decades, among them alterity, worldliness, and action. However, they persisted in her thought not as *philosophical* concepts, but rather through translation into decidedly political forms, which she would pursue as she examined the histories, variously, of totalitarianism, anti-Semitism, and public political process.

Though Arendt had recovered her youthful appreciation for philosophical inwardness by the time she returned to her Augustine manuscript in the 1960s, she did not return to it for intellectual reasons. "I got myself into something absurd," Arendt wrote to her friend Mary McCarthy in 1965, explaining that she had accepted an advance from a publisher who wished to release her Augustine study as a book. E. B. Ashton had produced a translation of the dissertation in 1963, which Arendt received and from which she apparently worked toward the project's revision. As she said to McCarthy:

> It is kind of a traumatic experience. I am re-writing the whole darned business, trying not to do anything new, but only to explain in English (and not in Latin) what I thought when I was twenty. It is probably not worth it and I should simply return the money—but by now I am strangely fascinated in this rencontre.[48]

The work never appeared during Arendt's lifetime, but she made substantial revisions to Ashton's translation. That Arendt kept working despite her doubts about the project's worth is notable, and is perhaps explained by the fact that Augustine had remained a presence in her life over the years. When she wrote *The Human Condition* he still served as a symbol of philosophy's devaluation of the *saeculum,* of the philosopher's refusal to value worldly actions and relationships except insofar as they reflected the transcendental. Yet *The Human Condition* also contained a note of surprising praise: Augustine was "the last to know . . . what it once meant to be a citizen."[49] In other words, Augustine was the last to understand "politics" in the elevated sense Arendt preferred and associated with the *vita activa* of the citizens of the ancient world. Augustine may have shared the traditional philosophical prejudice criticized throughout *The Human Condition*, bestowing upon the *vita activa* a second-order dignity because it facilitated the pursuit of the *vita contemplativa*, but at least he understood that the *vita activa* could mean "a life devoted to public-political matters."[50]

In *The Life of the Mind* Arendt returned to Augustine for something she had never rejected, namely his theory of mental representation, which prepared the mind for reflection without the aid of the senses. Augustine held that we effectively replicate vision internally, images stored in memory becoming "visions in thought," but crucially changed in the process. As Arendt put it, "the thought-object is different from the image, as the image is different from the visible sense-object whose mere representation it is."[51] It is the task of the imaginative faculty to transform items from memory's storehouse into elements "suitable for thought," but in the process the faculty grows, giving us the capacity to understand ideas unconnected to any sense-object. In this text Augustine's account of thinking as a withdrawal from sensual experience means that action is interrupted: "All thinking demands a *stop-and-think*."[52] In Arendt's last work, such withdrawal was not only the root of philosophy's unworldliness, but also a necessary precondition for the activities of "willing" and "judging," and not only for philosophers but for everyone.

But the imaginative faculty needs something to compel it to choose this or that image from memory's store; this is the will, one of the trio of faculties Arendt planned to cover in *The Life of the Mind*.[53] In her section on "Willing," Arendt returned to Augustine as "the first philosopher of the will," highlighting the "practical" dimension of his thought, in stark contrast to her prior presentation of Augustinian love. Augustine, wrote Arendt, had always been motivated by the goal of happiness; when he failed to secure it, he turned to religion. A "pragmatic concern for private happiness" thus drove him.[54] Augustine's philosophy of the will dealt with the essential divisions in our will—some traditions (such as the Manichaean, which Augustine followed in his youth) gloss as our possessing both an "evil" and a "good" nature—and is too complex for easy rendering here. However, at the end of the

Confessions, Augustine suggested that it is love itself that unifies our will, allowing the will to function as the "spring of action" toward an object.

In short, in the context of a series of lectures whose goal was to reassess the *vita contemplativa*, Arendt found ways to redeem Augustine's legacy, much as in his own meditations Augustine had understood the tormented and divided will to be potentially "redeemed" by love. Arendt, without reversing her decades-earlier judgment on the relationship between Augustinian *cupiditas*, *caritas*, and "love of the neighbor," had determined that even if Augustine's thought led in an unworldly direction, it contained an element critical for action in the world. Closing her discussion of Augustine as the "first philosopher of the will," Arendt thought back over her subject's life-long obsession with mortality (which Arendt had discussed in her dissertation in terms that directly recalled Heidegger's "being-towards-death"). However, she observed that if Augustine had properly contemplated his own teachings on the will, he would have understood himself as she did, as a philosopher of *natality* rather than mortality, based on the analogy between our freedom to will spontaneously and the freedom and open possibility of a new birth.[55]

It would be convenient to think that in criticizing Augustinian *caritas* for its hostility to true alterity, the young Arendt of 1928 anticipated her later interest in a politics of public participation and foreshadowed her mature criticisms of philosophy as a retreat from the world. But she did not fight free from philosophy's gravity so quickly. Two years later, in a book review titled "Philosophy and Sociology: On Karl Mannheim's *Ideology and Utopia*,"[56] she considered the idea that scholars and other persons of letters should be engaged participants in public life, and found it unpalatable. In this critique of Mannheim's 1929 *Ideology and Utopia*, she was eager to defend philosophy's autonomy against the claim inherent in his "sociology of knowledge," namely that all thought is determined by social forces as well as cultural ones. In fact, Arendt's review recalls Adorno's more sharply worded critique of Mannheim's sociology of knowledge: "a sociology of knowledge fails before philosophy: for the truth content of philosophy it substitutes its social function and its conditioning by interests while refraining from a critique of that content itself."[57] And at this point in her career, for Arendt, the importance of philosophy's truth-content needed no explanation.

As Martin Jay points out, Mannheim's work should be understood as an attempt to engage with questions of value at a time when Germany's leading intellectuals saw around themselves a crisis of valuation. This was a crisis not merely of morals, but of the possibility of a secure account of values themselves. Neo-Kantian and Marxist models of value seemed equally pale in the wake of World War I's devastation, and other alternatives—existentialism as plausibly instantiated in the political theology of Carl Schmitt, for example, or variations on neo-Orthodoxy in both Protestant and Jewish circles— hardly stood as universally acceptable solutions, especially for thinkers with their roots in either Kantian philosophy or Marxism.[58] For some, the crisis derived from cultural issues; for others, from fissures running through German society, something that could be vouchsafed by little more than a backward glance at the short-lived revolutions following the Great War's end and at the growing tensions between workers and bourgeois throughout the Weimar years. Though social explanations for the crisis in values often appealed to Marxists, in *Ideology and Utopia*, the notably non-Marxist Mannheim linked society and culture in such a way that his work has been called the "bourgeois response" to Georg Lukács's *History and Class Consciousness*, that foundational work of Western Marxist thought. Where Lukács had granted the proletariat a privileged perspective for the acquisition of social knowledge (for the proletariat was both the subject and object of history), Mannheim granted a "synthetic" vision instead to the figure of the intellectual.[59] In *Ideology and Utopia* Mannheim suggested that while each intellectual's perspective necessarily possessed only partial validity, a "collectivity" of "free-floating" intellectuals could bring their views together in order to grasp the totality of the moment. As Mannheim described them, "intellectuals" were not individuals who remained in the academy but ones who operated outside of it, seeking public engagement. For Mannheim, contra Julian Benda, affiliation with classes and parties facilitated a beneficial engagement with the public world.

Arendt saw Mannheim's idea of synthesis as a derogation of the basic functions of philosophy and suspected that his "sociology of knowledge" harbored a utilitarianism that ultimately betrayed philosophy's purposes. As she put it, "Prior to Mannheim's question as to the social and historical location of the sociological formulation is the question as to the ontological circumstance in which sociological analyses are historically justified."[60] She did not suggest that intellectuals must be "rooted," a plausibly Heideggerian riposte, but she denied that he had satisfactorily dealt with his philosophical priors. Not only had Mannheim asked his questions independently of any preliminary philosophical analysis of his own methods, he ignored precisely the inquiry that would have determined whether or not his own analysis was itself a reflex of class interests: for Arendt, Mannheim's claims that the "sociology of knowledge" could be conducted on a free-floating basis seemed insufficient, and the sociologist of knowledge himself remained fixed in the sector of society from which he had tried to ascend.

Resting heavily on the notion of philosophy's inherent dignity, Arendt's review of Mannheim was far less nuanced than many penned by more mature scholars, particularly those associated with the Frankfurt-based Institute for Social Research, later known as the Frankfurt School. In her persistent belief in the possibility of an Archimedean point of view, she did not fall so far from Mannheim herself. However, Mannheim's book was not just about the relationship between intellectual expressions and class interests, or about the possibility of synthetic sociological knowledge from an Archimedean perspective, but about the role of the intellectual in society. Mannheim's Frankfurt School critics suggested that intellectuals could not simultaneously change society and produce true knowledge of it.[61] Mannheim's own depiction of intellectuals had been true, as Carl Boggs points out, to a certain "Jacobin" vanguardist sensibility, hoping to impose change from above—and yet from no particular position, neither that of worker nor of bourgeois.[62] Mannheim relied on the notion of an outsiderly elite, but at a time when—as Benda's 1927 *Trahison des clercs* shows—the alliances of many intellectuals with revolutionary and nationalist parties made it difficult to believe in their independent status. Given the fragility of Mannheim's claims, even as slight a criticism as Arendt's could have force.

An Emergent Jewish Critique of Public Life

Arendt would not approach public political life via philosophy, at least not at first. *Love and Saint Augustine* was the last study of philosophy (per se) Arendt would produce for more than thirty years. In 1929 she began to write a strikingly different book, a biography of the eighteenth-century lady of salon society Rahel Varnhagen, born Rahel Levin in 1771. Arendt had learned of Varnhagen through a friend of her student days, Anne Mendelssohn, who gave her Varnhagen's collected correspondence. That the Varnhagen study was to be a work of Jewish history is plain in Arendt's planned title, *Über das Problem des deutsch-jüdischen Assimilation, exemplifiziert an dem Leben der Rähel Varnhagen* (*On the Problem of German-Jewish Assimilation Exemplified in the Life of Rahel Varnhagen*). As it happened it would not be published for almost two decades, appearing in English in 1957 as *Rahel Varnhagen: The Life of a Jewess*, a title that merely gestured at Arendt's sharper intended meaning.[63] In between the project's beginning and its conclusion, Arendt would research and write the much better known and more influential *The Origins of Totalitarianism*, the study that established her reputation and against whose grand historical scope *Rahel Varnhagen* seems a miniaturist portrait of its heroine and her world, a rendering of the *Goethezeit* through the life of a woman who was too much an adherent to the Romantic movement for her own good.[64] Leagues apart in subject and methodology, the two works are nevertheless the dual products of a single and extended train of thought on Jewish history as a window onto the emergence of public political life in modern Europe. Arendt sustained this train through her years of statelessness and into her life in the United States. Both works examine the process of Jewish emancipation and assimilation. Both consider the way the resulting "modernization" of the Jews was influenced by an increasingly important division between public and private spheres of life. And both tellingly reveal that Arendt considered a range of attempted, and failed, versions of public life before she sat down to produce *The Human Condition's* account of "action."

Arendt's original intention was not to break from philosophy completely, but to adapt *Existenzphilosophie* to a historical case, and it may have been a gentle criticism from Jaspers that turned her more fully toward history itself. In the winter of 1929–1930, Arendt sent her teacher a written lecture she was about to deliver in which she proposed to treat Rahel's life from the perspective of *Existenzphilosophie*, examining what "Jewish existence" might mean. Jaspers responded that such an approach would "cut existential thinking off at the roots."[65] "Existentialism" could not take "Jewishness" as its content, but only existence itself: "The concept of being-thrown-back-on-oneself can no longer be taken altogether seriously if it is *grounded* in terms of the fate of the Jews instead of being rooted in itself."[66] Arendt responded immediately in hopes of correcting Jaspers's misconceptions: she meant only to explore the way a set of historical conditions—such as those in which Varnhagen had lived—could constitute a person's horizons of existence and experience.

But the study's real meaning for the relationship between teacher and student became clear in later correspondence. Arendt, commenting on Jaspers's study *Max Weber: Deutsches wesen im politischen denken, im forschen und philosophieren*,[67] expressed her incomprehension at Jaspers's characterization of Weber as possessing "Deutsches Wesen (German Being)," though from her vantage point as a Jew she felt unqualified to endorse or gainsay such a claim.[68] This earned her a troubled response from her teacher, who nevertheless had to acknowledge that his own appeal to "Germanness" had been an attempt to appeal directly to nationalistic sentiments among his readers, an effort to give "Germanness" an *ethical* rather than a nationalistic content, based on culture and not on race.[69] In the same letter, Jaspers (married, notably, to a Jewish woman) also placed a heavy burden on his student by saying that his interpretation of Germanness as "ethical" might be judged a success or failure based on Arendt's ability or inability to identify with German culture.[70] Arendt in return admitted her attachment to German culture provided it could be considered apart from any political or national body, and the disagreement between student and teacher eased.

Arendt and Jaspers's back-and-forth over the accessibility of German culture anticipated (and arguably may have shaped) a central theme of Arendt's study of Varnhagen, the "Problem of German Jewish Assimilation" announced in Arendt's original title. This was the success or failure of the project of German Jewish identity itself, a project that got underway in Varnhagen's time, when bureaucrats and intellectuals (*avant la lettre*), both Jewish and German, worked to secure civic emancipation for Jews. However, German Jewish identity had been a fraught affair even for its celebrants; it was never clear whether or not a form of distinctly Jewish communal life could be preserved against the pressure of assimilation. Furthermore, even emancipation's most ardent eighteenth-century Prussian advocates, such as the civil servant Wilhelm Christian Dohm, had understood that rights might be secured not for Jews as a class—not *as* Jews—but as individuals.[71] Dohm expected that the resulting *bürgerlich Verbesserung* (civic improvement) would ultimately lead to the erasure of Jewish particularity. By the time of Arendt's birth, that project had fallen under heavy fire from Zionist critics of European Jewish assimilation, and during her youth a decidedly post-assimilationist spirit developed within the younger generation of German Jews, as we have already seen through the lens of Strauss's involvement with Zionist youth groups. Arendt ultimately came over to the anti-assimilationist side, and while she certainly identified with Varnhagen, she also criticized Varnhagen's Romantic approach to Jewish identity as "quixotic" and ultimately doomed, in the process offering what was effectively a psychocultural, rather than a political critique of "German Jewish symbiosis."

German Romanticism, with its celebrations of privacy and inwardness, had seemed to promise the complete remaking of the self. The social barriers between Jews and non-Jews could seem to dissolve while one engaged in the introspective activities promoted by Romantic poets, novelists, and post-Kantian philosophers.[72] In more mundane terms, conversion and marriage to Gentiles were among the paths taken by many of Varnhagen's assimilatory contemporaries. Another path was to participate in the world of salon conversation, in which one could effectively "perform" a cultivated identity that transcended national identity. Education, and not only in German letters, was perceived to be a key; the language of many Berlin salons was French.[73] In fact, the project about which Jaspers initially expressed doubts was, by means of its critique of the political dangers of a cult of private experience, effectively a continuation of the very doctoral dissertation he had approved, though Arendt's project implicitly rejected his argument about Weber's Germanness: Arendt would argue that many German Jews had been led astray by the overall ethos of the *Goethezeit*, fooled into thinking that social success within the salons, or the performance of identity through literary activities, was the promissory sign of a coming German Jewish symbiosis.

Arendt's Varnhagen was born into a Berlin Jewish family and lacked, as Arendt noted, the "natural advantages" of physical attractiveness, intelligence, or (being Jewish) social position. But she was a real performer. She became an "insider" in the educated, artistic, and moneyed circles of Prussian society by sheer force of personality, and she understood this charm to be her own kind of "magic." In particular, Rahel possessed the gift of storytelling, "the art of representing her own life":

> the point was not to tell the truth, but to display herself; not always to say the same thing to everyone, but to each what was appropriate for him. She learned that only as a specific person could one say something specific in such a way that it would be listened to, and she learned that unhappiness without a title was double unhappiness.[74]

The lines between inner experience and outer, public and private, dissolved when one performed for friends by telling stories and putting oneself on display. This ability was crucial in the complex territory traversed by Varnhagen and other Jewish aspirants to salon society. During the late eighteenth century, the rise of Prussia's bourgeoisie and the resulting displacement of both the nobility and the intelligentsia created a need for new spaces in which elites might gather.[75] The Jewish *salonnières* were perfectly positioned to provide this space: "In the Jewish houses of homeless middle-class intellectuals [the nobles and Gentile intellectuals] found middle ground and an echo which they could not hope to find anywhere else."[76] It was the very fact that the Jews stood outside ordinary social life that made them the ideal hosts, at whose homes people from all walks of life could safely interact. Rahel's salon, for example, was graced by such prominent figures as Friedrich Schlegel, Clemens von Brentano, Ludwig and Friedrich Tieck, and Friedrich Schleiermacher.[77] The heyday of the salons passed, however, after Napoleon's victory over Prussian forces in 1806. Under the weight of the humiliating French occupation, interest in the salons dropped, diverted by real political concerns.

The pressures of politics meant that one could no longer truly live in the Romantic world of the imaginary. As Arendt put it, "The salon in which private things were given objectivity by being communicated, and in which public matters counted only insofar as they had private significance—the salon ceased to exist when the public world, the power of general misfortune, became so overwhelming that it could no longer be translated into private terms."[78] However, Prussia's defeat had greater negative consequences for Jewish *salonnières* than for their non-Jewish peers. An outbreak of anti-Semitism blocked many Jews from participating in the remaining salons, even as patriotic Prussians gathered and spoke out, in Arendt's words, "intellectually against the Enlightenment, politically against France, and socially against the salons."[79] Despite her disappointment at this turn, Rahel Levin continued to move in the highest circles of Berlin society, eventually marrying the non-Jewish August Varnhagen. And yet Rahel was important to Arendt not just because her story illustrated the limits of early Jewish assimilation in Prussia, but also because she felt troubled by her own liminal position between German and Jew. Rahel could not embrace her own Jewishness without becoming a social pariah, nor could she fully transcend it, except under the essentially theatrical circumstances of salon society, which did not translate into truly public space.

Rahel Varnhagen was a critique of the Romantic cult of inwardness, but it was also more than this. It was influenced by the myriad elements accompanying Arendt's awakening as a Jew, including sympathy for Zionism and an interest in the meanings of "pariah" status, as opposed to the position of the "parvenu." Arendt finished the bulk of the book before she fled Germany in 1933, and completed the final two chapters in 1933, guided by the Zionist critique of assimilation, "which I had adopted as my own and which I still consider basically justified today," as she wrote in a letter to Jaspers.[80] In this mood Arendt could celebrate a different dimension of Varnhagen's story, her ultimate acceptance of her own Jewish identity, which by report she proclaimed on her deathbed, realizing that "pariah" status had not been the tragedy it had often seemed during her life. However, even at the time of writing the bulk of the book, Arendt had been coming under the influence of Kurt Blumenfeld, her first tutor in Zionism and an increasing, fatherly presence in her life in the 1930s.

Blumenfeld, later known as the "father of post-assimilationist Zionism," was from an educated German-Jewish family much like Arendt's, and when they met in 1926 he was of a similar age as her mentors Jaspers and Heidegger. Ever since the 1912 German Zionist Federation conference at Posen, Blumenfeld had been a leading force in the German Zionist movement, pushing for a practical emphasis on the building of settlements in Palestine and the emigration of younger German Jews.[81] Blumenfeld's erudition and political acumen impressed Arendt, and she was likewise impressed by his understanding of Zionism as "Europe's gift to the Jews."[82] Confident that settlement in Palestine represented the only solution to the "Jewish Question," Blumenfeld also worked hard to present Zionism as a solution for Jews who were "post-assimilatory" and close to losing touch with that "Question" itself. The acculturation of many Central European Jewish communities had eroded many aspects of community life, aspects vital both for a resurgence of Jewish culture and for the development of resistance to anti-Semitism. Thus Blumenfeld was attentive to precisely the problematic situation in which young, university-educated Jews like Arendt found themselves: aware that they themselves were implicated in the Jewish Question, they nevertheless found it difficult to identify with many other Jews on the level of culture.[83] While Arendt and Blumenfeld would part company in later years over details of Zionist thought and practice, she took her initial understanding of "the Jewish Question" from him.[84]

If Blumenfeld served as Arendt's tutor in Zionism, she would find another deep influence in the writings of the turn-of-the-century French Zionist Bernard Lazare.[85] Like Herzl, Lazare had been a journalist working in France at the time of the Dreyfus Affair. While the Affair helped to inspire Lazare's Zionism much as it did Herzl's, Lazare's involvement in the ensuing debates was very different.[86] Recruited by Alfred Dreyfus's brother Mathieu to act as the journalistic voice of the Dreyfusards, Lazare wrote pamphlets proclaiming Alfred's innocence. He was also the first to employ the phrase "J'accuse," which Zola later made famous in his 1898 broadside of the same title, against Dreyfus's own accusers. It was from Lazare that Arendt took the terms "pariah" and "parvenu," crucial not only in *Rahel Varnhagen* but also in all her subsequent reflections on Jewish history. For Lazare as for Arendt, the "parvenu" is the Jew who aspires to become part of the Gentile world of social attainment and wealth. In contrast, and as Anson Rabinbach puts it, the self-conscious pariah lives "in the authentic awareness that only an outsider embodies the humanity that society otherwise denies."[87] Arendt found Lazare's celebration of Jewish pariah identity useful in contrast to Herzl's insistence on a program of political action based on the attainment of (what Lazare called) parvenu status, Jews successful in the Gentile world becoming an avant-garde that would later help the entire Jewish people.[88]

Not only did the binary pair "pariah" and "parvenu" serve Arendt as a conceptual matrix through which to understand all of German Jewish experience, it became the basis for much of her political thought—including thought that did not explicitly explore the Jewish condition. The dilemma of pariah identity would provide Arendt with much inspiration toward her mature theory of the political.[89] In the essay "The Jew as Pariah," written almost exactly between the initiation of the Varnhagen project and its publication, Arendt praised the pariah's consciousness of the political status of the Jewish people. Here she presented an imagined "hidden tradition" within Jewish history consisting of "self-conscious pariahs," from Heinrich Heine to Bernard Lazare to Charlie Chaplin and Franz Kafka. "In their own position as social outcasts," she wrote, "such men reflect the political status of their entire people."[90] But against such praise for self-consciousness, *Rahel Varnhagen* becomes a story of an inability to realize one's own political situation or locate, in disenfranchisement, a politically useful perspective; Varnhagen had never been able to understand pariah status in properly political, rather than purely internal or psychological, terms.

CHAPTER 8

From the Camps to Galileo

Rahel Varnhagen finally went to press in 1957, six years after Arendt had made her name with *The Origins of Totalitarianism*. That latter work culminated with a frightening vision of humanity stripped away under totalitarian rule, but much of it dealt with a trope Arendt also addressed in "The Jew as Pariah" and *Rahel Varnhagen*: the Jews, considered as a paradigmatic "pariah" group, responding to emerging forms of politics and public life during Europe's modernization. Curiously, many of the Jewish protagonists Arendt followed in *Origins* made errors that mirrored those of Rahel Levin, who had thought that her ability to overcome the "disability" of Jewish origin might carry over into the world beyond the salons. The moneylenders, court Jews and, later, bankers and political actors whom Arendt discussed in her book's first section, "Antisemitism," committed the error of focusing their energies on influencing elite circles of politicians. As a result, they missed the rise of mass politics all around them, the very medium in which anti-Semitism flourished. *Origins* culminated in a description of concentration camps in both Nazi Germany and Stalinist Russia, and it is perhaps for this description that the work is best known—but a large amount of the text was devoted to cases in which Jewish "parvenus" misunderstood the forms of mass political life that had left Europe vulnerable to totalitarian regimes.

By the time Arendt first assembled the manuscript of *Origins*, in 1945–46, the conditions of her life and work had changed many times. What she would later call a departure from "intellectual circles," as she put it in her 1964 interview on West German television, was the least of it. After being arrested by the Gestapo in 1933 and luckily released, she had fled to Paris, where as part of the Zionist organization Youth Aliyah she assisted in the transportation of Jewish children to Palestine. Captured and interned at a camp in Gurs in 1940, she managed to escape and cross the Spanish border with her husband Heinrich Blücher. The couple then made their way to New York, where Arendt studied English while writing articles for the German immigrant newspaper *Aufbau* and subsequently worked for the Conference on Jewish Relations and the Schocken publishing house. She continued to write and publish through this period, but aside from occasional work as a lecturer at Brooklyn College and the New School for Social Research, she was not primarily employed as an academic. *The Origins of Totalitarianism* was not written out of whole cloth. It included a great deal of previously published material written during a difficult period of itinerancy, and the final product included Arendt's 1948 *Partisan Review* article, "The Concentration Camps," one of her first efforts to deal with the awful revelation of the camps' existence. The disparate pieces of *Origins* thus reflect Arendt's travels both physical and intellectual, and the fact that the work places a great emphasis upon Jewish history and anti-Semitism reflects her engagements with Zionism and with Jewish cultural activism more broadly throughout the 1930s and 1940s.[1] She had become convinced that, as she said, "twentieth-century political developments have driven the Jewish people into the storm center of events," but her analysis would reach back much farther.[2]

Arendt's emphasis on Jews as political actors reveals the influence of Salo Wittmayer Baron, the influential Jewish historian who had rebelled against a consensus version of Jewish history dominant since the early nineteenth century, the *leidensgeschichte* (history of suffering) narrative. Arendt described this as "the belief that the Jewish people had always been the passive, suffering object of Christian persecutions."[3] Arendt's acquaintance with Baron, which became a life-long friendship, began in 1941 in New York when he encouraged her to write on the Dreyfus Affair for his journal *Jewish Social Studies*.[4] Baron was also among the founders, with Morris Raphael Cohen, Harold Laski, and Albert Einstein, of the Conference on Jewish Relations, which employed Arendt during her first years in New York City.[5] As Young-Bruehl points out, Arendt's research work for the Conference contributed directly to *Origins*.

Perhaps reflecting Baron's influence on her thought, in the "Antisemitism" section of *Origins* Arendt began by discussing the beginnings of emancipation in Western Europe, charting the economic role played by the Jewish bankers who facilitated the expansion of state bureaucracies. Echoing the chapters already written for the as yet unpublished *Rahel Varnhagen*, Arendt showed that the very structure of Jewish emancipation revealed the influence of "parvenu" Jews who had become "protected" prior to the passage of emancipation edicts, enjoying privileges that would only later be extended to the entire community.[6] Because of the importance of Jewish moneylending as a vector of political influence, Arendt devoted pages to Jewish economic history from the medieval period to the modern, from the Jews who functioned as moneylenders in medieval England and France up to Gerson von Bleichroeder's financial support for Bismarck's Prussian-Austrian war in 1866. Across the centuries, Arendt claimed, the tendency to think of politics as an affair of elites left Jews unable to understand the tensions between society and state emergent in the modern period. Even a prominent family like the Rothschilds, Arendt asserted, had shown little political acumen; her discussions of Jewish prominence were, in effect, a critique of the Jewish parvenu political actor.

The Dreyfus Affair served as the next crucial point in Arendt's history of anti-Semitism. While much of her discussion of the Affair concerned the social dimensions of the battle lines drawn between Dreyfusards and anti-Dreyfusards (for example, the importance of the military elites and Catholicism as hotbeds of anti-Semitism), the Dreyfus Affair naturally occasioned reflection on the role of the intellectual in politics. Arendt found few heroes among the Dreyfusards, although she did applaud Clemenceau for his view that it was a thinking person's task *not* to ascribe authority to the mob. He was able to hold as a bulwark the "old time Jacobin" abstract ideas of "justice, liberty and civic virtue," and Arendt was careful to note that men like Clemenceau and Zola had effectively crafted a novel model of public engagement.[7]

But the intellectuals were, for the Arendt of *Origins*, effectively a side issue. It was not by crystallizing *les intellectuels* as a social type, but rather by marking the rise of mob politics that the Dreyfus Affair provided, as Arendt put it, a "foregleam" of the twentieth century. If the term "intellectuals" was usually reserved for the Dreyfusards, who participated in a kind of politics of publication, these had their counterparts in the "strong men" who catered to the needs of the anti-Semitic mobs. It was unfortunate, Arendt said, that mob opinion was so often taken to be the voice of the people; this was partly the work of nationalists such as Maurice Barrès, Charles Maurras, and Léon Daudet, who claimed as much in their writings.[8] Born of exclusion from political representation, mobs were a temporary gathering of people from all strata of a society that (they felt) no longer heard them. The statements made by figures like Zola often acted as catalysts for mob violence (the stoning of Zola's windows, sometimes even the bombing of cafes where Dreyfusards

were known to congregate) and Arendt naturally recognized that such violence was not itself new. She identified a new style of organization and a
fixation on fiery leaders skilled at oration, as the novel qualities of the mob.
While Arendt did not say so explicitly, the mob and the Dreyfusards (as she
presented them) both imagined political life to be conducted outside of par-
liamentary settings. The mob sought to take politics into their own hands
while the Dreyfusards appealed to the "tribunal" of public opinion in hopes
that it might influence real tribunals.[9] Tellingly, when it came to the mob
Arendt was willing to indulge in what she usually saw as a methodological
crime in the writing of history—foreshadowing. As she put it in a 1942 lecture at Brooklyn College, "it is relatively easy today to recognize in the Dreyfus Affair the deadly disease of the Vichy Government."[10] The Affair had
done more than merely show that "in every Jewish nobleman and multimil-
lionaire there still remained something of the old-time pariah." It had hinted
at the subsequent shift, forced upon Jews across Europe, from pariahdom to
full dehumanization.[11]

The book's next section, "Imperialism," seemed to depart from Jewish history, but Arendt continued to place Jews at the storm center of events, observing the "boomerang" effects of imperialist expansion on Jewish-Gentile
relations back in Europe. The rise of a new form of imperialism in the nineteenth century had, in Arendt's view, made the wealth of latter-day Jewish
moneylenders (at this point, bankers) obsolete as a means of supporting the
growth of European states, and imperialism on the ascent made the international connections of latter-day "court Jews" (Jewish civil servants, now) less
relevant as well. The connections between prominent "parvenu" Jews and
European governance thus faded at the very moment in the late nineteenth
century when anti-Semitism began to become a political force, fueled by "in-
novations" in race science and by the increasing importance of the mob as a
form of social organization. Imperialism itself stemmed, in Arendt's view,
from the application of "bourgeois logic" to the international stage, "born
when the ruling class in capitalist production came up against national limitations to its economic expansion."[12]

Rich in detail, the Imperialism section focused on developments such as
"the scramble for Africa" of the 1880s, the development of "race thinking before racism" in South Africa, and the economic life of the Boer communities
there, and most especially the close relationship between imperialism and
capitalism, particularly the promotion of imperialist policies by a bourgeoisie just beginning to acquire political influence. Arendt saw imperialism as

having "politically emancipated" the bourgeoisie both abroad and at home.[13] This was because the same basically bourgeois values that drove imperialism were gradually brought from the "periphery" of empire back to its center, where the essentially private logic of capitalism became the only principle recognized in the public political sphere. What resulted, Arendt suggested (anticipating her later discussion, in *The Human Condition*, of the destruction of public and private life by "the social"), was a "leveling" that eliminated the difference between public and private. The value of an individual in the public sphere came to equal their economic worth, even as public life itself only became important as the sum of private interests.

Arendt rejoined her earlier critique of mob politics in the "Imperialism" section as well, claiming that an "alliance between capital and mob is to be found at the genesis of every consistently imperialist policy."[14] The mob was a natural outgrowth of bourgeois society, "never quite separable from it."[15] As Arendt had tried to demonstrate in "Antisemitism," mobs were the natural byproducts of late nineteenth-century political changes in that had left some represented and others unrepresented in the respective political theaters of France, Germany, and Great Britain. Indeed, for Arendt the politics of the mobs and of bourgeois society were intimately linked. Both groups seemed nihilistically to pursue politics without recourse to "higher principles" (such as the Jacobinism for which she had praised Clemenceau). In both bourgeois society and in mob behavior Arendt detected—and here she anticipated the larger claims of *The Human Condition*—the elimination of all that was truly political and public, beginning with the social spaces in which people might form purposeful and genuine relationships. It was on this basis that Arendt could claim that the mob's organization

> inevitably [took] the form of transformation of nations into races, for there is, under the conditions of an accumulating society, no other unifying bond available between individuals who in the very process of power accumulation and expansion are losing all natural connections with their fellow-men.[16]

The concept of race itself became attractive as a way to feign a connectedness that men could no longer experience through the bonds of true political life. Racial chauvinism was a sign of political incapacity.

The story of lost public space Arendt had begun to tell through her accounts of anti-Semitism and imperialism came together in the work's third section, "Totalitarianism." She described that phenomenon succinctly in an essay published after *Origins*, "Ideology and Terror," and later included as an epilogue in the 1958 edition of *Origins*: "By pressing men against each other total terror destroys the space between them; compared to the condition within its iron band, even the desert of tyranny, insofar as it is some kind of space, appears like a guarantee of freedom."[17]

Arendt devoted the third section of her book to chronicling the absence of a viable public in Nazi Germany or the Soviet Union under Stalin.[18] It was by examining the "mass," and its constituent unit, the "mass man," that Arendt would explain how an essentially unpolitical society might come about.[19] While the masses predated the rise of the Soviet Union and Nazi Germany, they served as a crucial precondition for their styles of rule.

Arendt defined the "mass" by describing the qualities it lacked. Masses developed when people "either because of sheer numbers, or indifference, or a combination of both, cannot be integrated into any organization based on common interest, into political parties or municipal governments or professional organizations or trade unions."[20] Most essentially, they were made up of individuals who have grown incapable of finding "common interest" with one another. The members of an older form of congregation, the mob, came from all levels of class society and could return to their former positions when the mob dissolved. In contrast, mass man could only come about once class identity, the only thing that kept him from losing himself in loneliness, had lost its meaning: "The chief characteristic of the mass man is not brutality and backwardness but his isolation and lack of normal social relationships."[21] Prior to the spacelessness of totalitarianism, present in its most extreme form in the concentration camps but not limited to them, was a process through which governments capitalized on the existence of men incapable of making use of political space.

While the prior account of *Origins* has emphasized the fragility Arendt saw in modern European variations of public life, it is also important to see the book as an intervention in an ongoing conversation regarding the nature of "totalitarianism," a term that had been used in English since 1929 to explain both Nazism and Stalinism, and which found far more widespread usage from the early 1940s onward. By the time Arendt began to write on the subject, a truly formidable array of writers, including Hans Kohn, Sigmund Neumann, Raymond Aron, Herbert Marcuse, Max Horkheimer, Friedrich Pollock, and of course Franz Neumann, in his influential 1942 *Behemoth,* had considered its valences. While many of these authors emphasized the growing parallels between Nazi Germany and Stalin's Soviet Union—and some had ideological reasons to apply it only to the Soviets—some also noted convergences between the Italian and German economies.[22] The deep insight Arendt's work shared with those of earlier authors was, simply put, that totalitarianism was a novel product of modernity, a sign of civilizational breakdown from within. Her own great contribution was not a total reformulation of "totalitarianism" as a term, but, first, the idea that its rise was connected to a gradual failure of public political life in Europe, and second, the view that even as totalitarianism closed off the space where freedom might be expressed, it opened a window onto the malleable nature of the human condition itself. The camps had illustrated the potential truth of nihilism and the need to work out the material conditions under which human life was more than animal. Arendt would attempt this in her next major work, *The Human Condition*, a work that was as much a critique of modernity as *Origins* and targeted the tradition of European political thought and its anthropocentrism as sources—but not direct causes—of the nihilism witnessed in the camps and at every level of life under totalitarian rule.

The Road to *The Human Condition*

Keenly aware of how far she had moved from her philosophical training, Arendt would remark to Jaspers that in *Origins* she had taken the "low road" to understanding the crises of modernity, rather than the "high road." She had identified social and political causes for the initial fragility and eventual decline of public life, rather than rips and tears or shoddy crafting in the fabric of what she would soon call "the great tradition." Arendt would take the latter approach in a series of meditations of the early 1950s, which began in an attempt to work through elements in Marx left unconsidered in her 1951 work. As Young-Bruehl notes, drawing from a grant proposal Arendt submitted to the Guggenheim Foundation in 1952, Arendt thought that she had successfully mapped all the elements "which eventually crystallize into the totalitarian forms of movements and governments," including "racism and imperialism, the tribal nationalism of the pan-movements and anti-Semitism," all of which were disconnected from "the great political and philosophical traditions of the West."[23] She had not dealt with those traditions directly, save by noting that their guardians (mainly, philosophers) had not examined the radical evil rampant under totalitarianism. In Arendt's view, totalitarianism was made possible not by an ideology of control well-ing up from the Platonic prejudices of philosophers (as Karl Popper had argued in his 1945 *The Open Society and Its Enemies*), but rather by the breakdown of the traditional social and political institutions of modern Europe. As Arendt noted in her 1952 grant proposal, she had purposely left out an adequate account of "the ideological background of Bolshevism," and she was seeking funding to support further research.

Arendt omitted Bolshevism because she understood Marxism to be a problem for the political and social (rather than intellectual) history of to-talitarianism she had offered, potentially overturning her implicit claim that totalitarianism did not well up from deep currents in philosophy. Willing to reconsider her methodological commitment, she recognized that Marxism was an outgrowth of the Western philosophical tradition, and proposed a sophisticated study of Marx's writings, as well as of pre-Soviet European Marxism and socialism and the Lenin and Stalin periods in the Soviet Union.[24] Arendt unsurprisingly never finished this project, which would have been truly overwhelming. Her narrower starting project, treating Bolshevism as a movement unto itself, gave way to the examination not only of Marx's treatment of labor and work (this would form the crux of the criticism of Marx offered in *The Human Condition*), but of European political theory and philosophy much more broadly. It was in the 1950s that Arendt effec-tively remade herself as a political theorist, with a speed made possible not only by her obvious gifts, but also by her growing reputation as a writer and scholar. She was able to present work at Princeton, invited to publish in *Partisan Review*, and to give a talk titled "Concern with Politics in Recent European Philosophical Thought" at the American Political Science Association 1954 conference. All this occurred before Arendt took her very first full-time teaching position in 1955, at Berkeley, where she lectured on political philosophy, and before she received an invitation to deliver the 1956 Walgreen Foundation Lectures at the University of Chicago, lectures on which *The Human Condition* would be based. But the Marxism project led to two other studies as well, *Between Past and Future*, which contains Arendt's treat-ment of the "great tradition," and *On Revolution*. Notably, the same year she wrote to the Guggenheim Foundation for funding, she took a trip to Europe, and her 1954 American Political Science Association talk would be influenced by her fresh exposure to the personalities of the Hegelian intellec-tual circles of postwar Paris, themselves engaged in experiments concerning the ideal relationship between thought and action.

Arendt had first written on the French existentialists in 1946, in a brief essay for *The Nation* that was more colorful than penetrating. There she captured the public excitement that surrounded existentialism as a cultural as well as philosophical movement, emphasizing the way individual writers moved readily between journalistic, literary, and philosophical production: "They are not members of university faculties but 'bohemians' who stay at hotels and live in the café—leading a public life to the point of renouncing privacy."[25] This was publicness as rebellion against the complacency Arendt attributed to the intellectuals of interwar France. Arendt named Sartre and Camus as the chief exponents of the new philosophy, naturally enough, and she attributed to their version of existentialism a rejection of *l'esprit de sérieux,* or the conservative view that life's dignity and meaning derives from a person's social station. She also found, by comparing Sartre's play *Huis clos* and Camus's novel *L'étranger,* a common denial of "the possibility of a genuine fellowship between men," a pessimistic outlook that was of a piece with the existentialists' portrayal of life as a succession of personal choices one makes and then abandons, as though playing a series of varying games. This was French existentialism as the rebellious, unserious attitude of angry young men, performing their solitude in public, a somewhat amusing phenomenon Levinas had also noted, in his response to Sartre.[26]

More biting than Arendt's account of solitude in Sartre and Camus was her closing reflection on the "modernity" of their thought. Having smiled on their revolt against *l'esprit de sérieux,* she turned to the vestiges of philosophy's "old concepts" that clung to the existentialists, vestiges Arendt called "nihilistic."[27] She did not qualify or explain her judgment, however, but referred to Sartre's 1945 public lecture, "L'existentialisme est un humanisme," in which the master-thinker of postwar Paris had been at pains to defend his philosophy against charges of nihilism.[28] Arendt seemed to imply that Sartre had failed to mount a successful defense. Nihilism and the failure to respond to it were not necessarily offensive to her on their own terms, but rather because of the heights of human self-assertion to which they could lead, and the predicaments that followed from those heights.

A few years later, Arendt dug deeper in her "Was ist existenz-philosophie?," a survey of figures ranging from Kant to Jaspers, whom she considered indispensable for understanding existentialism.[29] Existentialisms of every stripe, she suggested, responded to the separation between thought and Being that had been announced by Kant's distinction between noumenal and phenomenal realms. In fact, for her all modern philosophy, and perhaps paradigmatically Hegel, responded to that separation, often by attempting to "re-establish the unity of thought and Being." Materialist philosophies such as Marxism did so by explaining mind as a reflex of matter; in contrast, idealist philosophies explained matter in terms of mind. Most existentialist philosophies followed neither course, taking seriously the impossibility of unifying thought and Being and contemplating the resulting sense of homelessness that afflicts us on this earth. While Husserl might have attempted to establish a new form of humanism by building his phenomenology on the human representation of the surrounding environment, "conjur[ing] up a new home from a world perceived as alien,"[30] his humanism presented one of the unproductive paths down which existentialism would later lead, namely that of hubristic anthropocentrism. Perhaps unsurprisingly, Arendt used Heidegger to illustrate the other unproductive path: by interpreting *Dasein* as intelligible only in terms of temporality and thus mortality, Heidegger yielded the same nihilism Arendt saw in the voices of postwar Paris. In contrast to the humanism of Kant, Arendt said, which made of every individual a representative of humanity via the categorical imperative, Heideggerian existentialism made the predicament of the self into a replacement for being human.[31] Jaspers served Arendt, in this essay, as a hero and as an implicit antidote to Heidegger. Emphasizing the parallels between Socrates' maieutic method and Jaspers's philosophy of communication, she noted that like Socrates, Jaspers rejected the idea that philosophers deserved special prerogatives. He situated philosophizing not in some artificial, otherworldly space, but in the state of communication with other persons.

While Arendt did not say so directly, she seemed to make a weighty claim on Jaspers's behalf, namely that the philosophy of communication was a route out of the problem of nihilism that other existentialist philosophies encountered.

In her aforementioned 1954 "Concern with Politics in Recent European Philosophical Thought," Arendt extended these reflections on existentialism (and on its usual attendant, nihilism) while connecting them to an emergent criticism of the historical "great tradition" and the character of political thought within it; in fact, her reflections on that tradition were startlingly similar to those of Strauss. "Concern with politics," she began,

> is not a matter of course for the philosopher. What we political scientists tend to overlook is that most political philosophies have their

origins in the philosopher's negative and sometimes even hostile attitude toward the *polis* and the whole realm of human affairs. Historically, those centuries prove to be richest in political philosophies
which were least propitious for philosophizing, so that self-protection
as well as outright defense of professional interests have more often
than not prompted the philosopher's concern with politics. The event
which started our tradition of political thought was the trial and
death of Socrates, the condemnation of the philosopher by the *polis*.[32]

Aside from the very important distinction of rooting antipathy in philosophers rather than in the polis itself, Arendt's picture of the history of political philosophy resembled that of Strauss's "Persecution and the Art of
Writing," down to the portrayal of political philosophy as a subfield made
necessary by the fundamental difference between philosophers and other
members of the polis.

Contemporary political thought within philosophy was radically different. If Hegel's historicism "[had] given the realm of human affairs a dignity
it never enjoyed in philosophy before,"[33] inviting many in the nineteenth
century to march under historicism's banner, Arendt suggested that in the
twentieth century political events themselves served as provocations to philosophical reflection, making possible a "new science of politics," as she put
it, borrowing the title of a recent work by the political philosopher Eric
Voegelin.[34] Those events also brought an end to a faith in "wise men." For
those whose youth had been shaped by the memory of the Great War,
Hegel's thought provided some preparation for the shock of history, even
making events into "the tangible reality" of theoretical predicaments,[35] but
Hegel's philosophy of history held both danger and opportunity.

Heidegger's work stood as a case in point. In Arendt's view he had effectively extended Hegelianism into the twentieth century through his concept
of "historicity," and this despite his own criticisms of Hegel. Crucially, Heidegger's "historicity" could be differentiated from other versions of historicism in that it understood history *not* in "anthropological" terms (that is, ones
dealing with the level of the human experience), but rather in the inhuman
terms of ontology. The consequences of Heidegger's historicism for his relation to politics were complex, but Arendt observed one positive outcome. To
abandon any claim to wisdom meant turning back to the "classical and persistent problems of political philosophy."[36] As she said,

The abandonment of the position of "wise man" by the philosopher himself is politically the most important and the most fruitful result of the new philosophical concern with politics. The rejection of the claim to wisdom opens the way to a re-examination of the whole realm of politics in the light of elementary human experiences within this realm itself.[37]

Arendt only understood this positive turn as a consequence *following from* Heidegger's historicism. She reiterated a claim she had made earlier. Heidegger himself manifested the "old hostility of the philosopher towards the *polis*," and understood public opinion and the public realm to hide reality and obscure the truth: *Das Licht der Öffentlichkeit verdunkelt Alles.* By viewing the world through the lens of a de-anthropologizing version of historicity, Heidegger lost sight of "the center of politics—man as an acting being."[38] At the same time, Arendt criticized Heidegger's historicity (in another curiously Straussian moment) for leading to a "forgetting" of the more philosophical questions of political science: "What is politics? Who is man as a political being? What is freedom?"[39] These were questions that emphasized man's volitional nature or agency, which in Arendt's view Heidegger had totally ignored.

Arendt then surveyed the response to nihilism by contemporary Catholic philosophers such as Étienne Gilson, Jacques Maritain, Josef Pieper, and other defenders of the principle of "tradition"—all of which, for Arendt, could be summed up as the revival of Platonism, as though for her Christianity truly were "Platonism for the masses." Against chaos in both the political and intellectual realms, and against the nexus of historicism and nihilism, such traditionalists reached for the eternal. Ironically, the recovery of tradition on the parts of both Catholics and Platonists was facilitated by precisely those intellectual turns that they themselves despised: historicisms such as that of Friedrich Meinecke, as well as Heidegger's insistence on reading "old texts with new eyes" through the technique of *Destruktion*. What Arendt regretted about the return to tradition was, predictably, its blindness toward the contemporary world and its tendency to view contemporary political crises and atrocities solely in philosophical terms. In *structural* terms, this mistake was identical to Heidegger's: the traditionalists and Heidegger both abandoned the "anthropological" or human scale in pursuit of Being or the Eternal, and in so doing they lost sight of human agency. Not only that, by suggesting that a return to religion from secularism might "cure" the world, they ignored the real dimensions of political wrongdoing.

Opposite the Catholics and their laudable if flawed attempt to revive classical questions, stood the French existentialists. Arendt here repeated some of her observations of 1946 regarding existentialism's publicness, while criticizing that stance more harshly than she had previously. In 1954 the vogue for activism was a "retreat" *into* history and effectively away from political philosophy in its most traditional forms. In keeping with her anti-Hegelianism, Arendt was especially hard on Sartre's and Merleau-Ponty's commitment to historical systems, and somewhat easier on Camus's and Malraux's commitment to pure rebellion detached from any grand plot for world politics. Even the latter authors, however, still seemed to her to fall within the ambit of nihilism.

Tellingly, Arendt seemed to accept Sartre's claim that "existentialism is a humanism," which she had mentioned without much comment in 1946. But if humanism lacked a transcendental morality that kept it from lending dignity to human artifice itself, it would decline into mere anthropocentrism, often with a utopian tinge. Arendt would engage in very similar reflections in the introductory passages of *The Human Condition*, where she would consider the inner nihilism in technocracy; here she linked humanism and nihilism directly. Interestingly, Arendt was able to exonerate Jaspers from participating in this linked humanism-nihilism, precisely because of (and not despite) his status as a "convinced disciple of Kant." This was a subtle point given that Kant, too, was humanist in his orientation, and also implicated as a cause of the very predicament of modern philosophy, that split between *noumena* and *phenomena* that led many thinkers to nihilistic conclusions. As she had done in 1948, Arendt pointed to Jaspers's philosophy of communication as outside the common predicament of existentialism because it understood all truth to be situated within communicative exchanges. Jaspers (preoccupied with Kant's "political" question "What ought I to do?") identified communication as a key to such considerations of "doing" on the world stage, in a further agreement with Kant's vision of a truly "cosmopolitan" perspective. Reason, in Jaspers's philosophy, brought men together in conversations about practical matters, and the question of what counts as reason is effectively answered by the practical nature of the matters at hand. However, this was very different from any conviction that public discourse itself was somehow reasonable. As Arendt noted, "it seems rather obvious that 'communication'—the term as well as the underlying experience—has its roots not in the public political sphere, but in the personal encounter of I and Thou."[40] And she went on, arguing that for Jaspers "this relationship of pure dialogue is closer to the original experience of thinking—the dialogue of one with oneself in solitude—than to any other."[41] However, Arendt also concluded that Jaspers's philosophy of communication, based as it was on the experience of thinking rather than on the experience of public life, had not dealt with politics in a satisfactory manner. Arendt closed her address by saying that any new political philosophy would have to ask about the fundamental relationship between thought and politics, given humanity's basic social nature and, thus, the fundamentally social character of thought. It would only be toward the end of her career, however, in *The Life of the Mind*, that she would complete the arc of her reflections on the philosophy of communication, relating communication not to solitary thought but to thought reimagined as always already political.

The Human Condition

The book Arendt published in 1958, after years of meditation on Marx, the "great tradition," and postwar existentialist experiments with activism and politics, was no simple companion to *Origins*, but a work of political theory in its own right. *The Human Condition* would become the *locus classicus* for some of Arendt's most celebrated and controversial views, especially her endorsement of a model of public political life characterized by "action," the highest element in a tripartite *vita activa* that also included "labor" and "work." It was also in this book that Arendt's earlier ambivalence about the role of philosophers in the public realm became a full-blown critique. It was here that she first referred to the "parting of ways" about which she would indicate regret a few years later, in 1963's *On Revolution*. In *The Human Condition*, however, Arendt practically celebrated the split. Identifying wholeheartedly with actors rather than thinkers, she described a historical conflict between the *vita activa* and the *vita contemplativa* generated by "our tradition of political thought." This tradition, Arendt said, "grew out of a specific historical constellation: the trial of Socrates and the conflict between the philosopher and the *polis*."[42] Socrates had been the only one of the "great thinkers" of Greece so involved with thoughts of eternity that he never wrote his thoughts down for human posterity; thus his case could offer the greatest possible contrast between an emphasis on philosophy and one on politics.

Much like Arendt's earlier works, *The Human Condition* had a triadic structure. However, whereas *Love and Saint Augustine* and *Origins* were built with three sections each, *The Human Condition* transposed the triadic onto the level of theory through its central division of the *vita activa* into labor, work, and action. As Margaret Canovan points out, Arendt's analyses of these realms of life was phenomenological rather than empirical or logical, and displayed a Heideggerian character.[43] By labor, Arendt meant all activities that correspond to our physical needs, to the biological dimension of our lives most generally. Work, on the other hand, corresponded to the construction of an artificial world or "second nature" of artifacts (practical or aesthetic), which last longer than their makers and thus provide a dimension of intergenerational continuity. Action is distinguished from labor and work by the fact that it only "produces" human relationships, and that its medium is not grain or wood or metal, but simply speech. Action is the means through which we manage the plural condition of social life, the means by which we coordinate labor and work, but its political purposes are in Arendt's view nobler than natural or cultural ones.

One final characteristic of "work" held enormous importance for Arendt's analysis. At least in his utilitarian (as opposed to art-making) guise, the worker, "*homo faber*," is capable of building a world, but incapable of raising it to signification. In other words, the utilitarian mindset that drives forward the building of the world can also keep life in that world from acquiring any lasting meaning. As Arendt said, "This perplexity, inherent in all consistent utilitarianism, the philosophy of *homo faber* par excellence, can be diagnosed theoretically as an innate incapacity to understand the distinction between utility and meaningfulness, which we express linguistically by distinguishing between 'in order to' and 'for the sake of.'"[44] The only kind of world in which mere building can become a meaningful act is an entirely anthropocentric world, where "man" becomes an end in himself. It was the Greeks, Arendt's champions of political action, who rejected anthropocentricity by positing transcendental standards of value and denying the highest honors to mere craftspeople. Thus, action was preferable to work precisely because it recalled the possibility of a standard higher than man himself. There was, of course, an additional danger in the ideology of *homo faber*, the possibility of viewing political life as if it were malleable, plastic, and subject to design in the same sense as art or architecture. Simply put, this was the error of fascism.

But *The Human Condition* was not simply a study of what an optimal public might look like, but of the public's potential failures under the conditions of modernity. *The Human Condition* extended *Origins's* critiques of mob and mass behavior—themselves made possible through failures of publicness—by exploring a third version of collective life, "the social." The "mob" and the "mass," terms respectively associated with bourgeois and totalitarian society, displayed elements that would receive greater definition in "the social." As Hanna Pitkin points out, this term has an inherent quality of strangeness because of its hypostatization of the conventional term "society,"[45] and Arendt's choice of words should recall Heidegger's interest in the use of etymology as a tool for *Destruktion*. As Arendt said, for her, words were always "something like a frozen thought that thinking must unfreeze."[46] Arendt understood "the social" to explain the underlying logic by which society functioned, a logic obscured by conventional uses of the term "society." Notably, in the 1960s Arendt would praise the student movement, as instantiated by the Free Speech Movement at the University of California, Berkeley, as a positive sign that contemporary students understood how to engage in political behavior without falling prey to mob behavior, congregating rather than merely becoming an aggregate group.[47]

It was in *Rahel Varnhagen* that Arendt had first explored a conformist variant of "society," the conventional "high society" world that Rahel Levin struggled to join. However, at least as important as this "conformist" version of the social was an economic version, which had grown so dominant in Arendt's thinking by the time of *The Human Condition* that Pitkin can with justice say that *The Human Condition's* "the social" was "economics gone public."[48] For those living within "the social," all daily decisions had to be made from the standpoint of the preservation of the "animal" side of man. Borrowing Marx's definition of labor as "man's metabolism with nature," Arendt observed that men labored in order to live and to support their progeny.[49] Arendt was explicitly *not* claiming that it was somehow ignoble to make decisions motivated by the need to survive. Instead she was suggesting that when daily life becomes nothing more than the maintenance of life processes it ceases to be fully human.[50] Here it was not only Marx's division between the natural and agentive aspects of human life that guided Arendt's thought, but a distinction that Kant once struck between nature, understood as a network of causes and effects, and the world of human action and moral responsibility.[51] While Arendt's demotion of economic thinking often seems harsh and, to her critics, even elitist, it is important to bear in mind that it was not the end of economic thinking—the maintenance of life itself—but rather the means, simple calculation, that bothered her. She was concerned that this type of thought easily degenerated into mere behavior, to be distinguished from true action.

If "the social" was the opposite of "the political," the latter was characterized by actions that were the opposite of mere "behavior" and that always tended to disclose the personhood of the acting individual: "The public realm itself, the *polis*, was permeated by a fiercely agonal spirit, where everybody had constantly to distinguish himself from all others, to show through unique deeds or achievements that he was the best of all."[52] A basic state of "plurality" was a necessary condition for the practice of politics. It was, of course, the very distinctiveness of our individual goals and needs that made political communication necessary. At the same time, for Arendt living within "plurality" carried with it the further requirement of respecting the equality of one's neighbors.[53]

Thus true political action required the public: it could not be bureaucratic, nor could it be anonymous. The "public" Arendt had in mind was modeled on the theatrical political spaces of ancient Greece, in which one agonistically competed for glory and in which one's deeds were known not only by a few peers, but by many.[54] This "public" can be differentiated from a "mass media" version of the public sphere in which celebrities become famous, but where their true personalities are never disclosed and their actions become almost interchangeable. Nor did Arendt have in mind the small, geographically scattered but interested and intimate reading public of the "republic of letters."

Most forms of intellectual production fell outside the narrow definition Arendt set for political "action." In her Prologue, Arendt targeted the efforts of scientists (who were arguably engaged in a species of "work") to transform the human condition through technical feats. She imagined these scientists hoping, variously, for space travel, the extension of the human life span, and the creation of artificial intelligences. All were commonplace fantasies in science fiction magazines during the 1950s. No luddite herself, Arendt objected not so much to the desire to improve "man's estate," but to what she saw as the unpolitical attitude permeating contemporary scientific discourse: "For the sciences today have been forced to adopt a 'language' of mathematical symbols which, though it was originally meant only as an abbreviation for spoken statements, now contains statements that in no way can be translated back into speech."[55] This statement did not refer only to the development of "machine languages" for computing, languages that were just beginning to enter the popular imagination at the time of Arendt's writing, but

also to the absolute difference between the kind of thinking Arendt characterized as "technical," and the type she considered political.[56] Scientists,
she said, "move in a world where speech has lost its power."[57] In fact, for
Arendt, the growing importance of technical expertise represented the in-
cursion of the *oikos,* or at least of the economic logic that sprang from it,
into the political realm. Technocracy was not politics.

Arendt's critique of "experts" and their technologies, as many have observed, drew her close not only to Heidegger's critique of technological modernity, but to those of the Frankfurt School as well. But this was only part
of the broader critique of intellectual life she offered in *The Human Condition.*
However lofty their interests, intellectuals were vulnerable to the pull of the
logic of "the social," as Arendt described in the course of reflections on Adam
Smith that deserve to be reproduced in full:

> What the modern age thought of the public realm, after the spectac-
> ular rise of society to public prominence, was expressed by Adam
> Smith when, with disarming sincerity, he mentioned "that unprosper-
> ous race of men commonly called men of letters" for whom "public
> admiration . . . makes always a part of their reward . . . a considerable
> part . . . in the profession of physic; a still greater perhaps in that of
> law; in poetry and philosophy it makes almost the whole." Here it is
> self-evident that public admiration and monetary reward are of the
> same nature and can become substitutes for each other. Public admi-
> ration, too, is something to be used and consumed, and status, as we
> would say today, fulfils one need as food fulfils another: public ad-
> miration is consumed by individual vanity as food is consumed by
> hunger.[58]

What is of interest here is not only Arendt's selected quotation from Smith
(though it does demonstrate her consciousness of the social category of the
"intellectual"), but also the fact that she cited Smith's examination of the need
for fame on the parts of three different classes of "intellectuals" without then
commenting on it, save for her general reflection that one may speak of an
"economy" of admiration and compare it with money. Such must count
as an endorsement of Smith's view. The public realm is no longer viewed,
whether by scientists, lawyers, philosophers, or poets, as a space in which
one's work (and thus one's name) can be rendered glorious and immortal, but
rather as a market in which to merely accumulate capital. Intellectuals in the

modern world had, in Arendt's view, begun to betray the higher purposes to which the public realm was once put.

This mistranslation of "fame"—so that it became a form of currency rather than the politically relevant "reputation"—in no way derived from the inner nature of the life of the mind. It stemmed from the decay of a properly political attitude toward public life. However, throughout *The Human Condition* Arendt made it clear that she saw in all philosophers a refusal to take public life on its own terms. As in her 1954 lecture, Arendt aimed at Plato. From his perspective, and from Aristotle's, the *vita activa* could only seem to be an interruption of the philosopher's tranquility.[59] If it enjoyed any dignity whatsoever it was of the second degree: if tamed and kept from becoming disruptive, those citizens engaged in the *vita activa* might care for the needs of the bodies of philosophers, so that philosophical minds might be allowed to function undisturbed.[60]

Arendt's picture of Plato's and Aristotle's philosophical projects was a horribly cramped one. She felt no need to mention the distinctions between Platonism and Aristotelianism, and she emphasized not Plato's and Aristotle's search for knowledge and truth but rather contemplation's tendency to cut philosophers off from others. She cited Plato's statement in the *Theaetetus*, "For wonder is what the philosopher endures most; for there is no other beginning of philosophy than this," and interpreted it to mean that the Greek term *thaumazein* or, "the shocked wonder at the miracle of Being," represented the starting-point of all philosophy.[61] Tellingly Arendt emphasized the fact that the sense of wonder emphasized in Greek thought had been taken to be "untranslatable" into words, a state of affairs that rendered philosophers "speechless." The muteness of *thaumazein*, however, had political consequences. With the act of philosophizing itself deprived of any political effects by its "speechlessness," it was easy for the utilitarian priorities of *homo faber* to eventually assume control of intellectual life.

If philosophy had been tyrannical and thus opposed to "politics" since its origins in Greece, in the modern age it became antipolitical in a different but equally problematic way. Chiefly through the efforts of Descartes, philosophers began to take doubt, rather than wonder, as the point of departure for their philosophizing, going far beyond the "zetetic" skepticism familiar to Greek philosophers.[62] Descartes's injunction to begin philosophizing by withdrawing one's senses from the world had been inspired (so ran Arendt's shakily composed historical claim) by the invention of the telescope and Galileo's discoveries therewith, which challenged the "truths" that un-augmented human senses had previously supplied.[63] Descartes believed that he could be certain of his own existence only through introspection, and while Arendt noted a logical error in his formula *cogito ergo sum*,[64] she also held that Descartes's historical importance resided not in the Cartesian subject's certainty of its own being, but rather in the all-encompassing tendency of Cartesian consciousness more broadly considered.[65] For Descartes, sense-evidence was inadequate to ascertain the reality of any object in the world. It was thus necessary to "submerge all worldly objects into the stream of consciousness," and thus consciousness itself took on an importance that was greater than the outside world.[66] This was of course not "tyrannical" except perhaps in the figurative sense that it reflected, on the level of epistemology, a need for self-mastery. But the Cartesian retreat from the world of sensual appearances had deeply negative consequences for philosophy's relationship with the political world. This was not least because modern technology gave philosophers, like scientists, the dream of replicating, in the outside world, their subjective fantasies of a perfected environment for mankind: Cartesianism thus led to the utilitarian dreaming of *homo faber* as one of its natural consequences even as it allowed philosophy to fall below "the bar" of political reflection. Arendt was expansive—to put it mildly—in naming the lines of philosophical inquiry that suffered from this turn in Cartesianism. As she said, a "congruity" between what she termed "world alienation" could be seen in, variously, "English sensualism, empiricism, and pragmatism, as well as German idealism and materialism up to the recent phenomenological existentialism and logical or epistemological positivism."[67] Not all philosophers may have become "Platonists," but all seemed to have become Descartes's grandchildren. Of course, the Cartesian emphasis on consciousness merely re-created, on a new and more anthropocentric level, the old politically speechless experience of *thaumazein*. One remarkable dimension of the last phase of Arendt's career—as the next chapter will make clear—is that she revisited philosophy's starting points (including "shocked wonder at the miracle of Being") not in the spirit of castigation, not merely to deepen her earlier critiques, but to gain a new appreciation of the intimate relationship between the life of the mind and the lives of humans as social beings.

CHAPTER 9

One More Strange Island

In what would turn out to be the final phase of her career, Arendt focused her teaching and writing on philosophy, as if reflection on political themes had carried her over strange territories and back to the material of her student days. Arendt's return followed on the heels of her most tumultuous public engagement in the wake of *Eichmann in Jerusalem*, and it coincided with her greatest fame. It is therefore notable that publicness, the problem of audience, and the predicament of address all loomed large in her final lectures. However, the account of the public she produced here was built not on historical fact, but instead on theoretical speculation regarding the way publicness, appearance, and the instinct for display inform intellectual production. This was precisely the kind of recourse to interiority and theory she often criticized. She speculated not on what it meant to write for a potentially unpredictable public (giving oneself to the public world and all its contingencies, as Arendt had once said in her *laudatio* to Jaspers), but rather on what it meant, for thinking, that it was a private activity but nevertheless regulated the congress between the interiority of the self and the exteriority of the world in which we find ourselves. Arendt's return to philosophical reflection furthermore took place at a time when many of her teachers and friends were reaching the ends of their lives. Jaspers died in 1969, and Arendt's husband Heinrich Blücher died a year later. It was thus appropriate that her lectures were marked by melancholy and by the question of how one understands the events of life as something *more* than, in the words of Arendt's friend Walter Benjamin, a "pile of debris" accumulating behind us as we look backward.[1]

As we will see, Arendt found tools, especially in the writings of Kant, with which to sort through the tension between judgments of past events of a grand scale—such as she had addressed in historical writings such as *Rahel*

Varnhagen and *The Origins of Totalitarianism*—and judgment in questions of personal morality, such as she had addressed in *Eichmann in Jerusalem*. While the task she took up was to rethink the *vita contemplativa* itself, it turned out that the scene of judgment could serve as a kind of laboratory in which to observe how the operations of one's own mind are bound up with the operations of other minds. The central document produced by this turn was *The Life of the Mind*, an exploration of basic mental faculties that is classically Arendtian in its evasion of labels. This project was neither intellectual history nor political theory nor existential phenomenology, but it displays features of each. When Arendt's executor Mary McCarthy received what would become *The Life of the Mind*, it was a collection of lecture notes Arendt had used between 1972 and 1974 in her Gifford Lectures at the University of Aberdeen, portions of which she had also used in teaching her graduate seminars at the New School. While Arendt only completed the first two sections of the project, corresponding to the faculties of "Thinking" and "Willing," she had made considerable headway into a treatment of the third faculty, "Judging," in a 1964 graduate seminar on Kant's *Critique of Judgment* taught at the New School. These were posthumously published as the *Lectures on Kant's Political Philosophy*.[2] If Arendt's earlier historical works were imbued with a feeling for the futility, even the absurdity, of human accomplishment, *The Life of the Mind* and the *Lectures on Kant's Political Philosophy*, were more optimistic—but they restricted our potential accomplishments to the balancing of the mental faculties themselves.

Elisabeth Young-Bruehl calls *The Origins of Totalitarianism* a kind of historian's Guernica, "a mural of the nineteenth and twentieth centuries that you can never finish taking in."[3] By contrast, the artwork to which *The Life of the Mind* might be most fruitfully compared is Book Thirteen of Homer's *Odyssey*, "One More Strange Island." This Book tells the story of Odysseus's homecoming to his own island kingdom of Ithaka, which he approached in disguise, knowing what danger awaited him from the suitors who sought his wife Penelope's hand in marriage, and who each day as unwelcome guests depleted his flocks and stores. Returning to well-known philosophical territory, Arendt took a fragment from Heidegger's "What Is Called Thinking" as the epigram with which to introduce the work's first section, "Thinking," and Augustine's *Quaestio mihi factus sum* ("I have become a question for myself") as the epigram for Part Two, "Willing," which bore the additional title "The Discovery of the Inner Man."[4] But like Odysseus in disguise, Arendt revisited old friends as if an outsider, asking unconventional questions that led some reviewers of her work to question its validity as philosophical inquiry (notably, Arendt never claimed it was such).[5]

Such questioning was appropriate enough. If Arendt had a central task it was to recover the activities of the mind from the philosophers who had enjoyed the privilege of defining them for so long, and to offer a new understanding of their worldly function. While she acknowledged the wisdom of the philosophers whose work she discussed, she maintained her opposition to the *vita contemplativa* much as she had in *The Human Condition*. "The thinking ego" was how she described the vantage point preferred by philosophers, which led philosophers to misunderstand the nature and function not only of thinking and willing, but of philosophy as a practice always conducted in social space. Rather than speculate about "thought-trains" we might ride in order to imagine a rapprochement between "professional thinkers" and actors, she tried to demonstrate that the basic faculties so admirably developed by professional thinkers had a place beyond the narrow range given by their *déformation professionnelle*. "Thinking," "Willing," and "Judging" were the possessions of all, and they began in the realm of appearances, the natural habitat of all.

Arendt began her examination of the faculties by encouraging her audience to attend to the "withdrawal" from the world that was one, initiatory, stage of the process of Thinking, and a part of Willing and Judging, as well. This moment of dwelling in one's thoughts for a time characterized both the (in all other ways opposite) activities of Thinking and Willing, as well as Judging; detachment, in other words, is essential for mental life. Philosophers were those who held the moment of withdrawal too long, seeking an existence outside the world through what Aristotle had termed the process of *athanatizein*, or "immortalization," and which Arendt understood to be akin to death, because it meant taking no part in the experiences of fellow mortals. In *The Human Condition* she had similarly remarked on philosophers seeking to live "outside the world."

Arendt did not share Heidegger's view that the central activities of philosophical *theoria* and *contemplatio* bear within them an impulse to know in a way that also destroys, "a looking-at that sunders and compartmentalizes."[6] True, her own picture of philosophers abandoning external stimuli for internal ones, comported well with Heidegger's charge that philosophy was concerned with control. But Arendt understood the necessity of withdrawal even if she also feared the escapism to which it might lead. Among other things, it was a foundational element of spectatorship, a practice she explored in greater depth in her lectures on Kant.[7] There was a common impulse toward order, she said, in both the spectator who observes historical events (which spectators can always know more fully than actors can) and the Greek philosopher who views the *kosmos* as an ordered and harmonious whole.[8]

In *The Human Condition* the task of the spectator was necessary if the deeds of actors were to be recorded and celebrated, securing "immortality" in the collective memory of the political community. Such an account of spectatorship naturally reflected the interests of those invested in the *vita activa*. In *The Life of the Mind* Arendt took a different approach by weaving spectatorship directly into the subject's experience of the world, attaching it to the primordial experience of publicness prior to the withdrawal from the world that initiated Thinking. At the very beginning of "Thinking," Arendt claimed "nothing and nobody exists in this world whose very being does not presuppose a spectator."[9] We experience ourselves as if we had no reality if unobserved, despite the absurdity of such a claim. As she put it in almost Heideggerian terms, "To be alive means to be possessed by an urge toward self-display which answers the fact of one's own appearingness. Living things make their appearance like actors on a stage set for them."[10]

Arendt did not delay herself with a discussion of Heidegger's treatment of "appearance" in *Being and Time*, where "appearance" described the way an object might send an "emissary" of itself through traces or outward signs without displaying itself fully.[11] Instead, in an early section titled "The thinking ego and the self: Kant," she labored over a plausible substitute she found more relevant to her own task at hand, namely Kant's *Ding-an-Sich*, the "thing in itself" that causes appearances without itself appearing. Kant's thing in itself, she noted, inherently prioritized a transcendent object over its mere representation. Arendt acknowledged that there was a sense in which nature bore Kant out: we can observe organisms that present us with core phenomena and processes that are distinct from, and produce, their appearances. But she sought to reverse Kant's prioritization, observing that for Kant the *Ding-an-Sich* was intelligible not from the standpoint of the phenomenal world but rather from that of the thinking ego.

Through this discussion of appearance, Arendt implied that philosophy is submerged in the very world of appearances it yearns to escape, and that philosophers have both an instinct toward self-display and a tendency to understand truth on the model of appearance. Similarly, in her lectures on Kant's political philosophy, Arendt cited Kant's view that "it is a natural vocation of mankind to communicate and speak one's mind, especially all matters concerning man as such."[12] Thinking is submerged in the world despite itself, and more consequentially in a world of other persons. Drawing on Merleau-Ponty's concept of "perceptual faith," Arendt suggested that we are dependent on a kind of mutual recognition in order to be certain that what we perceive has an existence beyond our perception.[13] In other words, to live in a world of appearances is to be primordially in debt to others both ontologically and epistemologically.

While this emphasis on the world of appearance would run through Arendt's entire study, it received its sharpest formulation in her reflections on the nature of spectatorship, present both in her book's first two sections and in the lectures on Kant, which would have become "Judging." Her discussion of Kant's account of spectatorship illuminated one of *The Life of the Minds's* otherwise implicit arguments, namely, that reflective mental practice, either within the individual or most especially in public life, was not limited to circles of professional thinkers. But the full meaning of Arendt's discussions of spectatorship will be clearer following a brief account of what Arendt meant by Thinking, Willing, and Judging. The activity of Thinking connoted the activities of consciousness more than it did grasping a knowable truth. In this Arendt drew upon Kant's distinction between *Verstand* (the faculty of understanding or knowing) and *Vernunft* (reasoning). Thinking, for her, was an activity without an outcome, an inquiry into the meaning both of objects in the world and objects in the mind. In this respect, it resembled the autotelic "action" of *The Human Condition*. Willing, on the other hand, was naturally a matter of freedom—and while Arendt allowed that philosophers or "professional thinkers" had properly understood certain aspects of Thinking, she began her discussion of Willing by stating the need to recover the concept from such persons entirely; many philosophers had simply insisted that the faculty of the will was an illusion. Behind many philosophers' approaches to will was a mistrust of freedom itself, over which they tended to prefer rule-governed and thus comprehensible necessity. But Willing was also, Arendt said, the mental organ used in anticipating the future. As such it was not concerned with immediate objects so much as with projects, and with the temporality of the future, which was far too unpredictable for most philosophers' comfort and had the additional drawback of being virtual, not yet real.[14] In contrast to future-oriented Willing, which can deal with political events and political change, Thinking works only on objects that are, or have been, known.

What Arendt meant by "Judging" must be redacted from the lectures on Kant's political philosophy she gave in her final graduate seminars at the New School, in the fall of 1970. Here she attempted to draw out the understanding of participation in politics she took Kant to have been working toward in the *Critique of Judgment*, although he had died before he could fully develop it. Kant had presented a philosophy of the aesthetic sense beginning with the phenomenon of taste and moving to the articulation of a *"sensus communis."* Arendt held that the same judgment that governs our relationship with art objects also governs our relationship with the political events we witness as part of a community of spectators. She began with aesthetics. It might seem that we have feelings about the objects of taste (foods, for example) that are simply impossible to communicate (*De gustibus non disputandum est*), but the faculty of the imagination allows us to transform these sensed objects into representations. As representations they become objects of reflection, and we are then able to understand them as "beautiful."

If imagination is the faculty that enables this shift from finding an object pleasing to finding its mental representation beautiful, it is common sense that demands we compare our judgments to those of others, and demands that we render those judgments intelligible to others.[15] Unlike Thinking and Willing, which we exercise strictly as individuals, Judging is a communal activity, and unlike Thinking but like Willing, Judging deals with particulars rather than universals, although in doing so it reveals the way the particular case serves as an example of a general principle. Thus, Arendt would make much of Kant's principle of "exemplary validity," or, as she understood it, the way any given object conforms to our expectations for its shape and function, based on an ideal (i.e., a table).[16] Crucially, Judging was not "practical reason" intended to guide action, a point bound to irk many of Arendt's colleagues and students who hoped she might provide guidelines explaining how the *vita activa* was to be governed. Instead, Judgment is a state of engaged but impartial "contemplative delight."[17] And while Thinking and Willing were each tied to the world of appearances, Judging was in a sense more closely bound to that world, involving a kind of internalized scene of discussion with "imagined others," or, in other words, involving an appetite for a kind of public.

Intriguingly, the only exemplary philosopher Arendt mentioned as having balanced the conflicting activities of Thinking and Willing in his person was Socrates, who in her view combined in his person two "apparently contradictory passions, for thinking and for acting."[18] He was able to do this precisely because he was, in Arendt's terms, "not professionalized." Before Socrates's trial, which initiated the split between "men of thought" and "men of action," spectatorship had been the last activity those groups shared. In a sense, spectatorship contained an echo of Socrates's insistence on his own right to inquire, publicly, into the opinions of his fellow citizens.

Writing about Socrates, albeit briefly, allowed Arendt to convey exactly what she thought thinking in public provided. She had already noted, approvingly, that Socrates feared being at odds with himself more than he feared being in conflict with the public. Later in her lectures, Arendt described how Socrates made his efforts at internal harmony visible: "What he actually did was to make *public*, in discourse, the thinking process—that dialogue that soundlessly goes on within me, between me and myself; he performed in the marketplace the way the flute-player performed at a banquet." And critically, "it was sheer performance, sheer activity." In other words, and as Arendt put it in *The Life of the Mind*, Socrates merged theory and practice, never prioritizing what would later be called the *vita contemplativa*. Arendt's Socrates was thus a performer who offered those around him a chance to witness thought as event.

This was radically different from the version of "thought as event" articulated in the philosophy of history. Socrates performed thinking on an intimately human scale, in the marketplace of Athens. In contrast, modern thinkers only related thoughts to acts from a very different vantage, namely, the backward and abstract gaze of the philosophy of history. Hegel was naturally the principal architect of the approach, but Arendt understood the tendency to have begun with Kant. While Kant's considerations of spectatorship would earn Arendt's praise in her lectures on his political philosophy, and while in "Thinking" she applauded his lack of the "traditional philosophical vice" of opposition to the public,[19] she also noted that he had sometimes succumbed to the tendency to assess individual spectacles, such as political events or wars, from the perspective of the very longue durée development of the human species. He granted to impersonal nature's sweep the final judgment on the meaning of any individual event. This tendency also meant denying any individual historian or storyteller the ability to judge. In fact, in works such as the *Idea for a Universal History from a Cosmopolitan Point of View*, Kant had moved from the more engaged spectatorship of judgment to a retreat into his own version of the philosophy of history, governed by the "ruse of nature."[20] And Arendt smiled less on other German observers of politics, whose metaphorical elaborations of political events suggested what she termed an "immature" shift away from the human scale. Both Herder and Goethe drew on the image of a shipwreck on a violent ocean, the former using it to describe the French Revolution, the latter to describe the battle of Jena.[21]

In her lectures on Kant's political philosophy, Arendt was more explicit about the positive social role spectators might play. Going beyond *The Human Condition's* portrayal of the storyteller as the figure who fixes the significance of actions after "the fleeting moment of the deed is past,"[22] she claimed that

> The public realm is constituted by the critics and the spectators and not by the actors or the makers. [Although] this critic and spectator sits in every actor and fabricator . . . spectators exist only in the plural. The spectator is not involved in the act, but he is always involved with his fellow spectators. He does not share the faculty of genius, originality, or the faculty of novelty with the actor; but the faculty they have in common is the faculty of judgment.[23]

In this remarkable passage, Arendt imparts a quality of nobility to the public function of critical judgment that was absent from her earlier works. While interpretation and action are still as divided as they had been in *The Human Condition*, the actor's requirement for the spectator has transformed. Whereas in *The Human Condition* spectators were necessary if political actors were to secure the "immortality" of reputation carried into posterity, in Arendt's late lectures spectators were necessary if actions were to take place at all, reflecting her deepening conviction about the primordial nature of appearance. Furthermore, in the Kant lectures Arendt was even more stringent about the inherent plurality of spectatorship than she had been in "Thinking"; one could not view events at all if one did not take part in the *sensus communis* other spectators made possible.

One feature of Arendt's discussion of Kant on Judging helps us to clarify her rejection of activism for political theorists and her enthusiasm for the backward glance of the storyteller. Following a discussion of Kant as a *Weltbetrachter*, a world spectator for whom the full sweep of human affairs were meaningful, Arendt emphasized that for Kant the position of the onlooker never provided a basis for action.[24] Marx had called Kant "the philosopher of the French revolution," and intended no compliment by it, in keeping with his view that philosophers had done little to change the world.[25] In regard to the Revolution, Arendt said, "[Kant] never wavered in his estimation of [its] grandeur," "and he hardly ever wavered in his condemnation of all those who had prepared it."[26]

This apparent contradiction becomes comprehensible when we consider Kant's view that there are two scales on which to consider human events: the human and the natural, or perhaps the moral and the spectatorial. The latter allows us, as Kant explained in *The Contest of the Faculties*, to appreciate progress through the disinterested observation of "the game of great transformations."[27] However, Kant also believed that the people had no right to violent revolution given that it entailed means incompatible with morality; the question was not whether a tyrant might justly be deposed, but, rather, whether the act of revolution could be moral. As Arendt put it, "What you see here clearly is the clash between the principle according to which you should act and the principle according to which you judge."[28] The maxims of revolutionary acts can never be, as Kant put it, consistent with publicity, or, in other words, they would be opposed if made public. According to Kant's "transcendental principle of publicness," articulated in *Perpetual Peace*, morality is the coincidence of the private and the public, of the equivalence of the personal and private maxim with the moral law that everyone can express in public.[29] Notably, the "publicness" shared by the spectators whose judgments of the meaning of the French Revolution are linked through the *sensus communis* is very different from the "publicness" of Kant's transcendental principle, which concerns not the experience of a shared faculty, but a space of publicly accessible communication. Arendt affirmed Kant's double perspective on human events: "Had he acted on the knowledge he had gained as a spectator, he would, in his own mind, have been criminal. Had he forgotten, because of this 'moral duty,' his insights as a spectator, he would have become what so many good men, involved and engaged in public affairs, tend to be—an idealistic fool."[30] Such persons were guilty of the same ideological mistakes Arendt had observed many years earlier in her 1954 survey of the philosophers of postwar Paris.

True to her earlier animadversions regarding influence, Arendt's late retheorization of publicness was not connected to any desire for action. At a 1972 conference on her work organized by her student Melvyn Hill at York University, Arendt rejected the idea that political theorists had any responsibility to commit their works or to encourage commitment among their students. In response to one question she insisted,

I don't believe we [political theorists] have, or can have, such influence in your sense. I think that commitment can easily carry you to a point where you do no longer think. There are certain extreme situations where you have to act. But these situations are extreme . . . . And I think . . . the theoretician who tells his students what to think and how to act is . . . . My God! These are adults. We are not in the nursery.[31]

Arendt was, of course, not immune to the attractions of public life—this much the 1964 interview with Gaus had demonstrated—but she dismissed the idea of commitment before reflection. Curiously, in *The Life of the Mind* she criticized two thinkers whose views she could reasonably have been expected to find congenial, Jaspers and Buber, grouping them together as "philosophers of communication." She rejected a premise they could plausibly be seen to share, namely, that truth itself arises only in intersubjective space. In doing so she effectively backed away from praise she had showered on Jaspers in her 1958 *laudatio* to him. Then she had argued that the philosophy of communication situated all real philosophizing in an inherently political space; in *The Life of the Mind* she denied that one could extrapolate from interpersonal acts of communication to the scale of the political. It was a mistake, she said in "Willing," to think that "Aristotle's friend, Jaspers' Beloved, Buber's Thou, can be extended and become paradigmatic for the political sphere." [32] Learning to address, accept, and work with the primordial otherness discovered within the self, or with a proximate other person, does not help us to deal with the true alterity of political life, the "we" that "arises wherever men live together."[33] In other words, Arendt rejected social ontology as a key to politics just as she rejected any philosophy of history grounded in metaphysics, and for the same reason. Both ran roughshod over the dignity of life and communication as they are lived rather than theorized.

Religion and the Intellectuals

In 1950 the journal *Partisan Review* asked Arendt to respond to a few questions regarding what was termed, "the new turn toward religion among intellectuals and the growing disfavor with which secular attitudes and perspectives are now regarded." [34] Other respondents included poets, theologians, political thinkers, philosophers, and historians; W. H. Auden, John

Dewey, Clement Greenberg, Irving Howe, and Marianne Moore were all included and their remarks published. Arendt's answers to the *Partisan Review* questions were brief but suggestive, not least because here she was willing to entertain, at least for a moment, the journal's avowed interest in identifying trends among intellectuals (the term was taken to be self-explanatory). However, Arendt was unconvinced by the seriousness and extent of the religious revival among intellectuals, and by the importance of "the history of intellectuals," itself. The former, she suggested, should be seen as a temporary "interruption" in the rapid decline of religious belief within modernity, and the latter, she said, was much less significant than the "history of Western mankind in general." The flattering gesture of *Partisan Review* including her in a star-studded list of "intellectuals," did not compel Arendt to celebrate a category that obviously caused her discomfort.

Religion was not a subject that Arendt reflected on at length in her mature writings, intriguing given that she had written on religious thought as a doctoral student, and that in her later reflections on the relation between intellectuals and politics the decline of religion as a political force played an important role. In 1963, Arendt explained, in her seemingly cast-off footnote toward the end of *On Revolution*, that secularization had opened a political space in which the division between philosophers and politicians became meaningful. The under-articulated line of reasoning in the footnote is made clear in her *Partisan Review* contribution of more than a decade earlier: one did not have to reject religious teachings to be a philosopher, naturally enough, but to accept a particular religious credo without question would mean abandoning the perspective of traditional philosophy. When religion dominated the political realm and lent politics its legitimacy, philosophy could hardly be a threat, and thus the difference between "men of thought" and "men of action" was less meaningful; however, with the breakdown of religion's authority, the presence of philosophers became problematic once more.

Arendt did not, in *On Revolution*, say more about the political-theological theme she had introduced. However, clues to her views on political theology appeared throughout her other works. As mentioned previously, for Arendt revolution derived its force from the way it served as a reminder of religion's foundational and law-giving social effects, and yet this was *not* because her thought was indebted to that tendency that saw such a resurgence in the Weimar years political theology.[35] Peter Eli Gordon has noted that, given the widespread influence of such authors as Carl Schmitt, the absence of a debt to political theology in Arendt's concept of the political seems curious.[36]

Arendt never endorsed the position taken by her fellow Heidegger pupil Löwith, namely that politics was in effect a secularization of originally religious concepts and regulations. Nor was she a celebrant of the position taken by the intellectual historian Hans Blumenberg, for whom the "legitimacy of the modern age" itself derived from shaking off any theological residue from political life. Though a secularist, and in many ways a modernist, Arendt was clearly no champion of "the modern age," eager to show how it had freed itself from constricting and superannuated forms of superstition and belief. In *The Human Condition* she displayed her own brand of archaism by longing for an idealized Greek political practice. And when it came to discussing Jews, Arendt drew on no account of the "unworldly" character of the Jewish people—such as that supplied by what Gordon terms the "apolitical theology" of Rosenzweig—but definitively identified the Jewish people as actors shaping their own political history.

It is not clear, however, which of the two entangled elements preceded the other—if Arendt's interest in the divide between philosophy and politics actually derived from her version of the secularization thesis, or if her interest in philosophy and politics began first. To answer this question on the basis of when Arendt began to mention either theme produces only more confusion. Her first work, the dissertation on Augustine, introduced both at once, yet in that work she never suggested religion and philosophy had somehow been at odds with one another, either for Augustine or in the history of philosophy more broadly. Despite her emphasis on the conflict between what Augustine termed the "city of man" and the "city of God," Arendt did not explicitly describe this as a *political* conflict in the dissertation itself. But for the mature Arendt, the resurgent importance of the conflict between thinkers and actors derived from philosophy's basic competition with religion, from the way each dealt with social life from the standpoint of a nonhuman point of authority, on which human life was radically dependent (religion) or from whose perspective human life was entirely insignificant (philosophy). Either way, social life was to be regulated from a lofty position above the fray of political debate and opinion. For Arendt, the existence of true public political life depended on the absence of any interference from such views; Arendt sought to rid the public of any trace of metaphysics, whatever its source.

Arendt's engagement with the question of religion and her interest in the philosophy/politics divide came together in her understanding of the public, and to consider these issues together may cast a helpful light on Arendt's opposition to metaphysics entering the public realm. However, and, perhaps more interestingly, this line of inquiry can also help us to understand her ongoing interest in the figure of Socrates. The simplest reason for her fixation has been confirmed in this chapter already: Arendt saw Socrates's trial as the crucial point of inflection in political philosophy's history, marking a transition from a public philosophical practice characterized by the egalitarian exchange of *doxoi*, or opinions (Socrates's practice), to a private philosophical practice that divides truth from opinion and constructs an edifice of political philosophy in order to account for absolute differences between philosophers and non-philosophers (the practice inaugurated by Plato). While Arendt was no political theologian, in a 1954 talk given at Notre Dame she was happy to use religion for illustrative purposes, saying, "The gulf between philosophy and politics opened historically with the trial and condemnation of Socrates, which in the history of political thought plays the same role of a turning point that the trial and condemnation of Jesus plays in the history of religion."[37] This talk, "Philosophy and Politics," demonstrates that the account of Socrates Arendt would ultimately offer in *The Life of the Mind*— where Socrates served as, literally, a philosophical performance artist—had crystallized for her much earlier. In fact, the careful description of Socrates that Arendt here provides raises the question of why Socrates did not appear more often in *The Human Condition*.

Socrates's trial led Plato to "doubt the validity of *persuasion*."[38] Persuasion, Arendt said, came from *peithein*, "the specifically political form of speech," and it was sadly the case that Plato came to doubt that *peithein* had the power to convince Athenians that there was room for a philosopher in their midst. Along with persuasion Plato came to reject *doxa*, and to introduce the hard distinction between truth and opinion that would characterize political philosophy after him: Plato's "tyranny of truth," for Arendt. Arendt here endorsed one very popular reading of Plato's *Republic*, according to which Plato did advocate for rule by philosopher-kings. Plato, naturally, did not share the popular Greek view that philosophy could actually make someone unfit for life in the polis and unfit to lead it. Inspired by the idea that "the good" was not just absolute, but carried a sense of what is "good for" a particular human purpose, Plato took the ideas to serve as potential models for human laws. The *Republic*, for Arendt, presented a "strictly philosophical" argument that had nevertheless "been prompted by an exclusively political experience," namely, Socrates's trial and execution.[39] The Aristotelian distinction between persuasion and political speech, Arendt reminded her audience, descended from Plato's distinction between persuasion and dialectic, a distinction plausibly based on the memory of Socrates's trial. Notably, whereas persuasion seeks a mass audience, dialectic consists in dialogue between intimates.

Normally, and as evidenced in *The Life of the Mind*, Arendt blamed the philosophers and not the people of the polis for the conflict between the two groups. However, in "Philosophy and Politics" Arendt suggested that at the time when Socrates began his work, the people themselves drew a line between the nonhuman concerns of philosophers and those of the people. Most intriguingly, Arendt noted that Socrates was a problem for the Athenians not because he offered them a nonhuman source of wisdom, but rather because he denied that mortals can be wise, and thus denied the people a source of useful wisdom. Furthermore—and again anticipating her later claim that Socrates had overestimated his fellow Athenians—Arendt pointed out that Socrates made the mistake of addressing his fellows using not persuasion but rather dialectic. And here Arendt voiced the same opinion she offered in a third work of 1954, the essay "Understanding and Politics:" rule by persuasion would only be another form of violence, words serving as weapons. The transmission of truth through speech or writing, on the other hand, was not a type of violence for Arendt. Thus Socrates' constant performance of the search for truth (featuring, as noted before, self-consistency and self-knowledge) seemed, to Arendt, a resistance to violence. It had, she also noted, served as a kind of provocation to the polis in its sheer insistence that philosophy could be rendered relevant.[40]

Arendt's reflections on Socrates and Plato, as well as Aristotle, here shed some light on her contradictory statements in the 1964 Gaus interview. In particular, her remark that she did not want to have "influence" (a form of violence), but rather to help readers achieve a certain understanding, recalled her discussion of the phenomenon of friendship in "Philosophy and Politics," and, in particular, Aristotle's basically Socratic figuring of friendship as a space in which friends help one another to work out the truth in each other's opinions. And Arendt, in 1954, found in this presentation of friendship a motif that she would later find in Kant's *sensus communis*, namely, "seeing the world (as we rather tritely say today) from the other fellow's point of view."[41] This, Arendt said, was the essence of politics. While politicians might be understood as persons who can unite a variety of *doxoi*, Arendt noted that Socrates seemed to have a political vision of the philosopher's performative work. The task was to establish, by demonstrating how one could share opinions, and especially opinions as efforts toward truth, a "kind of common

world," a world of friends, "in which no rulership is needed."[42] The capacity
for friendship itself stemmed from the fundamental dialogue with oneself
that Arendt would explore in such depth in *The Life of the Mind*, and which
stemmed from the fact that we all "talk with ourselves" as though we were
two. As we have seen, Arendt found that Socrates' account of internal dialogue could be harmonized with phenomenology's account of the primordial character of representation: from the very start, we render thought as a
form of "appearance," or, in this case, "appearance" in the form of speech.
Indeed, in a strikingly anthropological argument (albeit never articulated as
such), Arendt conjured a deep correspondence between the mechanisms
of representation itself and the fact of human plurality in the world. Arendt,
in 1954, articulated more sharply a point that was nevertheless still present
in *The Life of the Mind*: the philosophical escape from the public realm represented by Plato and Aristotle was a false escape because plurality itself would
travel with the mind wherever it went. "I have to put up with myself," Arendt
quipped.[43] And the message of *The Life of the Mind* was in keeping with
Arendt's vision of Socrates, namely, that the task of philosophy was first and
foremost the therapeutic task of ensuring that we can live with ourselves, and
that the political purpose of philosophy was that we, as people capable of
"agreeing" with ourselves, will be people capable of agreeing with one another.

But this thinking about internal dialogue opened up one limited sense
in which Arendt could be called a "political theologian," albeit one utterly
unlike Schmitt. For Arendt, a Socratic account of philosophy's public task
would satisfy a need opened up by secularization, namely, for something to
take the place of a divine judgment of the morality of human actions. Plato
had posed well the question of conscience, asking whether, as Arendt had it,
"'a good deed, or a just deed, is what it is even if it remains unknown to and
hidden before men and gods,'" that is, if it never rises to appearance.[44] Arendt suggested that the Socratic practice, of beginning with that dialogue-
with-self that leads to agreement-with-self, can supply the conscience necessary
in a secular society. She also claimed that a philosophy that encourages the
development of conscience can also serve a function previously provided for
by religion. Arendt's implication was that the model of audience provided by
religion, in which one's actions were witnessed and would be rewarded or
punished by God, was replaced with the model of witnessing one's self. The
import of totalitarianism, she was careful to add, was precisely that it could
eliminate "not only secular but also all religious forms of conscience," by
eliminating freedom in both public and private life.[45] This did not, however,

mean that Arendt saw Socrates as a constant and perfect conversation partner. He could not be, for he frequently fell into a speechless state of wonder—*thaumazein*—which came, for Plato and Aristotle and for Arendt, to characterize the paralysis of philosophical reflection. In such a state he could not share his insights with others, nor help them strengthen conscience through the craft of friendship. But whereas Socrates had been able to make the transition from *thaumazein* to dialogue with himself to dialogue with others, Plato lost those fine distinctions, and "prolong[ed] indefinitely" the condition of speechless wonder itself.

But in the closing moments of the essay, Arendt pursued the question of philosophy's usefulness, of the way Plato's rendering of "the good" as "good for," in *The Republic*, set a precedent for subsequent generations to use philosophy as a source of "yardsticks" against which human life might be measured. Arendt submitted, much as she did in "Concern with Politics," that this broke down within modernity, generating the need for a new political philosophy that began not with *thaumazein* but with common sense. Thus did she set the ground for *The Human Condition*, with the desire to make "human plurality" itself an object of wonder. And just as Arendt had earlier compared Socrates and Jesus, here she cited the biblical precedent that God did not create Man in the singular, but in the plural of both genders: "male and female created He them." Arendt closed on a sentiment she and Levinas certainly shared, namely that "it is not good for man to be alone."

When We Are Different from One Another and Do Not Live Alone

It is perhaps fitting that a book on totalitarianism, a phenomenon Arendt did so much to explain, can help us to understand her vision of the scene of address between writers and readers. This is George Orwell's *1984,* which opens with a case of writer's block.[46] Trying to write a diary entry in a room monitored by an all-seeing "telescreen," Orwell's character Winston has good reason for being unable to write. The government under which he lives constrains all public expression. All private conversations and writings are scanned for potentially seditious content. However, Winston still finds the requisite resolve to write a message. He writes the following on a piece of paper he places in his desk drawer, with a small piece of dust atop it so that he might later see if the police have found his diary entry: *"To the future, or to the past, to a time when thought is free, when men are different from one another and do not live alone.*"[47] Life in a totalitarian society makes imagining a concrete future impossible; Winston's dedication to either past or future implies that what he is really concerned with is not a conversation with a reader in a different time per se (not the past, of course, nor even with the "future self" to whom a diary might be addressed),[48] but rather between an abstracted "humanity." As Orwell writes, "he was a lonely ghost uttering a truth that nobody would ever hear. But so long as he uttered it, in some obscure way the continuity was not broken. It was not by making yourself heard but by staying sane that you carried on the human heritage."[49] Winston effectively addresses his own humanity. And as Michael Warner rightly argues, the point of this scene in *1984* is the intimate link between publicness and the experience of internal freedom itself, the way the former makes the latter possible.

In her 1964 interview with Gaus, Arendt denied her desire to influence readers, implying she did not "look over her shoulder" for her readers while she was still at the typewriter. But whether or not we take her avowed rejection of influence at face value, she certainly wished to reach a public, whether to achieve some measurable effect or simply to be heard, coming into "full humanity" in the process. Arendt's praise for the figure of Socrates, especially for Socrates understood as an actor who performed the role of inquirer before his fellow citizens, bespeaks a desire to "transform the possible contexts of speech," as Warner puts it.[50] And her late description of the way publicness inflects thought, even as we pull away from the world through thinking's momentary withdrawal, certainly recalls Orwell's sense that the condition of publicness is bound up with our humanity. Where Orwell suggests that even a note no one will see can still be enough to keep us sane, Arendt implies that the representational nature of our existence means that even the most abstract thinking itself anticipates publicness by its very nature. Martin Jay described Arendt's thought as "political existentialism," which for him conjured her willingness to believe in the total malleability of the human condition, her "expressivist" understanding of political action in response to an instrumental one, and her inattention to ethical issues.[51] While Arendt's politics of autotelic action were far from the decisionism of a thinker like Schmitt—and while she was absolutely opposed to taking an "aesthetic" approach to politics, which would treat people as though they were moldable material for art-making—there is at least some justice in the label.[52] The Arendt of *The Life of the Mind* argues that publicness (but not "public life" in any sociologically rich sense) is part of the human condition, as such, and so the public dimension of her politics is existential in the strictest sense.

Arendt understood that the kinds of public political action she prized most highly were impossible without the right kinds of publics. After the great public challenge of the Eichmann controversy, for Arendt the life of the mind took on the character Warner assigns Winston's diary-writing, a way of summoning the ghost of freedom. Arendt had hardly given up on the public realm itself, but in Socratic fashion she asked whether or not the space between us can become the site of meaningful political exchange as long as the space within us passes without scrutiny. Arendt was no celebrant of the view that some readers have projected onto Orwell, that the best way to communicate a political message is simply to write clearly and to as large an audience as possible, appealing to their common sense.[53] The history of philosophy has no greater enemy of the faith in common sense than Socrates himself.

Importantly, an appreciation of Arendt's late internalization of the public helps us to understand that she took no part in what Warner calls the "commonsense view" contained within "the folk theory of democracy." According to this folk theory, to address oneself to "public opinion" means engaging with a potentially reasonable conversation partner.[54] The assumption that the public world is reasonable certainly seems like a basis for calls that intellectuals engage in public political debate. Arendt, who had no praise for the various folk-theories of the intellectual that piled up as the twentieth century moved on, believed that not reason, nor truth understood as reason's goal, but rather opinion drove public political life. And yet this view stood in tension with her occasional desire to play the expert's part herself, albeit an expert not on "truth," but on clarity of thought in matters easily clouded by ideology.

PART IV

A Missed Conversation

If he is one who philosophizes, why does he
relinquish his solitude and loiter about as a
public professor in the market? But above all,
what a dangerous beginning is this ambiguous
behavior!

—Martin Heidegger

When I talk to you about Hellas, I am really
talking about the twentieth century.

—Heinrich Blücher

CHAPTER 10

Toward a Jewish Socrates?

Alexandre Kojève, whom André Glucksmann called "the big secret of French philosophy . . . who formulates the leftist intellectual theory of *engagement*,"[1] once claimed that for Hegel "the conflict of the intellectual faced with action" presents us with "the only authentic *tragedy* that takes place in the Christian or bourgeois world: the tragedy of Hamlet and of Faust."[2] He meant that intellectuals and philosophers could not act without giving up philosophy, and generally chose to give up action instead. The result was an unfortunate delay in the progress of world history. Regardless whether or not one embraces Hegel or reads him as Kojève did, it is true that both Shakespeare's story and Goethe's enjoy a special legibility in the bourgeois world.[3] A philosophy student home from university and a mature scholar ashamed of his worldly inexperience are both excellent avatars of intellectual inactivity, available for endless romanticization as well as for regrets like Kojève's. But from the perspectives of Hannah Arendt, Emmanuel Levinas, and Leo Strauss, Kojève's references to Goethe and Shakespeare overlooked another authentic tragedy in the history of philosophy that deserved new twentieth-century readings. Call this the tragedy of Socrates, the philosopher who stood for the slippage between philosophy and the political community, and whose misadventures, trial, and punishment supplied as accurate a description of the modern thinker's problems as the "tragedy" of inaction.

For Strauss, Socrates's story was tragic because it underscored the gulf between philosophers and others who were unable to see anything but subversion in philosophy's skeptical methods. In turn, it illustrated the need for the practice of divided speech, which Socrates had initiated. For Arendt, his story illustrated the failure of his strikingly egalitarian efforts to aid his fellow Athenians by drawing out the latent truths from their opinions. However, in her later studies and lectures she seemed to hope that Socrates-like figures might do a valuable form of public work.[4] As she put it in one letter to Karl Jaspers, it was Plato, that voluble celebrant of the *vita contemplativa*, who drowned out the voice of Socrates, who had had his own ideas about the proper relationship between contemplation and action.[5] In his first major opus, *Totality and Infinity*, Levinas used Socrates to provide a counterpoint to a narrative often spun around Heidegger: if Heidegger was a seducer who did little but impose his own ideas on his students (so ran the common story), Socrates "prevailed over a pedagogy that introduced ideas into a mind by violating or seducing (which amounts to the same thing) that mind."[6] For all three, Socrates' story contained lessons about the purposes and limitations of philosophy in the public realm. Regardless how frequently they wrote on Socrates (Strauss and Arendt mentioned him often, Levinas relatively rarely), he served as an ideal symbol of the way tragedy could lurk in the complex relationship between philosophers and their audiences as much as in philosophers' failures to take arms or engage in grand historical projects. There were tragedies of misrecognition and misunderstanding, tragedies of misguided pedagogy and tragedies of banal popularization. And of course there were tragedies, like Heidegger's, of political judgment and action. Naturally, Arendt, Levinas, and Strauss felt the need to respond to history's catastrophic turn in the first half of the twentieth century, to the horrors of the Holocaust, and to the way barbarism seemed to rise whenever civilization faltered. They considered the question (very popular among historians, philosophers, and political theorists after Hitler's rise to power, and familiar to us because of its appearance in Adorno and Horkheimer's *Dialectic of Enlightenment*) of whether the *vita contemplativa* had been complicit in civilization's failure.

Socrates' tragedy mattered because, in its dramatization of the meeting between philosopher and fellow-citizen, it offered a challenge to philosophers that had to be taken into consideration *prior* to the question of whether or how to take political action, whether that question was posed by Kojève, Sartre, or any other celebrant of the engaged "intellectual." It made publicity seem fraught and fragile. And behind the apparent fragility of publicness stood other stories. These included stories about liberalism, as dependent on the idea of the public as it was on the idea of the private person, and very fragile during Arendt, Levinas, and Strauss's youth—and stories about the history of the Jews in Europe, who had been left exposed and vulnerable by the failure of the liberal order. The precariousness of the modern Jewish condition in Europe found a distant mirror in the fragility of Socrates' relationship with Athens.

"Coincidence," Adam Gopnik writes in a short book on Abraham Lincoln and Charles Darwin, who happened to be born on the same day, "is the vernacular of history, the slang of memory—the first strong pattern where we begin to search for subtle ones."[7] This is an intriguing claim because it suggests that coincidence, which we know counts for nothing but the sheer contingency of our lives, may nevertheless lead to verifiable meaning. Surrounded by noise, we delight in signal. To choose perhaps the oddest coincidence linking the lives of this book's protagonists, Strauss, and Arendt's second husband Heinrich Blücher (a non-Jew and as an adult a committed Marxist) were once part of the same Zionist youth organization. This was the Blau-Weiss, among the first groups of its kind in Germany. It is unclear if they ever met. That a non-Jew would join the Zionist youth was of course exceptional, and it appears that the young Blücher did so to advance his own political development. Blau-Weiss's constituency was typically well educated, and there would have been opportunity for good conversations about politics. Strauss's own relationship with Blau-Weiss was, as Michael Zank observes, originally characterized by the enthusiasm of a new convert. This feeling was quickly replaced by disillusionment regarding the quality of solidarity and shared experience (*Erlebnis*) that Blau-Weiss attempted to imbue in its members through collective activities like hiking, camping, and singing. Strauss came to see the very notion of common experience as inimical to the activity of critique, a position that resonated with Heidegger's anxiety about the stultifying effects of everyday beliefs held in common, and with Arendt's later views as well.[8] There is something funny about the juxtaposition. Blücher joined a Zionist group (whose *Erlebnis* he could not have shared by virtue of his background) effectively in pursuit of a kind of learning, which, of course, is a traditional Jewish value. Strauss left that same group, complaining that *Erlebnis* had turned into a barrier against critical reflection for Zionists.

Of course such coincidences could occur because Arendt, Levinas, and Strauss were well positioned for them, first by birth and geography, later by aptitude and interest as young scholars, and ultimately by exiles that began either as voluntary resettlement (Strauss, Levinas) or as flight (Arendt). The shared experience of losing one's home would loom large in all of their writings, almost as large as their shared interest in the relationship between philosophy and society. That phrase could be differently turned, becoming "the question of the political purposes of philosophy," purposes that were likely (but not necessarily) to be played out in public life. As we have seen, they often addressed this by discussing the figure of "the intellectual." Of the three, only

Levinas sustained a relatively positive view of such persons, calling them to action (albeit the mysterious "action" of passivity) in his final major work, the 1974 *Otherwise Than Being,* but resisting the notion, promoted by many of his generation in France, that intellectuals should become political activists. However, Arendt and sometimes Levinas seemed to perform the role of the intellectual regardless of their own ambivalence. Certainly, all three shared a sense of the complexity of public political life. There could be no simple transmutation of philosophical insights into political ones; theory did not flow into practice and the effort to make it flow was the mark of totalitarianism. And all three used the term "an intellectual" as a screen for the projection of judgments about the relationship between the *vita contemplativa* and the *vita activa,* continuing a tradition initiated during the Dreyfus Affair. What is especially interesting about their uses of the term is precisely its non-centrality in their writings; none was like C. Wright Mills, who lavished much energy on the subject during the 1950s, and none penned a single work on the subject comparable to Max Weber's 1919 "Science as a Vocation." The term "an intellectual" is marginal, fugitive in their works. "Intellectuals" show up in seemingly casual contexts or, as in the case of the ending of Levinas's *Otherwise Than Being,* at moments that call for dramatic emphasis rather than argument. The term sometimes seems symptomatic rather than intentional, but symptomatic in a very useful sense: it offers us a glimpse of deeper efforts to sort through philosophy's place in the human realm, efforts that began when this book's protagonists read Heidegger's writings and listened to his lectures.

Arendt's, Levinas's, and Strauss's interest in the relation between philosophy and politics was, in part, a response to Heidegger's failure to address politics directly in his philosophy and in great measure a response to the affront of his Nazification. Samuel Moyn has suggested that Heidegger's account of the social in *Being and Time* contained two latent possibilities, communitarianism and universalism.[9] The former presumes we are so essentially social that if our communal lives are inauthentic so shall be our selves; historical communities, rather than appeal to some transcendent principle, will supply us with norms and standards to live by. The latter would take the sociality of the self as a universal condition and prioritize some version of sociality as an eternal concern of the self ("care," or *Fürsorge,* would be Heidegger's term for this) without presuming that it is the community—such as the "community of fate" the earlier Heidegger seemed to promote in his writings and, plausibly, his political choices—that supplies the self with what it needs.

Being and Time itself performs a transition from an initial consideration of care for the other, to an ultimate endorsement of belonging to one's community or generation (a generation is, after all, the ultimate "community of fate"). None of this translated into a full account of "the political," though the communitarian option proved disconcertingly compatible with Heidegger's later endorsement of National Socialism. It was as though Heidegger had simply leapt from the question of Being as the individual might pose it (on the way subordinating questions of others to the experience of that individual self) to the possibility of group commitment, speaking to a public while forgetting the political realities of public life. For their parts, Arendt and Strauss would react by drawing sharp lines between philosophy and politics. In so doing, they avoided precisely the confusion of politics and philosophy that Levinas's writings display. While Levinas developed concern for the other far beyond the "universalist" position of Heideggerian *Fürsorge*, he notably embraced that term itself. As he put it in an essay titled "Martin Buber's Thought and Contemporary Judaism," "It is certainly not from Heidegger that one should take lessons on the love of man or social justice. But *Fürsorge* as response to an essential destitution accedes to the alterity of the Other."[10] If Levinas's response to Heidegger combined the continued use of Heideggerian methods and ideas *and* the view that those methods and ideas were ethically flawed, the same could be said of Arendt and Strauss at many points.

It is useful to reiterate and expand upon the list of "strong patterns" linking Arendt, Levinas, and Strauss offered in the Introduction to this book. They were born within ten years of one another and pursued their educations (Arendt and Strauss entirely, Levinas in part) in Weimar Germany. They then experienced one or another form of exile, flight, imprisonment, or all three, the loss of family, and the need to establish a new home. That they went through these trials as Jews who came of age after the advent of Zionism, but before the establishment of the state of Israel, was far from incidental. All (at least for a portion of their lives) supported Zionism, but all were ultimately disappointed (to varying degrees; Arendt most consequentially, in *Eichmann in Jerusalem*) by the realities of the Israeli state, whose attractions did little to curb their own identification with the figure of the exile and with the pariah's perspective on society. And their youthful and mature intellectual interests overlapped considerably beyond their initial fascination with Heidegger's "New Thinking." They examined theology and philosophy, Jewish history, violence and authoritarianism, and the spectacle of Western civilization betraying itself in Nazism. They were critics of liberal political theory who lived under liberal democratic regimes of which they were often fond. All three loved at least some part of Greek philosophy, though Arendt struggled mightily with what she understood as Plato's autocratic tendencies and Levinas struggled with Plato's emphasis on "totality." From the thought of Husserl and Heidegger all three inherited the problem of the other, and while only Levinas would take up otherness as a matter for formal philosophical reflection, the idea of "the public" sometimes served each of them as a surrogate for the philosophical problem of alterity—in one formulation, the question of how we might be known, and our ideas recognized, by other minds. They spent at least a portion of their careers as outsiders either to the academic world itself or to the central social networks of their disciplines.

Returning to Gopnik's gloss on coincidence, it seems that when comparing Arendt, Levinas, and Strauss the question is how to save the subtle patterns of correlation between their ideas from the overpowering effects of the stronger patterns of correlation and contrast. The subtlest pattern is effectively this book's core theoretical claim: all three came to understand a form of literal or figural publicness as a permanent horizon for philosophical practice, a feature of the landscape that had always been present for philosophers, but pressed on thinkers differently in the twentieth century than it had done before. And if they recognized publicness as a modern condition and, along with the sanctity of the private person, part of the core of liberal thought, they did not embrace it as part of the progressive promise of liberal modernity. Rather, in thinking about the problem of the public they worked through their own critiques of liberalism as well as of tyranny.

While they could have become interlocutors, they did not, for reasons that were essentially circumstantial. Their sojourns in Heidegger's circle did not overlap: Arendt worked with Heidegger after Strauss (only a periodic student during Heidegger's time at Freiburg) had moved on to his postdoctoral research in Berlin. Levinas was a visiting student of Husserl's in 1928, meeting Heidegger there after Arendt had already moved on to write her dissertation with Jaspers at Heidelberg. Arendt and Strauss evidently did meet later, in Berlin, at the Preußische Staatsbibliothek. Strauss subsequently courted Arendt and was rebuffed, Arendt citing his conservative politics as a reason to reject him.[11] According to Elisabeth Young-Bruehl, this spurning was one cause of the much later rancor between the two at the University of Chicago, where both taught during the 1960s. Little evidence, however, supports Anne Norton's contention that the never-realized potential erotic connection between Strauss and Arendt "shaped both philosophy and politics in America," a claim that rests on the questionable conceit that the two thinker's students have been as influential in political affairs beyond the academy as they have within the field of political theory.[12] In a 1954 letter to Arendt, Jaspers asked if she knew Strauss and if he were still alive. He seemed unaware of Arendt's past acquaintance with Strauss, suggesting that she may never have mentioned him. Arendt wrote back, offering a brief description: "Leo Strauss is professor of political philosophy in Chicago, highly respected. Wrote a good book about Hobbes (as well as one about Spinoza). Now another about natural law. He is a convinced orthodox atheist. Very odd. A truly gifted intellect. I don't like him. He must be in his middle or late fifties."[13] Strauss appears once more in the Arendt-Jaspers correspondence, some years later, apparently having been the one person at the University of Chicago who "agitated" against Arendt during the Eichmann controversy.[14]

Neither Strauss nor Arendt appears to have had much contact with Levinas, though all three had been visitors in Kojève's Hegel seminars in Paris during the early 1930s. Levinas and Arendt are known to have met face to face in 1970, when Levinas was awarded an honorary doctorate at Loyola University in Chicago, but they reportedly did not engage in any sustained dialogue. Levinas once indicated awareness of Strauss in an essay on Spinoza. Offering what could be charitably called a cramped summary, Levinas wrote, "The American philosopher Leo Strauss has in fact invited us to see a cryptogram in the whole of philosophy."[15] He never cited Arendt in any of his writings, nor did she ever make note of his work. Strauss, for his part, never mentioned or cited either Levinas or Arendt, in keeping with his practice of keeping his books and essays free of any mention of contemporary thinkers. Arendt cited neither Levinas nor Strauss. The list of scholars with whom Arendt, Levinas, and Strauss (or at least one pair out of the three) all came into contact is predictably long. It includes the Jewish historian Salo Wittmayer Baron, who employed the young Strauss as a research assistant and who became Arendt's life-long friend, the Catholic political philosopher Eric Voegelin, with whom Strauss corresponded at length and with whom Arendt crossed swords over *The Origins of Totalitarianism*, the historian of Jewish mysticism Gershom Scholem, and the polymathic Hans Jonas, whose works ranged over topics from Gnosticism to the philosophy of biology. It seems only natural that such social overlap should bring us to the cusp of counterfactual questioning, for to read these thinkers' works against one another is to imagine what they might have said to one another, whether or not we formalize the exercise by asking "what if?"[16]

This book's first three main parts have examined Strauss, Levinas and Arendt's attitudes toward the figure of "the intellectual," and it is useful to sum up those attitudes briefly here. For Strauss, this figure sprang from the modern tendency to instrumentalize not only knowledge but also publicness as a foundational part of civil society in the liberal democratic West. Central to his claim against "intellectuals" was that their medium, publicness, paradoxically *limited* freedom. Things printed, distributed, said, and known in public would always be judged in public, and often according to an ever-lowering set of standards. By contrast, the political philosophers who wrote esoterically were able to exploit the public dissemination of knowledge in order to spread their messages to the like-minded, even if it meant doing so across the generations. Levinas never renounced publicness, though he did resist activism. He rejected Sartre's transformation of "the intellectual" into an engaged political actor and he offered "prophetic witnessing," an idea whose roots lie within modern Jewish philosophy and the tradition of the Dreyfusard *intellectuels*, as an alternative. Late in his career he identified "intellectuals" as the bearers of his message of nearly performative vulnerability, personifications of his ethics without a politics. Arendt called for public life, but not one in which intellectuals were to play a special role, and yet it is difficult to argue that she was not an intellectual who wrote and acted in public herself. At the end of her career she held out a political role for philosophy that was essentially educative, for philosophy was part of the balancing-act that comprised the "life of the mind" and, thus, good preparation for political life. In thinking this way about philosophy's place in society, she was actually very close to both Strauss and Levinas, like her invested in their roles as teachers and capable of naming education as the means by which philosophy discharged its social obligations.

While as of this writing no single study has brought Arendt, Levinas, and Strauss together, some scholars have focused their attention on two of the three. Glancing comparisons of Arendt and Strauss are not uncommon. John Gunnell, in his *Political Theory: Tradition and Interpretation*, links them through their shared belief in the existence and breakdown of a "great tradition" of political thought, and Anne Norton, in her *Leo Strauss and the Politics of American Empire*, asserts that they shared "the same intellectual tastes." One edited volume, *Hannah Arendt and Leo Strauss: German Émigrés and American Political Thought After World War II*, supplies close studies of their work that might assist in the project of comparative reading.[17] A more substantial comparative study is Ronald Beiner's "Hannah Arendt and Leo

Strauss: The Uncommenced Dialogue," which points to a "tacit or latent" dialogue between Arendt and Strauss while working through the most obvious conflict between their views: ancient Greek politics or ancient Greek philosophy?[18] This conflict does not obviate correlations. For example, Beiner notes that *The Human Condition*, with its descriptions of a world degraded by the demands of *homo laborans*—the world overtaken, we might say, by human metabolism—harmonizes with central Straussian concerns such as the disappearance of political standards under modernity. If Strauss's appeal to natural right has no direct counterpart in Arendt's thought, certainly her understanding of the human condition as ringed about by permanent and unalterable "natural horizons" brings her close to the Strauss of *Natural Right and History*, albeit in a less normative mode.

The crucial turn in Beiner's argument comes when he attempts to frame the choice between Arendt and Strauss at the most abstract level of philosophical contrast: do we choose Kant with Arendt or Plato with Strauss? Where do we locate "what is transhistorically true," in the structures of our judgments or in the ideas we only ever approach asymptotically?[19] Quickly this question gets reframed again, as Beiner notes that this was *not* a theoretical matter, or not just a theoretical matter, for either Arendt or Strauss. In another rearticulation of the conflict (which, among other things, points to the potentially endless character of the Arendt-Strauss comparison), the question of what is "transhistorically true" for each—a question at the level of pure theory—turns out to be less significant than the question of the relation between philosophers and nonphilosophers. Strauss's ideal world (one he knew was *only* ideal and unrealizable) features a natural hierarchy in which philosophers stand above their less gifted fellow citizens, even if they do not wield political power directly. Arendt, on the other hand, did not think that the intellectually gifted or trained ought to have a special place in matters of governance. For Strauss, the political challenge of philosophers (i.e., their anxieties about their own survival as a human type) stimulates the growth of political philosophies. For Arendt there is no necessary danger from a world of fellow-citizens who merely find philosophers amusingly unworldly. Furthermore, for Arendt the issue of natural differences of talent is mitigated by our acceptance of something "artificial" in our political lives, namely the institution of "peerdom," which compels us to ignore, when engaged in public speaking and listening, the differences that are so important in private life. Arendt is Burkean in her insistence on the importance of an admittedly artificial cultural institution. I suggest that the breakdown of

Beiner's comparison of Arendt and Strauss on strictly philosophical grounds is significant, and reminds us that the latent conversation between them was less about the nature of philosophy and more about the comportment of philosophers in the public world.

Another focused comparison of Arendt and Strauss comes to us from Dana Villa, who moves from the same point of departure as Beiner. In his essay "The Philosopher Versus the Citizen: Arendt, Strauss and Socrates," Villa identifies a common ground consisting of the kind of skeptical judgment both Arendt and Strauss celebrate. Very helpfully, he notes Strauss's surprising "agreement with Arendt as to the *causes* of the conflict between philosophy and politics."[20] Simply put, "philosophical thinking requires a withdrawal from the world of appearances."[21] Arendt and Strauss shared an understanding of the nature of philosophy and agreed that, since Socrates, we have had to choose between the *vita activa* and the *vita contemplativa*. However, in a fashion consonant with their divide over the location of "what is transhistorically true," they disagree on the issue of opinion and truth.

For the Arendt of *The Human Condition*, opinions themselves are what matter in political life, which constitutes a sufficient horizon for meaning. Heidegger's attack on metaphysics had freed her to discount the pursuit of truth as an ultimate *telos* for critical practice, and, accordingly, she presented Socrates as a fellow citizen who through his *maieutics* helped others work through their own opinions and refine them, while helping them to build habits of self-reflection and self-consistency. For Strauss, Heidegger's rejection of metaphysics helped to establish a new "artificial pit" of valuelessness beneath everyday human affairs, his historicism effectively denying the permanent character of our fundamental problems.[22] Accordingly, Strauss's Socrates was less a fellow-citizen and more a teacher, philosophically important not because of his positive effects on fellow citizens, but because of his pursuit of knowledge of the whole—and this despite his acknowledgment that it always remains unknowable. The asymptotic progress from opinion to absolute knowledge (replacing opinions about the whole with genuine knowledge of the whole) is what matters.

It is certainly plausible to read Arendt and Strauss as Villa suggests we do, attending to their shared interest in the skeptical force of Socratic questioning. But Villa's comparison of Arendt and Strauss also underscores one of their basic differences from Levinas: both offer us accounts of what a healthy political community looks like, and in both the line between public and private life is crucial. Arendt describes a collectivity engaged in public, agonistic debate, whereas for Strauss the healthy community is properly ruled by a class known as "the gentlemen," who have themselves been properly educated by philosophers. They rule with an eye toward the underlying natural order rather than by regarding rules as merely conventional; they understand the proper "ends" of the political community and, having had their virtues cultivated by good teachers, they rule according to virtue. Levinas never drew a line between politics and philosophy; his eventual view that philosophy as practiced in the Western tradition *and* politics both stood on the side of totality, kept him from imagining a virtuous political order or community of agonistic agents. It is thus significant that whereas Arendt and Strauss understood Socrates as a thinker aware that true knowledge remained beyond him, Levinas placed Socrates in the same tradition of "philosophical egoism" as Heidegger, despite the fact that he broke from solipsism, at a formal level, in his own pedagogy.

In my chapters on Strauss and Levinas, I have drawn from Leora Batnitzky's *Leo Strauss and Emmanuel Levinas: Philosophy and the Politics of Revelation*, a work that deserves more detailed discussion here. Batnitzky rightly situates Strauss and Levinas as respondents to a broad "crisis of the West" evident in the wake of the Great War and to which so many writers attested, from Ernst Bloch to Walter Benjamin, Thomas Mann, and Oswald Spengler. The project of understanding Western thought in its dual constitution by Jewish and Greek influences ("Hebraism and Hellenism," in Matthew Arnold's well-known updating of a problematic originally introduced by Tertullian) was for both Levinas and Strauss made pressing by the experience of a pan-European crisis of values registered on the levels of culture and politics at once. They sought a diagnosis and cure in what they took to be the roots of the dual tradition they inherited.[23] However, in Batnitzky's view, Levinas's mature criticisms of the totalizing logic of Western philosophy (his attempts, say, to express Hebrew ethics in Greek letters) are unconvincing and belie his own complicity with that logic. He ultimately responds to the wreck of the West by becoming "a defender of a particular modern philosophical project that endows philosophy with social and political capabilities" while Strauss stands as "a critic of this project."[24] Levinas's apparent activism troubles Batnitzky, but she is more worried about a larger issue: such politicization originates in what she terms a particular "post-Christian philosophical framework." That framework was itself made not just possible but deeply influential through the development of metaphysics in the course of the German Enlightenment. In that process, philosophy, religion, and the potential civic functions of each ran together and their tasks became confused. In contrast, Strauss's attunement to medieval renditions of the line between philosophy and Judaism effectively inoculated him against any tendency to philosophy as having the kinds of political effects religion can produce. Because the confusion of the tasks of philosophy and religion keeps Levinas from recognizing philosophy's limits, he becomes, in Batnitzky's view, a failed reader of the Talmud and of the Jewish textual tradition most broadly. Batnitzky's Levinas attempts to find in philosophy political powers that—from an Orthodox Jewish perspective—only religious authorities could legitimately wield. Strauss, by contrast, emerges as a more productive reader of Judaism's political and legal content. It is Strauss's thought and not the secular grandchildren of the metaphysical enlightenment who can help us to understand the political function religion still plays, even in the secular West.

Levinas once described modern Jewish thought as a self-creating spiral that forms because modern Jewish thought's most basic impulse is to define itself.[25] Batnitzky's reading of Levinas and Strauss tries to break out of such a Nautilus-like growth of shell by opting for Strauss's interpretation of Judaism as law. As Zank has noted, Batnitzky's championing of Strauss is ultimately driven by an "interest in establishing a path toward a novel constructive Jewish theology of Jewish revelation as law, or Jewish law as revelation."[26] Batnitzky understands Judaism as her Strauss does, as a fundamentally political and legal affair, rather than one with ethics as its core—as Levinas (like Hermann Cohen and Martin Buber) understood it. At one point he called Talmudic science the "unfolding of the ethical order," rather than the interpretation of Law.[27] And yet if Levinas's definition holds true, neither he nor Batnitzky can be right. There is no way out of the spiral, for every time an essence is posited, the spiral simply enlarges. Neither Levinas's own understanding of Judaism as ethics nor Strauss's legalism is truly viable as a definition of Judaism in the modern West.

But one other dimension of Batnitzky's argument deserves mention. She understands Levinas to suffer from the bad, distinctly modern, and, more specifically, post-Enlightenment habit of endowing philosophy and philosophers with a kind of authority over civic life. The minimal form of this endowment would be that philosophers could vouchsafe the rational foundation of civil law. The maximal form would be that they could speak on issues of public import in a truly *ex cathedra* style. Batnitzky draws on the work of Ian Hunter to argue that this modern habit originated in the context of seventeenth-century university metaphysics in Germany, one goal of which was to "resacralise" the state. This movement opposed those civil philosophers whose goal was to divide religion from governance. According to Hunter, Gottfried Leibniz himself endorsed a certain model of the intellectual when he described a "prestigious way of life, that of the secular sage," and treated the intellection of concepts as part of the pursuit of spiritual perfection and even as participation in the divine itself.[28] As such, it gave one the qualifications to speak authoritatively on religious and civil matters. I disagree with Batnitzky's claim that Levinas was a late heir to this tendency. Certainly in his writings, philosophy and politics do seem to run together constantly, and he seems to ground his pronouncements on current events by calling on the authority of philosophy and monotheistic religion— precisely the same metaphysical logic that his own revisions of metaphysics should lead him to challenge. And yet, I have argued that "prophetic witnessing," Levinas's replacement for philosophical authority, was itself a public performance of powerlessness—hardly the endowment of philosophy with civic authority, and closer, ironically, to the anarchistic tendencies others have seen in Levinas. Furthermore, and unlike Arendt, Levinas never inquired into the possible *function* of the public and, aside from his comments on criticism as "the public's mode of comportment" in the 1948 "Reality and its Shadow," he left the public undescribed, as though it would be enough for it to serve as an audience for acts of witnessing

Publics Modern and Archaic

In a March 7, 1934, radio broadcast titled "Schöpferische Landschaft: Warum bleiben wir in der Provinz?" ("Creative Landscape: Why Do We Remain in the Provinces?"), Heidegger explained his decision to decline a professorship in Berlin: "This philosophical work does not take its course like the aloof studies of some eccentric. It belongs right in the midst of the peasants' work."[29] The city was not just the place of "aloof eccentrics." It was also where one traded the solitude of the countryside for the experience of publicness Heidegger had attacked seven years earlier in *Being and Time*. "In the public world one can be made a celebrity overnight by the newspapers and journals. That always remains the surest way to have one's ownmost intentions get misinterpreted and quickly and thoroughly forgotten."[30] The obvious incongruity between Heidegger's complaint about newspapers and the fact that he was communicating over the more recent contrivance of radio was only the surface of the irony; a listener with an intimate knowledge of the 1927 *Being and Time* might have recalled Heidegger's suggestion that the radio was part of modernity's "speeding-up of things" and "conquest of remoteness." He had characterized it as a prosthetic by means of which "*Dasein* has so expanded its everyday environment that it has accomplished an un-distancing of the 'world'—an un-distancing that, in its meaning for *Dasein*, cannot yet be visualized."[31] This was not praise. Rather, the radio, like the newspaper, was part of modern media's production of a style of publicness that alienated the individual from her- or himself.[32] The implication was that Heidegger's deep philosophical work belonged in the peasants' space and at the pace of their labors. A rural clock should regulate it.

While Strauss praised Heidegger for facing a contemporary crisis of values, his teacher faced it by turning to the past. For Heidegger, the public and the urban were tied to the modern. He had been born in 1889, during the great industrializing push that transformed Germany, but he was a native of rural Messkirch, far less touched by the urbanization that would make Berlin the world's third-largest city by 1920, and he maintained his preference for rural settings throughout his lifetime. He was certainly aware that cities like Berlin were filled with public spaces (trains, parks, cafes, the street itself) that were defined by newspaper reading. At the turn of the century and increasingly thereafter, the newspaper was the medium through which many Berliners understood their environment.[33] Newspapers effectively provided their readers with constant running narratives about their cities, supplying information about politics, crime, the arts, and, of course, the economy. By the end of the nineteenth century, most inhabitants of German cities read newspapers daily, sometimes more than daily due to the evening editions. The city's "newspaper density" was greater than that of any other city in Europe.[34] By 1926, the journalist Hans Brennert could write, "Every hour in Berlin flings millions of newspaper pages onto streets, into houses, into officers, banking suites, factories, taverns and theaters."[35] It was precisely this invasive quality of the media that seemed to animate Heidegger's commentaries on the public in *Being and Time*, just one year after Brennert, but in the comforting solitude of his cabin in the Black Forest. As Benedict Anderson points out, the only thing linking the diverse events reported on the front page of a newspaper is the day's date: the medium thus reinforces the point that temporality is all, and journalism's temporality is (or was, in 1927) faster than any other form of writing.[36] The newspaper was, in effect, an inescapable urban clock.

For Arendt, Levinas, and Strauss, the public belonged to no single period of time. In some of its forms it was as modern as print (and they engaged primarily with its modern instantiation), but it was also as ancient as the agora. Each of them sustained elements of Heidegger's antipathy toward public life in their own work, while also considering the ways in which the scene of address, the meeting point between private and public, had always been a condition of philosophical practice—in fact, in the later works of both Arendt and Levinas, we get the impression that exposure to others is a permanent part of human experience, woven through the very fabric of our language and thought, touching both with a "trace" of our possible relationships with other persons. And even as they rebelled against Heidegger's influence, they asked a question he had asked both implicitly and explicitly in his earlier writings: what was the proper time of philosophy? Could it, should it, move at the ever-accelerating speed of modernity? Tellingly, in an August 15, 1946, letter to his friend Löwith, Strauss complained both about the modern city ("the famous atomic bombs—not to mention at all cities with a million inhabitants, gadgets, funeral homes, 'ideologies'—show that the contemporary solution, that is, the completely modern solution, is *contra naturam*") and about newspapers; he spoke of his desire to warn his students "*what* sort of rubbish is praised by idiots in *The New York Times, Tribune,* etc." [37] [Strauss's emphasis.] It might be tempting to understand Heidegger's instrumentalization of philosophy during his Nazi rectorship as an attempt to bring philosophy "up to speed"—up to the speed of Germany's political transformation—but Heidegger's relationship with National Socialist Party policy suggests otherwise. Heidegger may, for a time, have understood the National Socialists as the vanguard of Germany's future, but by the mid-1930s he saw that, rather than confronting the dilemmas of industrial modernization (which he had previously credited Hitler with doing), the Nazis were embracing the factory and of course the airplane and the tank. Heidegger's post-*Kehre* ("turn" in this case indicating a transition in thought) philosophy was as "worldly" as the thought of *Being and Time* in the sense that it wrestled with *Dasein's* temporal and worldly horizons, but it was hardly an effort to consider *Dasein* at a rapid modern tempo.

Nor would Heidegger's students construe their own various projects as attempts to bring philosophy "up to speed," though they clearly felt the need to respond to pressing twentieth-century problems. Many of them, including Arendt, Levinas, and Strauss, would engage in a form of modern archaism, reaching into the past for elements of traditional or ancient thought or culture, which they then employed in intellectual projects that were themselves modernist in important respects.[38] Arendt's interest in an agonistic version of public Greek politics, Strauss's celebration of the "medieval enlightenment" over its modern counterpart, and Levinas's use of the Bible and Talmud all conform to this pattern. As Strauss put it in his talk, "The Problem of Socrates," "every concern for the past which is more than idle curiosity is rooted in a dissatisfaction with the present." But, he continued, the point was that *no* present could be truly satisfying.[39] The dynamic of archaic modernism can never be fully worked through, and is conducted with a consciousness that the past does not represent a stable and final chronological position of authority from which we might resolve our present crises. Archaic modernisms imply a commitment to a form of historicism.

There was of course a deep conflict between Heidegger's vision of publicness, a leveling-down in which all the serious content of discourse gets lost, and the notion of the public as a kind of permanent reasonable tribunal that became attached to the figure of "the intellectual" at the time of the Dreyfus Affair and after. Heidegger's concern had been dual—to posit that public life is inauthentic and keeps the individual from a real relation with himself (and with *Dasein*), and to figure the public as a space of unintelligibility, or rather, a space in which discourse gets leveled down to a kind of intelligibility beneath the level of serious thought. These are very different concerns, though the latter can be understood to contain a critique of the very principle upon which the figure of "the intellectual" was always taken to function. Michael Warner has suggested that we should understand "publics" less as concrete social groups and more as "terms of intelligibility;" we would then become aware of ourselves as part of a public defined by shared terms of understanding. Likewise, to address a public is to "engage in struggles—at varying levels of salience to consciousness, from calculated tactic to mute cognitive noise—over the conditions that bring them together as a public."[40] Ironically, the public Heidegger had imagined in *Being and Time* was defined by a failure of intelligibility on the deepest of levels. This same duality surfaces in Arendt's attacks on the failures of publicness in mass society—such as the ones she described in that document of Western Civilization's decline, *The Origins of Totalitarianism*—and her celebration of a public process conducted by peers who share terms of intelligibility, in *The Human Condition*. We can likewise observe it (albeit iterated on an entirely different level) in Strauss's notion of exoteric writing, which preserves a divide between those who truly understand and those who can only grasp the superficial presentation of a text. But in Strauss the Heideggerian concern for authenticity disappears, replaced by a heightened effort to understand what counts as intelligibility both for the general public and for two other important types of persons—gifted youths who might wake up to the intricacies of an esoteric text, and their older, fully trained counterparts, the philosophers. Esoteric writing is premised on the worry that the public might understand the skeptical lessons of philosophical texts, which would endanger the weak agreements about politics, religion, and morality that bind society together. In contrast, what remains perplexing about Levinas's approach to this issue of intelligibility is precisely the tension between the ethics he understood as "Hebrew," in the sense of being derived from monotheism's rendition of the encounter with the Other, and the "Greek" language in which the witnessing of that encounter had to be expressed. Greek was a universal language, universally intelligible. Yet it would seem that for Levinas, what mattered was not that the content of a witness's speech was understood, but rather that the suffering to which they bore witness was registered and acted upon. He seemed inspired by the Dreyfus Affair, but it was to affect and not reason that he appealed.

Notably, Arendt and Strauss both aligned the objectionable dimensions of publicness with modern technology, as Heidegger had. Both were critics not of technology per se but of the technocratic mindset that governs our expectations for technology to reshape social life. Arendt's *The Human Condition* and Strauss's *Natural Right and History,* works that present radically different and contrasting accounts of modern publicness (but that, as this work has argued, agree that modern publicness is readily debased) should be understood to share in a critique of technocratic thinking. For Strauss (an outspoken critic of technocracy since his days on the staff of the journal *Social Research*), this critique was yoked to his critique of Kojève's hopes for a "world state," which Strauss was developed at the same time as he mused over the historical transition from classical to modern conceptions of natural right:

> Aristotle did not conceive of a world state because he was absolutely certain that science is essentially theoretical and that the liberation of technology from moral and political control would lead to disastrous consequences: the fusion of science and the arts together with the unlimited or uncontrolled progress of technology has made universal and perpetual tyranny a serious possibility.[41]

Strauss's complaint regarding the dangers of science's theoretical nature taking on material form, made in the 1949 Walgreen Lectures that would become *Natural Right and History*, would find its echo eight years later in Arendt's own Walgreen Lectures which became *The Human Condition*. Scientists, Arendt claimed, "move in a world where speech has lost its power."[42] In other words, they have lost their capacity to participate in public political life even as their specialty, the perfection of technical processes, became increasingly important for the regulation of mass society. Notably, where Heidegger's concerns about technology (which developed, as Stuart Elden has shown, in part out of Heidegger's early thought on measurement and calculation[43]) emphasized the way modern technology obscures our potential authentic relations with Being, for Strauss and Arendt technocratic thought obscures the true nature of political life. In Strauss's view such thought enabled tyranny, and while Arendt did not associate science and technology with tyranny per se, there was an implied relationship between the image with which she opened *The Human Condition*—the launch and orbit of the Soviet satellite Sputnik—and the "artificial world" of the camps established for the victims of totalitarian regimes. As Benjamin Lazier notes, Sputnik (which Hans Blumenberg called a "beeping artificial world") was more than an effort to escape the Earth's gravity, and even more than an effort to reach an Archimedean perspective on the terrestrial horizon of all human experience. It inevitably recalled the effort to create "a new world fit to compete with this one," which Arendt had claimed was the aim of the twentieth century's rabid new forms of governance.[44] Arendt said much the same about scientific experiments in *The Human Condition*: "the world of the experiment seems always capable of becoming a man-made reality."[45] The relation between science and totalitarianism may have been abstract and formal, but it was real: *homo faber*, the maker of artificial things, can run amok. Strauss said less about science than Arendt did (though his anxieties about the Atomic Age are apparent in his aforementioned correspondence with Löwith, and his doubts about the progressivist attitude of modern science are legible throughout *Natural Right and History*), but the relationship between the "world state" and the artificial moon, Sputnik, is clear enough. In *On Tyranny*, Strauss had insisted "present-day tyranny, in contradistinction to classical tyranny, is based on the unlimited progress towards the 'conquest of nature' that modern science makes possible, as well as on the popularization or diffusion of philosophic or scientific knowledge."[46]

Certainly, the Arendt of *The Human Condition* and the Strauss of *Natural Right and History* both turned to nature, or *physis*, to provide humans with a form of law or *nomos*, and they enjoined their readers to accept the relative permanence and inalterable character of nature's law. Also clear is a surprising parallel between Strauss and Arendt's thought, a parallel that begins to appear in their productions of the mid-1940s through the late 1950s: both associated healthy political life with a comparatively small scale of *demos*, as if echoing not just Heidegger's deepening appreciation of nature but also his dislike of "massiveness" as an attribute of the modern age.[47] Strauss insisted to Kojève and Löwith that the nation-state would not be surpassed by larger political bodies, and Arendt presented a model of the public that required relative intimacy and prohibited anonymity—else how could it possibly function on the agonistic principle she imagined? In keeping with their Heideggerian objections to technocracy, both displayed scorn for social scientists who employed the (originally European) tools of positivism and historicism, and who sought to interfere with political life as if they were engineers. For both of them, "intellectuals" were individuals capable of drifting, as Philip Rieff once put it in a frank assessment of midcentury American social science, from "the New School [for Social Research] to the Rand Corporation."[48] They shared the conviction that the modern mania for measurement as a tool for governance—certainly made necessary by the sheer scale of modern societies—corrupted the nature of politics itself. In this they echoed Heidegger's view that modernity had lost sight of the Greek idea articulated by Protagoras, that "man is the measure of all things" or that humanity supplies its own standards for political life.

While Strauss did not couch "Persecution and the Art of Writing" as an investigation of the social effects of technological change, in a certain sense it was one, for he was well aware that the printing and publishing revolution in early modern Europe had greatly expanded the possibilities for popular education.[49] But as mentioned in Chapter 2 of this book, at the outset of his 1941 essay, Strauss had noted the small number of thinkers who enjoyed access to modern media: "What is called freedom of thought in a large number of cases amounts to—and even for all practical purposes consists of—the ability to choose between two or more different views presented by the small minority of people who are public speakers or writers."[50] Something had slipped between the rise of the children of Gutenberg and *Social Research* or, more properly, between the Enlightenment enthusiasm for popular education (if

popular education were effective, "no one would suffer any harm from hearing any truth," as Strauss put it[51]) and the twentieth-century jargon of involvement in public life, so popular among "intellectuals." That slippage was
simple enough: a belief in the linked nature of intellectual and social progress, a belief that could, in turn, lead (as Strauss explained in *Natural Right
and History*) to the instrumentalization of intellectual life. In Strauss's view,
the Enlightenment faith in the public's ability to mature (to use its own
reason and escape what Kant once termed *unmündigkeit,* immaturity) had
gone unrewarded. The Enlightenment's liberal bias and prejudice on behalf
of natural science had produced a style of thought that, in place of a truly
educated public, had produced instead "public opinion," which was in fact—
so Strauss argued at the outset of *Natural Right and History,* extending the
position he had taken in "Persecution and the Art of Writing"—mere public
dogma. Here it is important to return to the issue of intelligibility in order to
clarify Strauss's point: the problem is not one of communication (which would
be a problem of language or the style of expression), but of understanding, of
thinking deeply about what was communicated. Public speech about the nature of things, including public political speech about the nature of the polis,
was little more than what Heidegger had termed "*gerede,*" or idle chatter.[52]

Socrates effectively comes to us as a literary character through the writings of Plato and Xenophon, [53] but while he says so very much (especially in
Plato's middle and late-period dialogues), he nevertheless has struck many
as silent, especially regarding himself. As Kierkegaard puts it in *The Concept
of Irony,* "Socrates' life is like a magnificent pause in the course of history:
we do not hear him at all." This made him a perfect character, in a sense, a
blank page that could be rewritten again and again. Unsurprisingly, Arendt,
Levinas, and Strauss's varied portrayals of Socrates all take note of his relationship with authority. In Strauss's writings he appears as a teacher; Arendt
greatly downplays Socrates's personal authority in *The Life of the Mind,* where
he appears as a fellow-citizen who helps his fellows to investigate their own
opinions. In Levinas's *Totality and Infinity* his teachings circumvent any problematic or "violent" pedagogical method. At stake in each of these portrayals is the question of how the philosopher should behave, both in politics and
in relation to interlocutors or students.

Such invocations of Socrates are, of course, a great theme of the history
of philosophy and social thought. Michel Foucault made him into an expert
on the "care of the self;" Nietzsche castigated him as a rationalist who "murdered" the spirit of tragedy in ancient Greece, but acknowledged that his

antipathy was driven by a close identification with Socrates; Hegel made him a symbol of a new era of reason, not a gadfly, but rather an "extension of the existing civic structures" of Athens, as Miriam Leonard puts it.[54] For the counter-Enlightenment thinker Johann Georg Hamann, Socrates was an irrationalist at heart, while for Hamann's counterpart on the other side of the Enlightenment debates, Moses Mendelssohn, to identify with Socrates had both philosophical and political meanings, as it helped Mendelssohn to present his thought as buttressed by universal reason rather than by revealed religion. Socrates-identification could thus serve as a tool in the campaign for Jewish integration into Europe, with rationalism providing a tempting common ground for Jews and their European neighbors. When Strauss accused modernity of *Sokratesvergessenheit* (forgetfulness of Socrates and his questions), he referenced, consciously or unconsciously, a host of philosophical and political issues including ones pressing for Jews.

Strauss knew that his own understanding of Socrates was partly motivated by a rebellion against Nietzsche's earlier reading of their ancestor. In his 1958 lecture series "The Problem of Socrates," he agreed with Nietzsche's characterization of Socrates in *The Birth of Tragedy* as "the proto-type and first ancestor of the theoretical man." But he would not follow Nietzsche in thinking that Socratic rationalism meant commitment to a world-shaping progressivism.[55] Socrates did not stand for unrestrained rationality, but rather was the origin of the principle of doubled speech Strauss would develop into the doctrine of "esoteric writing." In "The Spirit of Sparta or the Taste of Xenophon"—among other things, a preparatory exercise for "Persecution and the Art of Writing"—Strauss had found a "deliberate distortion of the truth" in Xenophon's Socrates.[56] Influenced by al-Farabi, Strauss understood Socrates's esoteric discourse to be a defense against the city's harsh punishment for impiety; neither Socrates nor Xenophon believed in the city's gods.

The distinction between Arendt's and Strauss's presentations of Socrates is, as Villa points out, roughly equivalent to the distinction between a teacher and a peer, though the differences run deeper than the issue of authority. Like Strauss, Arendt associated the trial of Socrates with the beginning of the "great tradition" of political thought, and with the splitting of the path of thinkers from the path of actors as the prejudice on behalf of contemplation grew stronger. She blamed not those who Strauss termed "the vulgar," but rather philosophers themselves for preferring ideas to men: Socrates might have been condemned unjustly, but not because of a general allergy to skeptical inquiry among the Athenians. Her Socrates was the last great philosopher

to operate before the start of a decline whose effects were still felt in Arendt's own day. Not only was he, in *The Life of the Mind*, the last to combine
passions for thinking and acting. In her "Some Questions of Moral Philosophy," he appears spending his days in the marketplace, "the same marketplace which Plato's philosopher shuns explicitly."[57] Here we see another
great divide between Arendt and Strauss on Socrates: Strauss did not distinguish greatly between Socrates as a historical figure and Plato's Socrates
(he effectively wrote on Socrates as a literary figure), whereas Arendt insisted on the difference between them. Thus in *The Life of the Mind* Arendt
complained about Plato attributing views to Socrates that were foreign to
him, such as having him declaim, in the *Theatatus*, that great philosophers
never knew how to get to the marketplace at all.[58] The principle of authority
Plato bequeathed to European intellectual history was intended to compen-
sate for the perceived failures of persuasion, and this seed grew into the prejudice against spontaneity, openness, and unpredictability that Arendt saw
running through the Great Tradition like a red thread.[59] Furthermore, in
Arendt's descriptions of Socrates, we learn that he was always interested primarily in the opinions of others as they *appeared*—that is, were stated—in
public. He was not interested in the distinction between metaphysical truth
and worldly appearance that Plato would later project back onto his teacher.

Perhaps most important, Arendt's Socrates internalizes a principle of appearance or publicness even as he also externalizes or makes public the
thinking process. This had implications, she noted, for the problem of hidden crimes: Socrates held that each should see himself as a witness to his own
actions, and also as a tribunal of judgment for them. Socrates was not only
in the polis; the polis was in him. She liked to quote Socrates's statement that
it was better "to be in disagreement with multitudes than, being one, to be in
disagreement with oneself." Rather than protected by a principle of esoteric
speech, Arendt's Socrates was vulnerable—"entirely unprotected, open to all
questioners, to all demands to give an account of and to live up to what he
said," as she put it, "the figure of *the* philosopher."[60] In fact Arendt was not
erasing the public-private divide at all, which would have run against her own
celebration of that distinction in *The Human Condition* (on consideration she
is just as reliant, but differently reliant, on the distinction as Strauss). She was
demonstrating the continuum between internal and external life, the linkage
between the parts of thought that Thinking, Willing, and Judging represent,
and recasting them as different parts of the self. In the *Lectures on Kant's*

Political Philosophy, Arendt united Socrates and Kant in the belief that critical thinking meant opening one's views to "free and open examination," and she quoted Kant's observation that "every philosophical work must be susceptible of popularity; if not, it probably conceals nonsense beneath a fog of seeming sophistication." Indeed, Arendt took Kant to be extending Socrates's principle of self-consistency through the enlarged mentality of the *sensus communis*. The project of recovering from *Sokratesvergessenheit*, for Arendt, meant not recovering "the problem of Socrates" in the sense of Strauss's divide between philosophers and other persons, but rather overcoming the prejudice that considered philosophy a private practice not subject to the rules governing other forms of human thought, including the rule of appearance and the expectation of perception—the internalization of publicness. "Even Socrates, so much in love with the marketplace, has to go home, where he will be alone, in solitude, in order to meet the other fellow."[61]

Levinas's writings of the early 1960s seem decidedly ambivalent regarding Socrates's status as a figure of philosophical authority. On the one hand, Socrates prevails over a tendency among philosophers to teach either through force or seduction. In other words, the persuasive character of Socratic *maieutics* functioned for Levinas, as it did for Arendt, as an alternative to authority—and *Totality and Infinity* was a work preoccupied by the question of whether philosophy could engage with the world without dominating that which it sought to describe and understand. The implications for the educations of young philosophers were obvious. One trained by domination would never be able to think freely. Ten years before *Totality and Infinity*, in the 1951 "Is Ontology Fundamental," Levinas had mentioned Socrates in the course of arguing that thought is so inextricably tied to its expression that it does not exist *without* being expressed. "But," he wrote, "expression does not consist in somehow pouring a thought related to the other into the mind of the other. We have known this—not since Heidegger, but since Socrates."[62] Heidegger had missed a point concerning both pedagogy and communication, one Socrates had understood.

But despite his openness to alterity at the level of *maieutics*, Levinas's Socrates was not awake to alterity at the level of theory in the same fashion as Arendt's Socrates, or, for that matter, Strauss's. Both were thinkers for whom the limitations of all human knowledge placed them in a persistent relationship with a form of philosophical other, namely, knowledge of the Whole itself. In contrast, Levinas wrote in *Totality and Infinity*:

> Western philosophy has most often been an ontology: a reduction of
> the other to the same by interposition of a middle and neutral term
> that ensures the comprehension of being.
>
> The primacy of the same was Socrates's teaching: to receive noth-
> ing of the Other but what is in me, as though from all eternity I was
> in possession of what comes to me from the outside—to receive
> nothing, or to be free.[63]

Socratic philosophy was as much an egology as the rest of Western philosophy, and this, evidently, despite all that is laudable in Socratic pedagogy. In
the essay "Freedom of Speech," originally published in the journal *Lettres
Nouvelles* in 1957 and later in *Difficult Freedom*, Levinas similarly placed
Socrates in a Western tradition of thinking about language "in which the
word counts only because of the eternal order which it manages to bring to
consciousness;" in other words, totality. Socrates was, Levinas implied, "apha-
siac" in his treatment of language, falling into a trap of coherence that elimi-
nates the possibility of "prophetic speech."[64] Levinas did not develop this
treatment of Socrates further and one could easily miss its radical character.
He was effectively arguing that Socrates, the greatest enemy of common sense
in the history of Western philosophy who nevertheless spoke in the language
of the marketplace, spoke in the language of the public *in Heidegger's sense*: his
speech was just as occluded as what Heidegger called *Gerede*, or "idle chatter."
    But Levinas would effect a striking reversal not long after completing *To-
tality and Infinity*. Despite his criticisms of Socrates in that book, in his 1961
"Heidegger, Gagarin and Us," he paid Socrates what we can safely say was
the highest compliment Levinas could give: comparison with Judaism. The
full passage is crucial to understanding the meaning of Levinas's about-face:

> Technology wrenches us out of the Heideggerian world and the su-
> perstitions surrounding *Place*. From this point on, an opportunity
> appears to us: to perceive men outside the situation in which they are
> placed, and let the human face shine in all its nudity. Socrates pre-
> ferred the town, in which one meets people, to the countryside and
> trees. Judaism is the brother of the Socratic message.[65]

Oddly, whereas in *Totality and Infinity* Socrates had seemed a stand-in for
Heidegger as a thinker of totality whose model of truth dealt not with human multiplicity, but with the singularity or totality of the philosopher's

own consciousness, here Socrates received a treatment more consonant with Arendt and Strauss's emphasis on his urban location and concern with human action. Suddenly set against Heidegger, Socrates now exemplified an interest in the experiences of others in all their uniqueness, an interest Levinas associated (as he had since his internment at Fallingpostel) with Judaism. While Levinas was no simple celebrant of technology, in his essay on Gagarin's flight he celebrated human mastery over "Place" (he was obviously thinking of Heidegger's *Ort* as described in the post-*Kehre* essays) as an escape from the pagan context of Heidegger's thought. He understood the Archimedean point of orbit—the same Archimedean perspective on human affairs Arendt and Strauss were rejecting in their criticisms of technocracy—*not* as a spot from which to achieve a totalized perspective, but rather as a point of access to "the human face . . . in all its nudity," or, in other words, as the particular that afforded access to the infinite ethical relation. Surprisingly, for a thinker of the Atomic Age so concerned with domination and capable of writing worriedly about the possibility of nuclear war, Levinas expressed optimism regarding the "new technological possibilities" and "new forms of knowledge" that Gagarin's orbit might open up. The tension between the Socrates of *Totality and Infinity*, who is complicit with a philosophy of totality that is in turn complicit with war and politics, and the Socrates of the Gagarin essay, is striking, and suggests that the idea of Socrates as a *teacher* may have attracted Levinas more than Socrates's putative egology repulsed him. While Levinas cited neither Xenophon's nor Plato's account of Socrates, in particular, it seems likely that the Socrates of *Totality and Infinity* is the one we encounter in Plato's middle and later dialogues.

What unites Arendt, Levinas, and Strauss's portrayals of Socrates is an interest in scenes of address and exchange—in the public character of Socrates's work—and what divides them is the question of the value of publicness, and what thinking in public made Socrates do. There is no deceit in Arendt's or Levinas's Socrates, of course, for they were not animated, as Strauss was, by a mistrust of the polis and its public life per se, but rather by anxieties about the fragility of modern forms of publicness. And Strauss returned to the scene of Socrates's life and work more frequently—one might say, more compulsively—than did Arendt or Levinas, justifying Robert Pippin's suggestion that Socrates drinking the hemlock could count as the iconic crucifixion moment in a "religion" based on Strauss's thought, that for Strauss the figure of Socrates captured the isolation that endures when philosophers live in political community with nonphilosophers, even as that figure captured a form of openness for Levinas and, for Arendt, an appetite for action. The contrast between the moderate political attitude Strauss advocated, based on the story of Socrates,[66] and Levinas attaching Socrates to a technological narrative involving space travel, could not be starker. Notably, there is not exactly a "quarrel" between ancients and moderns in this version of Levinas— nor is there such a quarrel in the Arendt who teams Socrates with Kant.

But even more importantly, behind these differing portrayals of Socrates stand different attitudes toward the metaphysics for which Socrates, in Plato's dialogues, became a mouthpiece. Arendt's rejection of metaphysics leads her to focus on Socrates's self-consistency and dialogue with himself; Levinas's portrayal of Socrates in *Totality and Infinity* was marked by precisely the same tension that attended his discussions of Platonic metaphysics in that text. Levinas understood there to be an egology in Plato's thought at the same time as he described his book as Platonist and identified his own "infinity" with Plato's insistence in the *Republic* that the Good lies beyond being.[67] While Plato seemed to Levinas to promote the suspect notion of autonomy in his discussions of the needs of the body,[68] he also wrote that "Plato nowise deduces being from the Good: he posits transcendence as surpassing the totality."[69] The remaining question was how to move from Plato to ethics, and Levinas's comment on Socratic *maieutics* suggested a pedagogical method by which to do just that.

In no case did any of the three suggest that Socrates used philosophy to buttress a claim to moral authority; he was *not* "an intellectual" in the popular sense of expecting his insights into transcendental affairs to license interventions in public debates. When Strauss, in *Natural Right and History*, wrote of Socrates founding political philosophy by calling "philosophy down from the heavens and forc[ing] it to make inquiries about life and manners and good and bad things," he meant inquiry and not authority.[70] Strauss's Socrates, in other words, resists what Levinas would term "totality," even as he turned toward the truth of the Whole and away from what Arendt termed "opinion." Meanwhile, Levinas's own rejection of the distinction between truth and opinion ("The idea of infinity is the mind before it lends itself to the distinction between what it discovers by itself and what it receives from opinion," he wrote in *Totality and Infinity*[71]) implied that he would seek ethics where Arendt sought the relative truth of appearances, in other persons and in the expressions of their faces and words.

Much as classical natural right, and Socrates as a philosopher thereof, served Strauss as a measure against the groundless conventionalism of modern

natural right, so did Socrates serve Arendt as a counter to a particular negative trend in modernity: our loss of the capacity for productive solitude. In
an August 20, 1954, letter to her friend Mary McCarthy, written during her
engagement with Marx and the Great Tradition, Arendt referred to the "fee-
bleminded thoughtfulness of intellectuals," and the forgetting of Socrates's
wisdom due to the fact that no one is truly alone anymore. In other words, in
the modern world everyone had lost Socrates's first lesson, which had to do
not with a dialogue with others but with himself, which is necessary before
any real speech in public is possible. As she wrote, sarcastically, "Our friends,
craving for philosophic 'information' (something which does not exist) are
by no means 'thinkers' or willing to enter the dialogue of thought with themselves."[72] A few years later, Arendt would conclude *The Human Condition* with
a quotation from Cato the Elder that, to the most casual reader, could be
taken to contravene the book's extensive arguments on behalf of action:
"*Numquam se plus agere quam nihil cum ageret, nunquam minus solum esse
quam cum solus esset*"—"Never is he more active than when he is doing
nothing, never is he less alone than when he is by himself."[73] These lines
themselves recall the capacity for productive thought Arendt had already
begun to see in Socrates, which would become the more formalized portrayal of internalized publicness we see in *The Life of the Mind*. And while
Arendt surely would have had little patience for Levinas's devaluation of
freedom in favor of bondage to ethics, she certainly agreed with his view
that action—in the sense of Sartrean *engagement*, perhaps—was so easily
corrupted that one had to engage in detached thought in preparation for it.
Against Kojève's orientation toward action, Arendt, like Levinas and Strauss,
prioritized something ironically also present in Kojève's reading of Hegel:
an insistence on self-consciousness that included awareness of the shaping power of publicness, without which the actions of intellectuals (were
they countenanced at all) would be meaningless.

Reading Exiles, Hermeneutic Jews

Not historians, Arendt, Levinas, and Strauss were nevertheless all readers of
Jewish history who never shared Moses Maimonides's view that the subject
was "*bizbuz zeman*," or a "waste of time."[74] Interpreters of all three have made
strikingly similar claims about their interests in past and contemporary Jewish experience: Arendt (or Levinas, or Strauss) was Judeocentric in the sense

of taking Jewish history and, most specifically, the experience of exile as a point of departure for broader claims about politics and ethics. Leon Botstein has argued that Arendt's account of a Jewish "pariah" identity was not only an attempt to describe a historical Jewish type, but also a developmental step toward her theory of political action. The qualities she attributed to properly political speech in *The Human Condition* were extrapolations from "the exceptional dimension of Jewish history" or, in other words, in Botstein's view, "action" was not a borrowing from ancient Greek politics at all but "the Jewish experience generalized."[75] Jewish history was the acorn, Arendt's political theory the oak. Such arguments must strain not to reduce a thinker's oeuvre to their own identity. If we embrace the thesis that Levinas's vision of the Other did not originate in his Judaism, we should be cautious of interpretations of Arendt and Strauss that reduce their thought to a reflex of Jewish historical experience. Still, there is good reason to think that Jewish history influenced Arendt, Levinas, and Strauss's thinking on the issue of publicness and on the role of the intellectual in public life. In particular, Jewish history provided a privileged understanding of just how fragile liberalism could be, a point most clear on the surface of Strauss's writings, but, as we have seen, present in Arendt and Levinas as well. It had been on the basis of liberalism's relegation of religion to the place of private confession that Jews were granted Emancipation in Europe and, in the views of some it had been liberalism's weakness that led to its collapse in Germany and to the rise of Nazism. Nor were Arendt, Strauss, or Levinas celebrants of the terms of Emancipation, though they recognized its necessity; each in their own way they celebrated Jewish distinctiveness and objected to the assumption, so common among eighteenth-century proponents of Emancipation, that visible Jewish difference (and the Jewish people qua people) would simply fade away over time.[76] It was also liberal democratic society that made the public so very important for politics, and made participation in public political debate a foundational part of "the intellectual's" identity. Despite their interests in Zionism, they were hardly enemies of Diasporic Jewish life, and, in fact, the figure of the Jew as estranged from her or his environment—as an exilic presence or even, in terminology that has become familiar, a form of "difference"—served as an imaginative resource in their readings of both textual traditions and contemporary political realities.

Of the three thinkers, Levinas was simultaneously the least historically minded and the quickest to invoke the motif of Jewish "election" and exemplarity. As he put it, "Judaism is an essential modality of every human being," effectively harmonizing with the Sartre of *Anti-Semite and Jew* for whom the Jewish case offers us an "intensification" of the predicament of human "thrownness" and freedom considered most broadly. In the short essay "Israel and Universalism," he insisted that the meaning of Jewish election was "exceptional duties" rather than "exceptional rights," the bondage of which one becomes aware when one feels the call of morality. Even if this kind of morality is universally applicable, in Levinas's view, it is never experienced as a universalism but rather as a particularism, an "election."[77] Levinas's development of this reading of Jewish election was not only a response to the version of "rootedness" and even "enchainment" he associated with Heidegger's thought, nor a development out of his view, formulated at Fallingpostel, that Judaism was an openness to the ethical demands made by the presence of the Other, but also a response to Sartre's treatment of the Jew, which had made that condition less intrinsically significant and translated it into the most universal terms possible. It was only toward the end of Sartre's life that the inner meaning of that gesture became apparent, disclosed to his assistant Benny Lévy in conversation in 1978: "It is me that I was describing when I thought I was describing the Jew, a type who has nothing, no land, an intellectual."[78]

Four years previously, in *Otherwise Than Being*, Levinas had effectively produced this same equivalency between the deracinated Jew and the intellectual who places her or himself hostage on behalf of the sufferings of others. His statement, like Sartre's, reproduced signal elements of discourse on Jews deployed at the time of the Dreyfus Affair. As Sarah Hammerschlag argues, at the end of the nineteenth century the idea that the Jew is roughly equivalent to the landless intellectual had been a mainstay of the anti-Dreyfusard Maurice Barrès, for whom the term "les déracinés" described all the groups that threatened France, including (after the term came into widespread use) "*les intellectuels*," but also Protestants and Jews. Rootlessness was the problem and its solution was for native French Catholics to acknowledge their own roots, celebrate them, and insist on their right to exclude foreign influences from French cultural and political life.[79] The problem with the Jews was not their foreign origins alone—the fact that, for example, even the Jews who served as loyal civil servants of the Republic had ancestors from Eastern Europe—but the fact that they lacked a deep relationship with some particular soil, somewhere. In his attack on the universalistic interpretation of "fraternity" within the French revolutionary triumvirate of virtues, Barrès identified universal brotherhood (a notion contrary to his own understanding of nationalism) as an idea crafted by Jewish intellectuals.[80]

Naturally, the upshot of this theory was that the Jews themselves had crafted the ideology of the French Revolution itself, and it was unsurprising that they were granted citizenship in the Revolution's wake.

Notably, in that same document, Barrès—credited with giving new popularity to the term "an intellectual" shortly after its use by Clemenceau—offered a definition of such persons in which their figural "rootlessness" was very important: "Intellectual: an individual who is persuaded that society must be founded on logic and who fails to recognize that it rests in fact on anterior necessities and may be at odds with individual reason."[81] Of course, Levinas's ultimate invocation of "the intellectual" in 1974 was diametrically opposed to Barrès's "logic." Levinas proposed a different set of "anterior necessities," namely, responsibility for the sufferings of others that impinge upon us as a form of bondage long before we "come to ourselves" as rational subjects. But Levinas certainly agreed with Barrès that the Jew and the intellectual both need not feel the "anterior necessity" of the love of place, as given its most dramatic illustration in Levinas's "Heidegger, Gagarin and Us." Levinas had, by this time in his career, long celebrated an ethics whose first requirement was the condition of deracination itself.

For Levinas—like Arendt and Strauss a decidedly post-liberal thinker on Jewish questions—the idea that the chosen and exilic condition of the Jewish people was a precondition for ethics had an important corollary, one with which Arendt and Strauss emphatically agreed: Jewish difference must not disappear through the processes of assimilation and normalization. In his 1959 essay "How Is Judaism Possible?" Levinas stressed the importance of public Jewish visibility and of the refusal to surrender Judaism to the invisible status of confession, with no significance for Jews beyond the home or the synagogue. This visibility was of course no normalization. Rather, it evoked Rosenzweig's antipolitical account of Judaism as "a recovery, the joy of self-possession within universal trembling, a glimpse of eternity in the midst of corruption." Up until now, Levinas wrote, Judaism "has been the victim of history; it has not taken on its cruelty."[82] This same language would inflect Levinas's contribution to the "Treblinka Affair," "Honor Without a Flag," and throughout many of Levinas's later "confessional" writings he would insist on Jewish visibility (a form of Jewish publicness) while denying any properly political status to it. The result was nothing less than a celebration of symbolic "exile" from politics, which famously ran aground when Levinas attempted to treat the state of Israel as though it were worthy of the same putatively ethical status as Diasporic Jewry. There was no plausible way he could deny that, by the time of the Sabra and Chatila massacres in 1982, the state had come to constitute the same form of political ontology (or Barrèsian rootedness) he had always attacked, yet he insisted on continuing to describe the project of the Israeli state as an ethical one. This, of course, was only one illustration of the inherent instability of defining Judaism as an ethics and tying it to the condition of exile.

In contrast, Arendt placed no explicitly universal weight on the idea of Jewish election. This need not contradict Botstein's claim regarding Arendt's use of the "pariah" as the basis of a political theory that would serve to describe non-Jews as well as Jews; it merely meant that though the Jewish historical experience played a critical role in her developing political thought, she declined to formally elevate the exilic Jew to the status of political exemplar. A glance at *Rahel Varnhagen* and *The Origins of Totalitarianism* shows that it was in Jewish history that Arendt found examples of the dilemmas of publicness and privacy that she would attempt to resolve in her mature political theory. It was not in *The Life of the Mind* but in these earlier works that she began to speak of the internal "dialogue of the two-in-one," which she ultimately attached to the figure of Socrates.[83] The question both works raised was, effectively, which social and political conditions facilitated such a dialogue in private along with healthy discourse in public? Not, of course, the circumstances of German Jewish assimilation traced in the Varnhagen project, or the circumstances of imperialism, anti-Semitism, and the weakening of Europe's liberal nation-states, all described in *The Origins of Totalitarianism*.

Published after the Varnhagen book was drafted and while Arendt was drawing together material that would become *The Origins of Totalitarianism*, "The Jew as Pariah: A Hidden Tradition" (1944) was an attempt to bring to light what Arendt saw as the antidote to the banal and failed adaptation strategies mapped in those other works: a political rather than a social response (i.e., assimilation) to the "Jewish Question" was called for.[84] Written just after Arendt's personal break with Zionism in 1943, this essay was influenced by the work of Lazare, whose perspective on the Dreyfus Affair Arendt had found salutary ever since Blumenfeld introduced her to his writings. Arendt particularly preferred Lazare to Herzl, with whom she could never fully agree because of her enduring commitment to the Diaspora. Not only did Arendt support Lazare's affirmation of Jewish identity within the Diaspora (she was in this sense a cultural Zionist), she believed that if the Jews were to obtain a physical homeland it would be a step toward increased equality in the Diaspora—and that the existence of Diasporic Jewish communities would help prevent the transformation of a Jewish state into a race-state on the European nationalist model. Written as Levinas was giving his emerging ethics the name of Judaism, and while Strauss was developing his thought on the "hidden tradition" of esoteric reading, Arendt's essay emphasized the importance of affirming one's political position as a Jew and *not* on any universalizing grounds as in Zola's defense of Dreyfus.[85] In this she narrowly anticipated the thought driving Sartre's speech at the Alliance Israèlite Universelle: it was necessary for one to accept the position one was placed in by anti-Semites and then defend oneself from there. One could not, in other words, endorse the hopes of the Dreyfusards and expect abstractions to prevail. As she put it, the promise of equality held out by assimilation had proven "treacherous," and the freedom ensured by emancipation merely "ambiguous."[86] On this point she was entirely aligned with both Strauss and Levinas.

Arendt's antidote was pariah identity itself, a solution to the ultimately unsatisfying dreams of assimilation. It was not exactly a way of being visibly Jewish for political purposes; the parvenu sought and received more in the way of attention, though its claims on politics were (as *The Origins of Totalitarianism* illustrated) fundamentally utopian. As Arendt put it in her 1946 essay "Privileged Jews," the parvenu type sought to use money, influence, or education to become an exception to all anti-Jewish prejudice, escaping into a "paradise of rights and liberties."[87] The pariah was "excluded from society and never quite at home in this world," as she put it, and bore a kinship with the poet.[88] But she credited Lazare with seeing that the marginality of the pariah would help the Jew to address the Jewish Question in public speech, and to respond when that question was hurled by anti-Semites, if he could only accept his own position rather than escaping into the fantasy world occupied by "*schlemihls*" like Varnhagen-nee-Levin. What divided Arendt's vision from Levinas's vision of the Jew as deracinated exile is confirmed, however, by her remarks on Kafka's Zionism, also in "the Jew as Pariah." After a long reflection on the failed attempts at assimilation made by the protagonist of Kafka's novel *The Castle*, Arendt suggested that Kafka's political stance had nothing to do with nationalism, but rather with the view that the "abnormal" situation of European Jewry had to be transformed, that they could not truly live human lives in an exceptional condition. Arendt understood full well that the perspective of the pariah was not to be maintained—indeed, she concluded her essay by remarking that "the same angry sea," or, in other words, Nazism, had engulfed both parvenu and pariah Jews alike. The remaining Jews could not truly choose to isolate themselves in the fashion of the pariah, but must rather function "in consort with other peoples," defending themselves as Jewish citizens of whatever state, and by the potentially universal political principle of rights. In *The Human Condition*, Arendt would formalize the division between the two realms she had already explored in her writings on anti-Semitism, politics, and the social, a division she thought was especially visible from the perspective of the pariah. And if the value of pariah writings like Kafka's lay within the political insights they disclosed and the power of language they embodied, nevertheless in *The Human Condition* Arendt would insist that properly political public speech was made possible not by conditions of exile, but rather by the supportive but always separate *oikos*, the household. Symbolically, at least, her archaic modernist recovery of the Greek polis as a model, expressed a central modern Jewish wish for political participation through speech.

If Arendt's defense of Jewish particularity fit neatly into (and perhaps informed) her arguments on behalf of human plurality—her insistence that we cannot, and should not, choose which peoples we will share the world with—Strauss expressed a very different version of exemplarity when he said "the Jewish problem, as it is called, is the simple and available exemplification of the human problem." This statement came in the course of his 1962 talk at the University of Chicago's Hillel House, "Why We Remain Jews: Can Jewish Faith and History Still Speak to Us?," now best read as a companion to the Preface to *Spinoza's Critique of Religion*, written in the same year, in which he described the "theologico-political predicament" facing German Jews in the Weimar years.

During his talk Strauss discussed the same predicament of assimilation Arendt named as one (failed) way out of the problem of social discrimination, and he likewise concluded that it was doomed to failure. He reviewed historical cases in which many Jews had considered themselves secure—medieval Spain, or Germany prior to Hitler's rise to power—only to find that they had been mistaken, as when the *conversos* found themselves accused of being "of impure blood," discriminated against as Jews even after conversion to Catholicism. However, Strauss said, one could only truly prohibit discrimination by abolishing the private sphere altogether—that is, abolishing liberal society's foundational division between public and private—and like Arendt he looked to totalitarianism (in his case, the Soviet Union) for an example of the disastrous consequences, for Jews, of abolishing those divisions.

As if with a sense of resignation, Strauss said, "there is nothing better than liberal society," that is, nothing better than its "uneasy" legal equality that nevertheless left room for social discrimination. It offered Jews who could not run away from their backgrounds even if they wished to, the best solution possible; the Jewish condition was "exemplary" in the important sense that it could not truly be resolved, much as other human problems did not admit of any ultimate solution. Though he stated his respect for political Zionism and reflected on his youth in the German Zionist movement, Strauss also stated that if Zionism took itself seriously (that is, took seriously the idea that Judaism was not "culture," but revealed legislation), it would have to become religious Zionism, something that had become impossible for most Jews— even for those who, like Strauss himself, called themselves atheists while continuing to recognize the wonder of the revealed legislation of Judaism. Here, Strauss implied that Judaism dealt with something he had, intriguingly but not in definitive terms, mentioned in the course of his only lecture on Heidegger: the mystery of Being itself.

Strauss's own use of Jewish exemplarity was closer to that of Levinas than to that of Arendt. As he put it, the Jewish problem exemplified the human problem, illuminating our forsaken and unredeemed condition in this world. The Jews were the "chosen people" in this sense, and if their story were properly told, "the whole of the other things would come out." This reflects more than the difference between Arendt's basically historical approach to the Jewish condition, from which she extrapolated to make political-theoretical claims that then became ahistorical in *The Human Condition* and the works that followed it, and Levinas and Strauss's more frankly ahistorical approaches. It also reflects Strauss's tendency to see the problem of threatened Jewish theological belief—not just the problem of assimilation, but the problem of science he had mapped in *Spinoza's Critique of Religion*—as exemplifying modernity's challenge more broadly. We "remain" Jews (we remain stuck in the same human predicament) precisely because the modern solutions to the effectively eternal problems of meaning on the one hand, and political life on the other, do nothing to address those problems at the important basic level. There are no "clean solutions" to the human problem, and liberal democracy remains the best political model for which we can hope.

But regardless of the differences in their readings of exile—Arendt would naturally have regarded Strauss's philosophical pariahs as *luftsmenschen*, or escapist "lords of dreams"—what Arendt, Levinas, and Strauss held in common was what Eugene Sheppard has called a feeling for exile's "forgotten virtues,"[89] virtues made necessary by adaptation to illiberal environments and hostile audiences, and to conditions in which one is exposed to structural or literal forms of violence. It was the crisis of liberalism they witnessed during their youths that made naïve faith in public politics impossible for them in their maturity.

Crucially, Arendt, Levinas, and Strauss's shared particularism ran against the universalism sometimes taken to regulate public life in Western democracies. They all thought, in other words, against the very logic that underlay the figure of "the intellectual" at the time of the Dreyfus Affair, which was also the logic that had governed Jewish inclusion in European life. Of course they diverged over what one could make of the public, after universalism's apparent failure. To reimagine the public as a crucial space for the flourishing of human plurality without recourse to universalism—which in a sense is what Arendt and Levinas both did—seemed implausible to Strauss. While Arendt and Levinas essentially shared his view that philosophy (defined, admittedly, very differently for each) was a practice apart from politics, and like him they refuted any instrumentalist attempt to engineer political life on rational terms, they denied that it was so incompatible with the medium of opinion that filled the public realm. This was in part because, whatever their debts to archaism and their doubts about specific turns modern thought and politics had taken, they did not share Strauss's vision of modernity as an epoch of pure decline.

Indeed, the figure of the intellectual offended Strauss for reasons clarified by attention to his belief that moderns (and, in particular, modern Jews like himself) were trapped in a theologico-political predicament, an uncertainty about whether authority floated in the heavens or had to be built by hand on Earth, if it could be found anywhere at all. While Levinas was willing to use the language of "prophetic witnessing" to describe the ethical labor of intellectuals addressing the public, Strauss could not thusly run the tasks of philosophical ethics and religion together. Modernity's decline was not exclusively the result of secularization, thought Strauss, but he had used the term "Epicureanism" throughout his career to describe a broad arc of thought that began in Greece with the critique of religion and ended, in the twentieth century, with a hedonistic modern subject blind to virtues other that the gratification of his own appetites: the "last man."

Arendt joined Strauss in his interest in secularization. As she asked in *The Human Condition*, tying secularization to Sputnik, "should the emancipation and secularization of the modern age, which began with a turning-away, not necessarily from God, but from a God who was the Father of men in heaven, end with an even more fateful repudiation of an Earth who was the Mother of all living creatures under the sky?"[90] The Arendt of *On Revolution*, who had intimated in a footnote that it was religion's declining public authority that revealed the conflict between philosophy and politics, was also the Arendt who understood the decline of political theology to have the rejection of all given creation as its possible successor. That is, our preference for artificial and thus predictable worlds, something on display among those who term themselves "intellectuals," leads us away not only from true politics, but from the realities of our nature as creatures on this Earth, where Heidegger might have said we find ourselves "thrown" and where Arendt said we recognize our origins and ends.

One of her solutions to the problem, one whose validity Strauss himself could not recognize, was to help us see the human realm of political action as worthy of wonder, every bit as mysterious as religion and as fascinating as philosophy. What was for Arendt the realm of natality and collective action was bedlam or the "vanity fair of the intellectuals" for Strauss. But her other solution might have appealed to Strauss more. This was to learn a lesson from Socrates as she herself had described him, allowing conscience to take the place formerly occupied by religion. When we are our own publics, as Socrates was part of his own public, we observe our own actions at all times, and we would not wish to live with a murderer, a liar, or a thief our whole lives. The inward turn each thinker took, whether it led to conscience or to Platonism, was actually not so different from Levinas's turn toward alterity, which involved the experience of the deep limitations of the self. It led to the recognition that the public and the private might be real, historically emergent categories on one level, but they were also interpenetrating realms of experience, on another. One could discover the public in private meditation; one could discover private communications in the most widely publicized broadsheet. The intellectual question, the question of what role such persons were supposed to play in public life, inspired new ways to think about the passage between private and public experience, a passage very well travelled before the arrival of "the intellectuals" themselves, and a passage to which all who think seriously are committed.

Conclusion

To return to the scene that began this book, there was irony in Arendt criticizing "intellectuals" on West German television in 1964, much as when her teacher Heidegger attacked modernity in his address, "Why We Stay in The Provinces"—and delivered this address invisibly through the air, by radio. In Arendt, Levinas, and Strauss's century, news was swift and philosophy was slow. The discrepancy between the perceived pace of current events and the perceived pace of the life of the mind was often written into the definition of the role of "the intellectual." Intellectuals spoke to fast-developing issues out of a slowly built reserve of knowledge and authority. They were sometimes characterized as representatives of timeless (and, notably, premodern) wisdom, even when their letters, editorials, and essays appeared at the pace of newspaper journalism. Theirs was the apparent power to move from one temporality to another and to illustrate by their actions the proper relation between modes of thought and modes of life, even as their efforts helped to bridge a different chasm, between politics and wisdom. Heidegger himself had complained about modernity's speed, and he took particular note of the pace of news; for him the competing geographies of country and city were also competing temporalities, the countryside still offering resistance to the "un-distancing" of modern media.

Heidegger's perhaps intrinsically antimodernist idea that there are two speeds, one for minds and another for media, followed his students into their own mature work, even when they hoped to make up for their teacher's failure to reflect upon political life. If in the twentieth century writers from all points along the political spectrum summoned "the intellectual" as a means by which to make reason and history rhyme (or, in chronological terms, synchronize), Arendt and Strauss rejected this particular philosophical and cultural project. Similarly, Levinas's embrace of the figure of the intellectual was not an effort to match the time of politics (the "time of the nations," as he might put it; "the nations" in the sense of *ha-Goyim*, as opposed to the Jews) with the time of philosophy. Instead, he made intellectuals into standard-bearers for an

ethics incompatible with politics. In other words, for this book's protagonists, ambivalence about intellectuals was often the surface expression of a
deeper ambivalence about the status of philosophy (whether conceived as an
otherworldly metaphysical enterprise, or as a form of ethics prior to metaphysics) in modernity.

The historical tension between the speeds of politics and philosophy has
often turned up as a problem for political theorists, one they are tempted to
resolve in order to produce desirable political or philosophical effects. For
some there has emerged the notion that theory, done right, will possess the
temporality of action.[1] If taken seriously, this implies that a theoretical account of class struggle (for example) should flash up like revolutionary orga-
nizing or, perhaps—in some academic imaginaries—just before revolution
itself, as an anticipatory call to action. For other theorists, the hope is that we
might find, or return to, a truer form of politics whose slower tempo would
match the pace of theoretical reflection.[2] It is important to note the oddness
of these efforts to unify very different categories of human endeavor, because
they often seem natural and intuitive to those engaged in them. Throughout
this book I have suggested that Arendt, Levinas, and Strauss are "good
to think with" because they resist the synchronizing style of thought that
seems to follow the figure of the intellectual through history. For them the
disjuncture of philosophy and politics, the permanent separation of the respective "times" of these pursuits, thwarts efforts to transmute the one into the
other, and enjoins us to think more carefully about their connections and
disconnections. But their accounts should not be taken as final or authoritative,
any more than their accounts of philosophy as otherworldly and metaphysical should be taken as final. Although I risk falling subject to Strauss's own
critique of historicism by saying so (i.e., historicism is itself an historically
situated position, and thus contains the seeds of its own undoing), I have
written this book on the premise that theories of the relationship between
philosophy and politics (much like specific definitions of either philosophy
or politics) are themselves historical artifacts subject to emergence and
dissolution, cases to study rather than permanent rules to follow.

I have argued that careful consideration of Arendt, Levinas, and Strauss
does not lead to prescriptive claims about the role played by philosophers,
political theorists, and other thinkers in public life. Such consideration leads
instead toward questions about the relationship between philosophy and
what we could call, at some risk of generality, "social practice." In following its protagonists through their mid-twentieth-century careers, first in

Germany and then in the United States and France, this book has also followed its own inward trajectory, moving from the problem of "the intellectual" to meditations on the way the life of the mind is shaped by a never-ceasing transition between public and private states, between meditation and conversation. This trajectory promises to refocus our vision if we place our trust in it. If in the past we have often asked, "How do intellectuals gain and wield influence, and in whose interest?" another, more sophisticated, question emerges: "How is the life of the mind affected by the fact that the minds of professional thinkers are situated in human bodies in a social world, with all the desires and frailties that come with this?"[3] Some commentators have pursued very similar questions about intellectuals, but usually with the intent of demonstrating that the desire for knowledge can readily be corrupted into a desire for power.[4] Such a focus on desire has its place, whether one hears the word "desire" in a Hegelian or a psychoanalytic key (or both), but it can have a distracting effect, drawing attention away from the force and internal validity of a thinker's own questions. This book has, by contrast, emphasized how an appreciation of worldliness led to a reassessment of the life of the mind itself. It is to Arendt's great credit that her final major effort was to understand thinking as conditioned by a kind of internalized publicness, rather than to pretend that the meeting of philosophy and politics always forces a choice between them and thus led to a parting of ways between types of human actors.

Readers may be surprised that this book has not dealt with the contributions of one social theorist who has devoted much of his career to understanding the connections between philosophy and political life, namely Jürgen Habermas. The main justification for not treating him here is the calendar—Habermas (born in 1929) is part of a younger generation of European thinkers; a secondary justification is that Habermas, as a non-Jew, was differently attuned to many of the experiences that shaped Arendt, Levinas, and Strauss's responses to publicness and modernity. However, there are both historical and theoretical reasons to ask what Habermas might make of Arendt, Levinas, and Strauss's respective views on intellectuals and public life. Habermas studied with Arendt's contemporaries in Germany, acknowledges her influence on him, and responds to many of the same currents in German intellectual life to which she, Strauss, and Levinas had themselves responded—including Heidegger's profound inattention to politics and his troubled account of sociality. The young Habermas wrote a now-famous book on the category of publicness, *Strukturwandel der Öffentlichkeit. Untersuchungen zu einer Kategorie der bürgerlichen Gesellschaft* (*The Structural Transformation of the Public Sphere: An Inquiry into a Category of Bourgeois Society*), which appeared in 1962 in German and, after its author became influential, was published in 1989 in an English translation. Habermas's many later productions, from *Legitimation Crisis* to the *Theory of Communicative Action* to *Between Facts and Norms*, have treated not only the social facts of public discourse, but also many topics of interest to Arendt, Levinas, and Strauss: the nature of communication and its relationship with reason, the philosophical and political legacies of the Enlightenment, and, of course, the possible functions of reason in public speech.

Habermas is often taken to be a champion of public discourse, of the universality (if not the purity) of some aspects of a faculty called reason—"the unity of reason in the diversity of its voices," as he titled one exemplary essay[5]—and of procedural liberalism. His own writings on politics, religion, and current events have established him as one of Europe's foremost public intellectuals (to give in now, in this Conclusion, to a term I have resisted throughout this book). Thus it makes sense to expect that a conversation between Habermas, Arendt, Levinas, and Strauss would turn into a contest between a view of philosophy and publicness as helpmates, and a set of contrary claims regarding the messiness, the noise, and the potential dangers of public life, claims that are at root about the incompatibility of public political life with philosophy. Habermas could be taken to stand for the synchronization of philosophy and publicness—but here this comparative effort breaks down, for Habermas fully understands (and has meditated upon) the impossibility of such a synchronization being completed, and he shares Arendt and Strauss's criticisms of instrumental reason—down to its manifestation in technological problem-solving.[6] And if Habermas champions reason, he does not seem to believe in the possibility of a "completed" rationality, either through reason's internal development or its piecemeal advancement through historical events. For him, history is an unchosen set of terms and terrains upon which philosophy must function.

All this said, a comparative account of Habermas and this book's protagonists might be extremely productive, especially if it were not staged as a contest between celebrants and critics of public reason. Such a comparison would allow us to ask how different the dyad of philosophy and publicness looks when approached from a postmetaphysical perspective such as the one Habermas proposes, influenced in part by his readings in Anglo-American analytic thought and the philosophy of language more broadly; conversely, it raises a question that owes something to Derrida, namely, whether invoking "the intellectual" always reflects a particular style of metaphysical thinking. And such a comparison would also invite a historical accounting of Habermas's late twentieth and early twenty-first-century thought on publics and intellectuals, and encourage us to ask what wishes and drives have shaped his more hopeful approach to the problem.

This book, whose energies bend toward demythologizing the figure of the intellectual, is not a call to abandon the thoughtful public discussion of books, politics, economics, films, social problems, and so forth. My sympathies are with those who desire a flourishing media ecology, a constant exchange of ideas and opinions. Instead, I have attempted to ask what the fantasies, hopes, and wishes that attach to the intellectual can teach us about specific moments in twentieth-century European intellectual history. If the figure of the intellectual represents a form of wish fulfillment (reason and history rhyme; truth will out; justice will prevail over corruption; the cold state apparatus can still be infused with ethics), I want to understand what those wishes are. I also want to know (it is hard not to have normative concerns about such things!) if those wishes are "good for us," or what other, better, wishes they might foreclose. The writings of this book's three protagonists have, of course, all been taken up in conversations among philosophers and political theorists, who sometimes want Arendt's, Levinas's, or Strauss's thought to "cash out" as a model for comportment in public life. My own interest has been more in the "symptomatic" aspects of conversations about intellectuals than in, as sociologist Zygmunt Bauman puts it, the "legislative" aspects of those conversations. I am more interested in the impulse to legislate than I am in legislation itself.[7]

Thus, if my book has not left its reader with a succinct definition of "the intellectual," to replace the ones Arendt, Levinas, and Strauss challenged, it is purposeful. That category is always being recovered and cast down again. It has no stable footing. Manifestos and dirges on behalf of "intellectuals" tell us more about those who craft such texts than they do about the role itself. Likewise, this book has aimed to make the category of "the public" seem more and not less ambiguous. Is "the public" a collective subject? A set of interlocking theatres or discursive spheres? A word to describe the feeling that one is part of a community of interest? This definitional ambiguity is part of the historical interest of the term, part of the reason to leave "the public" undefined but always on our minds. If publicness is all around us, if all scholars potentially become intellectuals when they engage with audiences beyond the academy, all the more need to consider these matters carefully, to interpret our desires for publics and intellectuals, as well as the histories of those desires. The twenty-first-century republic of letters has already undergone substantial transformations at the time of this book's completion (one and a half decades into that century) and it will doubtless undergo many more.

Perhaps most obviously, our increasing ability to share information and opinions over the Internet, delightful for some and dreadful for others, represents a new mutation in the genes of publicness, and it calls for new interpretations of the task of the intellectual as well. Notably, the sense of a crisis of culture (i.e., a diminishment of attention spans, the shortening and shallowing of essays) against a background of technological change, may spark precisely the same redefinitions of the intellectual that attended earlier political and cultural crises over the last century. Given that "the public" and "the intellectual" will stay with us as short-hands used to express our hopes and fears for the meeting of culture and politics, Arendt, Levinas, and Strauss are good companions to keep with us, too. Arendt's attempt to recast publicness, Strauss's skeptical attack on the public, and Levinas's idealistic appeals to the figure of "the intellectual," can all serve as lessons for us, both because of what they got right and what they got wrong. If their answers sometimes fail us, their questions do not. These questions force us to ask by which stars we orient our lives both contemplative and active—by our opinions? by our truths? by our bonds with others?—and with what kinds of publics we must share our thoughts. Their stories remind us that we never face a simple choice between public life and private thought, but rather a collective life constituted and troubled, but also made vastly more promising, by the tension between them.

NOTES

Introduction

1. With the exception of Emmanuel Levinas, who appeared several times on French television, none of this book's central figures made notable use of television or radio to reach their audiences. Though they were active during the period Regis Debray associates with the rise of "media intellectuals," they were not such, themselves. See Regis Debray, *Le pouvoir intellectuel en France* (Paris: Ramsay, 1979). For an examination of the role of television in constituting the persona of "the intellectual" in postwar France specifically, see Tamara Chaplin, *Turning on the Mind: French Philosophers on Television* (Chicago: University of Chicago Press, 2007).

2. The interview was originally published under the title, "*Was bleibt? Es bleibt die Muttersprache,*" in Günter Gaus, *Zur Person* (Munich: Ost, 1965). It was translated by Joan Stambaugh and republished in *The Portable Hannah Arendt*, ed. Peter R. Baehr (New York: Penguin, 2003) as "What Remains? The Language Remains"; see 11. On Arendt's views on Nazification and subsequent de-Nazification, see also her letter to Karl Jaspers of July 9, 1946, published in Hannah Arendt and Karl Jaspers, *Correspondence 1926–1969* (New York: Houghton Mifflin, 1993), 47; henceforth referred to as AJC. It is important to point out that Arendt was leaving out an important category of intellectuals, namely, literary writers. As Ehrhard Bahr notes, the vast majority of the Weimar Republic's prominent writers chose exile rather than seek to make a personal compromise with the new Nazi government. See Ehrhard Bahr, *Weimar on the Pacific: German Exile Culture in Los Angeles and the Crisis of Modernism* (Berkeley: University of California Press, 2007), 14.

3. "What Remains? The Language Remains," 11.

4. Arendt did not surmise that the theories of intellectuals found an eager audience within the National Socialist government itself. In a 1946 review of Max Weinreich's influential book *Hitler's Professors*, Arendt argued against Weinreich's thesis that "German scholarship provided the ideas and techniques which led to and justified unparalleled slaughter," suggesting that of the "quite a few respectable German professors" who "volunteered their services to the Nazis," none found that their work was appreciated. See Hannah Arendt, "The Image of Hell," *Commentary* 2, 3 (1946), republished in Hannah Arendt, *Essays in Understanding, 1930–1954: Formation, Exile and Totalitarianism* (New York: Schocken, 1994), see 201–2.

5. Leo Strauss, *Natural Right and History* (Chicago: University of Chicago Press, 1950), 58; henceforth cited as NRH.

6. A note on the distinctions between the terms "an intellectual" and a "public intellectual" is useful. There is a loose consensus among scholars that, from the time of the Dreyfus Affair on, the term "an intellectual" always already implied publicness, and that the compound term "public intellectual," popularized in North America toward the end of the twentieth century, is curious

because its first word effectively duplicates the original sense intended by its second. From the mid-nineteenth century on in Britain, France, and Germany, the label "intellectual" (used as an adjective or a noun) was understood to imply a social function, and most often it was used in the plural to refer to a distinct group within society. It was Russell Jacoby who gave the term "public intellectual" its lasting popularity. See Russell Jacoby, *The Last Intellectuals: American Culture in the Age of Academe* (New York: Basic, 1987). On the origins of the style of thought reflected in this term see Stanley Aronowitz, *Taking It Big: C. Wright Mills and the Making of Political Intellectuals* (New York: Columbia University Press, 2012).

7. For reasons I discuss in what follows, little comparative work has been done on any twosome out of the trio. But see Leora Batnitzky, *Leo Strauss and Emmanuel Levinas: Philosophy and the Politics of Revelation* (Princeton, N.J.: Princeton University Press, 2006) and Peter Graf Kielmansegg, Horst Mewes, and Elisabeth Glaser-Schmidt, eds., *Hannah Arendt and Leo Strauss: German Émigrés and American Political Thought After World War II* (Cambridge: Cambridge University Press, 1997). Samuel Moyn briefly surveys correlations between the early Arendt and Levinas in his *Origins of the Other: Emmanuel Levinas Between Revelation and Ethics* (Ithaca, N.Y.: Cornell University Press, 2005). See Chapters 4–6 for a more extended discussion of the above works and others.

8. On the motif of the "lure of Syracuse," see Mark Lilla, *The Reckless Mind: Intellectuals in Politics* (New York: New York Review of Books, 2001).

9. Michael Theunissen, *Der Andere: Studien zur Sozialontologie der Gegenwart* (Berlin: de Gruyter, 1965), in English, *The Other: Studies in the Social Ontology of Husserl, Heidegger, Sartre, and Buber*, trans. Christopher Macann (Cambridge, Mass.: MIT Press, 1984).

10. For one effort to understand the commonalities between Heidegger's students, including Jewish ones, see Richard Wolin, *Heidegger's Children: Hannah Arendt, Karl Löwith, Hans Jonas, and Herbert Marcuse* (Princeton, N.J.: Princeton University Press, 2001). And see especially Samuel Fleischacker, *Heidegger's Jewish Followers: Essays on Hannah Arendt, Leo Strauss, Hans Jonas and Emmanuel Levinas* (Pittsburgh: Duquesne University Press, 2008).

11. On the problematic logics shaping the canon of "modern Jewish thought," see Martin Kavka, "Screening the Canon, or, Levinas and Medieval Jewish Philosophy," in *New Directions in Jewish Philosophy*, ed. Elliot Wolfson and Aaron Hughes (Bloomington: Indiana University Press, 2010).

12. See Leora Batnitzky, *How Judaism Became a Religion: An Introduction to Modern Jewish Thought* (Princeton, N.J.: Princeton University Press, 2011).

13. See Emmanuel Levinas, "How Is Judaism Possible," in *Difficult Freedom: Essays on Judaism*, trans. Seán Hand (Baltimore: Johns Hopkins University Press, 1997); henceforth DF.

14. See Robert Pippin, *Pippin, Idealism as Modernism: Hegelian Variations* (Cambridge: Cambridge University Press, 1997), 212.

15. Ibid., 213.

16. See Peter Eli Gordon, *Rosenzweig and Heidegger: Between Judaism and German Philosophy* (Berkeley: University of California Press, 2003), 3.

17. Stefan Collini, *Absent Minds: Intellectuals in Britain* (Oxford: Oxford University Press, 2006).

18. However, readers eager for a definition of "the intellectual" contemporaneous with Arendt, Levinas, and Strauss's maturity, would do well to consult Edgar Morin's "Intellectuels: critique du mythe et mythe de la critique": "The intellectual emerges from a cultural base and with a socio-political role . . . . Thus the intellectual can be defined from a triple set of dimensions: (1) a profession that is culturally validated, (2) a role that is socio-political, (3) a consciousness that relates to universals," *Arguments* 4, 20 (October 1960). And see J. P. Nettl's discussion of Morin in "Ideas, Intellectuals and Structures of Dissent," in *On Intellectuals*, ed. Phillip Rieff (Garden City, N.Y.: Doubleday, 1969).

19. See Peter Winch, "Introduction," in *The Political Responsibility of The Intellectual*, ed. Ian Maclean, Alan Montefiore, and Peter Winch (Cambridge: Cambridge University Press, 1990), 4.

20. See Ernst Gellner, "La trahison de la trahison des clercs," in Maclean, Montefiore, and Winch, 17, and Julian Benda, *La trahison des clercs* (Paris: B. Grasset, 1927).

21. See Gellner, 20–21.

22. See Jacoby, and Richard A. Posner, *Public Intellectuals: A Story of Decline* (Cambridge: Harvard University Press, 2001). One exemplar of the "advocacy" approach can be found in Edward W. Said's *Representations of the Intellectual* (New York: Vintage, 1994). While Jacoby, Posner, and Said all ultimately endorse some version of intellectual involvement in politics—even when they mourn the absence of public intellectuals—Mark Lilla has taken a very different tack in his aforementioned *The Reckless Mind: Intellectuals in Politics*. Displaying clear debts to Strauss, as well as a Benda-like insistence on the transcendental orientation of the intellectual, Lilla argues that many of the twentieth century's politically engaged intellectuals in fact betrayed their own higher purposes by turning a blind eye to totalitarianism and political brutality. For an extended discussion of Lilla and other contemporary writers on public intellectuals, see Benjamin Aldes Wurgaft, "Within Sight of Syracuse," *Minnesota Review* 68 (Summer 2007): 159–65.

23. One example is Bruce Robbins's *Secular Vocations*, which takes it for granted that the social role of the intellectual is defined by a tension between a transcendental objective (frequently, the pursuit of knowledge for its own sake) and a set of social engagements that may seem to present compromises on, or even betrayals of, that objective. See Robbins, *Secular Vocations: Intellectuals, Professionalism, Culture* (London: Verso, 1993). Robbins is especially helpful when he explores the logic of the "decline-ist" narratives supplied by Jacoby and others: "The argument that intellectuals in the independent, public sense no longer exist has also been an argument, in other words, by which the arguer, who remembers the greatness of intellectuals past, shows in so doing that he himself (it almost always is a he) retains a true intellectual's public voice and truly, legitimately speak for the public. In a paradox worthy of Groucho Marx, he implicitly claims to belong to a category that he is asserting no longer has any members" (13). Like Robbins, Michael Warner has written in an effort to strip away some of our assumptions about public intellectual life; see his *Publics and Counterpublics* (New York: Zone, 2004), to which I will return later in this book. Suggesting that both "intellectuals" and "publics" should be understood as products of discourse, Warner focuses his attention on the way publics are wished into existence by a writer or speaker. Another of Warner's central contributions is to distinguish the concept of a public from that of an audience. An artist may seek to affect an audience, to bring it to tears of laughter or cries of joy, but a public may respond in deeper ways, and the term "public" suggests a political body in a sense that "audience" does not.

24. It should be noted that this book largely ignores the important perspectives on intellectuals supplied by sociology. This merits some explanation because it was sociology that produced the first significant studies of what Florian Znaniecki once called "the social role of the man of knowledge." Indeed, some of the groundwork for historical studies such as this one was first laid by sociologists such as Edward Shils, Alvin Gouldner, Lewis Coser, Seymour Martin Lipset, and others—not to mention Max Weber, Émile Durkheim, and Karl Mannheim. Nevertheless, the sociological approach to the study of intellectuals seems more appropriate for studies that investigate the social *fact* of intellectuals who engage in political life, and less helpful for studies like this one, in which it is the *idea* of the politically engaged intellectual that is being investigated. Because I remain agnostic about the definitional boundaries around the intellectual, I largely avoid any extended discussion of the sociological literature on intellectuals in politics—except, naturally enough, where Arendt and Strauss respond to that line of inquiry themselves. Critics not only of sociology in general but especially of the application of sociology to the activities of intellectuals, they had much to say against what Mannheim once dubbed the

"sociology of knowledge," and once in the United States they both scorned the American tradition of writing the sociology of intellectual life, of which Shils was among the greatest champions.

25. J. P. Nettl once noted that while the term "an intellectual" has been defined and redefined by numerous commentators, it nevertheless retains a telling ambiguity: "Is the intellectual an institution, a collectivity, a role, a type of person, or what? The failure to surmount the definitional hurdle produces as many explanations as there are implied definitions." Nettl, in Rieff, 55. In a similar vein, Peter Allen observes that the term "an intellectual," as it has been used in the twentieth century, roughly parallels the nineteenth-century term "gentleman," in that it "is more likely to tell us something important about the time in which it was used than about the social phenomenon it was meant to describe." See Peter Allen, "The Meanings of 'An Intellectual': Nineteenth- and Twentieth-Century English Usage," *University of Toronto Quarterly* 55, 4 (Summer 1986): 342–58, 355.

26. See Allen. On the "Public Moralist"; see Stefan Collini, *Public Moralists: Political Thought and Intellectual Life in Britain* (Oxford: Clarendon, 1991). On Victorian debates over the status of intellectuals, see T. W. Heyck, *The Transformation of Intellectual Life in Victorian England* (London: Croom Helm, 1982), a work Allen attempts to revise somewhat but does not entirely replace.

27. See, e.g., Victor Brombert, *The Intellectual Hero: Studies on the French Novel, 1880–1955* (Chicago: University of Chicago Press, 1960).

28. See William M. Johnston, "The Origin of the Term 'Intellectuals' in French Novels and Essays of the 1890s," *Journal of European Studies* 4, 43 (1974). Both Johnson and Brombert note that, prior to the early 1880s, there is little evidence for any use of the term *l'intellectuel* in French letters. The 1863–1877 Littré dictionary, for example, contains no such noun.

29. Brunetière, "le *Paris* de M. E. Zola," *Revue des Deux Mondes* 146 (April 15, 1898), 922–34.

30. Or as Allen puts it, "The force of Clemenceau's usage lay precisely there: he made explicit the long-simmering question of the social role of highly educated people and he did it in a context that ensured his use of the word would claim the attention of an international audience" (348).

31. Brombert, 33.

32. See Ernst Ferdinand Klein, "On Freedom of Thought and of the Press: For Princes, Ministers and Writers," trans. John Christian Laursen, in *What Is Enlightenment? Eighteenth-Century Answers and Twentieth-Century Questions*, ed. James Schmidt (Berkeley: University of California Press, 1996).

33. See Immanuel Kant, "An Answer to the Question: What Is Enlightenment?" trans. James Schmidt in Schmidt, 58.

34. On Kant's debate with Hamann, see Garrett Green, "Modern Culture Comes of Age: Hamann Versus Kant on the Root Metaphor of the Enlightenment," in Schmidt.

35. The classic work on this transformation is Fritz Ringer, *The Decline of the German Mandarins* (Cambridge: Harvard University Press, 1969).

36. See ibid, 5.

37. For a very different treatment of these debates, see Anson Rabinbach, *The Human Motor: Energy, Fatigue, and the Origins of Modernity* (Berkeley: University of California Press, 1990).

38. "Culture" and "Science," respectively, but note that "Wissenschaft" is often used to describe formal, disciplinary research, including research in the humanities or social sciences.

39. See Ringer, 103.

40. Thomas Mann, *Reflections of an Unpolitical Man*, trans. Walter D. Morris (New York: Frederick Ungar, 1983), 10. Mann's pejorative use of the term was far from unusual. Gertrud Bäumer, in "Die Intellektuellen," *Die Hilfe* 25, 28 (July 10, 1919), described the intellectual as marking "a failure of culture," claiming to speak in the interests of people from whom they have in fact become estranged. See Gertrud Bäumer, "Die Intellektuellen," in *The Weimar Republic*

Sourcebook, ed. Anton Kaes, Martin Jay, and Edward Dimendberg (Berkeley: University of California Press, 1995).

41. Mann, 16.

42. Ibid., 22.

43. See Bengt Lofstedt, Review of Dietz Bering, *Die Intellektuellen: Geschichte eines Schimpfwortes, Language* 55, 3 (September 1979): 743–44.

44. See Gordon, 201, and Ethan Kleinberg, *Generation Existential: Heidegger's Philosophy in France, 1927–1961* (Ithaca, N.Y.: Cornell University Press, 2007) 14. For an extended discussion of "Mitsein" see Lawrence Vogel, *The Fragile "We": Ethical Implications of Heidegger's "Being and Time"* (Evanston: Northwestern University Press, 1994). And see Moyn, 59–62, for a discussion of the origins of Heidegger's *Mitsein* out of a response to his own teacher Edmund Husserl.

45. Leo Strauss, *On Tyranny* (Chicago: University of Chicago Press, 2000), 212; henceforth OT.

46. See Moyn, 64.

47. See ibid., 58.

48. Karl Löwith, *Das Individuum in der Rolle des Mitmenschen: Ein Beitrag zur anthropologischen Grundlegung der ethischen Probleme* (Munich: Drei Masken, 1928).

49. See Theunissen, 172, and see Moyn's discussion of Theunissen, 67.

50. Martin Heidegger, *Being and Time*, ed. John Macquarrie and Edward Robinson (San Francisco: Harper, 1962), 165. Note that for "The light of the public obscures everything," the translation Arendt provided for *Das Licht der Öffentlichkeit verdunkelt alles* in her collection *Men in Dark Times* (New York: Harcourt, Brace, 1955), ix, Macquarrie and Robinson offer "by publicness everything gets obscured." In the above I have preserved Arendt's translation.

51. See Martin Heidegger, "The Self-Assertion of the German University," in *The Heidegger Controversy: A Critical Reader*, ed. Richard Wolin (Cambridge, Mass.: MIT Press, 1993), 32.

52. Ibid., 31.

53. Gordon, 28.

54. For an account of Heidegger's critiques of modernization, see Michael E. Zimmerman, *Heidegger's Confrontation with Modernity: Technology, Politics, and Art* (Bloomington: Indiana University Press, 1990).

55. See Fleischacker's Introduction in Fleischacker.

56. On Arendt's relationship with Heidegger, see Elisabeth Young-Bruehl, *For Love of the World* (New Haven, Conn.: Yale University Press, 1982), henceforth FLOTW, and (more controversially) Elzbieta Ettinger, *Hannah Arendt/Martin Heidegger* (New Haven, Conn.: Yale University Press, 1997). On Levinas's efforts to "rehabilitate" Heidegger, see Moyn. On Strauss's responses to Heidegger, see Eugene Sheppard, *Leo Strauss and the Politics of Exile: The Making of a Political Philosopher* (Waltham, Mass.: Brandeis University Press/University Presses of New England, 2006); Steven B. Smith, "Destruktion or Recovery? Leo Strauss's Critique of Heidegger," *Review of Metaphysics* 51, 2 (December 1997); and William H. F. Altman, *The German Stranger: Leo Strauss and National Socialism* (Lanham, Md.: Lexington, 2010). See also Benjamin Aldes Wurgaft, Review of Altman, *Notre Dame Philosophical Reviews* (June 2011).

57. See Sheppard, 38, and also Daniel Doneson, "Beginning at the Beginning: On the Starting Point of Reflection," in Fleischacker.

58. See Doneson, 109. This sentence, which Strauss's own student Seth Bernardete called his "Golden Sentence," may be found in his *Thoughts on Machiavelli* (Chicago: University of Chicago Press, 1958) on page 13, and refers to the "surface" of a text. For Doneson it is section 7 of *Being and Time* in which Heidegger performs the critical reading of Husserl that inspired Strauss's Golden Sentence. Thus Strauss's Sentence in fact owes a fundamental debt to Husserl's phenomenology, which Strauss understood in the following terms: "all philosophic understanding must start from our common understanding of the world, from our understanding of the world as

sensibly perceived prior to all theorizing." Leo Strauss, "Philosophy as Rigorous Science," in *Studies in Platonic Political Philosophy* (Chicago: University of Chicago Press, 1983), 31.

Chapter 1. Moderns and Medievals

Part epigraph: Leo Strauss, "Farabi's Plato," in *Louis Ginzberg Jubilee Volume* (New York: American Academy for Jewish Research, 1945) 357–93, 377.

1. Strauss, NRH, 58.

2. Leo Strauss, "An Introduction to Heideggerian Existentialism," in *The Rebirth of Classical Political Rationalism: An Introduction to the Thought of Leo Strauss*, ed. Thomas Pangle (Chicago: University of Chicago Press, 1989), 40.

3. Leo Strauss, *Spinoza's Critique of Religion* (New York: Schocken, 1965), Preface, 1.

4. Allan Bloom, "Leo Strauss," *Political Theory* 2, 4 (1974).

5. See Sheppard, *Leo Strauss and the Politics of Exile*, 21.

6. NRH, 34.

7. Leo Strauss, *Persecution and the Art of Writing* (Chicago: University of Chicago Press, 1952), 186.

8. OT, 77.

9. See Leo Strauss, "On Classical Political Philosophy," in *What Is Political Philosophy and Other Studies* (Chicago: University of Chicago Press, 1988).

10. Ibid., 61.

11. Ibid., 41.

12. Ibid., 54.

13. Ibid., 61.

14. See Strauss, "Persecution and the Art of Writing," in *Persecution and the Art of Writing*.

15. Leo Strauss, *Die Religionskritik Spinozas als Grundlage seiner Bibelwissenschaft Untersuchung zu Spinozas Theologisch-Politischen Traktat* (Berlin: Akademie-Verlag, 1930). For convenience all citations—unless the German is referred to explicitly—will be to the already cited English translation, *Spinoza's Critique of Religion*, denoted SCR.

16. SCR, 174.

17. Ibid, 20.

18. Ibid.

19. See Sheppard, 49.

20. Franz Rosenzweig, *Der Stern der Erlösung* (Frankfurt am Main: Suhrkamp, 1996, 1988); in English, *The Star of Redemption*, trans. William W. Hallo (New York: Holt, Rinehart, and Winston, 1971).

21. Interestingly, when Strauss took his distance from Rosenzweig it was precisely because while he applauded Rosenzweig's emphasis on Jewish experience as the starting-place for a philosophy of Judaism, he criticized him for starting with the "sociological" fact of the existence of the Jewish nation rather than with "God's Law," which Strauss took as the determining fact of Jewish experience. See SCR, 13.

22. The essay is translated into English as Hermann Cohen, *Ethics of Maimonides*, ed. and trans. Almut Sh. Bruckstein (Madison: University of Wisconsin Press, 2004), 23.

23. Julius Guttmann, *Die Philosophie des Judentums* (Munich: Ernst Reinhardt, 1933). Here I cite the English translation as *Philosophy of Judaism*, trans. David Silverman (Northvale, N.J.: Jason Aronson, 1988), 357. Guttmann's critique of Cohen recapitulated, albeit in a different key, Martin Buber's earlier complaint that Cohen's rendition of Judaism as a system of concepts ignored the reality of the Jewish nation. See Martin Buber, "Begriffe und Wirklichkeit," *Der Jude*

5 (July 1916): 281. Notably, in his "Living Issues of German Postwar Philosophy," Strauss made a comment that recalled Guttmann's critique of Cohen, although Strauss placed the blame for the depersonalization of the Divine squarely on Kant's shoulders: "It was hard not to see that the question of the existence or nonexistence of a personal God, Creator of Heaven and Earth, was a serious question, more serious even than the question of the right method of the social sciences. If the question should be answered, if it should even be understood as a meaningful question, one had to go back to an age when it was in the center of discussion—i.e, to pre-Kantian philosophy," Leo Strauss in Heinrich Meier, *Leo Strauss and the Theologico-Political Predicament* (Cambridge: Cambridge University Press, 2006), 130–31.

24. Guttmann., 47.

25. Leo Strauss, *Philosophie und Gesetz: Beitrage zum Verstandnis Maimunis und seiner Vorlaufer* (Berlin: Schocken, 1935); *Philosophy and Law: Contributions to the Understanding of Maimonides and His Predecessors*, ed. and trans. Eve Adler (Albany: State University of New York Press, 1995), 43. Except where noted, citations are to the English edition.

26. Guttmann, 342.

27. Strauss, *Philosophy and Law*, 59.

28. Ibid., 73.

29. Leo Strauss, "Ecclesia militans," *Jüdische Rundschau* (Berlin) 30, 36 (May 8, 1925), reprinted in Leo Strauss, *Gesammelte Schriften*, ed. Heinrich Meier (Stuttgart: Metzler, 1996), 2: 351–56; also translated and republished in *Leo Strauss: The Early Writings, 1921–1932*, ed. and trans. Michael Zank (Albany: State University of New York Press, 2002).

30. Isaac Breuer, *Das Jüdische Nationalheim* (Frankfurt am Main: Kauffmann 1925), 353.

31. Immanuel Kant, *Religion Within the Limits of Reason Alone*, ed. Theodore M. Greene, trans. Hoyt H. Hudson (New York: Harper, 1934), 85.

32. On Schmitt's interest in the medieval see John P. McCormick, *Carl Schmitt's Critique of Liberalism* (Cambridge: Cambridge University Press, 1999).

33. In 2009 the journal *Constellations* published a May 19, 1933, letter Strauss sent to his friend Karl Löwith, a letter that has since become infamous. In that letter Strauss seemed to affirm the virtues of fascism with the remark "There is no reason to crawl to the cross, neither to the cross of liberalism, as long as somewhere in the world there is a glimmer of the spark of the Roman thought." See *Constellations* 16 (2009): 82–83. Notably, almost two months later Strauss wrote to Schmitt asking him if he could provide an introduction to Charles Maurras, the anti-Dreyfusard and principal thinker behind the Action Française. Strauss's letter to Schmitt is reproduced in Heinrich Meier, *Carl Schmitt and Leo Strauss: The Hidden Dialogue*, ed. and trans. J. Harvey Lomax (Chicago: University of Chicago Press, 1995), 127–28.

34. Leo Strauss, "Anmerkungen zu Carl Schmitt, *Der Begriff des Politischen*," *Archiv für Sozialwissenschaft und Sozialpolitik* (Tübingen) 67, 6 (August–September 1932): 732–49. For ease, all citations provided here are to the translation of Strauss's Notes published in Meier, *Carl Schmitt and Leo Strauss.*

35. Ibid., 94.

36. Leo Strauss, *Philosophie und Gesetz*, 31 and 31n. And see Meier's discussion in Meier, *The Hidden Dialogue*, 30 n. 32.

37. Strauss in Meier, ed., *Gessamelte Schriften*, 101.

38. See Luc Ferry, *Rights: The New Quarrel Between Ancients and Moderns*, trans. Franklin Philip (Chicago: University of Chicago Press, 1990); Steven B. Smith, *Reading Leo Strauss: Politics, Philosophy, Judaism* (Chicago: University of Chicago Press, 2006); recently, William H. F. Altman, *The German Stranger: Leo Strauss and National Socialism*, and see also Benjamin Aldes Wurgaft, "How to Read Maimonides After Heidegger: The Cases of Levinas and Strauss," in *The Cultures of Maimonideanism*, ed. James T. Robinson (Leiden: Brill, 2009).

39. Strauss, *Philosophy and Law*, 74.

40. Daniel Tanguay, *Leo Strauss: An Intellectual Biography*, trans. Christopher Nadon (New Haven, Conn.: Yale University Press, 2007).

41. On May 1, 1946, two years after Kraus committed suicide in Cairo, Strauss wrote to Kraus's friend Charles Kuentz in search of the documents Kraus had prepared following their collaboration: "I have worked together with Kraus on Farabi, and we studied together the al-milla and al-fadila, and the paraphrase of Plato's Laws in particular. When we were both in Berlin, I ordered photographs of the mss. Of these works, which Kraus later took to Cairo in order to prepare an edition and translation. These must be among his papers . . . . I should appreciate it very much if, in accordance with the plan of your institute, you would let me have these materials at your earliest convenience." Kuentz evidently did not find the documents, but Strauss continued his own work on al-Farabi as a key to reading Maimonides and Plato. The fragment of Strauss's letter is reprinted in Joel L. Kraemer, "The Death of an Orientalist: Paul Kraus from Prague to Cairo," in *The Jewish Discovery of Islam: Studies in Honor of Bernard Lewis*, ed. Martin Kramer (Tel Aviv: Moshe Dayan Centre for Middle Eastern and African Studies, 1999).

42. "Eine vermiate schrift Farabis," 1936, in Strauss, *Gesammelte Schriften* 2, 175–76. "Quelques remarques sur la science politique de Maimonide et de Farabi," *Revue des Études Juives* 100 (1936): 1–37, trans. as "Some Remarks on the Political Science of Maimonides and Farabi," *Interpretation* 18, 1 (1990), 3–30.

43. See Strauss, "Farabi's Plato," in *Louis Ginzberg: Jubilee Volume on the Occasion of His Seventieth Birthday* (New York: American Academy for Jewish Research, 1945) and republished, in an edited version, in *Persecution and the Art of Writing*. Citations are to the latter version.

44. Ibid., 370.

45. Ibid., 377.

46. Strauss, "An Introduction to Heideggerian Existentialism," 30.

47. See Karl Löwith, "The Political Implications of Heidegger's Existentialism," Wolin, trans. in Wolin, *The Heidegger Controversy*, 172.

48. Wolin, "Preface to the MIT Edition," *The Heidegger Controversy*, xi.

49. See Shadia B. Drury, "The Esoteric Philosophy of Leo Strauss," *Political Theory* 13, 3 (August 1985): 315–37.

50. See Allan Bloom, "Leo Strauss," and Eugene F. Miller, "Leo Strauss: The Recovery of Political Philosophy," in *Contemporary Political Philosophers*, ed. Anthony de Crespigny and Kenneth Minogue (New York: Dodd, Mead, 1975).

51. SCR, 12.

52. Carl Schmitt, *Political Theology: Four Chapters on the Concept of Sovereignty*, trans. George B. Schwab (Chicago: University of Chicago Press, 2005), 36.

53. Friedrich Nietzsche, *Beyond Good and Evil*, trans. R. G. Hollingdale (Harmondsworth: Penguin, 1972), 113 (emphasis in original).

54. Strauss, "An Introduction to Heideggerian Existentialism," 27.

55. OT, 212.

56. See Tanguay, 124.

57. See Dana R. Villa, *Arendt and Heidegger: The Fate of the Political* (Princeton, N.J.: Princeton University Press, 1996), 9–11. See also Charles R. Bambach, *Heidegger, Dilthey, and the Crisis of Historicism* (Ithaca, N.Y.: Cornell University Press, 1995), 197–98, for an excellent explanation of how Heidegger transformed Martin Luther's principle of *destruire* to create *Destruktion*.

58. "Introduction to Heideggerian Existentialism," 27. See Sheppard, 55, and see Bambach.

59. Löwith in Wolin, 169. Löwith also claimed that "The philosophical definition of Dasein as an existing *factum brutum* which 'is and must be' (*Being and Time* §29)—this sinister, active Dasein, stripped of all content, all beauty, all human kindness—is a mirror image of the 'heroic realism' of those Nazi-bred, German faces that stared out at us from every magazine" (181). Next to these reflections of his friend, which he almost certainly would have read, Strauss's reflections on Heidegger's Nazism seem restrained.

60. See Max Weber, *The Theory of Social and Economic Organization*, trans. A. R. Anderson and Talcott Parsons (New York: Oxford University Press, 1947), and see Christopher Adair-Toteff, "Max Weber's Charisma," *Journal of Classical Sociology*, 5, 2 (2005): 189–204, and Charles Lindholm, *Charisma* (Cambridge: Blackwell, 1990).

61. "Kurt Riezler," in *What Is Political Philosophy?*, 246. No researcher working on the history of the Davos disputation has ascertained whether Strauss was present for the conference itself. See Peter Eli Gordon, "Continental Divide: Ernst Cassirer and Martin Heidegger at Davos, 1929—An Allegory of Intellectual History," *Modern Intellectual History* 1 (2004): 219–48. Notably, Strauss's reference to the "mythoi" of Heidegger echoed other claims that Heidegger was at root a mystic. In a 1945 statement to a peer review committee that was then contemplating his "denazification" or rehabilitation for teaching, Heidegger's colleague and former friend Karl Jaspers reflected, "He often proceeds as if he combined the seriousness of nihilism with the mystagogy of a magician." But for Jaspers as for Strauss, Heidegger's mysticism was at root uncommunicative: "Heidegger's manner of thinking, which to me seems in its essence un free, dictatorial, and incapable of communication, would today be disastrous in its pedagogical effects." See Jasper's statement in the report of the Freiburg University denazification commission, reproduced in Hugo Ott, *Martin Heidegger: Unterwegs zu seiner Biographie* (Frankfurt: Campus Verlag, 1988), 305ff. And see Richard Wolin's discussion of Jaspers on Heidegger, in Wolin's Introduction to *The Heidegger Controversy*, 3. Perhaps the most famous formulation of Jaspers's complaint about Heidegger's "incapacity for communication" is Theodor W. Adorno's *The Jargon of Authenticity* (Evanston: Northwestern University Press, 1973). See also Ernst Tugendhat, *Self-Consciousness and Self-Determination* (Cambridge, Mass.: MIT Press, 1986), 187.

62. Wolin, "Introduction," 15.

63. Virgil, *Aeneid*, Book I, Lines 148–54.

64. Virgil, *The Aeneid*, trans. John Dryden, (New York: Collier, 1909).

65. See Sheppard, 37.

66. Emmanuel Levinas, *Is it Righteous to Be?*, ed. Jill Robbins (Stanford, Calif.: Stanford University Press, 2001), 186.

67. Strauss, "An Introduction to Heideggerian Existentialism."

68. On Heidegger's reading of Kant at Davos, see Gordon, *Rosenzweig and Heidegger*, 283, and Gordon, *Continental Divide: Heidegger, Cassirer, Davos* (Cambridge, Mass.: Harvard University Press, 2010).

69. Strauss, "An Introduction to Heideggerian Existentialism," 29.

70. Michael J. Inwood, *A Heidegger Dictionary* (New York: Wiley-Blackwell, 1999).

71. It is unclear if Strauss was aware of Heidegger's *The Question Concerning Technology*, which sounded similar themes, when he lectured on Heidegger's thought. While that essay would appear in its original form as "Die Frage nach der Technik" in Heidegger's 1954 *Vorträge und Aufsätze*, Strauss's latest reference in his lecture is to a work published in 1953. However, Heidegger's critical reflections on "science," albeit in the more generalized form of German *Wissenschaft*, dated back to two presentations of 1929: his reflections on Kant during his debate with Ernst Cassirer, and his inaugural lecture at Freiburg, "Was ist Metaphysik?" ("What Is Metaphysics?"). Strauss may have been familiar with both.

72. Strauss, "An Introduction to Heideggerian Existentialism," 46.

73. Leo Strauss, "A Giving of Accounts: Jacob Klein and Leo Strauss," *The College* (St. John's College Magazine), April 1970, 4.

74. Leo Strauss, *Thoughts on Machiavelli* (Chicago: University of Chicago Press, 1958), 13.

Chapter 2. The Exoteric Writing Thesis

1. Leo Strauss, "Persecution and the Art of Writing," in *Persecution and the Art of Writing*, 36.

2. Thomas Mann, "The Living Spirit," *Social Research* 1, 1 (1/4) (1934); Emil Lederer, "Freedom and Science," *Social Research* 1, 1 (1/4) (1934).

3. Ibid., 35.

4. See Sheppard, 88–90, for a detailed discussion of the Graduate Faculty at the New School for Social Research in the late 1930s.

5. See Peter Rutkoff and William Scott, *New School: A History of the New School for Social Research* (New York: Free Press, 1986), 146.

6. Ibid., 1.

7. Ibid., 12.

8. Thorstein Veblen, "The War and Higher Learning," *The Dial* 65 (July 18, 1918): 45–49.

9. Alvin Johnson to Clara Mayer, October 25, 1950, New School Archive. As Claus-Dieter Krohn suggests, for Johnson the founding of *Social Research* also signified his institution's ascension to a more serious status. Claus-Dieter Krohn, *Wissenschaft im Exil: Deutsche Sozial- und Wirtschaftswissenschaftler in den USA und die New School for Social Research* (Frankfurt am Main: Campus Verlag, 1987). Johnson argued that Chicago and Harvard did not achieve such status until they began to release, respectively, the *Journal of Political Economy* and the *Quarterly Journal of Economics*. See Krohn, 98.

10. Sheppard, 91.

11. See ibid., 92.

12. Alvin Johnson, "Foreword," *Social Research* 1, 1 (1934): 1.

13. Emil Lederer, "Freedom and Science," *Social Research* 1, 1 (1934): 319; Hans Speier, "Germany in Danger (Concerning Spengler), *Social Research* 1, 1 (1934): 231; Paul Tillich, "The Totalitarian State and the Claims of the Church," *Social Research* 1, 1 (1934): 405; Thomas Mann, "The Living Spirit," *Social Research* 4, 3 (1937): 265.

14. Ibid., 92.

15. On Strauss's assessment of Plato's "correction" of Socrates in the *Laws*, see Tanguay, 92.

16. Leo Strauss, "The Spirit of Sparta or a Taste of Xenophon," *Social Research* 6, 4 (1939): 519.

17. Ibid.

18. Ibid., 532.

19. In their *The Truth About Strauss*, Catherine and Michael Zuckert describe the multiple and surprising parallels between Strauss's interests and those of Jacques Derrida. To their list— which includes an emphasis on the multiplicity of a text's meaning, the need to return to classical philosophical works and read them afresh, and of course debts to Heidegger—we might add a consciousness of the philosophical implications of writing itself. Strauss's essays of the 1930s and early 1940s anticipated, in their account of the advantages of writing philosophical works rather than simply engaging in oral dialogue, some of the insights of Derrida's *Of Grammatology*. See Catherine and Michael Zuckert, *The Truth About Leo Strauss: Political Philosophy and American Democracy* (Chicago: University of Chicago Press, 2006), 103–11.

20. Strauss, "A Taste of Xenophon; or, the Spirit of Sparta," 535.

21. Ibid., 536.

22. Strauss, *The Political Philosophy of Hobbes: Its Basis and Its Genesis* (Oxford: Clarendon, 1936), 160–61.

23. Strauss, *Gessamelte Schriften* 3:549–50.

24. Sheppard compares Strauss's essay to Freud's *Moses and Monotheism*, in which Moses appeared not as an Israelite but as an Egyptian; thus it was another attempt to "de-Judaize" an important figure in Jewish history. See Sheppard, 107.

25. Strauss, "Literary Character of the Guide of the Perplexed," in *Persecution and the Art of Writing*, 47.

26. Ibid., 56.

27. "Persecution and the Art of Writing," in ibid.

28. Ibid., 32.

29. Ibid., 25.

30. Ibid., 23.

31. Ibid.

32. Ibid., 33.

33. Ibid., 34.

34. Ibid.

35. See Sheppard, 58.

36. See Rutkoff and Smith, chapter 4.

37. Alvin Johnson, "The Intellectual in a Time of Crisis," *Social Research* 4, 1 (1/4) (1937): 282.

38. On the Frankfurt School in exile see Martin Jay, *The Dialectical Imagination: A History of the Frankfurt School and the Institute of Social Research, 1923–1950* (Berkeley: University of California Press, 1973).

39. Zygmunt Bauman, *Legislators and Interpreters: On Modernity, Post-Modernity and Intellectuals* (Oxford: Polity Press, 1987), 4.

40. Percy Bysshe Shelley, *A Defence of Poetry* (Boston: Ginn & Co. 1891), 46.

41. The University in Exile's economists were a central pillar of the school-within-a-school, and the potential applicability of their expertise fueled Johnson's hope that his faculty would make contributions beyond the academy. For a full discussion of this point see Krohn, *Wissenschaft im Exil*.

42. Nils Gilman, *Mandarins of the Future: Modernization Theory in Cold War America* (Baltimore: Johns Hopkins University Press, 2003), 25. On modernization as a theory of history see Gilman, 62.

43. Notably, Strauss's rising disquiet over Hegelianism, which would later find its fullest development in the stridently anti-Hegelian NRH, could be detected in a review of C. E. Vaughan's *Studies in the History of Political Philosophy Before and After Rousseau*, which he penned for *Social Research*. In this work Vaughan asserted, as Strauss put it, "his belief in a continuous progress 'towards a goal which itself is essentially progressive." The review perhaps unsurprisingly recalled Strauss's central criticism of Julius Guttmann, namely that Guttmann had merely imposed modern categories useful for his own work, on thinkers who had not thought in such categories. Leo Strauss, Review of Vaughan, *Social Research* 8, 1 (1/4) (1941).

44. See Gilman, 56.

45. See ibid., 59.

46. Strauss, *Persecution and the Art of Writing*, 23.

47. As Strauss certainly knew, Milton's tract included a series of statements directly recalling Xenophon's observation that Lycurgus's laws for the promotion of public virtue could not in fact eradicate private vice—as Milton put it, "Banish all objects of lust, shut up all youth into the severest discipline that can be exercised in any hermitage, ye cannot make them chaste that came not thither so." And Strauss could easily have recognized Plato's notion of philosophy being the progress from "opinion" toward "wisdom" in Milton's "opinion in good men is but knowledge in the making."

48. It seems likely that Strauss drew material from a book review of Karl Löwith's *From Hegel to Nietzsche*, which he wrote for *Social Research*. The review appeared in *Social Research* 8, 1 (1/4) (1941): 512–16.

49. Plato, *Republic* 372 c–d.

50. With the terms "open" and "closed" society, Strauss was drawing on terminology employed by Henri Bergson in his 1934 *The Two Sources of Morality and Religion*, trans. R. Ashley Audra and Cloudsley Brereton, with assistance of W. Horsfall Carter (Notre Dame, Ind.: University of Notre Dame Press, 1977), and this before the arrival of Karl Popper's more famous 1945 work *The Open Society and Its Enemies*. Bergson had distinguished between all-inclusive and open forms of religion and closed ones that could produce stronger feelings of social cohesion among adherents. While Strauss nowhere mentions Bergson in "German Nihilism," it is notable that Strauss had to effectively secularize a description of religion in order to adequately describe different types of civilization.

51. Bergson, *Two Sources*, 33.

52. Ibid., 33.

53. *Persecution and the Art of Writing*, 7.

54. Ibid., 7.

55. Ibid., 21.

Chapter 3. Natural Right and Tyranny

1. NRH, 12. Strauss references Plato's *Minos* 314h10-315.

2. Ibid.

3. OT, 236.

4. Ibid.

5. Ibid., 4.

6. Ibid., 7.

7. Ibid., 8.

8. Ibid., 11.

9. Ibid., 15.

10. Ibid., 21.

11. On Kojève's understanding of Hegelian recognition, see Judith Butler, *Subjects of Desire: Hegelian Reflections in Twentieth-Century France* (New York: Columbia University Press, 1987), 76–77.

12. See OT, 90.

13. For a discussion of eros in political and intellectual life deeply influenced by Strauss, see Lilla, *The Reckless Mind*.

14. OT, 79.

15. Ibid., 82.

16. Thomas Babington Macauley, *The History of England from the Accession of James II*, V. 8 (London: Longman, Brown, Green and Longmans, 1855), 70.

17. OT, 76.

18. Kojève's response was translated and published as "Tyranny and Wisdom," in OT, 139.

19. Ibid., 139. Notably Strauss refuted both examples in his response to Kojève; see ibid. 189.

20. Ibid., 145.

21. Ibid.

22. The ironies of Kojève's choice of the term "Epicurean" ran deep, for Strauss had long been strikingly critical of Epicurean philosophy itself, while aware of the correlations between his own thought and Epicureanism. See Benjamin Aldes Wurgaft, "From Heresy to Nature: Leo Strauss's

History of Modern Epicureanism," in *Dynamic Reading: Studies in the Reception of Epicureanism*, ed. Wilson Shearin and Brooke Holmes (Oxford: Oxford University Press, 2012).

23. Kojève in OT, 151.

24. Ibid., 163.

25. Ibid., 166.

26. Ibid., 176.

27. The "Restatement" was actually directed not to Kojève alone but also to the political theorist Eric Voegelin, who wrote a critical review of Strauss's study couched in terms of the definition of the concept of tyranny itself, which Voegelin felt had transformed radically since the classical period. See Voegelin, *Review of Politics*, 1949, 241–44. Voegelin and Strauss themselves carried out an extensive correspondence worthy of study, but which lies beyond the scope of my present work. See *Faith and Political Philosophy: The Correspondence Between Leo Strauss and Eric Voegelin, 1934–1964*, ed. Peter Emberley and Barry Cooper (Columbia: University of Missouri Press, 2004).

28. Ibid., 204. In fact, Strauss acknowledged, in the face of Kojève's claim that recognition was central to philosophy, that classical authors understood the dangers of the unratified independent mind, but he also pointed out that the very friendships one seeks out in order to gain ratification were problematic, bound to lead to "the cultivation and perpetuation of common prejudices by a closely knit group of kindred spirits" and therefore "incompatible with the idea of philosophy," for there was no place for prejudice in philosophical practice. See ibid., 195.

29. Ibid., 205.

30. Ibid., 194–55.

31. Ibid., 186.

32. See ibid., 210.

33. Ibid., 239.

34. Strauss to Kojève, September 11, 1957, in OT, 291.

35. Strauss, "Restatement," in OT, 212.

36. See Strauss's letter to Kojève of January 16, 1934, published in OT, 223, and see also Strauss to Kojève, September 4, 1949, published in OT, 244.

37. Heidegger translated Aeschylus's "techne d'anangkes asthenestera makro," the words of the titan Prometheus in the play *Prometheus Bound*, as "but knowledge is far less powerful than necessity."

38. Ibid. In a letter of September 19, 1950, Kojève indicated that he agreed wholeheartedly with Strauss's conclusion, and only suggested that Strauss's comment on Heidegger could be extended: "the fundamental difference with respect to the question of being pertains not only to the problem of the criterion of truth but also to that of good and evil." Published in OT, 255.

39. Ibid., 178.

40. Ibid.

41. Max Horkheimer and Theodor W. Adorno, trans. Edmund Jephcott (Stanford, Calif.: Stanford University Press, 2002), 1.

42. Strauss, NRH, 259.

43. Ibid., 260.

44. On Heidegger's *Question Concerning Technology*, see Zimmerman, *Heidegger's Confrontation with Modernity*.

45. NRH, 4.

46. NRH, 109. See also NRH, 109–13, 154, 168, 169, 170, 172, 177 n, 188–89, 264–65, 279, 311; on Lucretius in the same volume see 112–14, 168, 264, 271 n.

47. On Strauss's investment in the concept of heresy see Benjamin Lazier, *God Interrupted: Heresy and the European Imagination between the World Wars* (Princeton, N.J.: Princeton University Press, 2008).

48. SCR, 19.

49. NRH, 89.

50. Ibid, 34.

51. Ibid., 199–200.

52. NRH, 298.

53. Ibid., 301.

54. Ibid., 294.

55. Leo Strauss, "What Is Liberal Education?" in *Liberalism Ancient and Modern* (Chicago: University of Chicago Press, 1968), 5.

56. Ibid., 4.

57. Ibid., 9.

58. Ibid., 13.

59. Ibid., 10.

60. Ibid., 20.

61. Ibid.

62. Strauss to Kojeve, May 29, 1962, OT, 308–9. To this short list we might add the 1964 preface to *The Political Philosophy of Hobbes*, reprinted in Leo Strauss, *Jewish Philosophy and the Crisis of Modernity*, ed. Kenneth Hart Green (Albany: State University of New York Press, 1997).

63. On this issue, see Michael L. Frazer. "Esotericism Ancient and Modern: Strauss Contra Straussianism on the Art of Political-Philosophical Writing," *Political Theory* 34, 1 (February 2006): 33–61. The phrase "immunity of the commentator" appears in Strauss's essay, "Farabi's *Plato*," 375, and in the Introduction to *Persecution and the Art of Writing*, 14.

64. Jacques Derrida, "Violence and Metaphysics: An Essay on the Thought of Emmanuel Levinas," in *Writing and Difference* (London: Routledge, 2002), 192.

65. Leo Strauss, "Why We Remain Jews," in Strauss, *Jewish Philosophy and the Crisis of Modernity*, 320.

66. Ibid., 327.

67. Sheppard, 120.

Chapter 4. Growth of a Moralist

Epigraph: Emmanuel Levinas, *Is It Righteous to Be?*, 224

1. DF, 151.

2. Ibid.

3. Blanchot was, of course, referring to Nietzsche's *Untimely Meditations*. Levinas was sufficiently "untimely" that in a 1992 interview he was able to mourn the passing of the Soviet Union, which he had never celebrated in earlier writings. See *Is It Righteous to Be?*, 197.

4. On the tension between moralists and ideologists in postwar French thought, see Tony Judt, *The Burden of Responsibility: Blum, Camus, Aron, and the French Twentieth Century* (Chicago: University of Chicago Press, 2007).

5. DF, 154.

6. Ibid., 155.

7. See especially Howard Caygill, *Levinas and the Political* (London: Routledge, 2002), Simon Critchley, "Five Problems in Levinas's View of Politics and the Sketch of a Solution to Them," *Political Theory* 32, 2 (April 2004): 172–85, and Philip J. Harold, *Prophetic Politics: Emmanuel Levinas and the Sanctification of Suffering* (Athens: Ohio University Press, 2009).

8. For the original, see Jacques Derrida, "Violence et métaphysique: Essai sur la pensée d'Emmanuel Lévinas," *Revue de Métaphysique et de Morale* 69, 3 (1964) (Part I) and (Part II): 322–54, 425–73, published as "Violence and Metaphysics" in *Writing and Difference*.

9. See Critchley, 178.

10. Caygill not only argues that Levinas's ethics were influenced by the values of the French revolution—he goes further, suggesting that Levinas articulated a full-fledged political theory that involved rethinking the relationship between fraternity and liberty in the republican tradition, finding ways to use the former to limit the latter. Instead of conceptualizing fraternity in universal terms (all men are brothers), Levinas conceptualized fraternity in terms of alterity (our radical responsibility to the other, created by the relationship of exteriority itself). In many ways this chapter would be impossible without Caygill's insights into the political context of Levinas's ethics. However, this chapter's argument deviates from Caygill's insofar as it affirms the antipolitical character of much of Levinas's ethics.

11. See Michael Winock, "Les affaires Dreyfus," *Vingtième Siècle* 5 (1985): 19–37, and "Une question de principe," in *La France de l'affaire Dreyfus*, ed. Pierre Birnbaum (Paris: Gallimard, 1994), 543–72.

12. Emmanuel Levinas, *Alterity and Transcendence*, trans. Michael B. Smith (New York: Columbia University Press, 1999), 82.

13. François Poirié, *Qui êtes-vous?* (Lyons: La Manufacture, 1987), 70.

14. Emile Zola, "J'accuse," *L'Aurore*, January 13, 1898.

15. As Tamara Chaplin points out, following an 1809 Napoleonic decree, all *lycées* offered a year of instruction in philosophy. Philosophy was, in a loose sense, linked to French citizenship. See Chaplin, 29.

16. On Levinas's role in this process, see especially Ethan Kleinberg, *Generation Existential*.

17. See Julian Bourg, *From Revolution to Ethics: May 1968 and Contemporary French Thought* (Montreal: McGill-Queen's University Press, 2007).

18. See Sarah Hammerschlag, *The Figural Jew: Politics and Identity in Postwar French Thought* (Chicago: University of Chicago Press, 2010).

19. Ibid., 17.

20. Levinas, "The Other, Utopia and Justice," in *Is it Righteous to Be?*, 224.

21. Ibid.

22. Levinas with Raoul Mortley in Raoul Mortley, *French Philosophers in Conversation* (London: Routledge, 1991), 18.

23. Löwith, "The Political Implications of Heidegger's Existentialism," in Wolin, *The Heidegger Controversy*, 169.

24. For Levinas's appreciation of this point in Bergson, see Emmanuel Levinas and Philippe Nemo, *Ethics and Infinity* (Pittsburgh: Duquesne University Press, 1985), 27.

25. Henri Bergson, *Creative Evolution*, trans. Arthur Mitchell (New York: Palgrave Macmillan, 2007), 366.

26. In one late interview, Levinas was even able to imply that Bergson's understanding of durée anticipated Heidegger's accomplishments: "Isn't the ontological thematisation by Heidegger of *being* as distinguished from *beings*, the investigation of being in its verbal sense, already at work in the Bergsonian notion of durée, which is not reducible to the substantivity of beings?" Emmanuel Levinas, *Entre Nous: on Thinking-of-the-Other* (New York: Columbia University Press, 1998), 223.

27. Moyn, *Origins of the Other*, 38.

28. See Jean Hering, *Phénoménologie et philosophie religieuse: Étude sur la théorie de la connaissance religieuse* (Paris: Alcan, 1926).

29. Ibid., 188.

30. For a full discussion of Brunschvicg's neo-Kantianism, see Alan D. Schrift, *Twentieth-Century French Philosophy: Key Themes and Thinkers* (London: Blackwell, 2006), 7.

31. The engagement with Husserlian phenomenology led Levinas to his interest in the encounter with the other person, but partly because, as Moyn argues, Husserl's earlier work on

intentionality did not automatically open onto a consideration of interpersonal experience at all. Husserl chose to augment his theory of intentionality with a "more fundamental theory of the primacy of the cognizing ego," which inevitably led him to Descartes and to the solipsism Descartes had bequeathed to Western philosophy. See Moyn, *Origins of the Other*, 42.

32. See Emmanuel Levinas, *The Theory of Intuition in the Phenomenology of Edmund Husserl*, trans. André Orianne (Evanston, Ill.: Northwestern University Press, 1995), 216–18. And see Adriaan Peperzak's discussion of Heidegger's influence on Levinas's reading of Husserl in *Beyond: The Philosophy of Emmanuel Levinas* (Evanston: Northwestern University Press, 1997), 40.

33. It is worth wondering whether or not Levinas's criticism of Husserl is entirely fair, given that in his *Ideen*, Husserl emphasizes the importance of lived experience or *Erlebnis* over the theoretical knowledge provided by representation.

34. See Peperzak.

35. Levinas, *The Theory of Intuition in Husserl's Phenomenology*, 59, 64.

36. See Caygill, 25.

37. This essay was originally published in the *Revue Philosophique* 57 (1932) and was subsequently republished as part of *En découvrant l'existence avec Husserl et Heidegger*.

38. Levinas himself made the equation of "the philosophy of Hitlerism" and Heideggerianism in a "Post-Scriptum" written for the English translation of "Some Reflections." See Emmanuel Levinas, "Some Reflections on the Philosophy of Hitlerism," trans. Seán Hand, *Critical Inquiry* 17, 1 (Autumn 1990): 62–71. For convenience I cite Hand's translation; the original *Esprit* essay has been republished in French with an essay by Miguel Abensour as *Quelques réflexions sur la philosophie de l'hitlérisme* (Paris: Payot & Rivages, 1997).

39. Ibid., 64.

40. Ibid., 8–9.

41. Caygill, 33.

42. Levinas, "Some Reflections on the Philosophy of Hitlerism," 65.

43. Ibid., 65.

44. Ibid., 69.

45. Emmanuel Levinas, "L'inspiration religieuse de l'alliance," *Paix et Droit* 8 (1935).

46. See Mounier's *Personalism* (Notre Dame, Ind.: University of Notre Dame Press, 1970) for his presentation of the essentials of his doctrine.

47. J. M. Domenach in *Aussprache* (February 1952). This note was republished in the *Bulletin des Amis d'É. Mounier* 3 (April 1953): 13–16.

48. *Esprit* 8 (May 1933): 2333–34.

49. *Recherches Philosophiques* 5 (1935/36): 373–92. For the sake of ease I cite Bettina Bergo's English translation: *On Escape* (Stanford, Calif.: Stanford University Press, 2003).

50. Ibid., 49.

51. Ibid.

52. Ibid., 50.

53. Ibid., 51.

54. On Rosenzweig's account of philosophy's "flight" from mortality, see Gordon, *Rosenzweig and Heidegger*, 175.

55. Levinas, *On Escape*, 50.

56. Ibid.

57. Levinas, *Is It Righteous to Be?*, 35.

58. Emmanuel Levinas, "L'actualité de Maimonide," *Paix et Droit* 15, 4 (April 1935): 6–7.

59. Ibid.

60. Ibid.

61. It is in the context of this response to Heidegger's location of transcendence within the world, and Levinas's rejection of this as "paganism," that we can best understand Levinas's later

essay, "Heidegger, Gagarin et Nous" ("Heidegger, Gagarin and Us"), published in 1961 in *Information Juive*, the same year that Levinas's *Totality and Infinity*—which, as Levinas's second dissertation, was presented to its examiners as an exercise in Platonism—was published. In the essay, Levinas repeated his association of Heidegger's philosophy with paganism as he engaged with his teacher's famous postwar attacks on technology. If, according to Heidegger, technology threatened our relation to the world, and thus to Being, Levinas criticized this prioritizing of "world" as an immature antiprogressivism, "camping in the mountains." His title refers to the historically important flight of the Russian cosmonaut Yuri Gagarin, the first human to orbit the earth, which for Levinas symbolized man's ultimate mastery over himself, his lack of reliance on Place. The flight of Gagarin away from the place-world of Heidegger thus becomes legible as man's search for meaning beyond himself. The essay appears in English as "Heidegger, Gagarin, and Us," in DF.

Chapter 5. Resisting Engagement

1. See Kleinberg, *Generation Existential*, 246, and Raul Hilberg, *The Destruction of the European Jews* (Chicago: Quadrangle, 1961), 401.

2. See Marie-Anne Lescourret, *Emmanuel Levinas* (Paris: Flammarion, 1995), 134.

3. Ibid., 89. On the significance of the *agrégation* for the history of French philosophy see Alan D. Schrift, "The Effects of the *Agrégation de Philosophie* on Twentieth-Century French Philosophy," *Journal of the History of Philosophy* 46, 3 (July 2008): 449–73.

4. Levinas, *Is It Righteous to Be?* 38.

5. See Ethan Kleinberg, "The Myth of Emmanuel Levinas," in *After the Deluge: New Perspectives on the Intellectual and Cultural History of Postwar France*, ed. Julian Bourg (Lanham: Lexington, 2004), 210.

6. For a detailed account of the AIU's early activities see Michael M. Laskier, "Aspects of the Activities of the Alliance israélite universelle in the Jewish Communities of the Middle East and North Africa: 1860–1918," *Modern Judaism* 3, 2 (May 1983): 147–71.

7. For the sake of ease I cite the English translation of the work: Jean-Paul Sartre, *Anti-Semite and Jew*, trans. George J. Becker (New York: Schocken, 1965). For an account of how *Anti-Semite and Jew* represents an application of Sartre's philosophy to politics, see Jonathan Judaken, *Jean-Paul Sartre and the Jewish Question* (Lincoln: University of Nebraska Press, 2006), 126.

8. Rosalind Krauss and Denis Hollier, who translated and published Sartre's talk, are careful to warn readers that the exact provenance of the text they translated is unknown. They presume it to be either a stenographic recording or a direct transcription by Alliance staff present at the talk. Jean-Paul Sartre, "Reflections on the Jewish Question: A Lecture," in Rosalind Krauss and Denis Hollier, eds., "Jean-Paul Sartre's 'Anti-Semite and Jew'," *October* 87 (special issue, Winter 1999).

9. Ibid., 4.

10. Susan Suleiman understands Sartre's use of the phrase "La question juive" as a deliberate attempt to reappropriate a term that had accumulated significantly anti-Semitic connotations. Despite Jewish uses of the phrase *Judenfrage*—such as Theodor Herzl's use of it in the subtitle to his 1896 *Judenstaat* (*Versuch einer modernen Lösung der Judenfrage*) (English: *The Jewish State: Search for a Modern Solution to the Jewish Question*) at the time Sartre used the phrase it would have carried heavy associations with the Holocaust. Suleiman points in particular to Robert Brasillach's dedications of an entire issue of his weekly *Je suis partout* to "La question juive" in 1938 in the field of cultural production, and, even more important, to the Vichy government's Commissariat Général aux Questions Juives, established in March 1941. Sartre hoped to transform the often anti-Semitic phrase to show that the existence of a "Jewish question" in social and political life is in fact the fault of anti-Semites rather than of Jews. Sartre wanted to transform this question into the "Anti-Semitic Question." Suleiman draws on Jacob Toury's important article, "'The

Jewish Question': A Semantic Approach," *Leo Baeck Institute Yearbook* 11 (1966): 85–106. See Suleiman, 203–4.

11. Sartre, *Anti-Semite and Jew,* 40.

12. Ibid., 55.

13. Ibid., 57.

14. For the sake of ease I refer to Mary Beth Mader's translation: Emmanuel Levinas, "Being Jewish," trans. Mary Beth Mader *Continental Philosophy Review* 40 (2007) 205–210.

15. Ibid., 208.

16. Ibid., 209.

17. Martin Jay, *Downcast Eyes: The Denigration of Vision in Twentieth-Century French Thought* (Berkeley: University of California Press, 1993), 276.

18. Jean-Paul Sartre, "What Is Writing?," in *What Is Literature?* (London: Routledge, 1997), 1.

19. Ibid., 4.

20. Ibid., 5.

21. Anna Boschetti, *The Intellectual Enterprise: Sartre and Les Temps Modernes*, trans. Richard C. McCleary (Evanston, Ill.: Northwestern University Press, 1988), 119. There have been critical Marxist responses to Sartre's utilitarian perspective on literature. For example, see Ernst Fischer's response to Sartre's claim that "much of Western art" is, in the face of poverty, a waste of time Fischer, *The Necessity of Art: A Marxist Approach* (Baltimore: Penguin, 1963).

22. See Boschetti, 109, for a more substantial discussion of this note of ambivalence in Sartre's relationship to Marxism.

23. Emmanuel Levinas, "La réalité et son ombre," *Les Temps Modernes*, 38 (November 1948), 771–789. In the following I cite the English translation, "Reality and Its Shadow" in Seán Hand, ed., *The Levinas Reader* (Oxford: Blackwell, 1989) 141; emphasis mine.

24. Ibid., 131.

25. While Levinas did not refer to Kant as a precedent for his view, he might well have done so. In the *Critique of Judgment*, Kant offered a sustained discussion of the way the spectator-critic provides the public context in which it becomes possible to judge artworks as beautiful, a discussion that notably inspired Arendt's late lectures.

26. Levinas, "Reality and Its Shadow," 130.

27. Ibid., 131.

28. See ibid., 132.

29. Ibid., 135.

30. Ibid., 141.

Chapter 6. Witnessing

1. Emmanuel Levinas, *Totalité et Infini: essai sur l'extériorité* (The Hague: Nijhoff, 1961), and in English, *Totality and Infinity: An Essay on Exteriority*, trans. Alphonso Lingis (Pittsburgh: Duquesne University Press, 1969), henceforth TI; references are to the Lingis translation. TI, 21.

2. For ease of reference I cite the English translations of these works. Emmanuel Levinas, *Existence and Existents*, trans. Alphonso Lingis (The Hague: Nijhoff, 1978); *Time and the Other*, trans. Richard A. Cohen (Pittsburgh: Duquesne University Press, 1987).

3. Furthermore, and despite the aforementioned shift in Levinas's understanding of solipsism between *Time and the Other* and TI, the former work still anticipates one feature of TI's discussion of solipsism. As Levinas writes in *Time and the Other*, "Solipsism . . . is the very structure of reason" (65).

4. Levinas's response to Sartre came after the 1945 lecture "Existentialism and Humanism" that marked a watershed moment in Sartre's career. In the minds of many commentators, the

lecture stands as the definitive moment when Sartre turned toward a politically directed philosophy. See Jean-Paul Sartre, *Existentialism Is a Humanism*, trans. Carol Macomber (New Haven, Conn.: Yale University Press, 2007).

5. *Time and the Other*, 30.

6. Ibid., 31–32.

7. Ibid., 39.

8. See ibid., 43.

9. See ibid., 51. Levinas reflected in a similar fashion in his *On Escape*, discussed in the previous chapter. He repeated one of that earlier essay's major points a few pages later in *Time and the Other*: "Identity is not an inoffensive relationship with itself, but an enchainment to itself; it is the necessity of being occupied with itself" (55).

10. *Time and the Other*, 57.

11. Notably the language of fecundity and birth is continued in TI. The most famous response to Levinas's deployment of these tropes, and to his romantic reification of "the feminine" (which already appeared in *Time and the Other*; see especially 85–87) can be found in Luce Irigaray's "The Fecundity of the Caress," in *An Ethics of Sexual Difference* (New York: Continuum, 2005). The movement Irigaray critiques in her work on Levinas—from death to the feminine to a new (and "phallologocentric") emphasis on "the son"—is already present in *Time and the Other*.

12. Levinas, *Time and the Other*, 84.

13. Ibid., 87.

14. Ibid.

15. Ibid., 60

16. Ibid., 61.

17. TI, 148.

18. TI, 113–14.

19. TI, 192–93.

20. See TI, 195. It is this emphasis on language that has invited numerous comparisons between Levinas and Martin Buber, not to mention Rosenzweig and numerous other theorists of what is commonly called the "dialogical." Levinas, at least the Levinas of TI, differed from other dialogic thinkers in his emphasis on the "asymmetrical" or nonreciprocal nature of the self-Other relation. In other words, for Levinas there was no "conversation" of equals running between myself and my Other: as he often put it, one is utterly powerless before the ethical law announced by the Other's proximity. In TI he wrote, "The fact that the face maintains a relation with me by discourse does not range him in the same; he remains absolute within the relation." Ibid. Conversely, perhaps the best evidence for seeing Levinas as a dialogic philosopher appears a few sections later: he wrote, "The essence of discourse is ethical." TI, 216.

21. "Reality and Its Shadow," in Hand, ed., 112.

22. Ibid.

23. TI, 196. Levinas cites Descartes explicitly as the source of his thought (197).

24. Naturally it is because Levinas articulated these putatively philosophical notions in quasi-religious language that commentators are so tempted to view them as, in fact, transported theological notions.

25. Ibid., 197.

26. See ibid., 198.

27. Ibid., 199.

28. The *reason* the Other's proximity issues in a commandment not to kill, or the exact nature of the power that undermines my power to kill, is extremely difficult to discern in Levinas's text. Detractors have often found his notion of an "ethics of the Other" problematic because of this; it seems not to enjoy strong justification at the level of close argument in TI.

29. Ibid., 201.

30. Ibid.

31. Ibid., 202.

32. Ibid., 212.

33. Ibid., 213.

34. See also Caygill, 69.

35. On this point, see especially Michael E. Zimmerman, *Heidegger's Confrontation with Modernity: Technology, Politics, Art* (Bloomington: Indiana University Press, 1990).

36. Levinas, "Sur l'esprit de Gèneve," *Esprit* 24 (1956): 96–98.

37. Ibid.

38. Ibid.

39. Ibid.

40. Emmanuel Levinas, "Principes et visages," *Esprit*, 28, 5 (May 1960): 863–865 and also republished in DF as "Principles and Faces."

41. Ibid., 865.

42. TI, 28.

43. See Rosenzweig, *The Star of Redemption*, 329.

44. See Samuel Moyn, *A Holocaust Controversy: The Treblinka Affair in Postwar France* (Waltham, Mass.: Brandeis University Press, 2005). See especially 112–21 for a discussion of Levinas's role in the Affair.

45. Steiner's claims went beyond those made either by Arendt or by her historical inspiration, Raul Hilberg's *The Destruction of the European Jews*. Steiner "went beyond either of these figures in raising the specter, not simply of general passivity or elite compliance, but that of murderous participation too." See Moyn, *A Holocaust Controversy*, 4.

46. "Honneur sans drapeau," *Nouveaux Cahiers* 6, 1966. The essay was republished as "Sans Nomme" ("Nameless") in the volume *Nommes propres* (Saint-Clément de Rivière: Fata Morgana, 1976); for the English translation see *Proper Names*, trans. Michael B. Smith (Stanford, Calif.: Stanford University Press, 1996). Citations are to the latter.

47. Ibid., 121.

48. As previously discussed, "witnessing" was an activity with great symbolic importance for Levinas from his writings of the 1930s on. It represented one of his important points of congruity with Emmanuel Mounier and the other writers of *Esprit*. Furthermore, Levinas's notion of "witnessing," developed in the 1930s, went on to influence his mature view of the Jews as a "witnessing people."

49. Levinas, *Proper Names*, 120.

50. Ibid.

51. Emmanuel Levinas, "État d'Israël et religion d'Israël," *Evidences* 20 (September–October, 1951): 3–6, and in English, "The State of Israel and the Religion of Israel," published in DF.

52. DF, 218.

53. Levinas, "L'espace n'est pas a une dimension," *Esprit* 36, (1968): 617–23; in English, "Space Is Not One-dimensional," in DF.

54. I quote the excerpt from De Gaulle's press conference included in Raymond Aron's *De Gaulle, Israel and the Jews*, trans. John Sturrock (London: Deutsch, 1969).

55. Levinas, "Space Is Not One-Dimensional," DF, 260.

56. Ibid., 263.

57. Ibid.

58. Aron had said much the same thing in his *De Gaulle, Israel and the Jews*: "As a French citizen I claim the right granted to all citizens of combining allegiance to the State with freedom of belief and of sympathy" (46).

59. See Judith Friedlander, *Vilna on the Seine: Jewish Intellectuals in France Since 1968* (New Haven, Conn.: Yale University Press, 1990).

60. See Eli Lederhendler, ed., *The Six-Day War and World Jewry* (Bethesda: University Press of Maryland, 2000), 126.

61. See Alain Finkielkraut, *Le juif imaginaire* (Paris: Seuil, 1980), available in English translation as *The Imaginary Jew*, trans. Kevin O'Neill and David Suchoff (Lincoln: University of Nebraska Press, 1994).

62. In DF. One of the great ironies of Levinas's career is that he himself had been an inspiration, both as philosopher and Jewish thinker, to many younger Jewish intellectuals who then sought to make *teshuva*. However, their attempts to "drop out" of French culture could not have been further from his own ideal goal for Jews living in France. Levinas, with his strict division between philosophical and "confessional" writings, was himself living closer to the "universal man in the street but Jew at home" model that many of his self-appointed followers subsequently rejected. The most famous of Levinas's adherents was, as is widely known, Benny Levy (Pierre Victor), who would go on to produce works of Levinasian philosophy and meditations on Jewish identity that have garnered both praise and criticism.

63. See Kafka's "Letter" as published in his collection, *The Sons* (New York: Schocken, 1989).

64. The story of this chant is rather more complicated than can be explained in these pages. The student leader Daniel Cohn-Bendit, born a German Jew, had been denied reentry into France by the government. The chant thus originated in a protest against Cohn-Bendit's exile from France. Remembering this protest, in which he had taken part, Finkielkraut said that he had participated with a sense of bad faith: even as a participant in his late teens he had been sufficiently self-aware to object to any appropriation of Jewish identity for the purposes of a political display.

65. Finkielkraut and Levinas were, in fact, alike in criticizing Sartre's essay. Their major difference, however, was that Levinas still posited (at least implicitly) various essentializing understandings of Judaism, throughout the rest of his career.

66. Emmanuel Levinas, "Comment le judaisme est-il possible?" in *L'Arche* (1959): 33–34, 57. And in English, "How Is Judaism Possible," in DF, 245.

67. Ibid.

68. Ibid., 246.

69. Ibid., 247.

70. Levinas was notably unwilling to offer a concise definition of Jewish "culture" to augment this reference to a cultural politics. He stated that Jewish culture is resistant to summary, and does not go any further than stating the centrality of Hebrew for Jewish education.

71. See Caygill, *Levinas and the Political.*

72. Jean Wahl, *Traite de metaphysique* (Paris: Payot, 1953), 562, trans. Alphonso Lingis.

73. Derrida, "Violence and Metaphysics," in *Writing and Difference*, 102.

74. Emmanuel Levinas, *Autrement au'être, ou au-delà de l'essence* (The Hague: Nijhoff, 1974), in English, *Otherwise Than Being, or Beyond Essence*, trans. Alphonso Lingis (Pittsburgh: Duquesne University Press, 1981), 46–48. Henceforth cited as OTB.

75. OTB, 42.

76. OTB, 64.

77. OTB, 6. See J. L. Austin, *How to Do Things with Words* (Cambridge, Mass.: Harvard University Press, 1978).

78. OTB, 10.

79. OTB, 77.

80. OTB, 159.

81. OTB, 160.

82. OTB, 166.

83. Sartre, Introduction to Frantz Fanon, *The Wretched of the Earth* (New York: Grove, 2004), 19.

84. Jean-Paul Sartre, *Plaidoyer pour les intellectuels* (Paris: Gallimard, 1972). Citations will be to the translation by John Matthews, "A Plea for the Intellectuals," in Jean-Paul Sartre, *Between Existentialism and Marxism* (New York: William Morrow, 1974).

85. Ibid., 232.

86. Levinas in conversation with Raoul Mortley, Mortley, *French Philosophers*, 18.

Chapter 7. Arendt's Weimar Origins

Part epigraph: Hannah Arendt, *The Origins of Totalitarianism* (New York: Harcourt, 1951), 613, henceforth cited as O.T.

1. Hannah Arendt, *On Revolution* (New York: Viking, 1963), 306. Arendt borrowed the phrases "men of thought" and "men of action" from classicist F. M. Cornford, citing him in *The Human Condition* (Chicago: University of Chicago Press, 1958); henceforth HC. For Arendt's uses of "men of thought" and "men of action" see HC, 12 and 17; at the latter, Arendt quotes Cornford's "Plato's Commonwealth," published in *The Unwritten Philosophy and Other Essays* (Cambridge: Cambridge University Press, 1950). For Cornford, the historical moment when this "parting of ways" began was the death of Pericles and the beginning of the Peloponnesian War. See also HC, 17–18, for Arendt's discussion of Socrates himself developing the view that politics did not provide for all humanity's higher activities.

2. This matched her self-image. While in later years she would primarily identify herself as a political theorist, in a letter to Karl Jaspers of November 18, 1945, written when she had been in the United States for about four years, Arendt described herself as "something between a historian and a political journalist." See AJC, 23.

3. LeRoy Leatherman, "Homage to the Secret-Bearer," *Sewanee Review* 72, 2 (Spring 1964): 329–34.

4. See Hannah Arendt, "Understanding and Politics," in Arendt, *Essays in Understanding 1930–1954: Formation, Exile, and Totalitarianism* (New York: Harcourt, Brace, 1994).

5. As mentioned in the Introduction, the interview was originally part of Günter Gaus's television program, *Zur Person*. See Joan Stambaugh's translation in *The Portable Hannah Arendt*.

6. Ibid.

7. See Warner, *Publics and Counterpublics*, 23.

8. Hannah Arendt, *Men in Dark Times* (New York: Houghton Mifflin, 1970), 20.

9. See O.T, 26.

10. Ibid., 23.

11. As I will explain in the next chapter's discussion of *The Human Condition*, Arendt's formulation of "action," as well as "labor" and "work," derived from a critical engagement with Marx. For Arendt, Marx had made the mistake of producing, as Dana Villa calls it, a "work model of action," or, in other words, an understanding of action as political because it allows for building institutions and the material conditions for political life. Action, for Arendt, is more like performance than it is like building. See Danna R. Villa, "Totalitarianism, Modernity and the Tradition," in *Hannah Arendt in Jerusalem*, ed. Steven Aschheim (Berkeley: University of California Press, 2001).

12. Hannah Arendt, "The Crisis in Culture: Its Social and Political Significance," in *Between Past and Future: Eight Exercises in Political Thought* (New York: Penguin, 1961), 225.

13. Gaus tended to interview, in the *Zur Person* series, figures of great political influence, including Konrad Adenauer, Henry Kissinger, and Gerhard Schröder.

14. AJC, 195.

15. On Arendt's public success and the reception of her legacy in regions philosophers seldom reach—such as having a Lufthansa jet named after her—see Walter Laqueur, "The Arendt Cult," in Aschheim, ed.

16. Arendt once noted, to one of her students, that underlying Kant's categorical imperative is a "real imperative:" "Don't contradict yourself." Arendt to Auraam-Makis Koen, July 3, 1972, Hannah Arendt Papers, Library of Congress.

17. See FLOTW, 328–99. As Richard I. Cohen notes, the response to *Eichmann in Jerusalem*, a "public airing of historical issues relating to the Holocaust," would include the publication of several books and more than two hundred articles both journalistic and academic. See Richard I. Cohen, "A Generation's Response to *Eichmann in Jerusalem*," in Aschheim, ed.

18. See, for example, Richard J. Bernstein, *Hannah Arendt and the "Jewish Question"* (Cambridge: MIT Press, 1996); Aschheim, ed.; Richard I. Cohen, "Breaking the Code: Hannah Arendt's *Eichmann in Jerusalem* and the Public Polemic-Myth, Memory and Historical Imagination," in *Michael* 13, ed. Dina Porat and Shlomo Simonsohn (Tel Aviv, 1993): 30–41. See also Seyla Benhabib, "Identity, Perspective, and Narrative in Hannah Arendt's *Eichmann in Jerusalem*," *History and Memory* 8 (1996): 147–53.

19. Scholem's letter is dated June 23, 1963; see *Der Briefwechsel: Hannah Arendt/Gershom Scholem* (Frankfurt: Suhrkamp Insel, 2010).

20. Gershom Scholem to Shalom Spiegel (Letter 119), July 17, 1941, Scholem, *Briefe*, I. 285.

21. Arendt's response is dated 20 July 1963; see *Der Briefwechsel*, ibid. Notably, their exchange then appeared in two newspapers—first the *Mitteilungsblatt*, no. 33, August 16, 1963, and then the *Neue Zurcher Zeitung*, on October 20, 1963.

22. For one reading of the meaning of Arendt's response to Scholem, see Judith Butler, "I Merely Belong to Them," *London Review of Books* 2, 9 (May 10, 2007): 26–28.

23. It is worth noting, against Arendt's refusal to speak from a Jewish perspective, that in a letter to Jaspers of 1946 she had written, "I will always speak in the name of the Jews." AJC, 68. Arendt's insistence on non-self-contradiction did not, naturally enough, preclude change over time.

24. Arendt suggested that one strategy used, in order to place European anti-Semitism itself on trial, was to call as an expert witness and commentator on historical anti-Semitism, the Jewish historian Salo Wittmayer Baron, himself a friend of Arendt's. See Hannah Arendt, *Eichmann in Jerusalem: A Report on the Banality of Evil* (New York: Viking, 1963), 19.

25. Neither Arendt nor Raul Hilberg, who examined the *Judenräte* in the 1961 *The Destruction of the European Jews*, saw their painful choices as a form of complicity with genocide. See Hilberg, *The Destruction of the European Jews*.

26. See, for example, Yisrael Gutman, "Arendt-Style Self-Hatred," *Yalkut Moreshet* 4, 6 (December 1966): 111–34. Norman Podhoretz summarized the common objections to Arendt in *Commentary*, as follows: "In the place of the monstrous Nazi, she gives us the 'banal' Nazi; in the place of the Jew as a virtuous martyr, she gives us the Jew as accomplice in evil; and in the place of the confrontation of guilt and innocence, she gives us the 'collaboration' of criminal and victim." Norman Podhoretz, "Hannah Arendt on Eichmann," *Commentary* (September 1963): 201–8.

27. Michael A. Musmanno, "A Man with an Unspotted Conscience," *New York Times Book Review*, May 19, 1963, 1, 40–41.

28. See Arendt, *Eichmann in Jerusalem*, 48, 135–37.

29. This accusation had its ironies. As I explain later in this chapter, Arendt had meditated at length on the theme of individualism in German Jewish history, in her biography of the *salonnière* Rahel Varnhagen.

30. See Seyla Benhabib, *The Reluctant Modernism of Hannah Arendt* (New York: Rowman and Littlefield, 2003).

31. As is well known, Ralph Ellison managed to convince Arendt that she had failed to understand the complexities of the situation in Little Rock, and the complexities of the African American struggle for equality more broadly. See Ralph Ellison in Robert Penn Warren, *Who Speaks for the Negro?* (New York: Random House, 1965), 343–44, and Arendt's letter to Ellison of July 1967, cited in FLOTW, 315–17, 519.

32. See Arendt's notes prepared for an interview with *Look* magazine, 1963. Hannah Arendt Papers, Library of Congress.

33. Hannah Arendt to Karl Jaspers, March 4, 1951. See AJC, 165.

34. See AJC, 690.

35. On this point it is useful to compare Arendt's interest in Augustine with that of her friend and generational colleague, Hans Jonas, like Arendt a German Jew drawn into Heidegger's circle. In 1930, he completed *Augustin und das paulinische Freiheitsproblem: Eine philosophische Studie zum pelagianischen Streit* (Augustine and the Pauline Problem of Freedom: A Philosophical Study of the Pelagian Controversy) a scholarly study in theology and religious history like his other important youthful work, *Gnosis und spätantiker Geist* (Göttingen: Vandenhoeck & Ruprecht, 1934), later translated into English as *The Gnostic Religion: The Message of the Alien God and the Beginnings of Christianity* (Boston: Beacon, 1958). Jonas appears to have been drawn, like Arendt, to writing on significant thematic elements of *Existenzphilosophie* such as loneliness, alienation, and longing, through the surrogate of their appearance in the religious texts of the ancient world. This was likely due to the influence of Jonas and Arendt's "other" shared teacher, Rudolf Bultmann, himself preoccupied by the "mythic" character of the life of Jesus and the relationship between mythology and theology. Both praised and scorned for abstracting the existential content of a religious doctrine from the "mythic" context in which its teachings developed, Bultmann veered toward what both Karl Jaspers—his interlocutor—and Jonas—his student— saw as a philosophical interpretation of religion.

36. See Moyn, *Origins of the Other*, 78–84.

37. HC, 65.

38. Bultmann was in fact close friends with Heidegger at the time Arendt attended his seminar, making Arendt's presence there understandable. Heidegger and Bultmann met weekly between 1923, when Heidegger accepted an appointment at Marburg and replaced Paul Natorp, discussing theology and philosophy, and the Winter semester of 1923–24, Bultmann and Heidegger co-taught a seminar titled, "The Problem of Sin in Luther." While Heidegger and Bultmann shared numerous intellectual interests—as well as students—they were divided on the issue of neo-Kantianism, of which Bultmann was a follower and Heidegger a devout critic. Despite this gulf, Bultmann was able to find inspiration in *Being and Time* for his theology of inner experience apart from the world. For a more complete account of the Bultmann-Heidegger friendship, see William D. Dennison, *The Young Bultmann: Context for His Understanding of God 1884–1925* (New York: Peter Lang, 2008), 133–38. See also Hans Jonas, "Is Faith Still Possible? Memories of Rudolf Bultmann and Reflections on the Philosophical Aspects of His Work," *Harvard Theological Review* 75, 1 (1982).

39. Hannah Arendt, *Love and Saint Augustine*, ed. Joanna Vecchiarelli Scott and Judith Chelius Stark, based on E. B. Ashton's translation (and Arendt's revisions of Ashton's translation) (Chicago: University of Chicago Press, 1996) 21. Henceforth LSA.

40. Plotinus, *The Six Enneads*, trans. Stephen MacKenna and B. S. Page (Chicago: Encyclopaedia Britannica, 1952).

41. The titles of the three sections of the work are far clearer in the original German edition, where they are given in Latin, than they are in the English translation: *Amor qua appetitas, Creator-creatura,* and *Vita socialis.*

42. Arendt, LSA, 10.

43. Arendt, LSA, 29, and see 51 for Augustine's view that "being" is by nature immutable.

44. LSA, 93.

45. Arendt's citation is to Heidegger, *Being and Time*, 279–304, sect. 46–52, in the Macquarrie and Robinson translation.

46. Martin Heidegger, "Vom Wesen des Grundes," *Festschrift für Edmund Husserl*, 1929.

47. LSA, 24; Arendt quotes Augustine's *Confessions* X, 33, 50.

48. Hannah Arendt to Mary McCarthy, October 20, 1965, published in *Between Friends: The Correspondence of Hannah Arendt and Mary McCarthy, 1949–1975* (New York: Harcourt Brace, 1995), 190.

49. HC, 14.

50. HC, 12. Arendt cites Augustine's *De civitate Dei*, xix. 2, 19.

51. See Hannah Arendt, *The Life of the Mind: Thinking and Willing* (New York: Harcourt Brace, 1981). Cited henceforth as LOTM. Citations to the work mention "Thinking" and "Willing," which have different paginations. See "Thinking," 77.

52. LOTM, 78.

53. As Arendt put it, "The 'attention of the mind' is needed to transform sensation into perception." LOTM, 100.

54. LOTM, 85.

55. On Augustine as the source of Arendt's understanding of "natality," see Stephan Kampowski, *Arendt, Augustine, and the New Beginning: The Action Theory and Moral Thought of Hannah Arendt in the Light of Her Dissertation on St. Augustine* (Grand Rapids: Eerdmans, 2008). For Arendt's mature use of the term, see HC, 176, 177. See also Patricia Bowen-Moore, Hannah Arendt's Philosophy of Natality (London: Macmillan, 1989).

56. Originally published as "Philosophie und Soziologie. Zu Karl Mannheim's *Ideologie und Utopie*," *Die Gesellschaft* 7 (1930): 163–76. The review has been translated and abridged in Anton Kaes, Martin Jay, and Edward Dimendberg, eds., *The Weimar Republic Sourcebook*. For the circumstances surrounding Arendt's review, see FLOTW, 83.

57. Theodor Adorno, *Negative Dialectics*, trans. E. B. Ashton (London: Routledge, 1990), 197–98.

58. Martin Jay, "The Frankfurt School's Critique of Karl Mannheim and the Sociology of Knowledge," *Telos* 20, (Summer 1974): 72–89; republished in Martin Jay, *Permanent Exiles: Essays on the Intellectual Immigration to America* (New York: Columbia University Press, 1990). Page citations are to the latter.

59. Ibid., 65.

60. Hannah Arendt, "Philosophy and Sociology: on Karl Mannheim's *Ideology and Utopia*," in Kaes, Jay, and Dimendberg, *The Weimar Republic Sourcebook*, 302.

61. See Jay, *Permanent Exiles*, 73.

62. See Carl Boggs, *Intellectuals and the Crisis of Modernity* (Albany: SUNY Press, 1993), 94.

63. Hannah Arendt, *Rahel Varnhagen: The Life of a Jewess*, ed. Liliane Weissberg, trans. Richard and Clara Winston (Baltimore: Johns Hopkins University Press, 1997). Henceforth RV.

64. Hermann August Korff, who coined the term "Goethezeit" to describe the period of Goethe's greatest influence in German literature, took 1770 and 1830 as his bookends, corresponding almost perfectly to the lifespan of Rahel Levin (1771–1833). See Herman August Korff, *Geist der Goethezeit* 1–4 (Leipzig: Koehler & Amelang, 1923–1955).

65. Karl Jaspers to Hannah Arendt, Heidelberg March 30, 1930; AJC, 10. On this moment in the Arendt-Jaspers correspondence, see Martine Leibovici, "Arendt's Rahel Varnhagen: A New Narration in the Impasses of German-Jewish Assimilation and *Existenzphilosophie*," *Social Research* 74, 3 (2007): 903–22.

66. Ibid.

67. Karl Jaspers, *Max Weber, deutsches wesen im politischen denken, im forschen und philosophieren* (German Character in Political Thought, in Research and in Philosophizing) (Oldenburg: Stalling, 1932).

68. AJC, 15.

69. See AJC, 17. Jaspers's letter is dated January 3, 1933.

70. "The word 'German' is so much misused that one can hardly use it at all anymore. I made the attempt, hopeless perhaps, to give it ethical content through the figure of Max Weber. That attempt, however, would have proved successful only if you, too, could say: That's the way it is. I want to be a German." Ibid.

71. The story of Christian Wilhelm Dohm's project is told in great detail in Jonathan Hess's *Germans, Jews and the Claims of Modernity* (New Haven, Conn.: Yale University Press, 2002).

72. See FLOTW, 87.

73. Crucially, for both Jews and Prussian Germans in the late eighteenth and early nineteenth centuries, self-cultivation, or *Bildung*, often was often understood in explicitly internal terms, as Goethe wrote in his *Wilhelm Meister's Apprenticeship* (1795–6): *"mich selbst, ganz wie ich da bin, auszubilden"* ("the development [or cultivation] of my individual self just as I am"). See Johann Wolfgang von Goethe, *Wilhelm Meister's Apprenticeship* (New York: Collier & Son, 1962), 274. As George Mosse has argued, such an understanding of education not only as *self*-education but as a process that continues over one's lifetime, "was an ideal ready-made for Jewish assimilation, because it transcended all differences of nationality and religion through the unfolding of the individual personality." George L. Mosse, *German Jews Beyond Judaism* (New York: Hebrew Union, 1985), 3. Ironically, however, throughout the nineteenth century it was precisely this transcendental version of *Bildung* that many elite German Jews came to associate with Jewish identity itself.

74. RV 117.

75. That some Jewish *salonnières* benefited indirectly from the rise of the bourgeoisie was ironic, for as many German cultural and social historians have noted, it was precisely the timing of the bourgeoisie's rise and the emancipation of the Jews that enabled the Jews to resemble Prussia's bourgeoisie themselves. See Reinhard Rürup, "Judenemanzipation und burgerliche Gesellschaft in Deutschland," (Jewish Emancipation and Bourgeois Society in Germany) in *Emanzipation und Antisemitismus* (Emancipation and Antisemitism), ed. Rürup (Göttingen: Vandenhoeck und Ruprecht, 1975), and Arno Herzig, "Das Problem der judischen identitat in der deutschen burgerlichen gesellschaft (The Problem of Jewish Identity in German Bourgeois Society)," in *Deutsche Aufklarung und Judenemanzipation* (The German Enlightenment and Jewish Emancipation) (Tel-Aviv: Universität Tel-Aviv, Institut für Deutsche Geschichte, 1980).

76. RV, 58.

77. Ibid., 57.

78. Ibid., 177.

79. Ibid., 124.

80. AJC, 196. Hannah Arendt to Karl Jaspers, September 7, 1952.

81. See Avraham Barkai, "The Organized Jewish Community," in *German-Jewish History in Modern Times*, vol. 4, *Renewal and Destruction 1918–1945*, ed. Michael A. Meyer and Michael Brenner (New York: Columbia University Press, 1998), 91–93. It was partly due to Blumenfeld's influence that the Zionistischen Vereinigung für Deutschland (ZVfD; in English, "Zionist Federation of Germany") and the Zionist labor movement were able to bridge certain of the ideological rifts between these organizations and collaborate in support of Chaim Weizmann.

82. See Hannah Arendt, *The Jew as Pariah: Jewish Identity and Politics in the Modern Age*, ed. Ron H. Feldman (New York: Grove, 1978), 147, 246.

83. However, it seems unlikely that Arendt ever shared Blumenfeld's view that Zionists ought to abjure political activity in the Diaspora. This view led him to condemn the mainstream German Jewish Centralverein (CV) involvement in Reichstag politics during the Weimar years, and even to refer to CV members as "assimilationists." See Barkai, 112

84. As Richard J. Bernstein shows, Arendt's identification with Zionism must be understood as a political choice rather than an ideological orientation per se; throughout her career Arendt was deeply skeptical of any political orientation that demanded commitment on an ideological level. See Bernstein, 105.

85. Arendt would edit a volume of Lazare's essays, *Job's Dungheap*, published in 1948. See Bernard Lazare, *Job's Dungheap; Essays on Jewish Nationalism and Social Revolution*, ed. Hannah Arendt, trans. Harry Lorin Binsse (New York: Schocken, 1948).

86. Unlike Herzl, Lazare had already been writing on themes important to Zionism during the years immediately prior to Dreyfus's initial arrest in 1894. A correspondent of the Russian Zionist Ahad ha-Am, Lazare had published a work on the history of anti-Semitism in 1892, *L'Antisémitisme, son histoire et ses causes*. See the revised edition of this work (Paris: Coston, 1969).

87. See Anson Rabinbach, "Hannah Arendt Writes 'The Jew as Pariah: A Hidden Tradition,'" in which she describes the forgotten tradition of Jewish 'conscious pariahs,'" in *The Yale Companion to Jewish Writing and Thought in German Culture, 1096–1996*, ed. Sander L. Gilman and Jack Zipes (New Haven, Conn.: Yale University Press, 1996), 606.

88. In Arendt's 1942 essay "Herzl and Lazare" (published in *The Jew as Pariah*), she glosses the difference between Herzl and Lazare in terms of their attitudes toward emigration as a solution to the Jewish Question. For Herzl, negating the diaspora and emigration out of Europe were primary goals, whereas for Lazare, "the territorial question was secondary," as Arendt put it. Said question was "a mere outcome of the primary demand that [Arendt quoting Lazare], 'the Jews should be emancipated as a people and in the form of a nation'" (128; quoting Lazare's *Job's Dungheap*). What Lazare sought was "not an escape from anti-Semitism but a mobilization of the people against its foes" (ibid.). Lazare's lack of antipathy toward the diaspora, like Blumenfeld's "post-assimilatory" attitudes toward the Diaspora, were more congenial to Arendt than extremist attempts—such as Moritz Goldstein's—to draw a line between German and Jewish traditions.

89. Leon Botstein contemplated this possibility in his "Politics, The Jews and Hannah Arendt," *Salmagundi* 60 (1983).

90. Hannah Arendt, "The Jew as Pariah: A Hidden Tradition," *Jewish Social Studies* 6, 2 (April 1944): 99–122, 100. It is interesting that in this essay Arendt criticized Lazare for precisely the rejection of parvenu identity that had initially drawn her to him. She claimed that it was Lazare's disdain for Herzl's parvenu politics that kept him from bringing his political projects to fruition.

Chapter 8. From the Camps to Galileo

1. Arendt noted that she collected material for the book over the course of over more than ten years. See the Preface to the "Antisemitism" section of OT.

2. O.T, 7

3. Ibid., 5.

4. See FLOTW, 168.

5. See ibid., 186, for details of the Conference.

6. O.T, 3.

7. O.T, 142. In his 1900 *Contre la justice*, Clemenceau complained, "What irony is this that men should have stormed the Bastille, guillotined their king and promoted a major revolution, only to discover in the end that it had become impossible to get a man tried in accordance with the law!" See Georges Clemenceau, *Contre la justice* (Paris: P.V., 1900).

8. O.T, 145.

9. Ibid., 149.

10. Arendt's Brooklyn College lecture is stored in the Library of Congress Hannah Arendt Papers archive, container 62. See page 3 of the lecture.

11. See O.T, 151.

12. Ibid., 170.

13. Ibid., 184.

14. Ibid., 201.

15. Ibid., 206.

16. Ibid., 209.

17. Hannah Arendt, "Ideology and Terror," *Review of Politics* (July 1953): 303–27.

18. To great controversy—and of course inviting the charge that she was becoming a "cold warrior"—in the Second Edition of O.T Arendt also suggested that Mao's China might become a third totalitarian regime. See O.T, 392.

19. One intriguing weak point in Arendt's portrait of totalitarian society was her refusal to account for the phenomenon of political authority. While she would deal with that concept in her later essay "On Authority," in OT she rejected the idea of the "authoritarian personality" as approached by the social scientists associated with the Frankfurt School. In Arendt's view, the fact that under totalitarian rule there were no reliable intermediate levels or grades of power and authority between the lowest individual and the supreme Leader, indicated that "authority" was not the best concept to describe the hierarchical arrangement of society under totalitarianism. See OT, 525, and for the Frankfurt School's studies of the authoritarian personality see Jay, *The Dialectical Imagination*, chapter 4. One of the great ironies of Arendt's rejection of the "authoritarian personality" is that her own concept of "the social," especially as it described a kind of behaviorism, resembled some of the Frankfurt School's early treatments of alienation in society.

20. O.T, 414.

21. Ibid., 421.

22. See, for example, Rudolph Hilferding's "State Capitalism or Totalitarian State Economy," *Modern Review* 1 (1947): 597–605.

23. See FLOTW, 276.

24. Ibid., 277.

25. Arendt, "French Existentialism," *The Nation* (February 23, 1946). Reprinted in Hannah Arendt, *Reflections on Literature and Culture*, ed. Susannah Young-Ah Gottlieb (Stanford, Calif.: Stanford University Press, 2007), 115–77.

26. As Jeffrey Isaac suggests, Arendt's judgment about Camus cannot stand; Camus's *The Plague* would mark a shift away from an emphasis on the individual to an investment in rebellion as a communal phenomenon made in response to the struggles of communities, as Camus proclaimed in a letter to Roland Barthes: "If there is an evolution from *The Stranger* to *The Plague*, it is in the direction of solidarity and participation." See Jeffrey Isaac, *Arendt, Camus and Modern Rebellion* (New Haven: Yale University Press, 1994), 16. Note, however, that *The Plague* would only be published in 1947, after Arendt had rendered her original judgment on Camus.

27. Ibid., 193.

28. See Jean-Paul Sartre, *Existentialism is a Humanism*.

29. Hannah Arendt, *Sechs Essays* (Heidelberg: Die Wandlung 3, 1948). The essay was translated into English and republished in *Essays in Understanding*.

30. Ibid., 165.

31. Ibid., 181.

32. Arendt, *Essays in Understanding*, 428.

33. Ibid. 430.

34. Arendt and Voegelin had, not at all incidentally, had a contretemps over *The Origins of Totalitarianism*, which Voegelin reviewed critically, stating that she had only created a portrait rather than an explanation of her subject. For Voegelin, Arendt correctly diagnosed "modern man" as afflicted by a spiritual disease, but she failed to grasp its true dimensions because of her focus on the economic and political roots of totalitarianism. Voegelin explained that this disease was a symptom of "modern immanentism," the belief that science and social organization might produce the immanent perfection of the human condition, heaven on earth; notably, Arendt's treatment of the camps led her to parallel meditations on the sheer malleability of the hu-

man condition, something Voegelin did not mention. In a defense of her book, Arendt refuted Voegelin's suggestion that one could explain totalitarianism through spiritual decline alone.

35. Arendt, *Essays in Understanding*, 431.

36. Ibid., 435.

37. Ibid., 432.

38. Ibid., 433.

39. Ibid.

40. Ibid.

41. Ibid.

42. HC, 12.

43. See Canovan's Introduction to HC, ix. It is worth noting that Arendt nowhere characterizes her own method as "phenomenological" and, in fact, describes phenomenology late in her book as one of the philosophical trends that have led philosophers down a dangerously subjectivist road, and away from the political world. See HC, 272. When considering Arendt's debts to Heidegger in this text, it is important to bear in mind that her decisive, if indirect, response to Heidegger comes relatively early: while describing the human condition as bordered by natality and mortality, Arendt noted that "natality, and not mortality, may be the central category of political, as distinguished from metaphysical, thought." See HC, 9. In addition to its obvious riposte to Heidegger's emphasis on "being-towards-death," this line is striking for its creation of a fence between politics and metaphysics *without* rejecting metaphysics or producing a critique thereof.

44. HC, 154. However, utilitarianism is only one dimension of the larger story of Arendt's concept of "work." Patchen Markell has offered a compelling interpretation of HC, one that exposes the expressive, art-making dimension Arendt also saw in the activity of *homo faber*. Part of the force of Markell's reading is that "work" has a dignity of its own, for Arendt, perhaps most visible in the later moments of HC's chapter on "work," where Arendt shifts from discussing objects of utility to discussing art objects. Furthermore, Markell is careful to show that the "walls"—to use his architectural metaphor—between Arendt's tripartite activities, were permeable, complexly joined, and far from perfectly stable. See Patchen Markell, "Arendt's Work: On the Architecture of the Human Condition," *College Literature* 38, 1(Winter 2011): 15–44.

45. See Hanna Pitkin, *The Attack of the Blob: Hannah Arendt's Concept of the Social* (Chicago: University of Chicago Press, 1998).

46. See LOTM, 171.

47. See Hannah Arendt, *On Violence* (New York: Harcourt, Brace and World, 1970).

48. See Pitkin, 11.

49. HC, 99. Arendt quotes Marx's *Capital: A Critique of Political Economy*, ed. Friedrich Engels (New York: Modern Library, 1906), 201.

50. Notably the force of Pitkin's argument regarding Arendt's debts to Marx is to show that Arendt failed to fully acknowledge those debts, or to even perceive the proximity between her own arguments and those of the figure she was intent upon criticizing in HC. See Pitkin, 140.

51. See Immanuel Kant, *Critique of Pure Reason*, trans. J. M. D. Meiklejohn (Buffalo, N.Y.: Prometheus, 1990), 252–56, 299–317.

52. HC, 41.

53. See HC, 175.

54. Arendt named theater as the art form that best exemplified political life, for it was in her mind the only art form that showed man in his concern for human relationships. See HC, 188. On the architectural spaces in which Greek philosophy was conducted, see Indra Kagis McEwen, *Socrates' Ancestor: An Essay on Architectural Beginnings* (Cambridge, Mass.: MIT Press, 1993).

55. HC, 4. Later in the work Arendt expressed another concern about mathematics, namely, that modern science since Descartes had been marked by an ascendancy of mathematical deduction over all other modes of thought. See HC, 277.

56. The history of the development of computers and computing languages is too complex to render in a potted form here. One of the first popularizations of the new research—one Arendt may very well have had in mind—appeared in 1950, when *Time* magazine ran a cover story on the Mark III computer, developed at Harvard University, with the caption "Can Man Build a Superman?" *Time*, January 23, 1950. See also Atsushi Akera, *Calculating a Natural World: Scientists, Engineers and Computers During the Rise of U.S. Cold War Research* (Cambridge, Mass.: MIT Press, 2007).

57. HC, 4.

58. HC, 56. Arendt cites Smith's *The Wealth of Nations,* Book I, Ch 10. See Adam Smith, *The Wealth of Nations* (New York: Modern Library, 2000), 123.

59. Significantly, Aristotle understood contemplation as a form of activity whose content could never be transferred via speech—thus it could never directly affect political life. See HC, 27, and Aristotle, *Nicomachean Ethics*, lines 1142a25, 117826 ff.

60. In keeping with her presentation of Christianity as "Platonism for the masses" in *Love and Saint Augustine*, in HC Arendt saw Christianity as perpetuating Plato's denigration of activity in favor of contemplation, only in a religious key.

61. See HC, 302.

62. Ibid., 274.

63. See HC, 280.

64. Arendt drew on Nietzsche's claim in *The Will to Power* that the Cartesian formula *cogito ergo sum* was in error because thinking can only grant us certain knowledge of the fact that we think; thus Nietzsche and Arendt assert that the formula ought to read *cogito, ergo cogitationes sunt,* and thus consciousness can assure us not of the fact that we *are* but only that consciousness itself *is.* See HC, 280 n 40.

65. Arendt's claims about Descartes were notably influenced by Alfred North Whitehead's *The Concept of Nature*, and his observation that for the Cartesian subject, "the mind can only know that which it has itself produced and retains in some sense within itself." That is, one can best know the product of one's own labors, specifically one's mental labors. See Alfred North Whitehead, *The Concept of Nature* (Cambridge: Cambridge University Press, 1926), 32.

66. See HC, 285.

67. HC, 272.

Chapter 9. One More Strange Island

1. See Walter Benjamin, "Theses on the Philosophy of History," in *Illuminations: Essays and Reflections* (New York: Houghton Mifflin Harcourt, 1968).

2. Hannah Arendt, *Lectures on Kant's Political Philosophy*, ed. Ronald Beiner (Chicago: University of Chicago Press, 1989). Henceforth cited as LKPP.

3. Elisabeth Young-Bruehl, *Why Arendt Matters* (New York: New York Review Press, 2006), 33.

4. The epigram from Heidegger reads: "Thinking does not bring knowledge as do the sciences. Thinking does not produce usable practical wisdom. Thinking does not solve the riddles of the universe. Thinking does not endow us directly with the power to act." *What Is Called Thinking?*, trans. J. Glenn Gray (New York: Harper & Row, 1968), 159. Notably, while in his *Rektoratsrede* Heidegger had referred to placing "science" rather than "thinking" in the service of action, and of "theory" rather than "thinking" being realized in practice, Arendt could easily have understood the author of the 1951 "What Is Called Thinking" as correcting his younger self of 1933.

5. For early reviews of LOTM, see George McKenna, *Journal of Politics* 40, 5 (November, 1978): 1086–88, and George Kateb, "Dismantling Philosophy," *American Scholar* 48, 1 (Winter 1979): 118–20, 122–24, 126.

6. Martin Jay, *Downcast Eyes: The Denigration of Vision in Twentieth-Century French Thought* (Berkeley: University of California Press, 1994), 270.

7. Arendt, LOTM, "Thinking," 92.

8. Ibid.

9. Ibid. 19.

10. Ibid. 21.

11. Heidegger, *Being and Time*, 29–31.

12. See Immanuel Kant, *Kant: Political Writings*, ed. H. S. Reiss (Cambridge: Cambridge University Press, 1970), 85–86.

13. See LOTM, "Thinking," 46. Arendt cited Merleau-Ponty's *The Visible and the Invisible*, ed. Alphonso Lingis (Evanston, Ill.: Northwestern University Press, 1968), 28.

14. Arendt, LOTM, "Willing," 13–14.

15. LKPP, 67.

16. Ibid., 76–77.

17. LKPP, 14.

18. LOTM, "Willing," 168.

19. LOTM, "Thinking," 83.

20. Ibid., 97.

21. Ibid., 141.

22. HC, 192.

23. LKPP, 63.

24. LKPP, 44–45.

25. Karl Marx, "Das philosophische Manifest der historischen Rechtsschule," in *Werke*, Karl Marx and Friedrich Engels (Berlin: Dietz-Verlag, 1958), 1: 80. And see Ferenc Fehér, "Practical Reason in the Revolution: Kant's Dialogue with the French Revolution," in *The French Revolution and the Birth of Modernity*, ed. Fehér (Berkeley: University of California Press, 1990).

26. LKPP 45.

27. See Kant, *Political Writings*, 143–48.

28. LKPP, 48.

29. Ibid., 49.

30. Ibid., 54.

31. Quoted in FLOTW, 451. See Melvyn Hill, ed., *Hannah Arendt: The Recovery of the Public World* (New York: St. Martin's, 1979), 433–44.

32. LOTM, "Willing," 200.

33. Ibid.

34. See "Religion and the Intellectuals: A Symposiumm," *Partisan Review* (February 1950).

35. On this point, see Samuel Moyn, "Hannah Arendt on the Secular," *New German Critique* 105 (Fall 2008): 71–96.

36. Peter Eli Gordon, "The Concept of the Apolitical: German Jewish Thought and Weimar Political Theology," *Social Research* 74, 3 (Fall 2007): 855–78.

37. See Hannah Arendt, "Philosophy and Politics," *Social Research* 57, 1 (Spring 1990).

38. Ibid., 427.

39. Ibid., 431.

40. Ibid., 429–30.

41. Ibid., 436.

42. Ibid. 436–37.

43. Ibid., 438.

44. Ibid., 439.

45. Ibid., 442.

46. This observation I owe to Michael Warner. See his "Styles of Intellectual Publics," in *Just Being Difficult? Academic Writing in the Public Arena*, ed. Jonathan Culler and Kevin Lamb (Stanford, Calif.: Stanford University Press, 2003).

47. George Orwell, *1984* (London: Secker and Warburg, 1987), 26–27.

48. See Warner, "Styles of Intellectual Publics," 106.

49. Orwell, *1984*, 28.

50. Warner, "Styles of Intellectual Publics," 108.

51. See Martin Jay, "The Political Existentialism of Hannah Arendt," *Partisan Review* 45, 3 (1978), republished in *Permanent Exiles: Essays on the Intellectual Migration from Germany to America* (New York: Columbia University Press, 1986).

52. A number of scholars have objected to Jay's characterization, especially because it seems to place Arendt in the same category as figures like Schmitt. See, e.g., Maurizio Passerin d'Entrèves in *The Political Philosophy of Hannah Arendt* (New York: Taylor & Francis, 1993), 84.

53. On this point see Warner's aforementioned "Styles of Intellectual Publics," which is intended in part as a repost to James Miller's essay, "Is Bad Writing Necessary? George Orwell, Theodor Adorno and the Politics of Literature," *Lingua Franca* 9, 9 (December/January 2000). There, Miller contrasted Orwell's accessible style and wide audience with the admittedly more difficult writing and narrower readership enjoyed by Adorno, whom Miller paints as a willfully obscure mandarin. Miller's real target was, in fact, theoretically dense and potentially "jargon-"laden writing produced by academics on the political Left, which he felt compromised those writers' political effectiveness. Warner's use of Orwell is meant to demonstrate that Miller's chosen champion, Orwell himself, understood that publicness was no simple matter. In fact, the scene of Winston's diary writing conveys the almost Adorno-esque notion that sometimes the most political radical gesture is not one that communicates, but one that secures understanding for an audience, however small.

54. For a substantial criticism of the notion that publics function in this way, see Warner's *Publics and Counterpublics*, a work notably indebted to Arendt, but also to feminist and queer theoretical work, invested in the political meaning of private life and private experience, with which Arendt's sharp public/private binary is at odds.

Chapter 10. Toward a Jewish Socrates?

Epigraphs: Heidegger, GA 29/30: 18–19; Blücher cited in Young-Bruehl, FLOTW, 434.

1. André Glucksmann, interviewed in *Nouvel Observateur* 992 (November 11, 1983), trans. Michael S. Roth; see Roth's discussion of Kojève in "A Problem of Recognition: Alexandre Kojève and the End of History" *History and Theory* 24, 3 (October 1985): 293–306.

2. Kojève in OT, 166.

3. Notably, Thomas Mann saw in his own Doctor Faustus a treatment of Nazi Germany: "A lonely thinker and searcher, a theologian and philosopher in his cell who, in his desire for world enjoyment and world domination, barters his soul to the Devil-isn't this the right moment to see Germany in this picture, the moment when Germany is literally being carried off by the Devil." Thomas Mann, *Thomas Mann's Addresses: Delivered at the Library of Congress, 1942-1949* (Washington, D.C.: Library of Congress), 5.

4. Jaspers once suggested to Arendt that the figure of Socrates was not just an intellectual inspiration, but relevant to her personal life. Her husband Heinrich Blücher, he noted, seemed in the mold of Socrates, and Jaspers went so far as to speculate that much as Plato needed Socrates for his ideas to take shape, Arendt needed Blücher. Karl Jaspers to Hannah Arendt, December 10, 1965; see AJC, 616. It may have been the painter Alfred L. Copley who first suggested the parallel to Jaspers; see Jaspers to Arendt, November 2, 1963; AJC, 529. Jaspers also cited Socrates to

Arendt when consoling her regarding the hostile reception to *Eichmann in Jerusalem*: "Truth is beaten to death, as Kierkegaard said of Socrates and Jesus," he wrote, and he went on to speak of her enemies "manipulating public opinion." Jaspers to Arendt, July 25, 1963; see AJC, 511–12. Mary McCarthy likewise thought of Socrates's trial during the Eichmann controversy. See her letter to Arendt of September 24, 1963, Arendt and McCarthy, *Between Friends*, 148–49.

5. Hannah Arendt to Karl Jaspers, July 1, 1956; see AJC, 288–89.

6. TI, 171.

7. Adam Gopnik, *Angels and Ages: A Short Book About Lincoln, Darwin and Modern Life* (New York: Random House, 2009), 8.

8. See Zank, ed., *Leo Strauss: The Early Writings*, 66.

9. See Moyn, *Origins of the Other*, 70.

10. In Levinas, *Outside the Subject* (Stanford, Calif.: Stanford University Press, 1994), 18.

11. See FLOTW, 98. Notably, some tellers of this tale cite not Strauss's conservatism, but his inadequate commitment to Zionism as Arendt's reason for rebuffing him.

12. Anne Norton, *Leo Strauss and the Politics of American Empire* (New Haven, Conn.: Yale University Press, 2004), 38.

13. Karl Jaspers to Hannah Arendt, May 14, 1954; AJC, 240. Hannah Arendt to Karl Jaspers July 24, 1954, AJC, 243–244. Notably, Jaspers responded with puzzlement that Strauss was "an atheist," indicating that he had taken Strauss's works to be those of an orthodox Jew, "providing justification for authority." "The style and tone of his books put me off," Jaspers added. Karl Jaspers to Hannah Arendt, August 29, 1954; AJC, 245.

14. Hannah Arendt to Karl and Gertrud Jaspers, November 24, 1963; AJC, 535.

15. Emmanuel Levinas, "Have You Re-Read Baruch?," in DF, 111.

16. On the potential uses of counterfactual inquiry in intellectual history, see Benjamin Aldes Wurgaft, "The Uses of Walter: Walter Benjamin and the Counterfactual Imagination," *History and Theory* 49 (October 2010).

17. See Peter Graf Kielmansegg, Horst Mewes, and Elisabeth Glaser-Schmidt, eds., *Hannah Arendt and Leo Strauss: German Émigrés and American Political Thought After World War II* (Cambridge: Cambridge University Press, 1995). Some individual contributors to the volume, such as George Kateb, do, however, attempt the task of comparison, in his case by inquiring into Arendt's and Strauss's respective influence on political theory in the United States. See George Kateb, "The Questionable Influence of Arendt (and Strauss)," in ibid.

18. Ronald Beiner, "Hannah Arendt and Leo Strauss: The Uncommenced Dialogue," *Political Theory* 18, 2 (May 1990): 238–54.

19. Ibid., 243.

20. See Dana R. Villa, "The Philosopher Versus the Citizen: Arendt, Strauss, and Socrates," in *Political Theory* 26, 2 (April 1998): 147–72. Villa expands on his essay in a project later published as *Socratic Citizenship* (Princeton, N.J.: Princeton University Press, 2001).

21. Villa, "The Philosopher Versus the Citizen," 156.

22. Ibid., 160.

23. On Western thought as a dual tradition constituted by Judaism and German thought, see Gordon, *Rosenzweig and Heidegger*.

24. See Batnitzky, *Leo Strauss and Emmanuel Levinas*, XX.

25. See DF, 27.

26. Michael Zank, "Review of Leora Batnitzky, Leo Strauss, and Emmanuel Levinas, *Philosophy and the Politics of Revelation*," *Notre Dame Philosophical Reviews* 4, 20 (2007), http://ndpr .nd.edu/news/25275.

27. See DF, 6.

28. See Ian Hunter, *Rival Enlightenments: Civil and Metaphysical Philosophy in Early Modern Germany* (Cambridge: Cambridge University Press, 2001), 104.

29. See the English translation as "Creative Landscape: Why Do We Stay in the Provinces," in Kaes, Jay, and Dimendberg, *The Weimar Republic Sourcebook*, 426–28.

30. Ibid., 427.

31. *Being and Time*, 140. Notably, in 1950 Heidegger would echo this criticism by implicating television in the gradual shrinking of the world; Arendt likewise reflected on the gradual shrinking of the globe via technology eight years later, in HC.

32. For two important textual sources for Heidegger's anti-publicness, see *Being and Time*, sections 27 and 38.

33. See Peter Fritzsche, *Reading Berlin 1900* (Cambridge, Mass.: Harvard University Press, 1996), 2.

34. Ibid., 16.

35. See Hans Brennert, "Gemeinde und Presse," in *Probleme der neuen Stadt Berlin*, ed. Hans Brennert and Erwin Stein (Berlin: Friedenau, 1926), 540.

36. See Benedict Anderson, *Imagined Communities: Reflections on the Origins and Spread of Nationalism* (New York: Verso, 2006), 33.

37. Leo Strauss and Karl Löwith, "Correspondence Concerning Modernity," *Independent Journal of Philosophy* 5, 4 (1983): 105–19, 108. It is relevant that Strauss's own anti-urbanism derived, in part, as Eugene Sheppard documents, from his own rural origins in a Jewish community where both traditionalism and German patriotism were prevalent. See Sheppard, *Leo Strauss and the Politics of Exile*.

38. On "modern archaism" see Gordon, *Rosenzweig and Heidegger*, xviii, 5, 23, 24. Gordon argues that Weimar thought was often characterized by a "doubled" relationship to tradition, a desire to reach into deep cultural wells of authenticity, but simultaneously to escape from what was ossified and constraining in the past. The archaic modernist thinker thus seems to undo the past and the "progressive present" by reaching simultaneously into both, a gesture that can produce a productive tension but also self-undermining effects. That this practice was widespread and certainly not specifically Jewish (though many Jews, including Rosenzweig, took part in it) is a point made by Gordon and confirmed in my own earlier discussion of Weimar medievalism in Chapter 1 of this book. Certainly, archaic modernist efforts have an important antecedent in Nietzsche's attempts to find a counter-agent to the poisons of modernity in ancient Greek thought and culture.

39. Leo Strauss, "The Problem of Socrates," originally presented in 1958 and published in *Interpretation* 23, 2 (Winter 1996).

40. Warner, *Publics and Counterpublics*, 12.

41. NRH, 23.

42. HC, 4.

43. See Stuart Elden, *Speaking Against Number: Heidegger, Language and the Politics of Calculation* (Edinburgh: Edinburgh University Press, 2006).

44. Benjamin Lazier, "Earthrise; or, the Globalization of the World Picture," *American Historical Review* 116, 3 (June 2011): 602–30.

45. HC, 288.

46. OT, 178. Nicholas Xenos points out that for the younger Strauss, Hobbes seems to present the individual citizen as a product of technology. See Nicholas Xenos, *Cloaked in Virtue: Unveiling Leo Strauss and the Rhetoric of American Foreign Policy* (New York: Routledge, 2008), 68.

47. See Elden.

48. Philip Rieff, quoted in Irving Howe, "This Age of Conformity," in Irving Howe, *A World More Attractive: A View of Modern Literature and Politics* (New York: Horizon, 1963), 259.

49. See Strauss, "Persecution and the Art of Writing," 33.

50. Ibid., 23.

51. Ibid.

52. Arendt was capable of making similar statements; see the Preface to her *Men in Dark Times*.

53. See Alexander Nehamas, *The Art of Living: Socratic Reflections from Plato to Foucault* (Berkeley: University of California Press, 1998), 102.

54. Miriam Leonard, *Socrates and the Jews: Hellenism and Hebraism from Moses Mendelssohn to Sigmund Freud* (Chicago: University of Chicago Press, 2012).

55. Strauss, "The Problem of Socrates."

56. See Leo Strauss, "The Spirit of Sparta or the Taste of Xenophon."

57. Arendt, "Some Questions of Moral Philosophy," in *Responsibility and Judgment* (New York: Random House, 2003), 92.

58. LOTM, 168.

59. Arendt, "What Is Authority," in *Between Past and Future*, 107.

60. LKPP, 38.

61. LOTM, "Thinking," 190.

62. See Levinas, *Entre Nous: Essays on Thinking-of-the-Other*, 7.

63. TI, 43.

64. See DF, 207.

65. Levinas, "Heidegger, Gagarin and Us," in DF, 233.

66. See NRH, 93.

67. Levinas cites *Republic* §509. Here Plato presents through allegory the division between the realm of sensible appearances and the realm of the eternal Forms. And see Jean-Marc Narbonne, *Levinas and the Greek Heritage* (Leuven: Peeters, 2006). Narbonne argues that in TI and other works, Levinas derived his understanding of many key terms—alterity, the "otherwise-than-being," and totality itself, from Plato. Narbonne's study seeks not only to read Levinas for his Platonism, but also suggests that Levinas represents one of the most recent historical developments of Platonism in continental philosophy. Levinas would then predate another of French philosophy's more recent champions of Platonism, namely, Alain Badiou. See especially Badiou's *Logiques des mondes: L'être et l'événement* (Paris: Seuil, 2006), as well as John Milbank's essay on the correlations between Badiou's and Levinas's Platonisms, "The Shares of Being or Gift, Relation and Participation: An Essay on the Metaphysics of Emmanuel Levinas and Alain Badiou," http://www.theologyphilosophycentre.co.uk/papers.php. However, a complete discussion of Levinas and Badiou would have to address the latter's criticisms of the former on the grounds of Levinas's Jewish particularism of the other—which Badiou effectively damns, praising instead the universalism of Paul the Apostle, in *Ethics: An Essay on the Understanding of Evil* (New York: Verso, 2001). This criticism of Levinas would naturally have to extend to Strauss and Arendt's respective Jewish particularisms, though they did not elaborate them in the same terms as Levinas did.

68. TI, 116.

69. TI, 103.

70. NRH, 120.

71. TI, 25.

72. Arendt, *Between Friends*, 22.

73. HC, 325.

74. Moses Maimonides, *Perush ha-Mishnah*, Sanhedrin, 10.

75. Leon Botstein, "The Jew as Pariah: Hannah Arendt's Political Philosophy," *Dialectical Anthropology* 8, ½, Special Issue on the Jewish Question (October 1983): 47–73, 62.

76. On Enlightenment-era debates over Jewish emancipation themselves see Hess, *Germans, Jews and the Claims of Modernity*.

77. DF, 176–77.

78. Sartre quoted in Benny Lévy, "Sartre et judéité," *Études Sartriennes* 2–3 (1986): 142.

79. For a more extensive discussion of Barrès "philosophy" of roots, which emphasized the instincts over the intellect, see Hammerschlag, 31–41.

80. See Maurice Barrès, *Scènes et doctrines du nationalisme* (Paris: Plon-Nourrit, 1925), 64.

81. Ibid. 57, and see Hammerschlag's discussion of this definition, Hammerschlag, 39.

82. DF, 254.

83. See O.T, 613.

84. Arendt, "The Jew as Pariah: A Hidden Tradition," For a deeper investigation of Arendt's view of the "pariah/parvenu" dyad, and of her complex relationship with Zionism, see Botstein, and Bernstein, *Hannah Arendt and the Jewish Question.*

85. And see Arendt's similar statement, made to Hans Morgenthau, that "if you are attacked as a Jew, you have got to fight back as a Jew," in Hill, *Hannah Arendt*, 333–34.

86. Arendt, "The Jew as Pariah: A Hidden Tradition," 99–122, 100.

87. Hannah Arendt, "Privileged Jews," *Jewish Social Studies* 8, 1 (January 1946) 7.

88. Arendt, "The Jew as Pariah," 109.

89. Sheppard, 54.

90. HC, 2. Note that Benjamin Lazier takes this quotation as both the beginning and end of his already cited *God, Interrupted.* His book is an indispensible guide to the way Arendt's German Jewish co-generationists (Strauss, Scholem, and Jonas, in particular) attempted to answer her question.

Conclusion

1. For one analysis of this phenomenon in political theory, see Patchen Markell, "The Moment Has Passed: Power After Arendt," in *Radical Future Pasts: Untimely Political Theory*, ed. Rom Coles, Mark Reinhardt, and George Shulman (Lexington: University Press of Kentucky, 2014).

2. See Markell, and see Sheldon Wolin, "What Time Is It?" *Theory & Event* 1, 1 (1997).

3. Here I am motivated by a similar question posed about the heroes of the Scientific Revolution, in the title of Steven Shapin's *Never Pure: Historical Studies of Science as if It Was Produced by People with Bodies, Situated in Time, Space, Culture, and Society, and Struggling for Credibility and Authority* (Baltimore: Johns Hopkins University Press, 2010).

4. So runs the argument of Mark Lilla's aforementioned *The Reckless Mind: Intellectuals in Politics*, which problematically indulges in a dichotomous characterization of the relationship between mind and body, and sides with the mind: "Those who possess self-control mate intellectually and commune with the ideas, which is philosophy's aim, while those who lack it purge their passions in the flesh," he writes, glossing the Platonic idea that political tyrannies are in turn the expression of rulers tyrannized by their own appetites (3).

5. See Jürgen Habermas, "The Unity of Reason in the Diversity of Its Voices," trans. William Mark Hohengarten in *What Is Enlightenment? Eighteenth-Century Answers and Twentieth-Century Questions*, ed. James Schmidt (Berkeley: University of California Press, 1996).

6. See Jürgen Habermas, *The Future of Human Nature* (Cambridge: Polity, 2003), and for an earlier set of his views on the subject, see his essay, "Science and Technology as 'Ideology,'" in Habermas, *Toward a Rational Society: Student Protest, Science and Politics* (Boston: Beacon, 1971).

7. See Bauman, *Legislators and Interpreters.*

INDEX

ACKNOWLEDGMENTS

"A preface is either a bit of autobiography or its evasion," a colleague astutely observes. This is also true of that underexamined micro-genre, the Acknowledgments page. Just a fragment of autobiography, then. I was raised in Cambridge, Massachusetts, in an academic home in which the question of the meaning and value of a life with books was always on the table, sometimes literally. This book's major questions—especially that of the relationship between academic life and the wider world beyond—come out of Cantabrigian *terroir*, and out of the anxieties felt by what sociologist Pierre Bourdieu called the "dominated portion of the dominating class," which often feels compelled to make arguments for its social relevance. I cannot fully map the origins of my drives and impulses, but I suspect that I became an intellectual historian because I was fascinated not only by the history of ideas but also by the complex predicament of intellectuals (however defined) in society.

My first and deepest expression of gratitude must be to my parents, Merry (Corky) I. White and Lewis D. Wurgaft. I was lucky to be born to them and to have them as my first teachers, and I am even luckier to count them, in my own adulthood, as friends. Each dedicated a book to me, and it gives me a deeper satisfaction than words can express, to dedicate this book to them. My thanks go out as well to other kin, defined by love and blood both: to Carole Colsell, to Gus Rancatore, to my sister Jennifer Robin White.

I have had many wonderful mentors from early youth onward. At the Cambridge School of Weston, Mary Page and Alorie Parkhill helped me find my first footing as a writer. At Swarthmore College, Nathaniel Deutsch introduced me to Jewish studies and then became my mentor and friend; he also moved from Swarthmore to UC Santa Cruz just as I moved to study at Berkeley, allowing us to continue our conversations—on topics ranging from Gnosticism to modern Jewish thought to shotokan karate—while hiking in the Santa Cruz mountains. Without his guidance I would have been lost many times over.

At Berkeley, I couldn't have asked for a finer advisor, mentor, and friend than Martin Jay, who guided me through the ways of European intellectual history and proved that a great scholar can still be a real *mensch*. John Efron, my advisor in Jewish history, modeled the historian's virtues of curiosity and patience, and introduced me to areas of historical inquiry I would have missed on my own. Judith Butler was a generous outside reader and always knew the direction in which my work was going long before I did myself. Tom Laqueur taught me to teach by his excellent example, and he and Catherine Gallagher introduced me to the subject of the counterfactual, now an enduring interest of mine and represented in this book's comparative chapter. David Hollinger gave me the idea of writing on Strauss in the first place. I would be amiss if I did not acknowledge the staff of Berkeley's History Department, especially Mabel Lee and Barbara Hayashida. Graduate school, my father told me before I went, equals "free time plus guilt." If my Berkeley experience proved him right, I was delighted to find that at Berkeley one can add "plus delicious food and bicycle rides in the hills" to the equation. And if moving to California turned out to be a good choice, my wisest decision thereafter was to enter psychoanalysis, and I owe deep and continuing thanks to my analyst Michael Zimmerman.

I was also the beneficiary of a network of intellectual historians who finished their own doctorates shortly before I began my own. They became conversation partners and generous readers of my early work, and they continue to set a standard for scholarship and philosophical engagement that leaves me, as one of them once said, simultaneously "elevated and humbled:" John Abromeit, Julian Bourg, Nils Gilman, Peter Eli Gordon, Ethan Kleinberg, Ben Lazier, Dirk Moses, Samuel Moyn, Eugene Sheppard, and Abraham Socher all deserve thanks. I was doubly fortunate that Peter Gordon and Sam Moyn, whose works have influenced mine (I will not embarrass them by saying how much, but to informed readers of this work it will be obvious) launched their book series at Penn at exactly the right moment for my book to be included within it—and at Penn, I wish to thank my editor, Damon Linker, for his timely and valuable guidance.

I wish I could thank by name all of the friends who saw me through my graduate education and the writing of this book. Special thanks for years of conversation and connection that helped bring this book into being: to my immediate *Doktorbruder* at Berkeley Knox Peden and to Leslie Barnes, Katie Peterson, Annika Thiem, Michael Allan, Allison Schachter, Ben Tran,

Yves Winter, Jade Schiff, Timothy Stewart-Winter, Catherine Fennell, Jordan Stein, Isabel Gabel, Simon Taylor, Jeremiah Dittmar, Sarah Stoller, and Sean Feit. A toast to the members of our once-upon-a-time intellectual history reading group, who endured my first treatments of this book's topic, and another toast to James Martel, who arrived at a critical juncture to help me navigate the waters of political theory. In Oakland, Gordy Slack and Adriana Taranta rented me an apartment and then gave me a home and a second family. For ten years now I have enjoyed the friendship of Ben and Liz Oppenheim, who prove the justice of Horace's reflection that a friend is half of one's soul, as do my childhood friends Alison Kotin and Jennifer Webb (I am delighted that my soul seems to deny basic mathematics, having so many halves).

As is so often the case for writers and scholars, my trajectory has been an itinerant one, and I have racked up debts to widely dispersed colleagues. Leora Batnitzky responded graciously to my readings of her work on Levinas and Strauss and asked challenging questions in response. Melvyn Hill met with me in New York to reminisce about Arendt, and our conversation ranged from Arendt to Buddhism to psychoanalysis. At Chicago, Joseph Cropsey (now passed) provided me with access to the Strauss archives, and Nathan Tarcov, who taught a course on Strauss at the time I conducted my research, welcomed my early readings of Strauss even as he demonstrated a knowledge of Strauss's texts I can only hope to approximate. Prasenjit Duara and his family hosted me in Hyde Park and regaled me with Chicago stories. Nicholas Xenos shared conversation about Strauss, as have Robert Howse, William Altman, and Thomas Meyer. François Noudelmann generously met with me in Paris to discuss the Sartre-Levinas dyad, and Levinas's biographer Marie-Anne Lescourret was kind enough to share coffee and reminisce about interviewing Levinas herself. Also in Paris, Gad Freudenthal contributed his medievalist expertise, helping me to better understand the legacy of Maimonides in Strauss's thought. David Myers was a personally and intellectually generous host at UCLA, providing me with a visiting research title and library card as well as sharp questions that prompted me to reformulate my arguments. My thanks to the staff at the Bibliothèque Nationale in Paris, the Leo Baeck Institute Archives, and the Special Collections Research Center at the University of Chicago Library; oh for a scholarly world in which librarians and archivists receive the respect and gratitude they deserve! I am grateful to have been able to present early versions of this book's argument at a number of venues: the New School for Social Research General Seminar, the New York Consortium for Intellectual History, and the History Departments at Williams College and UCLA.

A round of institutional appreciations for material support are in order. Thanks to the University of California Regents-Intern Graduate Fellowship, the Berkeley Jewish Studies Program and History Department for several dissertation research and writing grants that took me to Berlin, Paris, New York and Chicago, the Federal Foreign Language and Area Studies Fellowship (*a shaynem dank* for two years of Yiddish!), the Berkeley Chancellor's Dissertation Writing Fellowship, and the Mabelle McLeod Lewis Memorial Fund Dissertation Writing Fellowship.

At the New School for Social Research, where I was an Andrew W. Mellon Interdisciplinary Postdoctoral Fellow in 2010–2012, I wish to thank my colleagues, students, and friends in Historical Studies and Anthropology, who not only gave me a chance to work at one of the two institutions Arendt and Strauss shared, they helped me develop the first versions of many of the arguments made in this book. My gratitude goes out especially to Oz Frankel, Federico Finchelstein, Jeremy Varon, Neguin Yavari, Nicolas Langlitz, Hugh Raffles, Janet Roitman, and Miriam Ticktin. This manuscript was accepted for publication at Penn while I was a National Science Foundation Postdoctoral Fellow at MIT, pursuing my more recent interests in the history and anthropology of science—I thank Stefan Helmreich and Heather Paxson for their warm welcome and guidance as I explored new-to-me disciplines, years after the completion of my doctorate.

Heartfelt thanks is also due to the cafes and restaurants that offered me precious writing space, equally precious distraction and (of course) excellent coffee, throughout my writing process: Pizzaiolo (Oakland), Third Rail Coffee (Greenwich Village), Fix Coffee (Echo Park, Los Angeles), and Hi-Rise (Cambridge).

And to conclude these acknowledgments, I thank Shannon Supple, without whose love and support this book would have remained a café daydream.

Note: a small portion of Chapter 2 originally appeared in "Culture and Law in Weimar Jewish Medievalism: Leo Strauss's Critique of Julius Guttmann," *Modern Intellectual History* 11, 1 (2014): 119–46. My thanks to my editors and reviewers.

CPSIA information can be obtained
at www.ICGtesting.com
Printed in the USA
JSHW082126120723
44640JS00003B/547